George S. Messersmith

Diplomat of Democracy

George S. Messersmith

Diplomat of Democracy

JESSE H. STILLER

The University of North Carolina Press

Chapel Hill and London

© 1987 The University of North Carolina Press

All rights reserved

Manufactured in the United States of America

Library of Congress Cataloging in Publication Data

Stiller, Jesse H.

George S. Messersmith, diplomat of democracy.

Bibliography: p.

Includes index.

1. Messersmith, George Strausser. 2. Ambassadors—
United States—Biography. 3. United States—Foreign
relations—20th century. I. Title.

E748.M573S75   1987   327.2′092′4   86-24917

ISBN 0-8078-1721-X

To the memory of Benjamin J. Cutler
—A Dedicated Teacher

And to Ivy
—My Playmate in the "Hitery" Room

Contents

Acknowledgments

Many were the times when the research for this project hit a dead end or, in the writing, when the words did not come, that I dreamed of the day I would compose these acknowledgments, thanking those who helped me and had confidence in me and my often repeated assurances that the work would eventually be finished. But my most important debts were contracted long before I knew who George Messersmith was. If it is trite to say that I am grateful to be an American, grateful for the freedom and the opportunity to have followed my interests unhindered, it is surely not unhistorical. From grade school through doctoral studies, the City of New York's superb public schools made more of me than I ever hoped to become. The pride of my life has been my association with Professor Arthur M. Schlesinger, Jr., who supervised this work as a doctoral dissertation and continues on as friend and mentor. He encouraged me when my spirits flagged and patiently corrected my worst lapses of analysis and composition. Anything admirable in this work is a tribute to his inspiration and instruction. The errors and infelicities that remain are mine alone.

Archivists and librarians have been indispensable to this project. I am especially grateful to Mr. Stuart Dick and his fine staff at the University of Delaware library, who patiently guided me through the Messersmith papers. Mr. Dennis Bilger of the Harry S. Truman Library cheerfully and efficiently processed my many requests. Mr. Eric Neubacher of the Baruch College library expedited interlibrary loans. To all of the professionals who helped me at the National Archives, the Library of Congress, the Franklin D. Roosevelt Library, and the many university and public libraries where I did research, thank you.

Finally, some personal thanks are in order. My kin in Wilmington, Delaware, the Schwartzes, provided a warm bed and breakfast and, most welcome of all, plain warmth, during my months away from home in their state. To all the parents, brothers, sisters, nieces, nephews, and assorted friends, thank you for your patience and support. That I do not mention you each by name does not mean that I love you any the less. Last but not least there is my dear wife. She has borne up heroically under the prolonged strain and sacrifice. I hope she would say it has been worth it.

Introduction

"His name doesn't remind you of an American diplomat but a Nazi fighter plane!" sniped columnist Walter Winchell in December 1943.[1] The name in question belonged to George Strausser Messersmith, a distinguished thirty-year veteran of the United States foreign service whose finest moment, ironically, had come as consul general in Berlin exactly a decade before. That was when he was known as "the terror of Nazi Germany"—probably the most fearless and determined foe Hitler's gang faced, then or ever, among Western diplomats. If Winchell had lambasted his late mother, nothing could have provoked Messersmith to purer fury than linking him implicitly to the ideology he never stopped loathing with every ounce of his being. But Winchell undoubtedly knew not how sensitive a nerve he had touched. If he had heard about Messersmith's Berlin heroics ten years earlier, certainly nothing more of the sort had happened since to bring him back to mind. After Berlin he had returned to the accustomed obscurity of far-off places and the upper recesses of his country's largely invisible foreign-policy bureaucracy. That was the safest place for his sort of diplomat to be. Always heedless of appearances, consequences, or others where his principles were concerned, he was never a politician. Where others spun equivocations, he barked his mind. Where others soothed troubled waters, he never hesitated to make waves when the cause was right. No one who knew him was neutral about him. There was no hypocrisy in this man, and few pretensions. Sincerity suffused even his myriad platitudes. For every critic who deplored his lack of finesse and his blunt certitudes, there were admirers who hailed his independence, his courage, his high-mindedness. A diplomat who dared to be undiplomatic, he was at his best a shining example of American individualism in action.

But there was another side. Driven by ambition, for responsibility if not for glory, he was frequently obsequious and overweening in his pursuit of place. And it may be said that he loved too much the freedom that had helped make him what he became, was too blind to public opinion, and too quick to advocate extreme measures to defend freedom when he perceived it to be in danger, as he did throughout the 1930s and 1940s. Democracy was a living reality for him as it was for few others in his profession. Ill-born but well married, maleducated by comparison to his colleagues and counterparts, he had found that diligence brought constant reward and opportunity. His career attests to the fluidity of American society, for white males at least, during the first half of the twentieth century. Messersmith's dedication to the country in which he had had the good fortune to be born was pure and unstinting. And that led him to exaggerate the threat it faced: from without, in the form of German and then Soviet totalitarianism (forces he took to be almost identical), and from within. He was convinced that if freedom was not its own worst enemy, it was too easily exploited by those who were. What were really great strengths of American society—its openness and ethnic pluralism, for example—he saw as dangerous sources of dissension and indiscipline. His analysis often lacked perspective and balance. His preoccupation with the precariousness of democracy, which might have been apt when the American nation was young and alone, was at odds with reality when its power was second to none. And his advocacy of preemptive war against the Soviet Union as early as 1946, if acted upon, would have done great violence to American traditions and the liberties that meant so much to him.

If all of this is true, as I hope the following pages will show, why bother with him? For all of his sterling qualities, he never made policy or advanced beyond the role of agent of policy made by others. He was, as Winchell sneeringly insinuated, a figure of frankly second rank. By the time his private friendship with the allegedly pro-Fascist ex-king of Romania, Carol, caught the columnist's splenetic (but passing) attention, Messersmith was his country's ambassador to Mexico—a critical post but not a very visible one. His name was well known among diplomatic insiders—which Winchell evidently was not—but to few others. Scholarship as a whole would not be vastly poorer were he left to languish in the anonymity he favored in life.

The answers are several. First, there is the sheer interest of his career, one that took him to ten posts on three continents during tumultuous times. He observed and participated in events whose importance far transcended his own. He provides an avenue for exploring a number of critical episodes in American foreign policy—the history of United States wartime relations with Mexico, for example—that have not been given the attention they deserve. The story of his years in Berlin and Vienna reveals the impressions of a discerning (but not unerring) reporter on the rise of nazism and the origins of World War II. In short, we can learn much about his world through his eyes and activities.

There is a human dimension to his life as well. His passions were primarily professional, but not exclusively so. Reconstructing his inner life has been the most difficult part of this project. He gave little to go on, and left his biographer—because, I suspect, it never occurred to him that there would be one—to rely much more than either of us would have liked on informed speculation. What he called "personal" letters rarely were. Private considerations, he was quick to admonish others, had no place in the conduct of one's official duties. Yet occasionally even he slipped. The stresses of his life were too great for any mortal to suppress. And where he failed to prevent his feelings from showing through, he emerges, not surprisingly, as a whole and eminently human person—not always likable or admirable, but who, on balance, saw more and did more good in his life than most of us can hope to do in ours. He needs no more justification than that.

George S. Messersmith

Diplomat of Democracy

The Making of a Foreign Service Officer

"The distant and remote held a peculiar charm for me as a child," recalled George Strausser Messersmith in his unpublished memoirs. At an early age he displayed a restless energy that his native Berks County, Pennsylvania, would not long contain. There his forebears, Presbyterians from the Rhineland, had settled upon their arrival in the English colonies in the early 1700s, and there remnants of the clan remain to this day.[1] The Messersmiths, like most of their Pennsylvania Dutch neighbors, were enterprising folk. In the 1820s, John Messersmith, a tailor, along with fifteen other artisans, founded the Berks hamlet of Coxtown, dubbed "Crowtown" by local wags, an apt appellation for the handful of log cabins that the place remained for a generation. But the picture changed in 1857. After feverish lobbying by the townspeople, the East Pennsylvania Railroad decided to run its tracks through their streets. It marked a new beginning for Coxtown, which, accordingly (and shrewdly) changed its name to Fleetwood. Prosperity came almost instantaneously, and Messersmiths were part of it. In the late 1860s, John's son Charles, born in 1846, became a partner in a wadding mill. By 1870 he had twenty people on the payroll, and annual sales in excess of $100,000. Charles plowed his profits into real estate, an iron mine, and "a two-story frame tenant house," perhaps for his employees. He took a wife, Caroline Schaeffer, and built her a fine brick house. Then, in his crowning achievement, he bought out his partners and became the mill's sole proprietor.[2]

Then his world fell tragically apart. In May 1873 the Messersmith mill was destroyed by fire. Charles had to watch much of the family's property being carted off by his many creditors. Shortly thereafter, Caroline died, at the age of twenty-six. But the grieving widower

1

battled back. Salvaging opportunity from adversity, he became a partner in a new entrepreneurial venture: fire insurance. He took a new wife: Sarah (Sallie) Strausser, of another venerable Berks family, a widow with two children. Soon there were offspring of their own: George in 1883 and Robert two years later. And, if slow to recoup his fortune, Charles retained every bit of his standing in the community. He remained active in public affairs, serving on the town school board and a term as postmaster. But the effort to restore his credit and self-respect literally consumed him. In 1889, at the age of forty-three, Charles Messersmith died. Sallie was again a widow, with two young sons to raise and debts still to pay. Fortunately she was a strong and resourceful woman, "a most extraordinary mother," George later wrote. Somehow she managed to provide life's necessities for her brood, without neglecting their moral and intellectual growth. She introduced George to the novels of Thackeray, Scott, and Austen. By the age of eleven he had read them all, books that stirred his imagination with far-off places and people and imbued him with a fierce and absolute sense of right and wrong.[3]

George left nothing in writing about his father or his feelings upon his death. The son was always an intensely private person, especially on the record. He could hardly have remembered very much about Charles in any case, absorbed as the father was with his business affairs during the scant six years that George had him. Yet Charles's influence left its mark. George inherited his assiduity and civic-mindedness. And, as he passed into adulthood, the son exhibited the practical bent characteristic of Pennsylvania Dutchmen. This put a temporary damper on his wanderlust and set his thoughts to earning a secure living. Considering his mother's fondness for books and his father's involvement in public education, it is perhaps natural that George, upon graduation from high school, should opt for a career in the classroom himself. Teaching was a respectable profession and, most of all, one he could quickly and cheaply acquire at the state normal school at nearby Kutztown while living frugally at home. He completed the two-year Kutztown course of study and, in 1900, the eighteen-year-old Messersmith was hired to teach in the one-room schoolhouse in the village of Woodside, Delaware.[4]

He was not long for Woodside. Messersmith was a young man on the move. Opportunity beckoned in turn-of-the-century America, and he was determined to make the most of it. In 1902 he took a position as principal of the grade school in Felton, another small Delaware town. There he took a room with the family of John Bassett Moore, one of the country's foremost international lawyers. To his disappointment, Messersmith was never to meet the eminent Moore during his stay in Felton, but Moore did hear about him from his folks. He was later to provide Messersmith with critical career guidance.[5]

Staying with the Moores paid off in the short term, too. Among the well-to-do Delawarians to whom they introduced him were the Mustards of Lewes, another of the state's leading families. The Mustards would give him a wife, and much more. Robert Mustard had founded the Shanghai branch of the American Tobacco Company, and his brother Lewis, with his wife and three children, joined him in China for extended stays. Robert and Lewis's uncle was E. W. Tunnell, governor of Delaware during the 1880s, and a close associate of Thomas F. Bayard, secretary of state in the first administration of Grover Cleveland. It was through Tunnell that Bayard had met John Bassett Moore and brought him to the State Department in 1885.[6]

Messersmith's circle of contacts expanded again in 1903 when he moved to Newark, Delaware, to take on his third academic job in as many years. Though barely out of his teens, he was already a seasoned classroom veteran who more and more looked the part. At five feet, six inches tall, he was not an imposing physical figure, but his electric presence filled whatever space he was in. In the classroom he never stopped moving and rarely stopped talking. The Deweyites then in the vanguard of American educational thought would have frowned on his methods, for he was an old-fashioned authoritarian less concerned with cultivating experimentation and self-expression than in dispensing knowledge and morals in large doses. Darting to and fro behind steel-framed spectacles, his eyes were a withering force for classroom discipline. Nor did he encourage one-to-one intimacy with his charges. His natural scowl deterred all but the boldest from approaching him privately. Yet, because of the personality that gave them life, his methods worked. Only the very best could meet his standards, but all were the better for the striving. In later years, students gratefully recalled his contribution to their education. And Messersmith, whose school years profoundly affected his own habits, always considered his experiences in Delaware's classrooms as among the most satisfying of his life.[7]

And there were other satisfying sides to his time in Newark. He ingratiated himself into a coterie of junior faculty at the state college there, now the University of Delaware. W. Owen Sypherd, a professor of English and political science, became a dear friend and a professional collaborator. In 1905, as co-authors, they published an English grammar. Three years later, with Sypherd's assistance and encouragement, Messersmith completed a textbook in civics. His *Government of Delaware* is a soporific piece of pedantry that evokes sympathy for the generation of young Delawarians drilled in it. But the book brought its author considerable notice among the state's important adults. Capitalizing on this reputation, he started up a series of itinerant summertime seminars in school administration, which he turned to further professional and financial profit.[8]

Messersmith's regimen also allowed for diversion and occasional frivolity. Someone sponsored him for membership in the exclusive Southern Club in Philadelphia, where he hobnobbed with the leisure class on weekends. On the Newark campus he and his friends regularly laid their books aside for some spirited revelry. Nor was he immune to female temptations. According to stories his niece later heard, "George was quite a gay blade in his school days and always had an eye for a pretty woman." By 1911 he had begun seeing Lewis Mustard's eldest daughter, Marion, whom everyone called Marnie. A "plump, very friendly, not very bright, party-loving female," four years his junior, she was not the kind of partner he might have been expected to take. Yet, they came to love each other dearly. She toned down his too-serious side, aided and basked in his achievements, and admirably forebore their stresses. But theirs was never a relationship of equals.[9]

Messersmith's active Newark social life was one reason why he decided not to matriculate at Delaware College. He never earned a baccalaureate. Throughout his career there was considerable confusion, which he never saw fit to resolve, over his academic attainments. The State Department's *Biographical Register* put "Delaware College" next to his name without specifying what he was supposed to have done there. Elsewhere it was variously noted that he was "a graduate of Delaware College," or had "three years at Delaware," or had "taken a course at Delaware." Messersmith did apply for admission to advanced standing in November 1908, and passed the entrance examination. But his two years of vocational training at Kutztown left him deficient in the classics, sciences, and mathematics. The Delaware faculty committee reviewing his application recommended his admission upon completion of the appropriate remedial work.[10]

Messersmith declined the offer. There is no record of his ever doing coursework at Delaware. His decision to forgo further formal education was one he never had cause to regret. He continued to rely on the innate talents—vast self-discipline, a retentive memory, and a heart as stout as any—that had already brought him a large measure of success in one learned career, and would soon bring him more in another, all without a four-year diploma. And yet, more of the liberal arts would have done him good. His was not a well-rounded intelligence. He never developed a taste for the fine arts. Out from under his mother's guidance, his literary tastes had already turned unabashedly lurid. He had no identifiable hobbies.[11]

And he was a clumsy communicator. Throughout his life, Messersmith's excruciating English did him a disservice. Occasionally, when he actually set pen to paper, he showed some signs of rhetorical vigor. Early on, however, in the name of efficiency, he became a slave to the dictaphone, to the enduring stupefaction of all who read him. He let his "writings" go out essentially as he had spoken them, without serious editing, and Messersmith could go on almost indefinitely, even to busy and important people. On paper he plodded implacably along, earning himself the derisive sobriquet "Forty-Page George." Someone, somewhere should have taught him to be succinct; someone might have done so in the years of college he never had.

That Messersmith, despite his youth and indifferent academic preparation, could rise so fast in his chosen field speaks volumes about the competition. The fact was that the public schools in Delaware were shockingly bad, and the more conspicuously so by comparison to its neighbors. Aided by a new state constitution of 1897, which magnified the power of rural areas at the expense of Wilmington and Dover, Delaware's 290 local school districts had repeatedly beaten back the centralizing and professionalizing currents of Progressive reform, which were elsewhere raising and regularizing standards for teachers and pupils alike. By contrast, the Delaware schools continued to depend exclusively on property taxes, with the predictable disparities in expenditures per pupil and educational quality. But serious problems afflicted even the most affluent districts. In a scathing 1908 report, a statewide citizens' group blasted the schools as "antiquated and undeveloped . . . general and local supervision are alike unsatisfactory; the teaching staff is largely untrained [and] school buildings are seriously defective." Delaware, it concluded, "buys a low and cheap brand of education."[12]

Messersmith could attest to all of this personally. The headstrong young educator had inevitably come into conflict with his autocratic employers on the local school boards, who routinely interfered in classroom matters and were not accustomed to being defied. He later recalled one incident when, as a principal, he was threatened with the loss of his job and reprisals against his school unless he desisted from the expulsion of a well-connected student who was a discipline problem. Messersmith stood fast. The episode taught him never "to

let himself be influenced by fear of a scene or of personal unpleas-
antness" in doing what he thought was right. But it is a reasonable
conclusion that his rapid movement from one Delaware job to another—four between 1900 and 1904—was not entirely by choice.[13]

More confrontation lay ahead. In 1911 Messersmith, now principal
of the high school in the town of Lewes, was named secretary to the
reorganized state Board of Education, and vice president a year later.
In 1913 the board presented the Dover legislature with a plan for
the complete overhaul of the public school system along Progressive
lines. But despite determined lobbying by Messersmith and his colleagues, the forces of localism again prevailed.[14]

Messersmith took defeat hard, then and always. Thirty years old,
single, frustrated in his profession, he was "tired of struggling with
ignorant and prejudiced school boards." He had made powerful enemies as well as friends around the state in the course of his struggle for reform. He contemplated a clean break: Delaware, teaching,
bachelorhood. A government career in foreign service certainly promised to take him far away. As for Marion Mustard, she was a free
spirit and "would never be happy as the wife of a schoolmaster." The
globetrotting life appealed to them both.[15]

It almost remained but a wistful dream. Without adequate study
time, he failed the consular examination in mid-1913. Fortunately,
examinations for the diplomatic service were scheduled for December. This time, with some reading under his belt, Messersmith scored
third from the top among thirty candidates.[16]

In January 1914 he traveled to Washington finally to meet John
Bassett Moore, then State Department counselor, and to learn what
his diplomatic assignment was going to be. Messersmith strode confidently into the anteroom of Moore's office in the old State, War, and
Navy building. His confidence would soon be shaken. A dozen people were waiting to see Moore, but Messersmith was shown in at once.
After congratulating him for his success on the exams, Moore told
him that he had heard good things about him from Delaware, and
that the State Department was ready to assign him to Vienna as third
secretary at $1,200 a year. But "you are not going there," he contin-
ued, not if what Moore had heard about him was true. "I understand
that you don't have a penny of private income. [The Mustards] have
some means, but I am sure you are not thinking of trying to live on
[Marion] and her family. . . . I do not think you are that kind of
person." Messersmith recalled his saying that the diplomatic service
"was a fairly good career for a man who had plenty of money and
who did not care for business and who wanted a respectable way of
passing his time without having to do very much work." The diplo-

matic service was small, with promotions few and far between. Moore advised that he wait and retake the consular exams; hard-working middle-class men belonged with the consuls. When, after an hour of such talk, Messersmith politely reminded him of the crowd of callers waiting outside, Moore brushed him off. "All of those people," he declared, "are waiting there to get something. It is far more important that I give you this time to save you from making a mistake that may spoil a lifetime."[17]

Messersmith was at first unconvinced. Why undergo the ordeal of exams again when a diplomatic career was available for the taking? Certainly the marginally better salaries in the consular service— $2,000 a year to start, still $4,000 less than he was earning as a school principal—was not a deciding factor; for, whatever Moore thought, Messersmith was ready and willing to accept whatever his "comfortable" in-laws-to-be intended to contribute to his and their daughter's upkeep and happiness. There may already have been an understanding to that effect. But Moore, he soon recognized, had at least one compelling point. Consuls worked under civil service and the merit principle, free from the politics and patronage that vexed the diplomatic career. At this stage in his life, Messersmith was more confident in his abilities than in his connections, and was undoubtedly aware, if Moore did not make a point of telling him so, that he might have trouble fitting into the tonier diplomatic world, where the family and academic background he lacked mattered very much. No less an authority on the subject than Wilbur J. Carr, the chief of the consular service, advised him, when Messersmith sought him out, that the place for a man with his talents and attainments was with the consuls. So, albeit with some misgivings, Messersmith took and passed the consular exams, had a week of orientation in Washington, and, on 25 June 1914, was notified of his appointment as consul of class ten to Fort Erie, Ontario. Three weeks later, he and Marion were wed at Lewes. The young couple packed their belongings and left for their life abroad.[18]

Messersmith had chosen well in a spouse and a career. Under Carr's leadership since 1909, scientific management had come to the consular service. To promote accountability and coordination, consulates were subdivided by function, classed according to importance, and assigned specific jurisdictions. Equipment, furniture, and forms were standardized. An inspection corps periodically rated officers' performance. A new esprit d'corps surged through the ranks. Export-minded businessmen increasingly found that they could depend on the consuls in their quest for markets, and they in turn gave Carr powerful support in his battle for appropriations from Congress.

When the European war broke out in the summer of 1914, the consuls' Ivy League cousins in the diplomatic service were at a low ebb, decimated and demoralized by patronage, which had reached new heights in the Wilson administration. But Carr's outfit was as ready as any for the challenges the war would bring.[19]

The war was almost imperceptible at Fort Erie, a sleepy village of 900 permanent residents, facing Buffalo across the Niagara River. On a gray August day the Messersmiths took the short ferry ride, and then the shorter train trip into town. The tracks wended their way through a series of vacant lots piled high with garbage. "A more desolate, dirty, and discouraging scene could hardly have presented itself to a new consul," he recalled. "I dared not look at my wife . . . but saw she was in tears, and I felt very much like weeping myself." Their introduction to Fort Erie did little to lift their spirits. They found that a house befitting an American consul and his somewhat pampered bride cost his entire salary; the one they took was temporarily without gas and electricity. By candlelight, he recalled, they ate their first Canadian dinner out of several cold cans.[20]

Their first impressions proved somewhat misleading. The new consul and his wife soon settled comfortably into the Fort Erie life, which, as it turned out, boasted more than a little glamour during the summer months, when the population swelled with prosperous vacationing Americans. Moreover, Messersmith found unexpected opportunity to prove his worth to Carr. In 1914 Fort Erie was an object lesson in what consular reform was all about. The post had long been a patronage sinecure much coveted by men who wished a change of scenery without straying far from friends and business interests at home. Horace J. Harvey, Messersmith's predecessor, was a bankrupt Buffalo businessman seeking government sanctuary from his creditors. His long second career as a consul came to an abrupt end, however, with the visit of one of Carr's inspectors. In a closet behind his desk, Messersmith discovered Harvey's sin of wholesale omission: a decade's accumulation of official mail, still in the sacks. Messersmith dived into this formidable backlog, and kept Carr minutely apprised of his progress. This earned him a promotion to class nine, with a $600 raise in pay.[21]

And then the Erie quiet set in. Ignored by Harvey, Canadian and American traders in the area had mostly migrated twenty miles up-river to Niagara Falls, where one of Carr's energetic new breed was ensconced. Messersmith made constructive use of his abundant free time, studying hard until he had mastered the voluminous consular regulations to his satisfaction. He went so far as to draw up a list of suggestions for revisions. But, recognizing that such officiousness might not be appreciated from someone with barely a year on the job, he prudently, if uncharacteristically, kept his insights to himself.[22] All but one, that is. He recommended that the Fort Erie consulate be closed down permanently. The $10,000 a year it cost to keep up, he maintained, could be much better spent elsewhere. For him it meant giving up "a nice, comfortable post," but, he assured Carr, he was not interested in relaxation—only in the good of the service.[23]

This was admirable. It was also a self-interested gamble. With Fort Erie out of business—it shut its doors for the last time late in 1916— Carr had to find someplace else, and he hoped someplace more stimulating for him. Messersmith did not consider how many less appealing alternatives there were until he got word of his appointment, with no increase in grade or salary, to the consulate in Curaçao, Netherlands Antilles. Disappointment turned to indignation and fleeting thoughts of resignation when he learned how much better certain consular classmates of his had fared in this latest rotation. In Washington on leave, he complained bitterly to Carr, thus laying his motives bare. Carr sternly reminded him of his responsibility to serve in whatever capacity he was needed. In any case, he trusted that Messersmith would find challenges worthy of him in Curaçao.[24]

Carr spoke the truth. Blessed by the trade winds and the superb deepwater harbor at Willemstad, the capital, Curaçao was a bustling commercial center, a major entrepôt for the northern South American trade, and lately an important coaling stop for Panama Canal traffic. With the war, it had become a veritable hotbed of activity, licit and not. Taking advantage of Dutch neutrality, the many resident Germans served the fatherland by transferring their mercantile and banking holdings to Venezuelan and Colombian dummy corporations in order to circumvent the British blockade and blacklist. A brisk trade in contraband sprang up. The island crawled with spies and agents provocateurs.

Messersmith had more mundane problems to tend to first. The Curaçao of 1916 was a far cry from today's tourist capital. The new consul and his wife wound up spending their first several months at the best hotel the island then had to offer, a decidedly second-class establishment. Guests shared the single bathroom on each floor. Water was scarce because the Dutch government had steadfastly refused to finance improvements. When guests wanted to bathe, they paid 20 Dutch cents for a bucket of water, which was poured into a perforated tin can suspended over the tub. Messersmith recalled that "anyone who had the temerity to ask for a second bucket, even though he was willing to pay liberally for it, was frowned upon."[25]

The American consulate occupied three rooms off the hotel's lobby. The looks of the office mocked the dignity of the United States. Dirt and dishevelment reigned. The chairs were to be used at one's own risk. The files were a crazy quilt. The vice consul was a Dutch citizen who devoted considerably less time to his consular duties than to his outside business interests. His staff, such as it was, consisted of a Dutch clerk besotted by gin and one gimpy-legged messenger.

Messersmith took one look, and then did not stop. It took four long days and the hiring of several local laborers just to clear out the accumulated debris, but order was soon restored, and a staff worthy of the name assembled. Messersmith was ready for a consular inspector's visit later in the year, whose report commended "the up to date arrangement of the archives, files and correspondence . . . the business-like manner in which the office is generally conducted . . . [and] the excellent standing in the community which both office and officer enjoy as the result of his conduct and efforts."[26]

While tidying up the office, Messersmith was indeed making himself persona grata in Curaçaoan society. By early 1917 he informed the State Department "with absolute certainty that there is not a single local official with whom I am not on friendly terms. . . . The Governor of the Colony has invited me to his table oftener than any other consular officer here." He developed warm relations in the Jewish community, whose prominence in the island's trade dated to the sixteenth century. Messersmith pronounced them "excellent friends of the United States," and they reciprocated his admiration. One merchant tried luring him into his employ with a salary of $25,000—this when, as consul of class eight, he was earning $2,600, less than "the American boilermakers at the petroleum refinery under construction here." Money—the lack of it—was the one sore point in the Messersmiths' life together so far. They had her savings and a "small stipend" from her parents to supplement his salary. But it was not nearly enough to entertain on the scale he felt was appropriate to his position and ambitions. The free spirit in her made her a free spender, unaccustomed to budgets. Then there were Carr's tightfisted bookkeepers, who niggled over every nickel and dime Messersmith laid claim to for expenses. But, he later declared, he never gave the job offers a second thought. Committed to his work, he was determined to carry it out to the limit of their joint resources.[27]

Financial stringencies did not seem to hamper him in Curaçao, where he quickly distinguished himself for conscience as well as congeniality. His instinctive sympathy for the oppressed and dispossessed found expression in the plight of the Venezuelan exiles on the island. They were loyalists to former Venezuelan president Cipriano Castro in his ongoing rivalry with the incumbent, the equally despotic Juan Vicente Gómez. Many of the refugees were destitute because local employers feared that Gómez, the man who once announced his own death in order to punish those who would celebrate it, would retaliate against anyone hiring his enemies. After unsuccessful attempts to raise a relief fund in their behalf, Messersmith dug into his own pocket to set up a soup kitchen at the local prison. Gómez, one of history's pettier tyrants, later refused the Messersmiths visas for a vacation visit. But Messersmith became a minor hero on Curaçao.[28]

That was one reason why Messersmith enjoyed the quiet cooperation of the local authorities, despite their official neutrality, when the United States entered World War I. Anticipating that eventuality, Messersmith had already put in hours "prowling the waterfront with a notebook," and poring through countless documents, hoping to identify concealed German interests and trade. Once he had, he set to rooting them out with a zeal and resourcefulness that made him, by his own reckoning, "probably . . . the most hated man in that part of the world" among Germans and those in their employ. The United States was Curaçao's sole supplier of coal, and wartime regulations required the consul to inspect neutral ships for contraband before authorizing a withdrawal from the stockpile. Thanks to Messersmith's vigilance, more than a few merchant vessels rode out the war at anchor, collecting barnacles in Willemstad harbor.[29]

These activities put him at some personal risk, which he faced down with an intrepidness that became one of his trademarks. Early one morning at the waterfront, he was seized from behind by a knife-wielding assailant muttering, "You are becoming much too inconvenient for me." Only the timely arrival of some passersby, he recalled, saved his neck.[30]

Others had cause to regret the failure of the attempt on his life. In late 1917 Messersmith began to suspect that the German consulate on Curaçao was active in espionage. He noticed that "bright, young Germans" attached to the consulate as lowly clerks "suddenly and mysteriously" started disappearing "one by one." Messersmith informed Washington; but the matter lay dormant until a young Dutchman walked into his office with a disquieting story. He was a former employee of the German consulate, and had just received two inexplicable pieces of mail: an insurance policy with certain sentences underlined, ostensibly issued at Baltimore for goods to be shipped from Curaçao to Liverpool; and a letter confirming issuance of the policy, calling "special attention to the underlined parts." Having placed no such shipment or policy, the Dutchman was baffled. Messersmith's "intuition" told him that the documents were messages in code. After two weeks of intensive study and "literally sleepless nights," he had still not hit on a solution. He was about to "admit defeat" by sending the documents to Washington when the key came to him. By day's end he had deciphered the messages.[31]

Messersmith's surmise had been right from the start. The "bright, young Germans," having completed training, had gone to the United States as spies. Since commercial documents like insurance policies routinely passed the American censor, the German agents had been ordered to communicate through Curaçao, where the Dutchman would presumably—a huge presumption—bring the documents to his former comrades at the German consulate. They waited in vain. In September 1918 Messersmith was notified of the arrest in Cuba of German agent Albert Westphal, who had concocted the scheme. Although Messersmith modestly attributed his discovery not "to any skill on my part but rather to entirely fortuitous circumstances," that was clearly not so. His persistence had paid off with an important contribution to American counterespionage, as recognized in a commendation from Carr.[32]

Surcease from wartime duties came earlier for Messersmith than most, though under sad circumstances. In October 1918 his wife's father died. The Messersmiths returned to Delaware to help ease her mother's travails. They landed in New York two days after the armistice to spend the winter of 1918–19 with the grieving Mustards at Lewes. There rumors reached him that he would not be returning to Curaçao. In January Carr notified him that he was going to Antwerp, Belgium. Messersmith "jumped at the opportunity"—as though he had a choice—because "Belgium was a magic word in those days." Certainly it was a promotion over Curaçao, and the opportunity to prove himself, "which I had always hoped might come to me in the Service."[33]

There would be no magic for the Messersmiths at first. Boarding the army transport *Agamemnon* in New York, they were shown to a "palatial suite"—in which, as they discovered that night, the bedbugs reigned sovereign. The army's bill for Marion's fare and a cold, driving rain greeted them in Antwerp. The scene in March 1919 was one of general commotion amid the destruction wrought by four years of German occupation. The port itself was relatively unscathed, though, so that relief and evacuation efforts had converged on the place. Refugees came in a steady stream, clamoring for visas and entry to the United States. Afraid that common criminals and revolutionary agitators were rife in the ranks of the would-be immigrants, Washington beefed up its consular manpower to help ferret out potential malefactors. Messersmith and the two army intelligence officers who arrived with him were on a relief mission on behalf of overworked bureaucrats rather than displaced persons. Order at the consulate general soon returned. As for the expected flood of "undesirables and troublemakers," it never did materialize, he wrote proudly, "due to the energetic steps taken at the beginning."[34]

Visa control was but one of the problems, official and personal, that beset Messersmith during his first weeks in Antwerp. He was responsible for arranging port clearances and wharfages for the transports that jammed the harbor, and protecting from pilferage the supplies that piled up invitingly while awaiting shipment into the interior. The more than 4,000 American servicemen billeted in the city to run the supply and evacuation operations made for nearly that many headaches for him. He was besieged by indignant civilians who had been summarily displaced from choice hotel rooms by American officers or who were tired of having their sleep disrupted by carousing enlisted men.[35]

Messersmith could commiserate convincingly with the aggrieved, for he and his wife were also having a hard time of it in the economic anarchy of Antwerp in 1919. They knew the housing shortage firsthand. Their modest hotel suite was unheated save for an hour or two daily. He later recalled their having to scrimp even on food in order to hold their living expenses down to no more than twice his current $3,000 salary.[36]

The strain of work and personal finances soon got the better of him. One morning in February 1920 he was awakened by stomach pains. Bleeding internally, he was rushed to the American army hospital in Coblenz, Germany. From his bed he cabled Carr with the assurance that he would be back at his desk within two weeks. The State Department cabled back a bill for $10.53, the cost of his telegram and its response.[37]

Such indignities did nothing to speed his recovery. He "got weaker steadily" under therapy at Coblenz. Increasingly desperate, he agreed to undergo what was then a new and risky surgical procedure to repair the damage. In April 1920 surgeons constructed a new duct from the base of his stomach to the intestine. Messersmith felt so much better that he ignored doctor's orders and returned to work

after his promised two weeks. The result was a life-threatening re-
lapse. Ultimately he was forced to take an extended convalescence at
home.[38]

The ordeal changed his way of life. He became a model patient—
adhering religiously to his bland diet, never missing his morning
prunes. He chewed on cigars all day, but would light one, and only
one, after dinner, and swore off alcohol and caffeine forever. Not an
epicure in any case, he lost all interest in food and drink. Through
compulsive abstinence he hoped to protect himself from his compulsive industriousness, to prevent what had perhaps happened to his
father from happening to him. People noticed that he habitually
rested his forefinger over his wrist, monitoring his pulse. But by being so attentive to himself, it would be more than twenty years before
he would see the inside of a hospital again as a patient.[39]

By the time he returned to action in mid-1920, his "internal geog-
raphy altered," pressures at the consulate general had eased mark-
edly. The last of the American troops were packing for home, the
throng of visa seekers was thinning, and local law enforcement was
reestablishing itself at the waterfront. Antwerp was caught up in rebuilding and preparations to host the summer Olympic games. The
consulate general's main occupation became arranging accommodations and side trips for the luminaries who were to accompany
American athletes to Antwerp. All about was a palpable desire to
forget the war, which had lingered so long in the city, and get on with
the business of peace.

Now that the clutter of war was gone, Messersmith was appalled
to see how negligible the American presence at Antwerp really was.
Gateway to the rich markets of northern France and western Germany, Antwerp boasted a well-integrated rail-and-river network, and
an abundant, productive, and intelligent labor force. Wages were
relatively low, but, thanks to a dramatic decline in the cost of living
since 1919, Antwerp's workers, as Messersmith noted, were spurning
the Pied Pipers of socialism. More and more European manufacturers were setting up their plants in the city. Americans and American products, on the other hand, were scarcely in evidence. Before
the war American trade at Antwerp "was practically of no importance." And, although the immediate postwar brought many American ships to call, Antwerp was not regularly served by a single United States merchant line. Over 100 European lines competed among
themselves for scarce docking and storage facilities. Nor were Belgians quite clamoring for American products, which had a reputation for shoddiness and, due to high labor and transport costs and
the strength of the dollar, were uncompetitively expensive.[40]

What troubled Messersmith was that the American consulate general in Antwerp was doing next to nothing either to surmount these obstacles or to capitalize on the considerable goodwill Belgians felt for the United States and its role in their liberation and emergency feeding under Herbert Hoover. Relations between Antwerp city officials and Consul General Harry Morgan, Messersmith's chief, were "very poor." Unhappy in Antwerp, Morgan asked the State Department to transfer him and the supervisory consulate general to Brussels. Messersmith was given charge of the office in Antwerp.[41]

With his new authority, Messersmith redoubled efforts already begun to bring American business to town. Trade had special political connotations for Americans in the 1920s. Having spurned membership in the League of Nations, they argued—and none more emphatically than Carr's consuls—that commerce was the real key to world peace and prosperity. "Economic ties," Messersmith told a group of Belgian and American businessmen in 1922, "determine the nature of political relationships in our day." Trade to mutual advantage was "one of the surest safeguards of peace"; "a political grievance," he maintained, "is no[t] sufficient for war if economic ties between the countries concerned make it undesirable." He foresaw the growing interdependence of the world business community continuing to draw nations together and creating a climate of trust and stability in which political problems could be amicably settled, with or without the United States represented at Geneva. Truly, he told the businessmen, "you are among the pioneers in the movement for international peace."[42]

So fortified, he worked to expand opportunities for Americans in Antwerp. "This consulate," he announced in a letter sent to firms requesting information, "is desirous of doing all in its power to promote trade relations between the United States and this part of Belgium. . . . All specific inquiries will receive our careful attention, and representatives of American firms visiting the city are cordially invited to call at the consulate." Those who did found a small but active American community waiting to greet and assist them. In early 1921 Antwerp's American Club, founded by Messersmith, held its first weekly meeting. As its businessman-president wrote the State Department, the club "presents a united front on American interests which has certainly not failed to impress those in positions of commercial influence and the civic authorities in Antwerp."[43]

This unified front helped Messersmith gain a place in the harbor for American shipping. His every effort, he assured Washington, was "directed towards securing . . . the advantages, in the way of quays and warehouses, which were needed to meet the competition of other flags, [and] to assist in every way" American ships' captains. These efforts paid off quickly. By 1922 the State Department was receiving letters from private American shippers and the government's Emergency Fleet Corporation thanking Messersmith for helping them acquire permanent berths. By 1924 five United States merchant lines (all with "adequate terminal facilities," Messersmith reported proudly) called regularly at Antwerp.[44]

And their cargoes increased steadily in volume and value. By 1926 Belgian-American trade amounted to $130 million, compared to $56 million in 1913. Although Belgian statistics were not broken down by port of entry, most of this commerce was clearly coming through Antwerp, which in 1922 surpassed Rotterdam as the continent's preeminent port. The American consulate contributed materially to the boom. In 1921 alone Messersmith and his staff turned out 246 trade reports on items from spark plugs to varnish.[45] His key recommendation was that these wares be stockpiled at Antwerp, so that "orders of any size may be filled quickly." Many American exporters took this advice, and reaped the rewards of their good sense. By 1925 Antwerp was European headquarters and distribution center for many American corporations. Chrysler, General Motors, and Ford went a step further, building and operating assembly plants with a combined output of over 200 vehicles per day.[46]

Since the war's end Messersmith had transformed the consulate, as one who knew from personal experience put it, into "a model of efficient foreign service," "where every problem of Americans abroad received prompt, personal, and sympathetic attention." In 1913 the consulate's annual correspondence filled four boxes; in 1925 it was ten times that many. Letters and visitors from Antwerp to the State Department glowed with praise for him. "The right man in the right place," said one. "The most able and efficient consular officer with whom I have come in contact in Antwerp or other European cities," went another. The chief executives of the auto companies sent commendations. Messersmith's "most excellent" trade reports, wrote a New York firm, "covered the subject from every angle," providing "exactly what we require."[47]

Such reviews had impact on their readers in high places. William Phillips, undersecretary of state in the Harding administration, noted in 1923 that Messersmith was "one of our best younger consuls." He was a man in a hurry, too much so for some. Carr was properly impressed at first, but his well-developed proprieties were soon offended by Messersmith's enthusiasm in his own behalf. When Messersmith forwarded one batch of no fewer than seventy appreciative letters from firms that had received his trade reports, Carr clipped his wings: Messersmith should not waste the department's time with what were "probably . . . form letters." A week after his fortieth birthday, 11 October 1923, there came another depressing message from Washington, making Antwerp again the supervisory consulate general—Morgan had been transferred to Argentina—and naming Messersmith not consul general in charge, but rather, "consul in charge of the Consulate General pending assignment of a Consul General," suggesting that he would soon be relinquishing the top spot in Antwerp. It was a dispirited Messersmith whom Paul C. Daniels, a Yale undergraduate then contemplating what was destined to be a distinguished diplomatic career, called upon for advice in late 1923. "Young man," Daniels recalled him saying discouragingly, "the same talent, brains, and energy applied to something else will get you much further." But in June 1924 his promotion to consul general arrived, and all was well again.[48]

Messersmith was "overjoyed," yet apprehensive. He was now five years in Antwerp, which was as long as anyone could expect to remain at a post. He longed to stay. By now he understood full well "that an officer must be willing to serve at any post at which the Department may find it desirable to use his services." But, he wrote Washington, he believed he had a "special usefulness" at Antwerp that argued against his removal. The situation for American shipping was much improved, but dockside competition was still fierce. To switch officials now, even if the new man were "an officer of much more capacity than myself," he maintained, would be a mistake; American interests might suffer while the newcomer was acclimating himself and establishing contacts. If only Messersmith had "a year or two more," he felt that the American position at the waterfront could be consolidated.[49]

His ulterior purposes for wanting to stay were stronger still. After successive stints in the Canadian and Caribbean boondocks, the Messersmiths had found happiness in the many amenities of Europe and Antwerp. To better partake of the gracious life, he had acquired a working knowledge of French, to go with the Spanish he had picked up from Venezuelan friends in Curaçao and the German that was a second tongue in Pennsylvania Dutch households. And, once the runaway inflation of 1919 had subsided, they discovered that, with outside help, they could afford all that Antwerp had to offer. Belgium, he later advised a foreign service officer headed there, was "probably the cheapest of the advanced nations of Europe from the point of view of living and for what one gets for one's money." His salary was up to $7,500, but still they were spending, by his own estimate, "at least twice" that. His memberships in the local golf, tennis, and polo clubs were one major expense. It was the company, not the sport, that interested him, but in such circles appearances had to be maintained, and that was costly.[50]

He and his wife were also entertaining lavishly. Marion had blossomed into an adept and charming hostess who helped smooth her husband's rough edges and occasional tendency to excessive feeling and frankness in polite discourse. She kept reminding him to hold his tongue in society, in which they were playing a prominent part in Antwerp. Over 250 guests were in attendance at their September 1920 dinner-dance to mark the closing of the Olympics. Their doors were always open to visiting Americans, local officials, and businessmen. Guests frequently spent the night, a courtesy the Messersmiths could now extend without personal inconvenience. For the days of unheated hostelries were over. A twenty-six-room mansion with a full complement of servants was now home. He spent over $1,100 on freight charges alone—none of which was reimbursed—bringing furniture over from the States. In short, he had a considerable financial stake in Antwerp, a fact he hoped would "be of interest to the Department" if it was considering transferring him.[51]

As a foreign service officer reputed to have made do on his salary—one of a "handful in a field preempted by millionaires," a State Department critic remarked—Messersmith's finances deserve more than passing mention. For, as he himself admitted, the decline in the Belgian cost of living and his modest salary hikes do not square with the rather dramatic improvement in their material conditions. Marion had inherited a considerable sum upon her father's death, perhaps $200,000, and apparently some securities besides. And, although Messersmith never discussed it, there is evidence that the "small stipend" they had been getting from her parents became much larger in Antwerp and thereafter. In 1920 her widowed mother, Virginia Lee Hickman Mustard, came to live with them, which she would do sporadically until her death in 1945. Her granddaughters remember her as "a marvelous person," and George was a devoted son-in-law who graciously accepted her contributions to the household. This largesse helped them live in luxury abroad. He often protested to his superiors that he was a poor man, which, strictly speaking, was true enough. But the State Department, which had to consider such things in its assignment decisions, correctly assumed that he had family resources to draw upon. Financial freedom became an important factor in his professional success. Foreign service officers *could* live on their salaries, but not in the style the life required.[52]

Messersmith hated to leave that life in Antwerp, so rich in material and personal pleasures. "It is very seldom," he wrote Carr, "that we do not have several interesting people either for dinner or lunch." Family came for extended visits. The Messersmiths never had children. He once confessed to having lacked "braver[y] . . . in facing the responsibility" of fatherhood. From this eminently brave man, that is unpersuasive. Assuming that the decision to go childless was theirs, and not dictated by circumstances beyond their control, it was undoubtedly prompted by career considerations. In foreign service, with its transfers and uprooting, children were an especial burden.[53] Yet the Messersmiths' residences around the world often rang with youthful laughter. Clearly "not the type to romp with children," he was no less devoted to his six nieces and nephews on her side, and took a paternal interest in their upbringing. Her sister's two girls, Virginia and Ann Layton, were special favorites, and they grew more worldly and mature by their time, which was considerable, with the Messersmiths abroad. In Antwerp, Ann recalled, their uncle "had plenty of time to take us to all sorts of places for fun." There were language lessons, college courses, excursions through western Europe, tours of the galleries and public buildings, but also, more frivolously, horseback riding and skating. The girls loved to rib him "for being so pompous," and he cheerfully endured their teasing.[54]

So the American position at the waterfront may have been the least of the reasons why he dreaded a transfer. He was therefore deeply relieved when, in May 1926, Carr assured him that none would be forthcoming for at least a year. Two months later, State did an about-face: Messersmith was needed in Athens, Greece. The telegram so notifying him was not the usual summary directive, however. Messersmith was politely invited to "inform the Department if your arrangements are such as to make you available for the post." In a handwritten postscript, Secretary of State Frank Kellogg encouraged him to "feel entirely free to express your wishes."[55]

Messersmith expressed them. A transfer, he informed Kellogg, was less convenient than ever. After Carr's assurances, Messersmith had taken a new, still larger house. Canceling the lease meant a $900 loss. Already $1,500 had been spent on renovations and "special fittings practically useless elsewhere." He was sure that the department would "appreciate fully [the] circumstances which compel me to request [that] I be permitted [to] remain at Antwerp."[56]

He got his way and two more years in Belgium. They brought new satisfactions. "Practically a month does not pass," he reported in March 1928, "that a new American firm does not establish a branch

office here." Five did in that month alone. The American Club, now
with over 100 members, reflected this presence. So many American
manufacturers had set up shop in Antwerp that he started worrying
out loud about the impact on employment at home. Belgian exports
to the United States kept pace, rising now to almost four times the
1913 level. Messersmith himself had become a fixture in the city's
official life. In March 1928 he became doyen of the consular corps,
formalizing a place of honor that he already occupied in fact.[57]

Then it was over. In June 1928 there arrived "the not unexpected
but dreaded news" (as the president of the American Club put it)
that Messersmith was going "to another post which would take him
far away to another continent." He was to become consul general in
Buenos Aires. Messersmith expressed his appreciation to the State
Department for "having left me here long enough"—now going on
nine years—"to enable us to carry out at least the major lines of the
program . . . which I had laid out." It was where he was going that
irked him. In American foreign service, the worst European post—
which Antwerp assuredly was not—was considered preferable to the
best Latin American post, which Buenos Aires in many ways was.
The cosmopolitan Argentine capital, with its broad boulevards,
graceful architecture, and rich cultural life, was the closest thing
there was to London or Paris in South America. Messersmith's main
thought was how much these amenities would cost him. Befitting its
status, Buenos Aires also ranked at or near the top of the world's
most expensive cities. As far as he was concerned, it was a bad bargain. With considerable ill grace, he applied for a post subsidy. The
State Department had to remind him that the entire post appropriation for 1928 was $100,000, and that there were many others much
needier than himself: officers with dependents earning less than
$5,000 a year had to receive priority in doling out what little there
was.[58]

Messersmith's misgivings about leaving were matched by the dismay of his Antwerp friends and colleagues. They recognized that
his departure "would create an extraordinary void" in the city. The
municipal government held several dinners in his honor, where
the mayor saluted Messersmith's "unforgettable services." More kind
words, "in most cases undeserved," he reported modestly, came from
local businessmen and his staff. Years later a successor assured him
that "the memory of you and Mrs. Messersmith is still warm indeed
in all circles in Antwerp."[59]

After a short holiday in France and Germany, the Messersmith
entourage, with her mother and their two lifetime servants—the
housekeeper Mary and Arturo ("as good a cook as there is," his em-

ployer boasted)—set sail for Argentina. They arrived in October 1928 to a warm welcome from the United States ambassador, Robert Woods Bliss, and the American colony. Speakers at a Bliss-sponsored luncheon paid tribute to Messersmith's accomplishments in Antwerp. He returned the compliments: although sorry to leave Belgium, he told the group, Buenos Aires "was on his list of places he would wish to be appointed to . . . , first on the list in order of preference."[60]

That fiction proved hard to maintain in the face of the problems that now crowded in on him. Not the least of these was the dreaded cost of living, which, as anticipated, put a serious crimp in their lifestyle. They went from twenty-seven rooms to a cramped seven, and those in the capital suburbs. But without being any less concerned for himself, he was becoming progressively more concerned for colleagues without his resources, and more aware of the larger implications of their plight. It was "unquestionably undemocratic and contrary to the spirit of our institutions," he wrote Washington, that consuls had either to subsidize the government or live in poverty at expensive posts. It was false economy, too. Americans seemed not to care or understand how their interests and prestige suffered when their representatives abroad became charity cases.[61]

Four years earlier, in 1924, Congress had passed the Rogers Act, a landmark in State Department history. On paper it had consolidated the consular and diplomatic services into a unified Foreign Service. Carr became an assistant secretary of state. But Rogers gave the consuls in the field no succor. The only improvement in remuneration that it provided went to the diplomats, by way of reclassification with the somewhat better-paid consuls. Rogers made provision for representation allowances, but Congress refused to fund them. A pension plan was set up, costing officers 5 percent of their meager salaries off the top. If anything, the Rogers Act left the consuls poorer than before. And, it might be added, still poor relations in the State Department. In practice, the diplomatic and consular services remained separate and unequal. A new single promotion list was supposed to open diplomatic positions to worthy consuls, but the diplomats resisted, maintaining two lists. "There will be no 'weaving back and forth' between the two branches, as the consuls wish," Undersecretary of State Joseph Grew vowed. The diplomats continued to deride them as overweening clerks lacking polish and brains.[62]

The United States stationed no diplomats at Messersmith's previous posts. Buenos Aires was his first capital. There the consulate general and the embassy worked out of separate quarters, at arm's length. Bliss did not wish this arrangement disturbed. Having done his introductory duty, the good ambassador wanted nothing more to do with the new consul general. When Messersmith approached him to suggest consolidation and coordination, the ambassador turned overtly hostile. Bliss made his feelings clear, that "while the consulate was useful, it was not quite as respectable [as the embassy] and should not contaminate the embassy by too close proximity."[63]

So the State Department remained divided against itself, at the expense of consular egos and the national interest. Because diplomats alone could formally approach the government to which they were accredited, business and financial issues, which generally little concerned them, tended to suffer. Compounding the consuls' problem was the profusion of attachés in the employ of the United States Treasury, Commerce, Labor, and Agriculture departments. Faced with the often conflicting objectives of a half-dozen Americans claiming to speak for their government, foreign officials could not be blamed for being confused.

Bliss and the attachés were comparatively minor impediments to Messersmith's business in Argentina. What he faced there had no analogue in Belgium. History was a deadweight on United States–Argentine relations. In many ways, the two countries' chronic difficulties sprang from their similarities more than their differences. Since the 1880s they vied openly for leadership over a hemisphere to which neither was really oriented, culturally or economically. They competed for the same world markets for many of the same agricultural products, and protected their own producers against each other. Naturally Argentina's European trading partners supplied most of its manufactures and investment capital, Britain predominating.[64]

Argentine-American relations took a decided turn for the worse in 1917. Not only Argentina remained neutral during World War I; most of South America followed its lead. Argentine neutralism was a complex product of nationalism and ethnicity, but the people of the Allied nations were indifferent to sociological subtleties. Ill will accumulated and spilled over.[65] In 1926 the Coolidge administration gave way to ranchers' pressure and banned imports of fresh Argentine beef, ostensibly to protect American herds from the hoof-and-mouth disease allegedly endemic in Argentina. The Argentines, beholding perfectly healthy beasts, took the measure as a "deliberate insult," an act of economic warfare calculated to besmirch their reputation in world markets.[66]

Messersmith's arrival sparked fresh anti-Yankee pyrotechnics, rhetorical and all too real. Someone hurled a gasoline bomb through his office window, at a spot where he was lucky not to be sitting.

He reported spontaneous consumer boycotts of American products, encouraged by the British. Argentine authorities demonstrated their displeasure in various diplomatic ways. Messersmith spent hours cooling his heels in government offices.[67]

Personal relations eventually warmed up. Messersmith did all in his power to promote American business in the Argentine market, with a view to bringing the two nations together. The Argentines saw that his heart was in the right place, appreciated his ability to speak their language, and treated him accordingly. But politics and history conspired against the reconciliation he sought. It was a harbinger of things to come.[68]

After little more than a year in Buenos Aires, in October 1929, family tragedy again called Messersmith home. In late June, his brother Robert, a Marine Corps major, had died suddenly at Quantico, Virginia. No one would have guessed they were brothers to look at them. Bobby's features were soft, even pretty, but underneath he was a Messersmith and a marine. They had been close over the years; Messersmith keenly felt the loss. Their mother, who had buried two husbands already, now mourned a child. But his homecoming was not unrelievedly somber. Messersmith found himself a celebrity in Fleetwood. The townspeople opened their hearts to the local man who had already made good and whose future seemed still brighter. The Fleetwood fire hall sparkled that night in November, as old friends and neighbors gathered to fete him. There were speeches, gifts, and a performance by the high school orchestra. One of his Kutztown teachers delivered a homily offering Messersmith "as an illustration of how a man can succeed if he applies himself to his chosen profession."[69]

Three separate State Department actions over the next six months attested to how true this was, to how far Messersmith had come after fifteen years of government service. Carr designated him to represent the department at a series of trade conferences. During two hectic weeks of December 1929 Messersmith addressed groups in Baltimore, Chicago, St. Louis, Los Angeles, and San Francisco. Carr had chosen wisely. By being himself, Messersmith doubtless dispelled some negative preconceptions about State Department personnel. His own accomplishments, especially in Antwerp, were a convincing case for the consular service at large.[70]

Before Messersmith had settled back in Buenos Aires after this exhausting itinerary, Carr ordered him off to inspect State Department establishments in South America. Before 1924 diplomatic offices were outside the pale for Carr's inspectors, who held the title

consul general at large. The Rogers Act created the position of foreign service inspector, with authority to check up on the legations as
well.[71]

With this mandate and a female secretary, Messersmith left for Rio
de Janeiro, the first leg of his tour as inspector and administrative
troubleshooter. Arriving in late March 1930, he found the situation
"serious." Problem number one was the ambassador, Edwin V. Morgan, no relation to Harry Morgan from Antwerp. After eighteen
years in charge of the Rio embassy, Morgan took orders from no one.
He was another example of diplomatic superciliousness in action, "a
complete snob," Messersmith recalled. Morgan received the inspector
coldly, and informed him that "there was going to be no inspection,"
not without explicit instructions from Washington—which, in fact, he
had received. No consul would sit in judgment of him. The inspector
called in his secretary and, in the ambassador's presence, dictated
a telegram to Washington noting his refusal to cooperate. Morgan
fumed, but finally relented.[72]

As Messersmith discovered, he had everything to hide. Morgan's
operation was "a distinct discredit to our Government." The legation
offices were "dilapidated." The furniture was "old [and] in many
cases worm-eaten." Morgan's pending proposal for a new chancery
appeared to have been based, at least so far as location was concerned, upon considerations of "the personal convenience of the officers rather than that of the public." Messersmith recommended an
emergency grant for rental space and furnishings while a new plan
was being drawn up.[73]

His mission was not limited to questions of buildings and management. He had orders to investigate a number of nonadministrative
problems. Foremost in Rio was the case of the National City Bank of
New York. The bank, for violations of exchange regulations, had
been forced by the Brazilian government to post a $3 million bond.
National City cheerfully confessed its transgressions, but protested
being singled out for punishment: all the foreign banks in Brazil,
it argued, were "well known" violators of the same law. The bankers had found no ally in Morgan. After his residency in Brazil, he
had begun to think like a Brazilian even where Americans were concerned, an occupational affliction of foreign service (or too much of
it in one place) called "localitis." Morgan had an advanced case. "The
less the State Department knows about things of this kind," he told
an inquiring Messersmith, "the better." Actually, as the inspector discovered, the Brazilians were all too eager to settle. The bank soon
had its money back. Morgan received a stern reprimand from Washington. He died at his post before a new administration could replace

him. In accordance with his last will, he was buried in Brazil. The Brazilians even named a street after him.[74]

What impressed Messersmith as he continued on his tour was how well represented the United States generally was, officially and privately, in Latin America. Morgan happily proved the exception rather than the rule. So did National City, in taking liberties with local law. This was a tremendous relief for Messersmith. By the summer of 1930 the corporate pantheon of the 1920s had already been hacked into ruins by the victims of the Wall Street crash and the growing armies of the unemployed. Those who promoted capitalism for a living, like Carr's consuls, inevitably came to reexamine their own institutional loyalties. Servants of a now discredited regime, they were tainted by association with what, in the changed climate, was seen as the economic exploitation of weaker peoples, unsuspecting investors at home or barefooted *campesinos* to the south. But Messersmith found no evidence, or suppressed any he did find, to support the seamier allegations of misconduct or intervention by American business in South America.[75]

Having seen Brazil, Uruguay, Paraguay, and Chile, Messersmith was preparing to leave for Bolivia and Peru when welcome news arrived: his appointment as consul general in Berlin. It was, with London and Paris, the consular service's first prize, by far his "most important assignment . . . a realization of my ambitions." The prospect of leaving the many vexations of Latin America and returning to advanced society pleased him. But his tenure in Argentina and the abbreviated inspection tour was experience that prepared him for more critical Latin American assignments to come.[76]

☆ **II** ☆

Berlin

1930–1934

Messersmith arrived in Berlin to find the Weimar Republic in the throes of its final crisis. Germany had thrived on American loans during the 1920s. With the Wall Street crash, those loans were called in, and Weimar began to go under. By February 1930, 16 percent of the German workforce, some 3.5 million people, had no work, and their numbers were growing. Hard times bred political extremism. In September's Reichstag elections the Communists gained twenty-three new seats. The big winners, however, were Hitler's Nazis, whose delegate strength increased from 12 to 107. The balance of power now rested with Weimar's enemies. On the streets they clashed in bloody brawls. In the Reichstag they cooperated to paralyze the government of Chancellor Heinrich Brüning. Germany's experiment in democracy was doomed.[1]

Of course, officials of the beset regime and diplomats accredited to it continued to insist otherwise, and the most determinedly upbeat among them even believed it. In Messersmith the optimists found an active ally. He was never one to give up a fight, regardless of the odds, and, new on the scene, he did not yet appreciate how hopeless Weimar's position was. In his introductory speeches before various segments of Berlin's business community, he faithfully echoed Washington's current official line: positive thought and deed, he insisted, could still save the day. But this stubborn confidence ran headlong into the facts, which were telling a gloomier story. By 1932 he too was moved to admit that private initiative had run its course; and the events still to come were to destroy the remnants of his faith in the invisible hand.[2]

American public servants knew hardship personally during the depression. Dwindling tax revenues forced Congress to enact an across-the-board 10 percent cut in salaries for the fiscal year beginning July 1932, and another 15 percent the following year. The plight of the Foreign Service became still more desperate. Paid leaves went by the

26

board. The steady depreciation of the dollar further eroded purchasing power. Men in the lower grades were obliged to let insurance
policies lapse, to take children out of school, and to scrimp on food
and housing.[3]

By the end of 1932, according to his own careful estimate, Messersmith's $9,000 salary had lost almost a third of its real value. Money
meant altogether too much to him for him not to complain.[4] But
even as he did so, he was also acting selflessly to alleviate the very
real suffering of his staff, who lacked his outside resources. The official family at the consulate general continued on after hours almost
nightly at his dinner table. And this fostered an intimacy among
them otherwise inhibited by rank and protocol. Vice Consul Cecil W.
"Joe" Gray was a soft-spoken Tennessean who had come with Messersmith from Buenos Aires and would go with him to his next post.
Gray was a brilliant organizer and a clear thinker, traits that would
eventually bring him one of the least visible and most powerful positions in the entire American foreign-policy establishment: personal
secretary to another Tennessean soon to become secretary of state.[5]

Messersmith's second in command in Berlin was Consul Raymond
H. Geist. After winning a Harvard Ph.D. in English, Geist entered
the wartime navy, entering the consular service upon his discharge.
Appointed to Berlin in October 1929, he was to remain there for the
next eleven tumultuous years. During that period Geist would be an
unsung hero of American foreign service—unsung, that is, except by
Messersmith, who never failed to commend him to the State Department higher-ups. Geist's death-defying protection work in the stormy
days ahead and extraordinary political prescience made him singularly indispensable in Berlin; and that was why, despite Messersmith's
and others' patronage, his career lagged behind others less able than
himself. Finally, in 1940, he was brought home to head up a new
division of commercial affairs in the reorganized State Department.
In 1945, he moved on to Mexico City, where he was reunited with
the chief whose acquaintance he first made fifteen years before in
Berlin.[6]

Although only four years his junior, Geist became the closest thing
to a protégé Messersmith developed during his foreign service
career. He would have been a hardhearted man indeed not to be
touched by Geist's unabashed admiration for him. Geist consciously
modeled himself after the older man. "I have always tried to be an
apt scholar,"[7] he wrote him almost reverentially in 1934. This was
hardly typical of the men Messersmith had supervised so far. His
reputation as a martinet was already firmly established throughout

the service. One anonymous former subordinate recalled resentfully that "he couldn't help talking to you as though you hadn't done your homework." Geist was the star pupil who did do his homework, and one of very few who penetrated Messersmith's emotional shell as well.[8]

Geist and Gray made the civil-service-compensation crisis a personal one for Messersmith. He put Carr on repeated notice that the "splendid" dedication of his staff was being taxed to the limit. And he endeavored to ease their burden, albeit in a small and largely symbolic way, by better using what resources there were at his disposal. Efficiency, one of his abiding values, became a human imperative for him as well.[9] The thirty American consular offices scattered throughout Germany reported, at least in theory, to the consulate general in Berlin. But only with Messersmith's arrival was that authority enforced. He and Gray took to the road, increasingly to scale back operations and cut costs in line with the depression-related declines in business and tourism. At Cologne half the rented offices were let go. The consulate at Stuttgart moved into smaller quarters, and cheaper by $2,300 a year. While these savings may have been of no direct benefit to the hard-pressed consuls, Messersmith's leadership in their cause was surely a tonic for consular morale.[10]

The one redeeming aspect of government retrenchment for Messersmith was that the meddlesome commercial and agricultural foreign services were cut even closer to the bone. Commerce's appropriation was cut 50 percent; accordingly, half of its personnel were fired and twenty-six of its fifty-two foreign offices were shuttered up. By a May 1933 coordination agreement with the State Department, Agriculture and Commerce agreed to confine their remaining attachés to capital cities.[11] The immediate result for Messersmith was that a small horde of indolent bureaucrats descended upon Berlin, where they did little more than exercise his spleen. Few of them, he wrote disgustedly to Carr, put in "a day's work in a week. Most of them spend their time 'promoting trade' in some of the hotel bars," while consuls were doing the real work and struggling to hold body and soul together. In Messersmith the independent attachés were one day to find their master.[12]

What concerned Messersmith more immediately was the consolidation of diplomatic and consular operations in Germany, a move easily justified during the depression as an economy measure, but one, as he well knew, fraught with political and social implications. The "old line diplomatic officers" at the Berlin embassy, as elsewhere, he snorted to a friend, considered it "a desecration of the sanctity of the diplomatic establishment to associate it with so matter of fact an establishment as the consulate." The worst of them, fully the equal of Bliss in Buenos Aires or Morgan in Rio, was George Gordon, counselor of the embassy. An Alabaman educated at Harvard, Gordon was a consummate snob. With his "gray-white hair and mustache which looked curled, elegant dress, gloves, stick, and proper hat, a complexion of flaming hue, clipped, polite and definitely condescending accent," he was almost a caricature. Gordon would no sooner consort with consuls as equals than be seen in public in his underwear.[13]

The tide, however, seemed to be turning against him and his ilk. Diplomatic resistance to the Rogers Act had drawn the attention of Senate investigators, whose probe turned up the aforementioned pattern of brazen favoritism and discrimination against the consuls. With the dual promotion list and the diplomatic majority on the personnel board, only token numbers of senior consuls had been admitted into diplomacy under Rogers. To close its loopholes, Congress in February 1931 passed the Moses-Linthicum Act. Carr obtained important new powers, with which, according to one historian, he "strove constantly for commonality in the service: a single set of regulations, commissioning under both diplomatic and consular titles, and consolidation of diplomatic and consular work in capital cities."[14]

Then there was Gordon's chief at the embassy, the ambassador since 1930, Frederic M. Sackett, Jr. A former business executive and United States senator, Sackett was encumbered by neither diplomatic prejudices nor diplomatic experience, and so refused to deprive himself of Messersmith's clear talents and good judgment. He occasionally accompanied Messersmith on his consular inspection rounds. Such fraternizing irked Gordon no end, but Sackett learned much about conditions in the German hinterland, where a revolution was gathering force. Their travels together brought Messersmith and Sackett closer personally. But consular-diplomatic consolidation could stand on its merits. Messersmith had found an ideal facility in which to house it, the old Bluecher Palace near the Brandenburg Gate. It was sufficiently commodious for all the diplomatic and consular offices, and for the attachés, too, if and when circumstances permitted. Best of all, the owners, strapped for cash, were willing to let the place go for only $1.8 million. Recognizing the bargain, Sackett enlisted his erstwhile colleague, Senator Claude Swanson, to help expedite the transaction on the American side. In September 1931 the government took title. Gordon grimaced.[15]

But he soon had reason to smile. On the evening of 30 March 1932, just before the first Americans were due to move in, the Bluecher Palace was gutted by fire. The damage was assessed at $200,000. The debate over its fate was reopened. The building would sit and rot for six years while it was being decided in Washington whether to fund the repairs or to unload what some contended had been a white elephant from the first.[16]

The Bluecher rubble was a metaphor for the status of Foreign Service reform at the end of 1932. Budget cuts and making ends meet had largely preempted the reformist agenda. Some efficiencies, born of dire necessity, had been achieved. But Congress's democratizing initiatives had been blunted by the State Department bureaucracy into which Carr, the supposed agent of change, had been co-opted. His crusade for the consuls had partly been a personal one, for acceptance by those who by mutual agreement were his betters. Having achieved rank and power, he used them sparingly, so as not to offend. In November 1932 Messersmith complained privately about Carr's failure to prevent the "reactionary diplomats" from "educating and training a new class of snobs," among whom the "idea remains firmly fixed that a diplomatic assignment, no matter how low in grade, is more important than a consular assignment." The only solution, he was convinced, was for the department to take "the bull by the horns," implementing "constant and recurring transfers" between the services. Moses-Linthicum gave Carr the power to do just that, but, predictably for Messersmith, little came of it. In all 1932, only one senior consul was promoted to a diplomatic mission. The cause required more determined leadership than anyone currently on the scene could or would supply.[17]

The triumph of de-facto segregation at the State Department was a keen personal defeat for Messersmith and all the consuls. As he approached his fiftieth birthday, a time when many get to savor the success of their careers, his had reached an apparent dead end. He could look forward to a future of lateral transfers, or worse. For word had reached him that in agitating for himself and for reform he had again irritated Carr, not to mention the diplomats. With influential enemies and few friends at the State Department, Messersmith had reason to fear exile back to the boondocks, a fate not unknown to others who rocked the boat.[18]

If his superiors wished to punish Messersmith for his heresies, they soon had a pretext. In November it was announced that the renowned physicist Albert Einstein had accepted an invitation to do research at California's Mount Wilson Observatory. In response, several rightwing organizations in the United States publicly charged that Einstein was a Communist, and demanded that the State Department certify that extending him a visa would not endanger national security. Carr meekly complied, issuing the appropriate orders to the consulate general in Berlin. With Messersmith off on an inspection tour, Geist received Einstein and his wife on 5 December and, following instructions, questioned them about their politics. She refused to answer; and before he could, she got up and stalked out, her illustrious husband in tow. She then contacted reporters to denounce the "consul general" for "rudeness," and threatened to call off the American trip unless the State Department apologized and approved their visas within twenty-four hours.[19]

The incident set off a storm of criticism at home. Walter Lippmann derided Messersmith—who, of course, had missed the whole affair—as "The Perfect Bureaucrat," and demanded his recall. President Nicholas Murray Butler of Columbia University declared that his "heart wept for his country at the spectacle of what happened at the Consulate General in Berlin." The American Civil Liberties Union launched an investigation of State Department visa practice.[20]

Messersmith rushed back to Berlin at the first word of trouble. His investigation frankly laid the blame where it belonged: on the State Department—that is, on Carr—for insisting on "silly procedures" in order to satisfy domestic "extremists"; and on the Berlin journalists who had reported the Einsteins' complaints without getting the consulate's side of the story. He also concluded that the Einsteins were not entirely innocent victims—that they were trying to divert attention from very real Communist associations. The reality Messersmith and Geist had to face was that both their careers were in jeopardy. For it seemed entirely possible that Carr, having begun by truckling to representatives of the political right, would hand over Messersmith and/or Geist as a sacrifice to the liberal left.[21]

Happily, this was not to be. Messersmith's friends around the world wrote the State Department to the effect that if it were he who was rude, it must have been richly deserved. The Einsteins' visas were hastily processed. Aboard ship they admitted to reporters that they had perhaps overreacted, and that their inquisitor, whoever he was, did not deserve punishment. At a 10 December press conference Secretary of State Henry Stimson exonerated Messersmith and the consulate, and then telephoned Lippmann, who two days later published his apologies. Other newspapers did the same.[22]

Messersmith was so relieved that for a time, instead of brooding over his future, he counted his blessings. His friends had come through when he needed them, and, he wrote one, he was "eternally grateful" for their support and Stimson's. And when his thoughts once more turned to the question of his career prospects (as they very shortly did), he decided that the Einstein imbroglio had not been such a bad thing after all. Those who had wrongly accused him were at least a little in his debt, and his exoneration strengthened him in his belief in a righteous justice whose payoff for him personally could not be far away. It was only now, as 1932 came to a welcome and happy end, that he began to set aside and save his personal papers—an act of confidence, perhaps, in bigger and better things in store for him.[23]

Nor was this renewed self-confidence simply a product of faith. The year 1933 opened with an air of expectancy especially keen in Germany and the United States. In Washington the Democrats and Franklin D. Roosevelt prepared to assume leadership of a stricken nation. Their activism and optimism was contagious even 6,000 miles away in Berlin, and Messersmith took heart, for his depression-ravaged country and for his career. Major changes in the direction and makeup of the government could be anticipated with a new party taking over the White House in normal times, and these times were decidedly abnormal. The executive departments, dominated by Republicans for more than a decade, braced for the worst. Nowhere was the apprehension greater, and more justly so, than at the State Department. The senior diplomats remembered what had befallen them under the last Democratic administration, and Roosevelt, despite his Ivy League roots, was said to harbor no more affection for them. Whether the threat to their dominance would come in the form of political outsiders or men like Messersmith promoted from the ranks, or whether it would come at all, was still an open question. But the promise of greater fluidity and opportunity in the State Department was clearly at hand.[24]

Messersmith, for one, was buoyed to the point of entertaining wildly unrealistic thoughts of himself catapulting into a policy position in the new administration. He was never one to underrate himself. In this instance he wrote to a casual acquaintance whom he believed to have a line to Roosevelt, to the effect that he was just the man the president was presumably looking for to enforce the will of Congress at the State Department. To that end he boldly advised firing all the current assistant secretaries except for Carr, "in many respects the most valuable officer within the Department." But Carr needed someone at his side to "complement and work with" him, and occasionally to push him, and Messersmith, though "not eager to serve in Washington," was willing "to make the personal sacrifices involved" in an important cause. Roosevelt saw his letter, and took some of its advice: Carr was to be the only Hoover holdover in the upper echelons of his State Department. But that was as far as Roosevelt was willing to go—at the time.[25]

If Messersmith, still an unknown functionary, really considered himself anything but a very long shot for an assistant secretaryship in 1933, he was in deep trouble. He was, we may hope and trust, more actively concerned with who would become secretary of state, applauding when it turned out to be the junior senator from Tennessee, Cordell Hull. Messersmith had first met him a decade earlier, when then Congressman Hull stopped in Antwerp during a European junket. He had invited Messersmith to his hotel room that night for talks, a courtesy Messersmith never forgot. Hull, he recalled of that encounter, was "a saintly-looking man, with a charming, engaging personality, shy and modest." More importantly, Hull's worldview was congenial to consuls. He was convinced that "unhampered trade dovetailed with peace; high tariffs, trade barriers, and unfair competition with war." Throughout the 1920s and early 1930s Hull had crusaded against the rising tide of protectionism at home and abroad, repeatedly warning his congressional colleagues that economic nationalism would backfire disastrously, and cost the country markets and jobs. That prophecy had indeed come true. With Hull at the helm, the State Department was expected to do battle for expanded trade. Consuls figured to play an important role in that cause.[26]

While the Roosevelt team was being assembled, Germany continued to sink. Heinrich Brüning's government had fallen in May 1932, a victim of the worsening depression. His successor as chancellor, Franz von Papen, was "a well-bred buffoon" who proved to be the tool of a camarilla of military men and others with a common hatred for the republic. In the 31 July Reichstag elections, the Nazis easily outdrew seven other parties. Hitler rejected all overtures to form a coalition government, insisting upon terms that would effectively make him dictator.[27]

Pressure mounted. In late December Messersmith predicted "fireworks here pretty soon." Actually the momentous transfer of power took place peacefully. On 30 January 1933 Hitler was named chancellor. Germany would not know real peace again for a dozen years. On 27 February the Reichstag went up in flames. Civil liberties were suspended and leftists were arrested en masse. In 5 March elections Hitler secured a working majority in the relocated Reichstag, which promptly voted itself out of practical existence. Hitler now controlled the state. The first stage of the Nazi revolution was over. Where it was headed was anyone's guess. One thing was clear: the coming months would see events of extraordinary significance for Germany and the world.[28]

Ambassador Sackett had kept Washington well informed on these critical developments. But he owed his position to the outgoing Republican administration; and when he tendered his resignation to the president-elect, as was customary, it was accepted. By inauguration day he had departed Berlin.[29]

A replacement was not immediately forthcoming. Filling the embassy in Berlin proved more difficult than most for Roosevelt, partly because he sensed the significance of what was going on there in 1933. A second-rater would not do. But because of how costly and physically taxing the German mission figured to be, Roosevelt's first several choices, all leading liberals, declined his offer. Not until June did he finally find someone suitable and willing: history professor William E. Dodd of the University of Chicago. By the time Dodd closed out his affairs, briefed himself in Washington, and arrived in Berlin, it was the middle of July.[30]

Thus, for some 100 days the United States was without an ambassador in Germany. They were days of horrifying events and high tension. *Gleischschaltung*, the nazification of German life, began the moment Hitler took power. Leftists and Jews were purged from official life with ruthless avidity. Hitler and his henchmen proclaimed the New Germany, vowing to undo the Treaty of Versailles and to restore the nation to its place in the sun.

While politicians and bureaucrats maneuvered behind the scenes, violence reigned in the open. The Nazi party and its fighting arm, the brown-shirted SA (*Sturmabteilung*, or storm troops), conducted their revolution in the streets. The promise of pillage and jobs had placated that paramilitary force since 1921. Now more than a million strong, the SA considered its time at hand. Germany convulsed in lawlessness as Brown Shirt thugs indulged in kidnapping, assault, and murder for sport and profit. There were accounts to be settled in business, too. Party connections were exploited to secure positions and promotions, and to ruin competitors.[31]

Messersmith strove to make sense of this chaos. He and other close observers concluded that Hitler was nothing more than a low demagogue. The Führer apparently had no real ideology and no program to enact. He had committed himself to economic recovery and revisions in the postwar settlement, but these objectives were supported across the German political spectrum. When pressed on specifics, he had fallen back on "promising everything to everybody," a tactic he was living to regret. Finding himself unable to satisfy extravagant expectations, he had let his minions take the initiative. They were now out of control. In the relative vacuum of Versailles, the SA was the largest and most potent armed force in the country, and it had made clear that it would not submit to restraint. If Hitler accepted its challenge, Messersmith thought, he and his entourage would be swept aside by "real radicals."[32]

Messersmith's perspective would change with the events he was reporting. For now it was significant that he was reporting them at all, in lengthy regular despatches to the State Department. Political reporting was the embassy's responsibility; and Gordon, chargé d'affaires since Sackett's departure, did not appreciate the competition. But the ambassadorial vacancy at this critical time and place was Messersmith's chance to show what consuls could do beyond their accustomed realm of business and commerce, an opportunity he did not intend to let slip away. In violating the State Department's division of labor, he struck a blow for himself and for a truly unified Foreign Service.[33]

In the months ahead Messersmith upheld still higher ideals in the netherworld of Nazi Germany. Foreigners, he believed, had to impress upon the Hitler government that Germany's problems could not be resolved unilaterally, that while the world might view sympathetically the needs of a responsible regime, it would not be inclined to make sacrifices to help a regime that did not keep law and order on its streets. Indeed, as Messersmith wrote in March, Germany was seeking the lifting of Versailles restrictions at the World Disarmament Conference in Geneva, and was hoping for a reduction in interest rates on its foreign indebtedness at the World Economic Conference, scheduled for June in London. It had to be made clear that these claims on the world awaited Hitler's asserting his authority over the SA.[34]

By late March Messersmith could report some movement in this direction. Hitler's speeches suggested that he frowned on violence and was sensitive to adverse publicity. Foreign protest rallies, like that of 27 March at New York City's Madison Square Garden, and boycotts against German products, Messersmith reported, were creating "what was almost hysteria" in responsible German circles. Joseph Goebbels's propaganda machine tried to counter negative foreign opinion by enlisting prominent Jews and foreigners to praise publicly the Nazi revolution for its tolerance. Hitler denounced the troublemakers as Communists masquerading as Nazis. Prussian Interior Minister Hermann Göring, Foreign Minister Konstantin von Neurath, and Ernst Hanfstängl, the foreign press chief, all insisted that the reports of trouble on the streets were "lies" manufactured by "enemies" of the Third Reich, notably the Jews. On 28 March plans were announced for a boycott of German Jewish businesses as retribution for Jewish "slanders."[35]

Was this a regime seeking a rationale for persecution or one trying to restore order and satisfy world criticism? Messersmith leaned to the latter view. The boycott, he decided, represented an initiative by Hitler and the moderates to take control. An open crackdown on lawlessness would be too risky, but the announced action, Messersmith believed, might serve to preempt the SA's program. Indeed, the boycott proved almost a nonevent. Many Germans even patronized Jewish shops, in defiance of SA pickets. On 4 April the regime announced that the boycott had "achieved its purpose and therefore need not be resumed." Messersmith noted a sharp decline in anti-Jewish violence in the next days.[36]

There were other signs as well that the regime was amenable to reason, desirous of internal tranquillity, and not without goodwill toward the outside world. Random or calculated, SA ruffianism inevitably affected United States citizens and property. In early March several Americans vanished without a trace. Others were brutally attacked on the streets. The kidnappings and assaults continued as the month wore on. On the 31st, in one of several incidents that week, three Americans were seized and taken to an abandoned warehouse converted into an SA prison. They were stripped naked and forced to sleep on the freezing floor. The next morning they were beaten unconscious and dumped onto the sidewalk.

To this point, Messersmith's repeated protests to the local police had gone unanswered. The gendarmes were paralyzed by uncertainty as to whether the new regime was on the side of the victims or the thugs. What evidence there was, in fact, suggested the worst. "The police," Göring told a crowd at Essen on 11 March, "do not exist to protect the swindlers, scoundrels, profiteers, and traitors." The Brown Shirts had taken that message to heart. So had the police.[37]

But things were changing for the better. Messersmith prevailed upon American journalists not to transmit their reports of the 31 March incidents for forty-eight hours, in order to give the authorities a chance to act first. This time, with the apparent approval of the government, the police were "extraordinarily active, efficient, and rapid in the action which they took." Within the day, several SA men had been apprehended, "sharply reproved," and expelled from the organization.[38]

Although attacks on Americans did not cease, Messersmith was convinced that the regime wished them to. Hitler called for discipline and ordered a crackdown on offenders. On 26 April the Gestapo (State Secret Police) was established, with a budget of almost 4 million marks and a mandate to impose order. Geist was friendly with the Gestapo chief, Dr. Rolf Diehls. When informed that the United

Press correspondent, Dr. Paul Kecskemeti, had disappeared, Diehls launched an investigation. He phoned the next day with word that the journalist was again a free man. The SA, Messersmith reported triumphantly, "was no longer above the law."[39]

Messersmith also pointed to a moderating trend in Nazi economic policy. Here too Hitler seemed to have become a victim of his own cynicism. Just as the SA were wooed with promises of Jewish spoils, small businessmen and the unemployed had responded to Hitler's pledge to break up concentrated wealth. He had fulminated against corporations, landed estates, and foreign capital, all the while privately reassuring the upper classes. Now he was being called to account. He apparently appreciated, Messersmith observed, that the radical policies demanded by the masses would lead to "economic ruin and the reduction of Germany to a country of peasants," as well as the estrangement of big business, whose cooperation was essential to ending the depression. Moreover, the regime could not discriminate against foreign capital unless it was prepared to brave foreign censure and probable retaliation.[40]

Hitler seemed to have no ready answer to his dilemma. "The government," reported Messersmith on 25 April, "has no real [economic] program; it is drifting with the tide." The Führer's speech of 1 May, in which he was expected to outline his recovery program, contained only the usual empty encomiums to labor. Aside from token make-work projects, the regime as yet had done nothing to help the unemployed masses. "The situation of the individual German," Messersmith concluded, "has in no sense been made easier." And no relief was in sight.[41]

Local party leaders had their own plans. Acting, as one scholar puts it, "on the assumption that Hitler privately wanted them to do what the government could not do officially," they declared open season on "non-Aryan monopolists." A Combat League of Middle-Class Tradespeople, or Kampfbund, was organized. Brown Shirts enforced Kampfbund sanctions against chain and department stores, long the bane of small shopkeepers. That many of the large stores were entirely or partially American-owned seemed only to make them more tempting targets, as Messersmith soon learned. Several F. W. Woolworth outlets were put out of business. The Hermann Tietz store, Germany's second largest, had to drop its profitable restaurant concession. Store executives who resisted risked Brown Shirt picket lines or worse.[42]

Drunk with success, the Combat League took on larger quarry. Big industrial concerns soon came under pressure to replace Jews and moderates in upper management with party *kommisare*, usually, as

Messersmith observed, young incompetents. Foreign-owned firms again got special attention. In April the party decreed that government contracts would henceforth be restricted to "Aryan" companies—those certified as free of Jewish, Communist, and foreign influence. Approved vendors were listed in a party directory distributed to all government purchasing offices. American firms were left out. When the companies protested, party officials suggested that they fire all of their Jews, deposit funds equal to 54 percent of their total capital into the Reichsbank, and provide regular party kickbacks.[43]

On Messersmith's advice, all refused to submit to what he concluded was "systematized blackmail" and a clear violation of the antidiscriminatory provisions of the German-American commercial agreement of 1923. More importantly, the German government agreed with him and acted accordingly.[44] On 1 May Alfred Hugenberg, the economics minister, ordered "all independently placed *kommisare* removed" and urged businessmen to resist unauthorized interference. Göring publicly threatened to dissolve the Combat League altogether unless its meddling ceased. American firms suddenly received "clean bills of health" as "pure German firms." On orders from Hitler's deputy, Rudolf Hess, the department store pickets were removed. At the same time, Kampfbund cells began being absorbed into Dr. Robert Ley's German Labor Front, a process completed by mid-August.[45]

It was an impressive display of resolve and authority, indicative, as Messersmith wrote the State Department in early June, of "an almost unbelievable movement in the direction of moderation." Goebbels, who had emerged as among the most radical members of the ruling circle, now appeared to be on the eclipse. A respected insurance executive, Kurt Schmitt, replaced Hugenberg at economics. Schmitt promised foreign businessmen fair treatment. His speech before the German Trade Council, lamenting the removal of Jewish managers and emphasizing the importance of foreign trade, struck Messersmith as "the most constructive statement by any public man in Germany on economic matters."[46]

Although no definite economic policy had been established yet, Messersmith was "convinced of the [regime's] sincerity" in claiming not to want "foreign interests or capital disturbed." Despite popular and party pressure for repudiation, Germany continued to service its external debt. Foreigners were generally safe on the streets. So were the Jews. Messersmith had "reason to believe that Hitler disapproved of the general anti-Jewish action" and was "moderate in his views in this respect." The regime seemed to be reassessing its position on

Jews in the country's official and cultural life. The removal of Jewish artists like the conductor Bruno Walter had aroused such open public indignation that Messersmith felt safe in predicting on 23 May that they would be "gradually brought back to their old places."[47]

Amid all these healthy signs, however, militarism was flourishing. Germany seemed to have lost itself in pomp and pageantry. Uniforms had become the rage in fashion. Strident rhetoric spewed forth from pulpits around the country. Clearly Germany was a nation that did not crave peace. But Messersmith generously passed off the martial goings-on as a relatively harmless diversion for the unemployed that, like the April anti-Jewish boycott, aimed to steal the thunder of the party radicals. In fact, Hitler's announced foreign-policy objectives seemed eminently negotiable. Hardly a Westerner outside France in 1933 disputed his contention that modifications in Versailles were long overdue. Certainly there was room for talk among reasonable people, and Messersmith, as late as the early summer, was inclined to see the current German leadership as such. Germany had undergone a revolution, with the inevitable bloodshed and brutality, but he was convinced that "a good deal of the greatest danger is over." It would be "a trouble spot for a long time," but for now he believed that Germany's leaders could be dealt with.[48]

The first 100 days of Nazi Germany were a personal watershed for Messersmith. He had never lacked for opportunities to do good and meaningful work, but never before had so much hinged on the outcome. For a State Department that dreaded crises, it was enough that he had staved one off, by quietly and effectively defending Americans and their interests.[49] But of equal importance was the fact that he had not compromised his principles one iota in so doing. He had done no fawning for favors for American life and property. He had, rather, demanded what was due him and his country, had registered his unequivocal disgust at the assault on civilized values, had refused to acquiesce to the reign of brute force. He had set an example of courage and conviction that left knowledgeable Berliners, German and foreign, gaping with admiration or, in the case of the Nazis, frustrated fury. "Truly magnificent," one American witness to his heroics wrote of him. Among "his colleagues . . . he is practically regarded as having ambassadorial rank." Practically, but not quite. Another spoke of his "burning courage . . . and passionate devotion to democracy, decency, and truth."[50]

The Nazis had discovered right from the start that he was one foreigner they could not ride roughshod over. Those who tried had got back a taste of their own nasty medicine.[51] "Putzi" Hanfstängl was one who learned his lesson the hard way. With his Harvard edu-

cation, modest musical talent, and charming façade, Putzi had wan-
gled his way into Hitler's early inner circle. Messersmith heard that
the Führer kept him around mainly as a favor to Putzi's mother, who
had sheltered the then down-and-out Führer-to-be during his foot-
loose days in postwar Munich. Although "never more than a court
jester," Hanfstängl, Messersmith recalled, "thought that his position
as Hitler's favorite and his uniform permitted him to do anything."
Messersmith first ran into him at an American embassy reception.
Putzi dripped sarcasm. "Oh," he said, "so this is the famous Messersmith who knows everything that is going on and doesn't like it."
Boor that he was, Putzi started rubbing against the leg of the woman
seated at his side at the dinner table. The other guests tried to ignore
the scandal, but Messersmith, never fearing a scene, rose to denounce Putzi's behavior "in unvarnished language." The German, he
recalled, "was an exemplary guest the rest of the evening."[52]

To repay Messersmith for that humiliation, Putzi dedicated himself
to a crude revenge. Employing the favorite Nazi smear, he circulated
the rumor that Messersmith was a Jew—a falsehood that gained considerable currency. In February 1934 Putzi was still busily accumulat-
ing evidence of Messersmith's supposed "unfriendl[iness] to the German Government and the German people," hoping to make a case
for his recall.[53]

Others, to go by Messersmith's memoirs alone, employed less diplomatic means to get him out of their hair. Crossing the street outside
his office after one especially harrowing day, he remembered looking
up at a sedan (SA?) bearing down on him, swerving at the last minute
to avoid him. Some days later the prank was repeated in more deadly
earnest. He learned never to drop his guard, on the streets or in
conversation. Suspecting that the telephones in his office and home
had been tapped, he conducted his own campaign of misinforma-
tion, which worked so well that, according to his own information,
Goebbels "froth[ed] at the mouth" at the mention of his name. Certainly he had gained the Nazis' wary respect. Messersmith, a party
newspaper concluded grudgingly, was one non-Aryan who "approach[ed] the German spirit."[54]

With the apparent return of German sanity and the arrival of Ambassador Dodd, Messersmith anticipated a respite from the daily
pressures of life-and-death situations. The Dodd party—the ambassador and his wife and their two adult children—landed in Hamburg
on 13 July. Messersmith met the new envoy two days later. He "liked
Dodd from the outset." Gordon had a much unhappier introduction
to the new ambassador's plainspoken Americanism. Dodd told him in

no uncertain terms that work habits geared more to the social life than to embassy business would no longer be tolerated.[55]

Certainly Dodd was intellectually equipped for his mission. Thanks to his graduate studies at Leipzig, he was fluent in German and understood the German character in a way that few did. No one, Messersmith wrote later, "realized what was happening in Germany more thoroughly than he." Dodd's first analysis agreed that the current trend was toward moderation, a trend, Messersmith observed, to which Dodd himself contributed. The Nazis kept nagging him to get him to say something positive about the regime, but Dodd proved their rhetorical equal, parrying leading questions with his ready command of history to remind Germans of the futility of extremism. After Dodd had been in Berlin for a month, Messersmith assured the State Department that his appointment was "one of the wisest that could have been made."[56]

But the ambassador's limitations soon became clear. Just to look at him raised serious questions about his fitness for his post. Messersmith had had to call upon all his physical reserves to stand up to the Nazi steamroller; the short, slender, sixty-five-year-old Dodd "gave the impression of being rather fragile." So were his nerves, and in Nazi Germany that would not do. He struck Messersmith as a classic ivory-tower academic, with "little knowledge of economics or business" and "very little contact with some of the realities of life." Dodd made no secret of his disdain for the fine points and the finery of diplomacy. Determined to lead a life of Jeffersonian simplicity, he ordered Messersmith to find him inexpensive living accommodations. But Messersmith was convinced that the Germans "would not understand nor respect such modesty," and so arranged for him to get the royal suite at the luxurious Hotel Esplanade at less than half the usual rate. The naïve ambassador marveled that "six embarrassingly elegant rooms with beautiful furniture" cost him only 40 marks a day.[57]

Dodd's vendetta against indolence and ostentation at the embassy won him few friends there. Before very long the ambassador and the bulk of his staff, professional and clerical, had settled into a relationship of mutual distrust and distaste that only hardened over the years. In long, handwritten letters—Dodd suspected that the stenographers were feeding gossip about him to his embassy enemies—he inveighed to Roosevelt and Hull against his "wealthy staff people" who "think more of wearing good clothes than doing good work," men who made themselves "rediculous [sic] imitating Louis XIV." They reciprocated the sentiment.[58]

On the bright side, though not for Gordon, relations with the consulate general, home of the work ethic, were never better than under Dodd. He gave high marks to Geist, and praised Messersmith as "a good disciplinarian [who] keeps his staff in order" and "sense[s] things accurately." Best of all, "there is not a lazy streak in him." After Messersmith left Berlin, however, their friendship cooled, partly because Dodd correctly suspected that Messersmith sought his job. In 1936, drained physically and emotionally by the diplomatic mission that he and his many enemies agreed was a failure, Dodd wrote a bitter and irrational letter both denying and regretting having endorsed Messersmith for promotion.[59]

Tactical differences developed between them soon after Dodd's arrival. The first concerned Edgar Ansel Mowrer, Berlin correspondent of the *Chicago Daily News* and president of the city's foreign press association. Mowrer had irked the Nazis early on with the January 1933 publication of his Pulitzer Prize–winning exposé, *Germany Puts the Clock Back*. His despatches to the *Daily News* were in the same lurid vein. In April the Germans began to take aim. They imposed stiff restrictions on all foreign journalists, restrictions that would be lifted, they implied, when Mowrer resigned as their spokesman. He offered to do so, but his colleagues refused to hear of it. Messersmith delivered their decision to Göring, pointing out that the real problem was the lawlessness on the streets, not the honest efforts to report it. Sure enough, in the ensuing days the restrictions were relaxed nevertheless, and Mowrer stopped being harassed.[60]

Three months later Mowrer was again an item of controversy. In late July the attacks on American citizens and property resumed. As before, Mowrer reported the bloodcurdling facts, and the Nazis renewed their efforts to get rid of him. On two separate occasions, the German chargé d'affaires in Washington, Rudolf Leitner, demanded that the State Department arrange his recall. Leitner got back two long lectures on the virtues and constraints of the free press.[61]

Stymied on the diplomatic front, the Nazis resorted to physical intimidation, at which they excelled. Mowrer became the target of anonymous death threats. The police stationed guards outside his home, but warned that nothing further could be done to protect him. Fearlessly he carried on, forcing the regime to a more direct solution. The journalist and his wife were simply ordered to leave the country. Mowrer and Messersmith called on Dodd, hoping for his support in fighting the expulsion. The meeting went badly. Dodd came away convinced that Mowrer "was almost as vehement, in his way, as the Nazis," and that for the sake of the other foreign journalists, he ought to leave quietly. The question became academic for

Dodd when, on 20 August, Mowrer's publisher, Frank Knox, reassigned him to Tokyo. Two days later, at a meeting with Hans Dieckhoff of the German Foreign Office, Dodd agreed to urge Mowrer's immediate departure. Dodd did, and the journalist never forgave him for it. The Mowrers left Berlin a few days later. Messersmith alone among American officials, Mrs. Mowrer remembered, "left a dinner party to come down to the [railroad] station to embrace Edgar for the last time."[62]

The loss of the courageous Mowrer came just as the Hitler regime seemed to be throwing all restraint to the winds. The "almost unbelievable movement toward moderation" of early July reverted to the bedlam of March. Messersmith's respite was over almost before it began. Dossiers on Americans assaulted in the streets again piled up on his desk. A young American tourist couple were set upon in Leipzig. He suffered "internal injuries [from which] he may never recover"; she miscarried and "will never again be able to bear children." In Berlin an American medical researcher, hurrying to his office on Unter den Linden, made the mistake of not stopping to return the Nazi salute to a passing SA corps. Later that day a number of Brown Shirts paid him a surprise visit that reduced the physician to "a mass of raw flesh." Messersmith was summoned. He "took one look and got as quickly as I could to one of the basins where the doctor washed his hands."[63]

So it went. In late August the noted radio commentator H. V. Kaltenborn arrived in Berlin to prepare a series of broadcasts. In talks with Messersmith, Kaltenborn expressed the opinion that the reports of Mowrer and others must be greatly exaggerated. Four days later his wife and son, strolling the Berlin streets, were beaten bloody while two policemen ten feet away watched in amusement.[64]

The Germans were abandoning reason and cooperation on the economic front as well. American business interests suffered as in the spring, but now at the initiative of the regime, not over its opposition. By the end of 1933, the 1923 treaty, on which Messersmith had rested his case for relief, had been effectively abrogated. On 11 August the Commerce Ministry issued orders requiring travelers leaving the country to obtain permits if they wished to book passage on non-German transportation. By another decree, German firms were permitted a tax deduction for replacement machinery if and only if purchased from other German firms. Currency restrictions virtually banned the repatriation of profits. After promising equal treatment for all foreign bondholders, Reichsbank president Hjalmar H. G. Schacht concluded one settlement with Americans calling for 75 percent of the interest due them, followed by agreements granting

Swiss and Dutch bondholders 100 percent. On 18 September the regime announced preferential new import regulations for 1934. The American prune quota was reduced by two-thirds; Yugoslavia, by agreeing to accept German industrial products in compensation, had its quota doubled.[65]

In this climate the SA went back on the economic rampage, drawing upon the popular passions the Kampfbund had tapped. The department-store pickets returned. By November Messersmith estimated that some $40 million in American commercial investments were "a complete loss." The economic vigilantes organized and enforced a "buy at home" drive. Newspapers were pressured into eliminating foreign advertising. The SA published lists of businesses so rash as to patronize non-Aryan contractors. The value of American investments generally, Messersmith reported, "was constantly shrinking" under discrimination.[66]

German Jews bore the brunt of the renewed fury. Far from being restored to their positions, they were undergoing persecution, a horrified Messersmith observed, "of the most refined and deadly character," sometimes organized, and always blessed, by the regime. Expelled from the civil service and the professions, barred from public facilities, robbed and murdered with impunity—with all this, Messersmith concluded, "the life of the Jews has become absolutely impossible." He finally saw that making Germany *judenrein* was one of two objectives—the other being the annexation of Austria—on which the Führer was "absolutely implacable."[67]

Messersmith tried to fight back. But he could no longer count on the cooperation of the bureaucracy—indeed, he could count on its active hostility. Officials with whom he had worked constructively in the spring suddenly displayed symptoms of fanaticism. Dr. Roland Freisler of the Justice Ministry was typical. In April Freisler had helped liberate Americans ensnared by the SA. When Messersmith called on him in August, he found a different Dr. Freisler, who launched into the "usual Nazi harangue," his eyes becoming "those of a maniac." Gestapo chief Diehls turned a sudden deaf ear to Geist's problems. Göring expressed the same regret that Americans and their interests should suffer so, but he now proved unable or unwilling to deliver relief. Americans continued to fall in the streets.[68]

The time had arrived for formal protests. On 4 September, and then again in October, Hull warned Leitner that the State Department was considering advising Americans to stay out of Germany for their own safety. On both occasions Dieckhoff, responding for his government, offered pious "deep regrets," asserting unconvincingly that "these incidents did not indicate any anti-American or anti-foreign sentiment."[69]

Unsatisfied, Hull ordered Dodd to protest personally to Hitler. The ambassador was notably unenthusiastic about this assignment. Fearing a stressful scene with the cantankerous Führer, Dodd, as Messersmith remembered it, came down with what he claimed was the flu. But when Messersmith refused his request to substitute for him, Dodd had no choice but to do his duty. To his acute relief, Hitler was a gentleman during their 17 October talk, save for a brief tirade against Versailles. The ambassador felt the interview had been "favorable" because his nerves were intact. Messersmith recalled that the ambassador "recovered rapidly from his influenza."[70]

Dodd's quick recovery and temporary tender feelings toward the Führer were the only good that came of their talk. Hitler had promised him to "personally see to it that any [SA attacks on Americans] would be punished to the limit of the law." A few well-publicized arrests were made. Messersmith's evidence, however, was that those arrested were entirely innocent of the crimes in question. The real guilty parties had been held and then released, to continue wreaking havoc on German streets.[71]

Diplomatic representations did not satisfy American economic grievances, either. More than anything else happening in 1933, Nazi trade restrictions angered Hull, striking as they did at the most-favored-nation foundation of his traditional liberal economics. In September, fed up with Germany's "numerous colossal frauds" and flagrant violations of American treaty rights, he instructed Dodd to take all necessary steps to secure the "immediate and effective removal of discrimination against American trade." Again Dodd moved halfheartedly, his natural diffidence reinforced by his antipathy to the American "plutocrats" whose presumed interests he was being ordered to defend. In fact, in his representations he was openly sympathetic to the Germans, whose "exports to the United States," as he wrote Hull, "are only one-fourth of American exports to Germany"; it was understandable to him that Germany favored the trade and creditors of nations with whom it enjoyed a more equitable balance of trade.[72]

Dodd's failure to present American demands in "a forcible manner" infuriated Hull and his professional diplomats. Their hatred for Dodd and all he represented would assume rather unprofessional proportions. But Messersmith frankly doubted whether even a more emphatic approach than Dodd's would do much good under the circumstances. After everything that had happened since the summer, there was no more mistaking, at least for him, the true character of the Nazi regime. One British journalist, he wrote Undersecretary of State William Phillips on 29 September, "said that the motto of this revolution is 'Brutality, Mendacity, and Loquacity.'" Messersmith suggested an addition: duplicity. Indeed, he and others who had thought Hitler a traditional statesman open to reason had been deceived. Instead, he believed the worst was true: Hitler and his henchmen were "psychopathic cases [who] would ordinarily be receiving treatment somewhere." Moderates—he considered Göring one— had apparently fallen from power and grace. Schacht, Messersmith learned, had tried to impress upon Hitler the importance of world opinion, but, finding the Führer deaf to his appeals, "has about given it up. Schmitt has little influence except insofar as the internal [economic] situation is concerned," and even here was losing ground to radicals like Walter Darré and Robert Ley and to SA viligantism. Papen, the vice chancellor, was "nothing more than a messenger boy." Neurath, another respectable type, was being retained only "as a decorative and protective front because of the confidence that the diplomats here and chanceries outside have in him." Foreigners, Messersmith warned, were "playing the party's game" if they ignored the new reality of power in Germany.[73]

Where was Hitler headed? It was impossible, Messersmith admitted to Phillips, to predict Germany's future any more than "the keeper of a madhouse is able to tell what his inmates will do in the next hour." But the inmates had taken control of the madhouse. Once all domestic opposition had been crushed or co-opted, a process well underway, Hitler's aim was "to make Germany the most capable instrument of war that there has ever existed." Messersmith admitted he had been wrong: there was nothing insincere about Nazi militarism. Its manifestations were everywhere. "Wherever one goes in Germany," he wrote Phillips, "one sees people drilling, from children of five and six up to those well into middle age." Hitler Youth groups spent weekends under military instruction throwing "dummy hand grenades from a trench at dummy torsos of soldiers." Through the controlled media a "psychology is being developed that the whole world is against Germany and that it lies defenseless against the world." The "most extraordinary fairy tales" were current—that, for example, Germany's enemies planned to bomb the country at any moment. Investments in air-raid shelters were made tax deductible. Messersmith doubted whether Nazi propaganda had succeeded to the point where "the majority of the German people . . . desire war," but the fact was that in a matter of months millions of formerly apathetic Germans had been turned into zealots, ready to follow the Führer wherever he led them.[74]

On 14 October 1933 Hitler led them out of the League of Nations and the World Disarmament Conference, moves ratified by national plebiscite a month later. He regretted the necessity for such steps, Hitler told Germany and the world, but the lack of progress on general disarmament left him no choice. Germany's wish for peace, of course, remained "unshakable." Hitler said his greatest desire was for permanent reconciliation with France: "It would be a mighty occasion for all mankind," he declared, "if the two peoples could forever dismiss force from their mutual dealings."[75]

Many foreigners, Dodd included, credited Hitler's sincerity. Messersmith would never be tricked on that score again. He advised the State Department to "judge Germany by her actions rather than by the declarations of her leaders," which were intended to confuse world opinion. No matter what Hitler said, he "had no desire for peace unless it is a peace which the world makes at the expense of complete compliance with German desires and ambitions." His excuse for quitting Geneva was the purest hypocrisy, for what Germany "is interested in is not so much the other countries cutting down their armaments, as having a free hand . . . to go ahead and rearm herself."[76]

In the weeks ahead Messersmith reported important strides to do just that. German heavy industry again went full blast. Some factories had already been converted to turn out light arms and shell casings. Aircraft construction boomed, ostensibly for commercial use. To his disgust, American firms like Pratt and Whitney, Sperry Gyroscope, and United Aircraft were eagerly supplying components to this incipient Luftwaffe.[77]

In this context of massive militarization, German economic policy made perfect sense. The attacks on American firms, discrimination against American bondholders and trade, and currency restrictions, Messersmith told Washington, were elements of a plot to confiscate foreign property and attain economic self-sufficiency. He predicted that Germany would increasingly pay hard currency only for strategic raw materials, insisting on barter arrangements for consumer imports. The domestic economy was already on a war footing. Basic commodities like copper, petroleum, and textiles had come under government control, with rationing contemplated. German science was being mobilized to search for laboratory substitutes.[78]

By the end of 1933, then, Messersmith was convinced that this German regime was a genuine threat, not only to world peace, but to

everything civilized people held dear. "There is absolutely no humanitarian principle in this government," he wrote Phillips, and no
limit to its malign vision. Göring, one of the few top Nazis he found
capable of "normal conversation," had once matter of factly assured
him that all the land south of the Rio Grande would eventually be
Germany's. Perhaps he meant to quiet concerns that Germany had
designs on the United States proper; Germany apparently laid claim
to everything else. In the years ahead many would discount such talk.
Messersmith never forgot it.[79]

The situation was clear to him. To avoid the certain agonies of
a Nazi future, "in some way or other a more moderate Germany
must be restored." But how? Constructive diplomacy was predicated
on limited objectives he accurately adjudged absent here. Some
observers were predicting that hostile foreign opinion would ultimately either force Hitler out or force him back onto a moderate
course. Messersmith did not reject that possibility categorically, but
he warned that this was "a slender reed on which to lean." The Nazi
upheaval had dominated the foreign press for some weeks at the
beginning, but the world economic crisis and Roosevelt's astonishing
first 100 days had pushed it off the front pages. At best, outside
interest in German developments would be difficult to sustain, especially across the Atlantic.[80]

There was one sure solution. In his letters and despatches to Washington, Messersmith occasionally discussed the military option—
"forcible intervention" or "preventive war"—only to dismiss it as a
practical possibility. He knew full well how utterly unprepared the
West was, militarily and psychologically, to fight an enemy that was
not yet recognized as such. Instead he looked to Germans themselves
to undo what they had visited upon themselves and the world. In the
end, he believed, basic human instincts, moral and economic, would
reassert themselves, and the Hitler regime would be brought to a
merciful and inglorious conclusion. By late 1933, even the German
faithful were complaining about the material hardships demanded
by the new order. Messersmith acknowledged that unemployment
was coming down, but hastened to point out that wages were a pit-
tance while inflation was galloping ahead, especially for the many
consumer necessities in increasingly short supply. Nearly all the
country's cotton and wool was going into uniforms; manufacturers
were warning that the average German would be wearing "paper
clothes" by spring. Party taxes and dues were a further drain on
living standards. Germans were being asked to sacrifice a meal a day
in order to save food. Exporters were growing "panicky" as their
foreign markets dried up. And Messersmith could only see the crisis

going from bad to worse, until the deviant regime was overthrown in favor of a "government with an appreciation of the real principles and facts that form the basis of domestic and international exchange of goods and services," a government "with which we can deal in the ordinary way." It was "the only hope for Europe and for all of us."[81]

Hope was all it was. Already there was clear and disconcerting evidence that the Nazis might indeed be able to weather their economic crisis. "Somehow or other," Messersmith reported incredulously in October, Germany was making do. But, he assured Washington, it was only a matter of time—perhaps weeks—before Hitlerism succumbed to its internal contradictions and an ineluctable justice. Weeks became years, but still Messersmith held firm. As late as January 1938 he was still unready to concede that the regime was not going to fall of its own iniquity.[82]

The internal-collapse thesis was a comforting one indeed in the face of the international realities of the 1930s. For Messersmith understood not only what Hitler meant for civilization, but also how vulnerable it was to the threat he posed. The mood of 1933 had been displayed at the London Economic Conference over the summer. The weariness and wariness engendered by the depression, which the conference was convened to address, all but predicted its failure. It broke up with the industrial nations still more grimly committed to nationalism and finding their own individual solutions. In this climate, the concerted economic sanctions some were urging as a means of hastening Germany's economic collapse and political redemption were about as remote as military intervention. The fact was that a great many Westerners viewed Hitler as something of a blessing, or at least a mitigated evil; his oft-repeated boast that he had saved Germany and Europe from the scourge of Bolshevism was widely credited. And those who found him most repugnant were typically constrained by hopes both for expanded world (including German) trade and for preserving the peace.

The pieces were thus in place for the tragedy that was to unfold over the course of the decade. Messersmith recognized it, but he could not face it. Understanding all too well that the depressed West was unequal to the challenge of Nazism, he took tenacious refuge in the illusion that the problem would essentially dispose of itself. The democracies, in his view, needed only to maintain a kind of passive hostility—rejecting Nazi appeals for economic assistance and isolating the regime politically—until disintegration had run its course. For some two years, until well into 1935, the Western powers waited for that to happen. When it did not—when it became clear that Germany was growing stronger rather than weaker, and increasingly unified as a people—they saw no choice but to try to come to terms with it.[83]

It was not only Messersmith's credibility that suffered over the years for his dogged adherence to the internal-collapse thesis. The false sense of security it fostered may have been fatal for some individuals who turned to him for advice. His anti-Nazism nowhere stood him in better stead than with world Jewry. At a time when the State Department was suppressing his and others' reports of German anti-Semitism, Messersmith frankly spoke the appalling truth. "There is no greater crime in history," he wrote a prominent American Jew in September, "than that which the German government is committing against the Jews." And he told the Germans exactly the same thing. When Göring once retorted that Jews were also discriminated against in the United States, Messersmith stopped him short. There "might be social prejudices," but he had never heard any responsible American advocate "any interference with their completely equal rights in the Government, in the professions and in business and before the law." At the open insinuation that President and Mrs. Roosevelt were surrounded by "practically nothing but" Jewish advisers, Messersmith indignantly replied that "if the President had Jewish friends or Jewish advisers it must be because they were fine people and good citizens of our country." As for the First Lady, "she is an intellectual woman [who] moved in philanthropic and educational circles," and "Jews in the United States have taken such a fine and important part in such activities."[84]

Jews believed they had found a righteous Gentile, and they embraced him. Rabbi Stephen Wise, head of the American Jewish Congress, noticed him early and commended him unreservedly. "As far as there can be a Refuah [healer]," Wise wrote, "he is that for our unhappy people in Germany." The word got around fast. Messersmith became the Jews' man in the Foreign Service and later, as Justice Louis D. Brandeis wrote, "their only active friend among the higher ups in the State Department."[85]

Unfortunately that said more about the State Department than it did about Messersmith. In the context of anti-Semitism and indifference during the 1930s, his record on Jewish matters was relatively good. By any ethical standard, it was not good enough. He failed the persecuted when they most needed him. Hearing of his anti-Nazi exploits in Berlin had prompted Carr in June to remind him to enforce his country's restrictive immigration laws. But Carr's worries were unfounded. Upholding all law in the face of Nazi lawlessness was vitally important to Messersmith. Nor did the laws in question trouble him. After all, he wrote a friend, "we still have an enormous amount of unemployment at home"; refugees would presumably compete with Americans for jobs. His visceral Americanism, source of much that was admirable in him, had a selfish side that favored selective immigration policies even in good times. What had already happened in Germany was for him an object lesson in the fragility of democracy; he determined to do his part to keep out those who might become an added burden on democracy at home. Applicants for visas at the Berlin consulate general during his tenure found abundant sympathy and no disposition whatsoever to bend the rules in their favor. Some were served, but others who could have been were not. There were unfilled places in the German quota in 1933 and 1934, as there would be throughout the decade. Most Jews were turned away, back to a life that, as Messersmith knew so well, was "absolutely impossible" and getting worse every day.[86]

The thought that the Jews' pain would be short-lived helped allay any guilt he may have felt in this grim business. There was, he assured Jewish friends in Berlin, no reason for precipitate flight with the collapse of Hitlerism imminent. Even those qualifying for visas he advised "not to run away but stay here and adopt a policy of watchful waiting." By winter's end Hitler would surely be gone and normal life restored. Whether or not a single Jew chose to stay at his advice, he was encouraging an ultimately disastrous complacency among them.[87]

In December Messersmith made ready for leave from nine grueling Nazi months. Germany, he hoped, would be in different hands when he returned in the spring. In truth, he hoped not to be returning at all. In October he had learned that the American minister to Czechoslovakia, Francis White, intended to resign. Messersmith immediately decided that he was the man to replace him. Two recurrent themes in Hitler's speeches—expansionism and Aryan solidarity—persuaded observers who took him seriously that Czechoslovakia, with its long common frontier and many ethnic Germans, would become an early target of Nazi foreign policy. Washington needed accurate reportage from this likely hot spot, and Messersmith, with his profound understanding of nazism, believed he "could do a very worthwhile job at this Prague post."[88]

But it was more for himself that Messersmith coveted the post. Now fifty years old, he felt he had "to begin to think of my own health and future." He had proved himself in Berlin and waited long enough for the rewards to come his way. "There is nothing ahead of me in the consular branch." He could not "continue indefinitely" to carry the "heavy burdens" of a supervisory consul general. He was "satisfied that the time has arrived for me to transfer to the diplomatic branch where I can get a post as Minister in which I can be reasonably active and render useful service." Prague would be "a logical and proper step in my career."[89]

Unfortunately a great many others viewed Prague in the same appealing light. The post had proved too expensive for White to keep up, but that did not stop a long line of suitors from forming at its door. The competition for Prague was both personal and bureaucratic, and the stiffer for it. Under Roosevelt so far, the major European embassies as well as many of the secondary ones had gone to patronage. Determined to salvage something for the career, Undersecretary Phillips made a stand with Roosevelt over the vacancy in Prague. Career diplomats unhappy where they were—especially in Latin America—were encouraged to promote themselves for the post. Would-be diplomats bearing Democratic IOUs joined the contest. Roosevelt, in short, had a more fundamental decision to make first in whittling down the field for Prague.

Testing the waters, Messersmith was considerably unnerved to discover how much company he already had in pursuit of the post. He expressed particular dismay at finding fellow career men active in the race. Their overt politicking, he complained to a sympathetic Dodd, was both unbecoming and unprofessional. He suggested that his colleagues comport themselves as he claimed to be doing: politely declining offers of assistance from politically connected friends, or at least "doing nothing to encourage my friends to work on my behalf," standing on his record and trusting in fate.[90]

But he wanted Prague badly enough to grovel with the best of them. He had launched his own campaign for the post as soon as he learned it was coming open. There was a long personal letter to Boston businessman Edward A. Filene, asking him to speak to his friend Roosevelt. Filene sent a warm recommendation to Hull instead. In late November the department received a half-dozen letters from prominent Delawarians, which must have been prompted, touting him as "probably the most outstanding man in the Service today." Naming Messersmith to Prague, one leading Democrat wrote, "would please a large number of people in this State."[91]

Upon his arrival in New York on 11 December, Messersmith continued his quest. He met with leading businessmen, including Henry Morgenthau, Sr., Owen Young, Thomas Lamont, and Felix Warburg. He had a long lunch with Henry Stimson. Everyone evinced an "intense" interest in German developments and, encouragingly, an appreciation of his work in Berlin. Proceeding to Washington, he conferred with Carr, Sumner Welles (assistant secretary of state after a brief, tumultuous tour as ambassador to Cuba), and Francis Sayre,

Hull's chief trade adviser. He found Undersecretary Phillips and Jay Pierrepont Moffat, in charge of the division of Western European affairs, "extraordinarily interested" in his Nazi stories and "very appreciative of the information they are getting from Berlin," but noncommittal about Czechoslovakia.[92]

After some time in Delaware, Messersmith went to Fleetwood to spend the holiday season with his mother. What he wanted for Christmas, however, was Prague. He wrote Moffat thrice in a week with anxious inquiries. Not wanting to appear too eager, he always expressed his "ambivalence" about the post, but confessed the obvious: he was "hoping that the President will decide to send me there." Moffat assured him that the decision would soon be announced.[93]

By mid-January, without having heard anything further, Messersmith waxed optimistic in a twenty-eight-page letter to Dodd. He felt "sure that the Department has suggested me to the President as the career man for the post. Mr. Phillips and Mr. Moffat seemed to be very favorable indeed. I understand that Secretary Hull, before he left for [the Pan American conference at] Montevideo was very favorable. . . . My impression is that the President is very well informed, is quite favorable to my appointment, and will appoint me if he appoints a career man."

His intuition was on target at least in respect to Roosevelt. As early as November the president had spoken to Phillips "about promoting Mr. Messersmith to a legation." Roosevelt's sensitive antennae had homed in on the glowing reports about this combative consul who stood up to Nazi bullies. Jews and leading liberals, who rarely had a good word for the State Department, singled out Messersmith for repeated praise. Oswald Garrison Villard, influential editor of *The Nation*, brought him to Roosevelt's attention several times, and *The Nation* named him to its Honor Roll for 1933, "for upholding the rights of Americans in Germany."[94]

And he was a consul. Messersmith's longstanding burden had become his ticket to promotion. Many of candidate Roosevelt's preconceptions about the State Department received confirmation early in his first term. "Definitely unfavorable to the diplomatic side," reported Representative Edith Nourse Rogers (widow of the Rogers Act's author) of a 1934 conversation with the president, "but thought consuls were good." Already suspect for their elitism and Republican connections, the senior career diplomats in Washington were anything but contrite in their early relations with the Roosevelt White House, working feverishly, for example, to scuttle its plan to normalize relations with the Soviet Union. Then there was a warm spot in Roosevelt's Democratic heart for the salt-of-the-earth consuls, the

State Department's long-suffering underclass. At last Rogers and Moses-Linthicum had found an active, though often distracted, advocate at the White House. Messersmith, whom circumstances had thrust into the spotlight, was first in line for the payoff. For when the president learned of White's probable resignation, Messersmith came immediately to his mind as a replacement, "as a reward for his excellent work as Consul General in Berlin."[95]

The State Department also seemed to be on Messersmith's side. Responding to a letter of recommendation from Villard, Phillips assured him that "everyone of us in the Department is anxious to see him promoted to a ministership." Edgar Ansel Mowrer, who had a personal interest in Messersmith's being rewarded, reported to Frank Knox that State was "as full of admiration of [him] as we are." Mowrer concluded that if Messersmith wanted Prague, and if Knox and others "remember to back [him] up, he should have no difficulty about obtaining the job."[96]

He wanted it, all right, and his friends backed him up, and on 29 January Phillips called him in to offer him a post—as minister to Uruguay. Prague went to that charter member of the diplomatic fraternity, J. Butler Wright, whom Messersmith was to replace in Montevideo.[97]

What had happened? British historian D. K. Adams speculates that Wright pressed his claim on Hull during their time together at the Pan American Conference. But Phillips's support of his candidacy was more important than Wright's powers of persuasion. The undersecretary meant for Messersmith to have a ministership, but not Prague. It was one thing to put a consul in a legation and quite another for it to be among the choicest available. Messersmith could bide his time in the South American "swamps" and wait his turn. Phillips's diary conveys an almost malicious delight in denying the ambitious consul his desire.[98]

Roosevelt accepted the change in plans with good grace. Granting Prague to the career implied the obligation at least to consider its choice for the post, and Roosevelt had nothing personal against Wright. Hull, whom Wright had indeed served well at Montevideo, no doubt put in a good word for him. Roosevelt could take satisfaction in Messersmith's promotion to diplomacy whether it was to Czechoslovakia or to Uruguay.[99]

Messersmith seemed not to care one way or the other. Returning to Berlin on 9 March, he was, as Dodd observed, a "very happy" man. At last he was entering the diplomatic ranks, and he looked forward to building on the "splendid foundation" Hull had laid at the recent conference.[100]

Eight days later, happiness became elation. The American minister to Austria, George Earle, suddenly resigned to run for governor of Pennsylvania, and was planning to leave Vienna before the end of the month. Messersmith, not yet departed for Uruguay, was an obvious replacement. Phillips decided that "no one [was] better qualified . . . to fill this key position"—as though that were not as true for Prague. He saw Roosevelt on 16 March and "persuaded" him to approve the switch, "in view of the fact that [Messersmith] was probably better informed than anyone else at our disposal on the Nazi program and activities. . . ."[101]

Roosevelt had actually needed little persuasion. He was right pleased with this turn of events, which kept Messersmith in Central Europe, as he had intended. He was also pleased with himself, as John Gunther, then the Vienna correspondent of the *Chicago Daily News*, discovered in an interview some months later. "Ha, ha!" the president cackled. Messersmith's appointment "was a good joke on the State Department, wasn't it! Just think what the career boys will say! I've put a lowly consul into a diplomatic post. Ha, ha, ha!"[102]

Messersmith was too full of himself for mirth. For him, the change was "the most pleasant surprise of my life." Vienna would keep him "nearer old friends and in touch with a situation which I have been following so closely. . . ." He expressed gratitude to Phillips for "this mark of confidence which the President and the Secretary and you all have shown in me." Editorials in the United States press praised him and his promotion as an illustration, as the *New York Times* put it, .of "the advantages of our comparatively new system under which men of proven ability may pass from the consular to the diplomatic service."[103]

The news, according to the *Times*'s Berlin correspondent, aroused "conflicting sentiments" in official German circles. Although Messersmith "thoroughly understands the German viewpoint . . . he has been the most persistent and thoroughgoing contender for all that is due the United States, both in letter and in spirit, with whom the Germans have ever had to deal." For this "he has won their entire respect." But, the writer added, "they may not mourn his passing."[104]

Americans in Berlin and his many German friends were happy for Messersmith, as attested by their hurried flurry of farewell celebrations. But their joy was tempered by the unsettling recognition that truth and justice were losing a much-needed champion in Nazi Germany.[105]

☆ **III** ☆

Vienna

1934–1937

1

"In my earliest youth," wrote Hitler nostalgically in *Mein Kampf*, "I came to the basic insight which never left me, but only became more profound: that Germanism could be safeguarded only by the destruction of Austria." Austria looked entirely ripe for destruction in 1933. Conceived in defeat, like Weimar, independent Austria seemed near the same fate. For three centuries it had been the cultural and administrative center of the great Hapsburg empire; in 1919 it was instead a rump republic of scarcely 6.5 million. Tariff walls quickly erected by sister successor states Hungary, Romania, Czechoslovakia, Poland, and Yugoslavia choked off Austria's traditional markets. Political chaos almost immediately broke loose, with socialists battling the clerical-monarchist parties in the new parliament and in the streets. Rival militias—the rightist Heimwehr and the socialist Schutzbund—filled the vacuum created by the 1919 peace treaty of Saint-Germain, which imposed stiff limits on Austria's regular forces. By 1930 Heimwehr–Schutzbund skirmishes had escalated into veritable civil war. Then came financial disaster, with the crash of its premier bank, the Creditanstalt. Taking office in April 1932, Chancellor Engelbert Dollfuss inherited record unemployment, a grave budget deficit, and a disastrous trade imbalance.[1]

With his life's dream looming invitingly before him, Hitler in the spring of 1933 seized the initiative. At his disposal were 43,000 card-carrying Austrian Nazis, who on cue began agitating for representation in the Dollfuss cabinet and new elections. The Germans dropped leaflets from the air urging Austrians to rise against their tottering government. Nazi sabotage and terrorism made for frazzled nerves and the worst tourist season since the war. Trade and tourism from Germany dried up. Hans Frank, the Bavarian interior minister, publicly warned Dollfuss that the suppression of Austrian

National Socialists would force Reich Germans to "take upon themselves the task of assuring the freedom of their fellow Germans in Austria." When Vienna protested these threats, the Foreign Office in Berlin replied that Nazis did "not regard Austria as a foreign country." Planning ahead, the Führer named Reichstag deputy Theo Habicht to be Dollfuss's successor, and assigned him to the German legation in Vienna as press attaché, to ready himself for his next assignment.[2]

But Hitler underestimated his Austrian adversary. War hero, agrarian reformer, and hard-driving technocrat, the diminutive Dollfuss displayed courage and agility in defense of his country. He secured aid and guarantees from the Italian Duce, who was considerably unnerved himself by the Nazi revolution. But Mussolini exacted his pound of flesh in return. Dollfuss had to agree to undertake internal "reforms" of the sort that would transform Austria into a corporative state after the Italian model. Dollfuss, it should be noted, enthusiastically carried out his part of the bargain, dissolving parliament and outlawing the Schutzbund. With Italian backing and a free hand domestically, he rose to the German challenge. A nationwide manhunt for Nazi terrorists was launched. Habicht was unceremoniously expelled from the country, for seditious activities inconsistent with his diplomatic status. On 19 June Austria banned the Nazi party, arrested its officers, and put the rank-and-file to flight across the German border, where they regrouped into the so-called Austrian Legion. At Geneva Dollfuss described Austria's brave defiance of Nazi bullying, winning the country new admirers and visitors from the world over.[3]

Having weathered Hitler's initial assault, Dollfuss in early 1934 tried to reduce his dependence upon Italy, which worried him nearly as much. He appealed for British and French support, but the historic anti-Austrianism of France's allies Czechoslovakia, Yugoslavia, and Romania—the Little Entente—conspired against him. In the end his overtures westward elicited only expressions of "interest" in Austrian independence from London and Paris and angry warnings from Mussolini, who ordered him on with his "reforms." In February the Heimwehr took the offensive against the socialists. Three days of fighting, replete with artillery and spot executions, claimed nearly a thousand casualties, mostly leftists. It was the most brutal manifestation of the madness over Central Europe yet to assault the world's senses, and a bucket of cold blood on its sympathies. Despairing now of assistance from the West, Dollfuss signed the Rome Protocols, a mutual consultative pact, with Italy and Hungary. Austria was still independent, but its fate rested with the dictators in Rome and Berlin.[4]

2

The situation nonetheless seemed stable. Washington was in no evident hurry for Messersmith to take up his new post. The State Department found a special mission for him to do first. In late 1933 the American embassy, consulate general, and the various attachés in Paris had all moved into a new United States government office building on the Place de la Concorde. Paris, Carr noted, was State's "most conspicuous establishment," and so where it wanted to look its best. The new building was a good start, but visitors from Capitol Hill complained about overstaffing and inefficiency inside. The situation cried for a hardnosed organizer like Messersmith. So, on 14 April, Hull ordered him to Paris "for the purpose of studying and planning with the Ambassador [Jesse Isidor Straus] further economies in personnel and management."[5]

The department's people in Paris were not gladdened by this news. Straus, reported First Secretary J. Theodore Marriner, deeply resented the despatch of "an outsider, with no knowledge of the situation" to help direct "what the Ambassador very properly considers his own show." Only with difficulty had Marriner dissuaded Straus from "a violent, direct outburst to the President." He hoped that Messersmith's "personal tact will be sufficient to keep things smooth."[6]

It apparently was, for within two weeks a reorganization plan was ready for submission to Washington. It embodied many of Messersmith's longstanding objectives for the Foreign Service. The plan called for the embassy and the consulate general to be consolidated, for a promised savings of $50,000 annually in clerical costs and a much improved coordination. Consuls were to receive dual (diplomatic-consular) commissions; the consul general was to become the ambassador's chief commercial adviser; the first secretary was to assume the title of counselor and political adviser. But the attachés still could not be touched.[7]

The plan had something for everyone except the ten laid-off clerks. Counselor-to-be Marriner and pinchpenny Carr applauded. The prospect of diplomatic status cheered the consuls and distressed Undersecretary Phillips, who was nonetheless relieved that the embassy was to retain "a dominating position" in the new arrangement. Most of all, the plan appealed to Roosevelt as a step toward Moses-

Linthicumism and consular-diplomatic fusion. In August he ordered the reorganization into effect.[8]

On the morning of 18 May Messersmith and his wife and the two Belgian servants set out in the car from Berlin, arriving in Vienna in time for dinner. He looked forward to a week of rest and informal orientation before taking charge of the American legation. No sooner, however, had the Messersmiths checked into the fashionable Hotel Bristol (there being no official minister's residence) than came a message from Dollfuss, requesting an early introduction. So much for their holiday. The next morning Messersmith presented his credentials to the Austrian chief of state, President Wilhelm Miklas. After a long and "unusually cordial" talk, the American was driven to the chancellery on the Ballhausplatz. A cabinet meeting was just breaking up. Messersmith entered the conference room to find the Austrian chancellor emptying the ashtrays. "Well," he remembered Dollfuss saying with a broad grin, "you have caught me cleaning up." Messersmith could not help but chuckle, too.[9]

The mood turned abruptly somber, as they settled down and Dollfuss blurted out his fears for his country. Messersmith, heralded in Vienna as "the terror of Nazi Germany," was a predictably sympathetic listener. The Austrian chancellor expressed concern about a recent resurgence of Nazi terrorism, fearing that those small crimes were a prelude to invasion by the Austrian Legion. As bad as conditions were reported to be inside Germany, Dollfuss said, Hitler might be planning a diversionary foreign-policy coup against Austria. Messersmith agreed that Nazi Germany was on its last legs, that, with "the internal dissensions in the Party" and "the increasing economic and financial difficulties," Hitler had two months at most. The diplomat also agreed that a last-gasp German invasion was possible, but expressed confidence that Italy and France would rush to Austria's defense in that event and thus deliver the coup de grace to the Hitler regime. Austria, then, needed only to "hold on" and await Hitler's inevitable downfall.[10]

Messersmith surveyed the scene and concluded that Austria would indeed hold on. Under Dollfuss's ministrations the economy was well on the mend. The Creditanstalt had been reorganized. Bank deposits surpassed predepression levels. The schilling had been stabilized. Declines of 76 percent in the trade deficit and 16 percent in unemployment since December 1932 reflected the revival of industry, particularly steel and textiles. "Heroic efforts" by Dollfuss had almost eliminated the budget deficit. Impressed foreign bankers expressed a readiness to discuss a rescheduling of Austria's external debt.[11]

The internal political picture also inspired confidence. After their auspicious introduction, Messersmith and Dollfuss went on to develop an extraordinarily close personal relationship, which helped convince the American that Dollfuss was both an astute judge of character and badly misunderstood in the West. The purge of the socialists, Messersmith pointed out to Washington, had been forced upon him by Mussolini and, indirectly, by Hitler; Dollfuss had merely bowed to the dictates of national survival over his protesting conscience. The Austrian repeatedly assured Messersmith that the constitution would be restored once the Nazi threat had passed. Meanwhile the chancellor's essential goodness and force of personality were helping to heal the nation's wounds and uphold its sovereignty. Dollfuss, Messersmith concluded, deserved the West's support and understanding, not its censure.[12]

Nor, the American minister decided, were Major Emil Fey and Prince Ernst Rüdiger von Starhemberg, the Heimwehr leaders, the malevolent characters of repute. Despite their very real Fascist leanings, they, like Dollfuss, were patriots first. As evidence, Messersmith cited a 1 May cabinet reorganization, in which Fey agreed to relinquish the largely ceremonial vice chancellorship to the somewhat flighty young Starhemberg, who was better suited to the position. The shift, everyone agreed, presaged still more serenity on the political scene.[13]

Late June brought more good news. The announcement that Hitler and Mussolini were to meet for the first time, in Venice, caused consternation in Vienna, but Messersmith saw no chance for Italo-German rapprochement. The Duce, he assured Dollfuss, would never barter away Austria for Hitler's friendship. The Führer's overtures, Messersmith predicted, were bound to be scorned by a Mussolini who saw his German counterpart as "a very poor miniature of himself." The Duce, he believed, was too vain to openly embrace the Nazi upstarts.[14]

The conference outcome seemed to sustain Messersmith's analysis. Journalist friends of his stopping over on their return from Venice confirmed what history would show to be entirely erroneous reports in the Vienna press that Italian pressure had forced Hitler to disavow his designs on Austria. Still, coincidence or not, on 18 June Messersmith could report the sudden cessation of Nazi incendiarism. The next day the French foreign minister, Louis Barthou, arrived in Vienna. He publicly pledged "France's whole power" to defend Austria and Dollfuss. With the recovering economy, internal tranquillity, and foreign support, "the Austrian situation," Messersmith concluded on 28 June, "is one that need not give us great concern."[15]

Austria's best guarantee, the self-immolation of the Hitler regime, was reassuringly on track from Messersmith's perspective. In March the Germans formally petitioned Washington for trade talks, which he interpreted as further evidence of their imminent collapse. German behavior suggested otherwise. They arrived not on hands and knees, but rather, with a package of demands most unbecoming a supplicant. They wanted, among other things, concessions for their exports, credits with which to purchase American raw materials, and abrogation of the most-favored-nation clause in the 1923 treaty, so that Germany could make preferential deals with its neighbors.[16]

In frantic letters to the State Department, Messersmith urged rejection of the German overtures. He did so, he assured Phillips, mindful of the economic crisis at home and the importance of foreign trade to recovery. He appreciated that "we want an outlet for raw materials and that Germany is potentially one of our best customers for such materials." But the Nazi regime could not be trusted to honor its contracts or pay its bills. He questioned whether a "new treaty would be worth any more than the old one," which the Germans were systematically violating. In any case, the national interest dictated that "we must not give them any aid or comfort or support in any way," even if that involved certain short-term sacrifices. Messersmith's German business contacts agreed that "increasing economic distress" was the best way to "bring Germany to reason and make it possible for a decent government to be established." The United States, Messersmith contended, had "practically nothing to gain and much to lose" from a German trade agreement.[17]

One historian has suggested that Messersmith's letters persuaded the State Department to refuse the German bid. Top officials, however, reached that decision without his help. For Hull, reciprocity was practically non-negotiable. Messersmith's letters were of "extreme importance," as Phillips assured him, but mostly as ammunition against bureaucratic interlopers. Expanded bilateral trade with Germany had at least one champion in the Roosevelt administration. George N. Peek, the president's foreign-trade adviser, headed the government's new Export Import Bank (Eximbank). Peek's overriding objective was to dispose of price-depressing surpluses overseas, and he cared little about how or with whom such deals were consummated. Commodity-hungry Germany beckoned, and Peek was eager to grant it Eximbank credits to buy American copper, cotton, lard, and petroleum, lest it take its business elsewhere.[18]

The State Department objected—less because American taxpayers would be subsidizing German rearmament than because Peek's plans

collided with Hull's vision of multilateralism and general tariff reductions. The Trade Agreements Act passed by Congress on 5 June
1934 authorized the president to adopt either Hull's approach or
Peek's, or both, in order to revive American commerce: Peek's German initiative was widely seen as a precedent-setting assertion of his
economic nationalism, an attempt to "take over" the New Deal trade
program.[19]

It was in this context of bureaucratic competition for the president's favor that Messersmith's letters were pressed into service. The
State Department needed all the help it could get. Roosevelt swore
his devotion to liberal trade in Hull's presence, but, as Phillips observed ruefully, the president had "something of a New England
trader in him." Privately Roosevelt ridiculed Hull's panaceas. Generally suspicious of dogma, he could not see the point in spurning
certain immediate markets for uncertain future ones. But he was
increasingly concerned about the Nazi menace, a concern the State
Department skillfully exploited. On 5 July Phillips sent the White
House long extracts from Messersmith's letters, suggesting enticingly
that Hitler would fall, or be significantly weakened, if the United
States refused to treat. In an appended memorandum, Herbert Feis,
State Department economic adviser, asserted that it would "be difficult, if not impossible, for Germany to get along" without American
raw materials. Later in the year, a special State Department committee on relations with Germany came to the same conclusion, pointing out the inadvisability of trade negotiations or credits when the
"whole complexion of affairs may be quite different in a year or two.
It is not likely that the current German commercial policy can last.
. . ." In short, the regime would soon be forced to its knees if only
the United States held firm.[20]

The State Department's counterattack won the day. After initially
supporting a Peek plan to sell Germany 800,000 bales of cotton, Roosevelt swung against it. Peek's position was fatally undercut. He was
to leave the administration in November 1935.[21]

3

The cotton shortage was actually the least of Hitler's many problems in 1934. While the Hull-Peek contest was heating up, a German
power struggle was building to a bloody climax. Over the weekend
of 29 June–1 July the entire SA leadership was slaughtered at Hitler's order. The world recoiled in horror; to Messersmith, the purge
simply "showed the true murderous spirit of the Nazi regime." But

he was sure that Hitler's butchery would be futile. "The so-called cleansed government," Messersmith wrote confidently on 5 July, "will no more be able to solve Germany's problems than the form it presented a few days ago. The situation is bound to go from bad to worse unless help from the outside is given." And, given current world revulsion, outside assistance, Messersmith trusted, was less likely than ever. Germany was now "definitely isolated." If Germans had any "decency and honor," they would now rise up and rid themselves of their false prophet. "But if not . . . the economic and financial factors" would soon do the job.[22]

Within the month Hitler's blighted hand struck again. Summertime doldrums in Vienna, which usually occasioned complaint from those duty-bound to the city, were this year welcome relief from the civil war that had recently beset it. A blithe Dollfuss shooed foreign diplomats off on their holidays. The weeks ahead, he assured them, would be uneventful.[23]

Thus 25 July found only two ministers of major powers on the job in Vienna: newcomer Messersmith and the German, Kurt Rieth. A little after noon, Messersmith heard the startling radio bulletin that Dollfuss had resigned; Dr. Anton Rintelen, the Austrian minister to Rome, was reportedly the new chancellor. A putsch was clearly in progress, although it was as yet uncertain whether the insurgents were Nazi or Heimwehr. Rumors had Dollfuss and his cabinet being held prisoner at the chancellery.

By 5 P.M. local time this news was on its way to the State Department in the first of four cables Messersmith filed that fateful day. The third, transmitted at 10 P.M., reported Dollfuss's murder during the occupation of the Ballhausplatz by 150 Austrian Nazis. His captors had shot him twice in the neck and then watched him bleed to death on his office couch. But murder was all they accomplished. Dollfuss had been alerted to a plot during his morning cabinet meeting, which he had immediately adjourned. When the conspirators stormed in, expecting to seize the entire government, they found only the chancellor and two of his ministers. The rest of the cabinet reassembled elsewhere and established contact with President Miklas, who was vacationing in south Austria. Kurt von Schuschnigg, the minister of justice and education, was designated chancellor. Police and Heimwehr surrounded the chancellery. The insurrectionists were arrested as they tried to leave under a promise of safe passage arranged by Rieth and promptly disavowed by the government. Messersmith could retire for the night secure that the crisis had passed.[24]

The next morning, as the world awoke to the shocking news and the absentee diplomats scrambled back, Messersmith paid his condolences. At the Foreign Office he was taken aside and asked whether, in view of "the great friendship between the Chancellor and myself," he would care to view the body. He almost could not bring himself to do it. "I am one who knows righteous anger," he wrote years later, "but I cannot begin to describe the feelings which I had in the few minutes that I was in this room . . . with the man whom I had admired as a patriotic and courageous defender of the liberties of his country."[25]

Austria plunged into mourning. The 28 July funeral drew over a million people, who heard Miklas and Starhemberg delivering eulogies and pledging themselves to Dollfuss's policies. Schuschnigg, the new chancellor, was, as far as Messersmith could tell, "a sound man of determination and many good qualities," undoubtedly the "best man available." The populace seemed united behind him. Nazi radio appeals for a general uprising had been ignored on the 25th; Austrian patriotism was at an unprecedented high in its wake. "Dollfuss as a martyr," Messersmith declared, "has solidified the nation." He detected "a real unity of purpose" among the politicians, a willingness to "submerge personal rivalries and ambitions." Starhemberg was surprising everyone with his sudden diligence.[26]

These were all encouraging signs. But, as Messersmith wrote Feis on 31 July, "poor Austria's fate does not depend so much on her as it does on those who built this house in which she has to live." The abortive coup had demonstrated anew the extent of Austria's dependence upon its friends. At 4 P.M. on the 25th Mussolini had despatched four army divisions to the Austrian border to head off a follow-up incursion by the Austrian Legion. The Italian show of strength, Messersmith learned, had prompted Hitler to cancel the planned invasion at the last minute. Europe had skirted a precipice. Messersmith felt that the close call had sobered London and Paris, where it was "increasingly recognized that political peace in Europe rests on the maintenance of Austrian independence." Prospects now looked more favorable for a tripartite guarantee treaty, vital lest Austria remain a vassal of Rome.[27]

It even seemed possible—especially to Messersmith—that the shock waves would carry off Hitler, too. Germany's position, the diplomat wrote the day after the funeral, "has never been weaker"; it was totally isolated, "insecure and trembling." Perhaps the Reichswehr would now seize the initiative.[28]

He was disappointed again. Hitler barely broke stride. On 26 July the Führer published a letter denying involvement in Dollfuss's assassination, "which the Reich Government most sharply condemn and regret." He so wished to normalize relations with Austria, the

Führer wrote, that he was replacing Rieth with one of his "most intimate and trusted co-workers": Franz von Papen, who, according to Western accounts, had been targeted for execution during the Blood Purge, escaping with his life only through a last-minute reprieve.[29]

Hitler's pious platitudes cast sufficient doubt on German complicity to undercut world outrage and to disgust those like Messersmith who knew where the guilt lay. A week before the coup, he wrote in exasperation to Phillips, Goebbels had bragged to the Italian ambassador in Berlin that a Nazi government would be installed in Vienna within the month. Then there was Rieth's intervention, "one of the most extraordinary things that I have ever heard of." Rieth actually may have been the only high-ranking German without advance notice of the coup, which we now know Hitler had indeed approved and helped plan. But in 1934 the democracies did not want to know that.[30]

The fact that Hitler had survived both the SA challenge and the Dollfuss contretemps led Messersmith to revise, but not abandon, his forecast of Nazi downfall. His contacts in the German business community still told him that Hitler's days were numbered. But not even they were so sure anymore. Upon the death of the German president, Paul von Hindenburg, on 2 August, Goebbels announced that Hitler would assume that office as well if the nation approved by plebiscite. In a mass ceremony just hours after Hindenburg's death, the entire German army, offices and enlisted men alike, swore "unconditional obedience" unto Hitler. In the 19 August poll, nearly 90 percent of German voters blessed his consolidation of executive power.[31]

These unexpected life signs forced Messersmith to conclude that collapse was not imminent. "The present German regime," he wrote Phillips on 1 August, "is on its last legs, but it can last some months longer." The coming winter would surely accomplish what the previous winter had not; this time, cold and hunger would have their effect. "The German people," he insisted, "are a patient one . . . but once the conviction comes that the enemy may be on the inside, the regime . . . is not likely to be tolerated." As long as the world withheld sympathy and support, "she will crack and a prostrated Germany may learn humility."[32]

Until that happened, Austria would not be safe. Despite Hitler's crocodile tears for Dollfuss, Messersmith emphasized, Nazi Germany had "in no sense given up her aims." Hitler's only "definite convictions" concerned Austria, land of his birth, and the Jews. "He has," Messersmith explained, "felt an outsider in Germany until he can bring Austria as a gift to the Reich." The putsch having failed, Hitler was expected to adopt a more covert approach, as suggested in his 5 August interview with British journalist Ward Price. Hitler publicly challenged the Schuschnigg government to submit itself to popular vote, as he had done in Germany. The implication was that free elections would see a vast outpouring of repressed pro-German feeling. Of course, Hitler knew better; the Nazis were really calculating that elections would undermine Austria's fragile political unity. The Führer's new strategy, most diplomats agreed, was to bide his time until some combination of Austrian weakness and German strength enabled him to retake the initiative.[33]

The designated agent of this strategy assumed charge of his legation in October 1934. Franz von Papen was one of the regime's establishment front men, like Neurath and Schacht, who moved in European society in cutaways rather than khaki, serving the Nazi revolution by bemoaning its excesses. He always had an especially violent effect on Messersmith, who considered Papen in many respects the most despicable of all the Nazis. Fanaticism Messersmith could understand; for the unprincipled opportunism of the likes of Papen he had no use whatsoever. There was strong evidence that Papen's Berlin bosses felt the same way. The new Austrian foreign minister, Baron Egon Berger Waldenegg, conjured up a scenario in which Hitler's "most trusted coworker" would be gunned down by Nazis in Heimwehr uniform, simultaneously finishing the work of the Blood Purge and giving Germany a pretext for invasion. Optimistic suggestions that Papen's arrival presaged some shift in German policy tolerant of Austrian independence were early laid to rest. Introductory talks with Schuschnigg and Berger Waldenegg made it clear that Papen had brought no demarche from Hitler. Messersmith reported that Papen appealed to the Swedish minister for help in his "difficult mission," but refused to say what that mission was.[34]

Messersmith tried to prevail on other foreign representatives in Vienna to join him in ostracizing Papen on the social circuit. But such a moral boycott was contrary both to diplomatic etiquette and to the personal inclinations of the diplomats themselves, including even such staunch anti-Nazis as British minister Sir Walford Selby, on whom the suave Papen made his usual favorable first impression. Messersmith himself was obliged to invite Papen in for a protocol visit. He walked into Messersmith's office at the appointed hour and greeted him "like an old friend." Messersmith spurned his outstretched hand. Papen never offered it again, Messersmith explained later, "because he knew that I would not take it." The American sat tightlipped at his desk. Papen soon got the hint and left.[35]

The tables turned; Messersmith had to accept Papen's invitation. The German welcomed him magnanimously. "This time," Messersmith recalled his saying, "we are in my legation, and although you may not talk, I will talk and you will have to listen to me." Messersmith did not object. Papen "could be the most indiscreet man in the world"; he hoped that some secret would slip out. Indeed, he heard an extraordinary monologue. Claiming as usual to deplore much that was going on inside Germany, Papen admitted that Hitler had sent him "to see that the Anschluss was brought about peacefully." The Austrian government, he claimed, was in power against the will of its people, who really wanted to be part of Germany. He was on a mission of liberation that, he assured Messersmith, would succeed in putting Austria out of its misery.

Messersmith again had occasion for righteous anger. He had had "many experiences and surprising conversations," he told the German, "but never one like this." "Diplomacy," he continued, "has often been devious, but I have not known of any time in history where a man has been sent by his government to endeavor, under diplomatic immunity, to undermine [another] government and to destroy its sovereignty." Never again would Messersmith set foot in Papen's legation, which was a boon for his blood pressure. But he also cut himself off from an important source of diplomatic intelligence.[36]

Luckily for Austria, Messersmith assured everyone, Papen was "a great spinner of webs" who "usually gets tangled up in them himself"; his basic stupidity would foil him in the end. Messersmith recalled the bungling that got the then military attaché Papen thrown out of the United States for espionage in 1915. Nineteen years later, in the fall of 1934, there was the same old maladroit Papen, spending most of his time shuttling between Berlin, Vienna, Budapest, and Sofia, entertaining local Nazis. "It seems," Messersmith observed, "that he is to be Minister at a number of posts to which he is not accredited, with nothing to say at the post to which he is accredited," and nothing to do except to abuse his hosts' hospitality. He made an issue of his diplomatic status in Austria. According to his credentials, he was minister on unspecified "special mission." Papen had his cards engraved accordingly, and pressed his supposed precedence at official functions. His behavior created "more amusement than anything else" among his colleagues, Messersmith reported, but also serious embarrassment for the Schuschnigg government, which recognized no "special mission," and yet did not wish to offend Germany. Papen, of course, appreciated Austria's predicament and exploited it without shame. When, after months of indecision, the government finally prepared an updated diplomatic list showing Papen as a regularly accredited minister, he protested so vehemently that the list, still in proof, had to be withdrawn. An exasperated Berger Waldenegg told Messersmith that Papen "always counted on the other man's being a gentleman." Messersmith agreed that he was "absolutely impossible."[37]

By these and other offenses, the peripatetic Papen made himself a thorn in Austria's side. When the Saar plebiscite of 13 January 1935 went in favor of union with Germany, he assured the Vienna press that Austrians would vote likewise if only given the chance. Messersmith reported that Papen "opened a book at the German legation in which the 'enthusiastic'—to use his words—could inscribe their congratulations" on this latest Hitler triumph, which all German citizens in Vienna dutifully did. In June Berger Waldenegg told Messersmith that Austria was contemplating declaring Papen persona non grata. The American minister advised against the move. Why risk a crisis with Germany when Papen would probably soon be recalled? "He has been utterly inept here," he wrote Moffat. Messersmith was sure that Papen's bosses in Berlin were aware that his clumsy machinations were succeeding only in solidifying support for Schuschnigg.[38]

In fact, despite continuing internal problems—unemployment, the alienation of the socialists, and restiveness in the Heimwehr—Austria was rapidly recuperating from the 25 July trauma. Schuschnigg, Messersmith decided, was a worthy keeper of the Dollfuss tradition. His first months as chancellor showed that he was "highly intelligent with a penetrating mind." Although a neophyte in big-power politics, he "thinks clearly and will learn fast." What he lacked was Dollfuss's charisma. With "the air and manner of a scholar," noticeably uncomfortable around people, he would never inspire love. He often spoke longingly of his days in the education ministry. Messersmith suspected that his "inner mind" leaned toward a Hapsburg restoration as a bulwark against Germany and surcease from the burdens of his office.[39]

Whatever his ambivalences, Schuschnigg was on the job, working to broaden his support, both internal and external. The two were very much related, for the curtailment of Austrian democracy and the continued ostracism of socialists were prime impediments to Western assistance. Schuschnigg, Messersmith felt, was inclined to liberalize and conciliate, as Dollfuss had started to do before his death. But fear of antagonizing Mussolini and the Heimwehr, and of Hitler exploiting the return of party tumults, held the chancellor back.[40]

Although Austria remained a quasi-autocracy, the Western powers finally relented in its behalf. Meeting in Rome in January 1935, French and Italian representatives agreed to consult should Austrian integrity again be threatened. Britain adhered a month later. Austria's neighbors, including Germany, were invited to take a pledge of nonintervention. Messersmith hailed the accord's "far reaching significance": France and Italy, rivals in the Mediterranean, had "committed themselves publicly to work for peace in Europe." Rome, he believed, marked "tremendous progress"—and the "bitterest pill [the Germans] have had to swallow since Nazism came to power."[41]

State visits by Schuschnigg and Berger Waldenegg to Paris and London in late February 1935 left good feelings all around. The Austrians had nervously anticipated demonstrations, vilification, and pressure to liberalize at home. Instead, the opposition in both countries maintained a decorous silence; there were no mass protests; the Austrians received a sympathetic hearing and cleared up the misconceptions about Austrian "fascism." The delegation, Messersmith reported, returned home with evidence that "they have a good part of Europe behind them."[42]

Moreover, the winter tourist season, so important to Austria's economy, was shaping up brilliantly. The heir to the British throne, Edward, Prince of Wales, was taking his annual ski vacation at Kitzbühl. Thanks to the publicity, there was hardly a room to be had in the Austrian Alps. At the same time, the Austrian Nazi party was "shot to pieces," and pro-Anschluss sentiment "has never been so weak." In general, Messersmith reported on 19 March, the situation was "more satisfactory in practically every major respect than it has been during the past two years."[43]

For reasons Messersmith could well understand, the Austrian government did not share his confidence. "Yes," the impudent Papen had told Berger Waldenegg upon the latter's return from London, "you have your French and English friends now and can have your independence a little longer." Although Hitler had not publicly rejected the Rome call for nonintervention, there was no evidence that he had forsaken his aggressive designs either. Berger Waldenegg concluded that the Führer was stalling for time. Messersmith concurred. With Europe aligned against him, Hitler recognized that Germany had "to appear reasonable and willing to talk." But Messersmith was convinced that if "the solid front is maintained, Germany will have to sign" a nonintervention pledge after all. That would hand Hitler a diplomatic defeat that would "at least give [Austria] a breathing spell," and "increase the possibility of a more reasonable regime coming into power" in Germany.[44]

It was precisely because the Austrians did not think that the united front would hold up that they remained on edge. Schuschnigg had little faith in his supposed allies, individually or collectively. Royal vacations aside, he especially doubted British support—as well he might in view of Prime Minister Ramsay MacDonald's 11 March declaration that Britain had assumed "no military commitments, direct or indirect," in connection with the Rome agreement. French interests Schuschnigg considered too bound up with the Little Entente nations, which were obsessed with fear of restored Hapsburgs. This left the field to the Italians, whom Schuschnigg deeply distrusted. He was a native of the South Tyrol, detached from Austria by Saint-Germain and ruthlessly Italianized by Mussolini. Schuschnigg himself had been an Italian prisoner during World War I. Cultural and historical considerations reinforced his convictions about the two countries' basic incompatibility. Messersmith conceded that the relationship was not a natural one, "for after all Italy is a Latin country and Austria is a German country, and the two cultures do not mix easily." Convinced that Austria could not rely on the Rome signatories, Schuschnigg embarked on a policy of appeasement with respect to Germany, avoiding, as he put it, anything that "would give Germany a pretext for intervention," doing everything "to secure in some way Hitler's toleration of the status quo." As we shall see, this was to culminate in the Austro-German treaty of 11 July 1936.[45]

4

Facing a desk piled high with official paper, a goodly portion of which had come from the American legation in Vienna, Undersecretary Phillips could spare only a few words of thanks for Messersmith's coverage of the events of 25 July and their aftermath. "It must have been a thrilling time for you," he wrote with a twinge of jealousy on this sticky 15 August in Washington. Although it was also hot in the Austrian capital, the Messersmiths' leased house boasted a shaded garden ideal for alfresco entertaining. But by mid-August the excitement Phillips envied had already worn off. Messersmith had settled into a routine that was to continue undisturbed for the duration of his stay in Vienna.[46]

The truth was that American interests in Austria required only his occasional attention. Not that the United States was indifferent to Austria's fate. The Austrians knew, he wrote later, that "we had this deep and friendly interest [in the maintenance] of their sovereignty and integrity." But, as "great realists," they also knew that the United

States, resolutely isolationist, could offer them little more than moral support. Of this they did not need to be frequently reminded.[47]

Austro-American trade totaled a mere $17 million in 1934, of which 76 percent were United States exports to Austria. The Austrians periodically approached the State Department for help in rectifying the imbalance. Not wishing to jeopardize a good thing, Washington was consistently evasive. In February 1934 an Austrian trade delegation arrived with a long list of sought-after concessions. Assistant Secretary Francis Sayre agreed to examine their requests, but informed the Austrians that their timing was bad. The administration's foreign-trade program was still pending before Congress; the State Department lacked legislative authority to talk. Moreover, Sayre made plain that Austria was not at the top of the list for reciprocal trade agreements. Cordell Hull planned to begin with America's principal suppliers, especially those in a position to take more American farm products. Austria did not qualify on either count.[48]

In May 1935 Vienna tried again. Schuschnigg's minister in Washington, Edgar Prochnik, came armed with statistics showing that Austria was an important American source of magnesite and certain machine parts. These items, Prochnik suggested, might serve as a basis for trade talks. The department was unimpressed. In late June it formally declined to engage in treaty discussions on the grounds that the "amount of effort required to prepare for them would not be warranted in view of the limited number of products which Austria ships to the United States." With Congress and the press on guard against what would surely be construed as backdoor involvement in European politics, the State Department had no incentive to treat. In any case, the department pointed out, Austria stood to benefit under the most-favored-nation clause from the generalization of tariff concessions granted by the United States to other countries—provided, of course, that Austria did not start discriminating against American exports.[49]

Austria was thus unable to stem a small invasion of its market by the United States without losing its most-favored-nation treatment, vital if it was to boost sales in return. Minister Prochnik, who seems to have been more sympathetic to the Hull trade program than to his own government's difficulties, undercut his own representations by volunteering that Austrian factories were so accustomed to American raw materials that it would be impossible for Austria to divert purchases to countries that took more of its exports.[50]

Austrian exports to the United States did rise after 1 April 1935, the date of the executive order according it most-favored-nation status, but American exports rose faster. Few complaints of anti-American discrimination came to Messersmith's attention, and those that did he found either baseless or "of a very minor character." By mid-1936 the American trade position, he reported, was "very good, . . . about as good as we can expect it to be," almost embarrassingly good "in view of the very large favorable balance of trade which we enjoy with Austria." Messersmith's only worry was that the Vienna government would succumb to growing demands for import restrictions.[51]

Messersmith helped forestall that threat, partly by maintaining a low profile on all bilateral trade questions. He had decided, he wrote Moffat, "to keep silent" on the whole subject, "as the trade balance . . . is so tremendously in our favor that the less we say about it and the less we attract attention to it, the better it is." Americans with trade grievances would have to understand that "nitpicking" over "indirect and unimportant" discrimination might irk the Austrians and provoke the restrictions everyone wished to avoid. The best approach, he concluded, was for him to continue making himself scarce at the economics ministry.[52]

With the United States politically aloof and perfectly content with the commercial status quo, Messersmith and the Austrian government had precious little to say officially to each other. He met regularly with Berger Waldenegg, but Schuschnigg, unlike Dollfuss, rarely took him into his confidence. Their conference in November 1935 was the first in nearly nine months; and, by Messersmith's account, the entire forty-five minutes was taken up with the minor complaints of American journalists in Vienna.[53]

Administrative matters consumed some of his time. Messersmith had found the United States establishment in Vienna abysmally housed. Legation offices consisted of two converted flats; the consulate rented quarters elsewhere; the commercial and treasury attachés maintained still other premises. Messersmith was "distressed" by this "unbusinesslike and inefficient" arrangement, but not until late in 1934 did he find the time to address it. By November 1935 new consolidated offices were ready for occupancy. The attachés at first refused to move, but Messersmith finally prevailed. The whole American establishment, he noted proudly, was now housed for exactly what it had cost the consulate alone.[54]

As always, Messersmith was also looking out for himself. His gardened house on the Lustig Preangasse was comfortable, but in need of expensive renovations. He insisted, however, that personal finances "in no way" influenced his recommendation that the United States purchase the house for him. At $50,000, he thought it was simply too good a bargain to pass up. For that "ridiculously small sum," the government had an opportunity to acquire a first-class permanent residence for its ministers. "A poor man like myself can live in it," he declared, "but it is equally adapted for the purposes of a rich man."⁵⁵

Twice the State Department turned him down, claiming lack of funds. Then he learned that houses in Rio and Ottawa had just been purchased for mission chiefs who, he noted indignantly, "are in a much better financial situation . . . than I am." He would see about that. "I have the distinct impression," he wrote his colleague in Budapest, "that in order to get a thing through of this kind, one has to bring it to the attention of the right people in certain quarters." He wrote letters and had friends visit the department to recommend the purchase. He took photographs of the house and sent them to Roosevelt and Hull. The bureaucracy was no match for this. In December 1935 Keith Merrill, chairman of the department's buildings commission, came to inspect the place, and agreed to recommend the allocation of $100,000—$56,000 for the purchase (the price having gone up while Washington dithered) and $44,000 for "repairs, alterations, and furnishings." Final approval made for "a very nice New Year's message" for Messersmith.⁵⁶

He had problems with his staff. Aside from the excellent "Joe" Gray, the third secretary, Messersmith was saddled with two disreputable characters. Alfred W. Kliefoth had been Sackett's second secretary in Berlin. Transferred to Vienna in May 1933, he served as chargé d'affaires after George Earle's departure. Knowing that Kliefoth would be with him "almost took away the pleasure that [Messersmith] had felt in going to Vienna." The man was incompetent, and a pathological liar to boot. Shortly after his arrival, Messersmith heard that Kliefoth was telling Austrians that he (Messersmith) was a Jew. Messersmith was "dumfounded." He found it "almost inconceivable that [Kliefoth] should do such a thing, especially after our four years' service together in Berlin he knew quite definitely that I was not a Jew." He also believed, correctly, that Kliefoth was making "quite derogatory remarks about me" to American diplomats in Europe and to State Department officials. "He just cannot help this disloyalty and not sticking to the truth," Messersmith wrote Moffat, "as it is a temperamental failing which he has consistently shown." And he was "lying down on the job in addition."⁵⁷

Messersmith would not have it. In Washington in April 1935 he told Carr that he wanted Kliefoth out, suggesting helpfully that he be moved to a consulate and "closely watched." Just before Messersmith sailed back, he received an impertinent telegram from Kliefoth, "practically a royal command for me to return to Vienna so that he could go on his leave as planned." When Messersmith arrived soon after, Kliefoth bragged that his summons had turned the trick. That did it. "It is absolutely impossible for Kliefoth to return here," Messersmith fumed to Moffat. "I do not think that I could stand seeing him again." Kliefoth was shipped off to the consulate in Cologne.[58]

Consul General Ernest L. Harris was a relic of the old service, "a nice man," wrote Messersmith in November 1934, who "since I have been here has done really no work, and I doubt that he has done any for years." After a lifetime in government service, the sixty-five-year-old Harris was due to retire, quite against his will. Messersmith informed the department that Harris would probably ask for an extension in his employment, and advised against granting the request. "We have too many people who are deserving of promotion to keep men with his attitude."[59]

By September 1935 Harris had been separated from the service under a cloud of scandal. In early 1934, during the ministerial interregnum, he had secured from two Vienna banks loans totaling 170,000 schillings (about $8,500) supposedly for legation expenses, actually used and lost in currency speculation. Messersmith made the discovery when the bankers visited him to demand their money back. He was shocked and disgusted. "I did not trust Harris," he wrote Moffat, "but I did not think him capable of anything like this." The affair made him "almost physically ill." Harris was immediately recalled. Although Carr was eager to bring criminal charges, Harris's long and otherwise unblemished record won him a kind of reprieve. He was retired rather than fired, so that he would have a garnisheeable pension to be applied against his debt.[60]

In the meantime, Messersmith had also lost the able Gray, promoted to the department, with his blessings, as Hull's assistant. Messersmith would never have stood in his way, but he regretted the timing of his departure. For with Gray gone, the Vienna professional staff was reduced to a single diplomatic secretary, a thirty-year-old career officer on loan from his Moscow post. George F. Kennan had arrived in Vienna in January 1935 for treatment of ulcers aggravated by Russian food. After two months he was ready to resume work. In view of the depletion of Messersmith's staff, the department ordered Kennan to stay put until replacements arrived. By September, however, Ambassador William Bullitt in Moscow began clamoring for Kennan's return. Messersmith fought to retain him until at least one of the designated substitutes—Alan Rogers, a consul in Paris assigned to him as third secretary, and James Barclay Young, consul general in Lima-Callao, Peru, to hold a dual commission as consul general and first secretary—had arrived in Vienna. Rogers came first, in late October. Messersmith would have preferred to keep Kennan. "I need not tell you," he wrote a colleague, "with what regret I see Kennan leave here. He is one of the finest of our younger officers." For his part, Kennan came away deeply impressed by Messersmith's "combative stoutness" and dedication to principle. Looking back on it, he decided that Messersmith, "this dry, drawling, peppery man, his eyes always glinting with the readiness to accept combat, capable of being wrong like the rest of us, but stern and incorruptible in his fight for what he considered right and decent, was one of those chiefs who left an indelible mark on my concept of what American diplomacy could and should be."[61]

Shorthanded as Messersmith was for much of his stay in Vienna, he was hardly overworked. That was temporarily to his taste. After the strains of Berlin he had looked forward to leisure time with Marion and her family. Vienna was surely the fulfillment of this wish. The summer of 1934 brought a host of interesting visitors from home. A number of his colleagues from other European cities and the State Department came. So did Roosevelt's aide Harry Hopkins, sent by the president for a badly needed vacation-cum-inspection tour. Everyone was treated to the Messersmith hospitality and the Messersmith analysis of current events. Herbert Feis, who stayed a week in August, returned to Washington wishing, or so he wrote, he were back "wandering around the streets of Vienna with you, listening to you talk." The nieces, Virginia and Ann Layton, arrived for what Ann recalled was "a glorious year." "Uncle George"—as some colleagues had begun calling him behind his back—was in his glory. Rare was the weekend he could not get Marion and the girls into the car for trips to the countryside and neighboring capitals.[62]

These were happy days. The prestige and responsibility of his first legation gave Messersmith real satisfaction. Christmas 1934 promised to be an especially merry one. Early December brought Marion's sister's youngest, four-year-old Robert Barnes. Born in Berlin, Bobby had spent much of his young life with the Messersmiths, who felt "toward him as though he were our own." A week after his arrival in Vienna, the child was suddenly stricken with "some strange stomach ailment." Messersmith spared "no pains to get the best [medical] advice," but the doctors were baffled. Five days after his admission to the hospital, despite "loving care," the boy died.

Messersmith was almost choked with grief. Watching his nephew sink put him through "a veritable hell." "Not having any children of my own," he wrote poignantly to Moffat during the ordeal, "the little fellow has become very much a part of my life and it is heartbreaking to see a little one suffer and to feel so utterly powerless. . . . My whole household is absolutely broken up and I have not been any good for the last three or four days myself." He wanted Moffat to understand why there would be no letters from Vienna for a while.[63]

The day the boy died, Ann underwent emergency surgery herself. By the time she was up and about, her stay and her sister's were nearly over. Messersmith "dreaded" their departure. It left a void in his life, the more painful for the lack of official business. With the girls gone, he had more time on his hands than he knew what to do with. There were still weekend jaunts with Marion, and the social life she loved so well. But that life left him intellectually and temperamentally unsatisfied. He found Viennese society "boring." "It is strange," he wrote a friend, "how much the formalism of the old Court still weighs on certain aspects of official life here." He endeavored to liven things up, entertaining like a man with nothing else to do. In one month alone the Messersmiths gave five formal dinners for fifty or more, and, over two days, had 600 guests to tea. But the stultifying lethargy soon returned. "We are not having a very exciting time," he confessed in October 1936, "for there is not much going on here." Afternoon naps became a habit, out of character. He overindulged his literary predilection—Raymond Chandler and Dashiell Hammett were his current favorites—reading, he was rightly "ashamed to say," a book a day.[64]

And yet there was a deceptive air of perpetual crisis at the American legation—stenographers rushing about, typewriters clattering with the minister's communications to the State Department. Mission chiefs were supposed to report by despatch, and Messersmith filed more than his share. But he did more. Procedure, as he recognized, had drawbacks. Incoming despatches were routed to the appropriate regional or national desk at the State Department, where they were digested by junior officers of varying skill. What emerged was a précis of varying accuracy. Then too, some important reports were inevitably lost in the crowd of routine ones that clogged the diplomatic pipeline. Worried for the fate of his warnings on nazism, determined that they get through to the top in the form he intended, Messersmith had started writing long "personal" letters directly to the policymakers in late 1933. They encouraged him to continue. Moffat's successor in charge of the Division of Western European Affairs (EUR), James Clement Dunn, assured him that the letters were "very helpful in forming a picture of what is going on." When Phillips left to become ambassador to Italy in August 1936, Messersmith wrote to Assistant Secretary R. Walton Moore and to Hull, who more than once thanked him for his "careful, painstaking and diligent efforts to report fully." He swelled with pride on hearing "four or five times" from Moore that his letters had gone to the White House so that Roosevelt could "have my 'considered views.' "[65]

All this went right to his head and, characteristically, he overdid it in return. Compulsively thorough, Messersmith made it a point literally to "convey all of the interesting and worthwhile information which reaches me here." The results, he admitted, were "sometimes rather long" and "disjointed," often running thirty or more single-spaced pages. But he felt that "when we are passing through such an important period as at present, the Department will want to get all the information which I can get." Besides, "it is better to err on the side of giving too much rather than too little."[66]

He was mistaken, as he recognized with hindsight. Giving too much ran the risk that "the most important officers"—those to whom his letters were addressed—"would not read them" at all. Hull rarely did. Thirty pages of Messersmith's disorganized stream of consciousness was tedious work. His letters to Hull—and apparently his alone —were returned to the desk officers at EUR to be abstracted. Messersmith might have saved everyone the trouble.[67]

Phillips, Moffat, Dunn, and Carr did read their letters. Messersmith may have been better off if they hadn't. Those officials were of the school that judged diplomatic correspondence as much for form as for content—sticklers, as historian Waldo H. Heinrichs observes, for "precision, conciseness, clarity, an orderly structure of logic, and the avoidance of stylistic excrescences." Messersmith failed on each and every count. In Vienna he had the leisure to write carefully, but he persisted in dictating and rushing off rough transcripts, which made a bad impression. "Two more long letters from Messersmith," Phillips sniffed in his diary. "Very verbose, as usual." Once a consul, he implied, always a consul. It was Carr, who had spent much of a lifetime combating such prejudice, who finally ordered Messersmith in late 1936 to shorten his letters. Messersmith said he would try, "even if I think that in some ways their effectiveness may suffer." In any case, he wrote Moore on 22 December, "I have made a firm resolution to keep my letters shorter during the next year." Moore next heard from him three weeks later to the tune of fifteen pages. And Hull was no sooner back from the Pan American Conference in Buenos Aires than Messersmith hit him with two letters totaling thirty-one pages.[68]

Messersmith apologized profusely to Carr. "I hope that you do not think that I was not mindful of your good advice about the length of my letters." He had found it "difficult to keep them within a few pages [when] discussing such complicated situations." He promised to write less frequently, if not less copiously. Before he had a chance to make good, Roosevelt summoned him home to serve in the department. Only then, when he was on the receiving end, was he to learn how burdensome letters from the field could be.[69]

His line of argument also went down hard with his superiors, especially his plea for cooperation with the Soviet Union to stop Hitler. The State Department's European specialists by no means approved of what had been going on inside Germany since 1933, but there was a tendency to blame the worst of nazism, as originally had Messersmith, on the popular passions Hitler had unleashed but could not control. Washington and London were also plagued with guilt over the punitive Treaty of Versailles, whose oppressions Hitler never ceased to belabor. And there was considerable anxiety over Hitler's successor in case he did fall. If from the right, Junker militarism, which had already given the world a war, would be back in the saddle. A victory for the left, on the other hand, would be the biggest since November 1917, bringing, Phillips was convinced, "more chaos than ever" and, it was feared, the encirclement and eventual collapse of non-Communist governments in Central and Eastern Europe. Hitler was a known—and possibly lesser—evil.[70]

As Thomas R. Maddux and others have shown, Westerners also labored under serious illusions about Soviet Russia during the 1920s and 1930s, illusions compounded of popular hopes and fears and Soviet ideological window dressing. The class hostility of Western foreign offices that Maddux documents was reinforced by some slippery Soviet diplomacy and deliberate boorishness in contact with their capitalist counterparts. Despite lively debate over the relative influence of ideology and national interest in Stalin's diplomacy, nearly all the Europeanists in the State Department and in the field endorsed the conclusion that Soviet Russia was an unreliable ally and an unfit partner for the democracies in their security arrangements.[71]

Messersmith cut through this intellectual fog. He practically dismissed Marxism as an objective of Soviet diplomacy, and scoffed at the suggestion that the Kremlin was actively exporting revolution. "Nine tenths of the Communist agitation laid to the account of Moscow," he maintained, "has no connection whatever with that country." He even saw some evidence that Stalin was moving domestically away from collectivism toward a kind of state capitalism not unlike Mussolini's system. In fact, Messersmith was more and more convinced that Russia and Germany particularly were cut from the same cloth, alike "dictatorships based on the worship of force," under the thumb of nationalists posing as revolutionaries. Hitler's talk about having saved civilization from Bolshevism was also deception; in reality, Messersmith explained, the Nazis perceived in the Soviet "not such a dangerous social, economic, or political doctrine, but the system that presents its greatest obstacle to world supremacy. The two systems are almost identical in their objectives . . . and methods, hence their enmity."[72]

There was, however, a critical difference. "The ultimate aspirations of the Soviet regime," he wrote Phillips, "may be as dangerous to the peace in Europe as those of the present German regime," but the German threat was imminent and the Russian remote. Internally weak, beset east and west by greedy and powerful neighbors, Russia would not be in a position to make trouble, in his opinion, "for years to come." For the present, "no country . . . wishes peace and . . . has more reason to fear war than Russia." To its avoidance, Stalin was prepared to collaborate in good faith, purely as a matter of Russian self-interest. Purely as a matter of Western self-interest, Messersmith advised, his overtures should "not be spurned but [rather] availed of with, of course, always wide open eyes." After disposing of Hitler with Russian help, the democracies would then be free to turn to "the menace that might come from Moscow when that inert giant may feel himself strong enough to move and become aggressive."[73]

It was a sober and realistic analysis, delivered as events marched in the opposite direction. Inside Russia Stalin's terror ground into high gear, and Western conservatives thanked God, again, for the revival of the German bulwark. And in early 1935 Messersmith got the first incontrovertible evidence that the West lacked the will to stop Hitler, with or without Soviet assistance. The anti-German unity of Rome, repeated in April at the Italian town of Stresa, was instantly compromised by Britain's compensatory feelers to Berlin. On 26 February it was announced that the foreign secretary, Sir John Simon, was going to see Hitler on a mission of friendship. Messersmith was stunned. "It is almost inconceivable," he exploded to Phillips, "that at the moment of Germany's most complete isolation and at a time when her internal situation is in reality most critical, any move should be contemplated which will tend to add prestige to and prolong the life of a regime which has in it so much danger." On 16 March Hitler responded with an announcement of his own: the reintroduction of conscription, with plans for a peacetime army of 550,000. Britain condemned this first open violation of Versailles, and then asked Berlin whether Simon's invitation stood.[74]

More bad news awaited Messersmith in Berlin, where he stopped for a week in late March before sailing home on his first leave from Vienna. He had been tempted to drop everything back in December, when he got word from Fleetwood that his mother, just turned eighty-six, was "having one heart attack after another." But, he explained to Moffat, "there is too much dynamite stored about for me to leave here with any peace of mind." Fortunately his mother stopped having heart attacks—she was to live another three years— and Messersmith, having again demonstrated his dedication to duty, finally pronounced the situation stable enough for him to leave.[75]

He stayed up late that first night in Berlin, 20 March, listening to old friends tell a grim story. Another winter had come and gone, and by all accounts Hitler was stronger than ever. The economy limped along, but the populace seemed almost oblivious to their privations. Indeed, it was clear that Germany had taken further leave of its senses in the year since his last visit. Goebbels's propaganda had produced "popular hysteria"; Messersmith observed that Germans were "completely disoriented with respect to practically every social and economic problem and with respect to the outside world," and united behind their Führer. Perhaps most disheartening, the Reichswehr had submitted to the regime, in gratitude for the breakup of the SA and the rearmament program.[76]

As a result, Messersmith reported, "Hitler and his associates are absolutely drunk with power and their illusions, and believe that the whole world is afraid of them, and that no one will move against them no matter what they do." Simon's impending visit had produced euphoria in Nazi circles. In talks with Messersmith, the French ambassador, André François Poncet, could barely contain his disgust over recent British policy; his British counterpart, Sir Eric Phipps, whom Messersmith met on 25 March, was no less "melancholy."[77]

Despair was contagious. Messersmith departed Berlin "tremendously depressed." Everything was going wrong. Perhaps, on its rickety economic base, the expanding Nazi military machine would crack at the first show of resistance. Perhaps not. In any case, there were no volunteers to conduct the test. By the time the democracies woke up to the danger, he feared it would be too late for the United States. Given the present pace of German rearmament, he calculated nervously, as early as 1936 the confrontation with nazism could spill over and involve "us . . . in spite of all that we shall do to keep out."[78]

In his State Department discussions in April and May, however, he kept these forebodings and self-doubts to himself, insisting as before that the clock was running out on the Nazis. Messersmith was always a big one for sticking to his guns. His faith in human nature told him that Germans would eventually rediscover their consciences. But it was not merely for consistency's sake that he clung to a thesis that he wished was valid but increasingly knew was not. For he understood that when hope for internal collapse was gone, so too was the best rationale for keeping Germany isolated. To be sure, he was not yet alone in contending that Hitler was vulnerable internally, and thus, externally. As late as March 1937 Herbert Feis expressed doubt that Germans would put up with "ever harsher measures of economic control and coercion." From Cologne, Alfred Klieforth (born Kliefoth) concurred into 1938. And some officers at the Berlin embassy, like First Secretary Joseph Flack, still held that Hitler would not last. But they were a dwindling minority whose counsel was increasingly discounted. By the end of 1934 Ambassador Dodd, who had come to hate nazism with at least Messersmith's passion, had dropped his assumption of economic breakdown, joining those who gave the regime a long lease on life. Douglas Jenkins, Messersmith's successor as consul general, agreed. "When I came to Berlin," he wrote Hull in late 1935, "foreigners and many Germans still clung to the idea that the Nazis could not endure, and predicted the early collapse of the Hitler regime. I think I can say that few people entertain this thought today." Raymond Geist declared that "those prophets who predict a collapse in the near future are not well-advised." Writing to Moffat in January 1935, Geist, with accuracy uncanny even for him, predicted that "if Hitler lives, he will conduct the destiny of this nation for the next decade at least."[79]

As in Hull's battle with Peek, the question of Nazi longevity had important policy implications for the United States. The spring of 1935 found the German ambassador, Hans Luther, pressing the State Department again for trade talks, and, Messersmith observed nervously from the scene, "no rebuff seems to stop him." In the face of such rebuffs, Messersmith would have persisted himself. If anything, the negotiating climate was warmer than it had been the year before, when Hull and Phillips were advising Roosevelt that the end of Hitlerism was in sight. Now Peek was effectively disposed of, Nazi power had been further consolidated, and the new consensus at State, as Messersmith wrote in dismay to Dodd, was that "Hitler will be around for a long time and we might as well treat with them." Two years of halfhearted disapproval, of withholding "aid and comfort and support," Messersmith's prescription, seemed only to have made Germany more united and more belligerent. It was time to try a more openhanded approach in the hope that, as Feis later put it, "were Germany's immediate economic situation alleviated, it would accept the rules of a peaceful international society."[80]

Messersmith personally presented his dissent. His arguments were by now familiar, even tired, as usual a mixture of fact and fantasy: Luther's persistence bespoke his government's desperation; nazism could never be tamed; a treaty would recognize a regime hellbent on war and would undermine the efforts to preserve real peace. "Even if we cannot do very much in a positive sense to help this effort," he argued, "we should at least refrain from doing anything negative."[81]

In June 1935 representatives of the United States and Germany initiated an extension of the 1923 treaty of friendship, commerce, and consular rights. The State Department defended its handiwork as a practical necessity: Americans and their interests in Germany would otherwise suffer the loss of consular protection. In lunatic Germany that was no small matter, as Messersmith could attest. The Reich gained no special trade concessions; the most-favored-nation clause of the 1923 treaty was eliminated, disqualifying German products for generalization.[82]

Certainly the treaty was not the coveted breakthrough. Neither side would surrender its trade principles. Still, this treaty, any treaty, was a moral victory for nazism and a bitter pill for Messersmith. "Friendship" indeed. However it was justified, the treaty also legitimized and regularized German-American relations. Hitler, the State Department was saying, was in power to stay, an assumption that was henceforward to guide its German policy. It was a small breakthrough on the road to appeasement.

Attitudes were thus ossifying in Washington. By being gracelessly and interminably contrary, and slightly unhinged on the subject of Germany, Messersmith found himself outside the State Department mainstream. There he was to remain throughout the 1930s. But he was also getting encouragement from above. He had had fifteen minutes with Roosevelt, their first meeting, on the eve of his return to Europe the year before, and now again, 12 April 1935. Precisely what they said to each other cannot be known, for Messersmith made no memorandum and neither, according to custom, did the White House. But Roosevelt, who could be beguiling with people he loathed, was genuinely delighted to see him again. Recent intelligence told him that in sending him to Vienna he had not only tweaked "the career boys'" noses, but had made a splendid diplomatic appointment as well. Harry Hopkins's inspection report may have been decisive: Messersmith was the only American mission chief Hopkins said he met in Europe more than perfunctorily interested in conditions at home. This touched a sore spot with the president, who was deeply annoyed by Foreign Service types more eager to dissociate themselves from their country than to represent it. Messersmith, a proud product of American middle-class democracy, was something else again.[83]

A presidential relationship had begun, circumscribed by distance and bureaucratic considerations, but increasingly close nonetheless. In fact, these limitations may have helped bring them closer. Roosevelt often invited noncareer mission chiefs to write him directly from their posts, a practice that never ceased to annoy Hull. The Dodds of the world had little to lose—they were pariahs at the State Department anyway—but Messersmith and others in his position flouted procedure at their own risk. Hence, during either their 1934 or 1935 meeting, Roosevelt instructed him to continue writing to the State Department; he would order the letters to be forwarded to the White House. Responding retrospectively to the longwindedness charge, Messersmith recalled asking Roosevelt in 1936 whether his letters were serving their purpose. The president replied that he had "read them all" and that, regardless of what people like Carr might think, "I was not to shorten them." To the end of his days Messersmith wondered where the president "found the time to read them." In fact, only three substantive letters from Vienna, sent over by Moore in 1936, appear in the president's papers. Possibly the State Department deliberately withheld letters it preferred that Roosevelt not see; possibly too he saw others that were then returned to State.[84]

In any case, less of Messersmith was better and perhaps more influential than more of him. Regardless of how many letters Roosevelt actually read, they clearly had impact on his worldview and his estimation of their author. Messersmith always believed—Roosevelt, a great flatterer, may have told him so—that his letters were "the ones in which he placed the greatest dependence concerning developments in Central Europe," and the ones that were responsible for Roosevelt's early appreciation—by 1935, according to historian Robert Dallek—of the inevitability of United States–German confrontation. But there is absolutely no evidence, not in Dallek's definitive history or elsewhere, to support this extravagant claim, which speaks well for Roosevelt. The reports of people like Dodd, Claude Bowers in Madrid, and Robert W. Bingham in London, nonprofessionals all, carried at least as much weight at the White House and, as on the key question of Nazi staying power, were more often on the mark. What made Messersmith special to Roosevelt was the spirit of his analyses rather than their specifics. He was a career man with a progressive outlook, one of the very few who knew right from wrong as the White House understood it. "He is one of the best men we have in the whole Service," the president wrote a mutual friend in December 1935. "I count greatly on his judgment."[85]

5

With such or similar words of presidential encouragement offsetting his short shrift at the State Department, Messersmith returned to Vienna late in May 1935, a month sooner than planned. The depressing realities of Berlin back in March had been shunted aside by the two dominant impressions he took back to Europe with him from the states. The mood of economic recovery at home had exhilarated and comforted him. The New Deal, he wrote gratefully upon his return, had spared "our people . . . the social and political disorders which are disrupting this old continent." And one other thing had become absolutely clear to him: the American people wanted no part of the Old World's current tumults. New initiatives to promote world peace, as Roosevelt himself may have told him, were out of the question. Reconciling himself to this reality, Messersmith again suppressed others. He once more professed optimism that Europe's troubles would come to a head in time to be contained to the continent, and opined that, for the sake of reform and recovery at home, the United States could not and should not pull anyone's chestnuts out of the fire but its own. Washington, he counseled the State Department, might provide moral support for collective security, but the temptation to "actively participate . . . must be sternly resisted, for it can accomplish no permanent good in the old world, which must settle its own problems in the best way it can."[86]

The illusion of isolation fleetingly indulged in by Messersmith was never more seductive than in the last half of 1935. June witnessed the Anglo-German naval agreement, another breach of the then five-week-old Stresa front. Then Geneva was put to the test and found wanting in East Africa. By the time Messersmith returned from leave, Mussolini had amassed half a million troops for an invasion of Ethiopia (Abyssinia), scene of Italy's humiliating defeat in 1896. Western analysts guessed that he would strike at the end of the rainy season, in the fall.[87]

For London and Paris, the quandary was acute. On the one hand, Messersmith wrote Phillips on 6 August, they recognized that "Italy was treated like the black sheep of the Allied family at Versailles in the matter of colonial spoils and that she does need a place to expand." France especially regarded Ethiopia as a small price to pay to keep the Duce content and committed to the anti-Hitler front. On the other hand, the democracies could not "permit the roughshod way in which Mussolini has been proceeding," not without making a mockery of collective security and the League of Nations, of which Ethiopia was a full member.[88]

No third state was more affected by these developments than Austria. For it, Messersmith saw, an Italo-Ethiopian war would be a "catastrophe." The diversion of Italian forces from the Brenner would leave the door ajar for Hitler. If Geneva imposed sanctions, Austria would be forced to choose between collective security or its protector. Mussolini might be driven into Hitler's embrace; and the Führer would surely make Austria the price of his friendship.

Yet Messersmith assumed that Mussolini would pull back before it was too late. Austrians and their friends, like Messersmith, tended to see the Duce through glasses colored rose by his heroics on 25 July 1934. Messersmith's Mussolini, for all his bluster and bombast, was a realist with the courage to act, then rare qualities among European statesmen. It followed that he would abandon the Ethiopian project when pressed by his Stresa partners, appreciating, as Messersmith concluded on 6 June, that the German threat and "the Austrian situation and cooperation with England and France are far more vital to Italy than Abyssinia."[89]

This proved all wrong. The Duce was more interested in glory than security, and understood that trying to resist Hitler's absolute determination to have the Anschluss might deprive him of both. He had invested too much in the African buildup to turn back, even for a generous negotiated settlement. Instead he made "the reaction to his Abyssinian policy the test-case for his future attitude toward other European countries." While the West threatened sanctions, Hitler was muzzling German criticism of Italy and rejecting an Ethiopian bid for arms. This attitude was noted and appreciated in Rome.[90]

As diplomatic prospects dimmed, Austria groped for the guarantees that would permit it to stand with the West against Italy, in defense of collective security. But Berger Waldenegg returned from Geneva empty-handed and, in a 19 September talk with Messersmith, "hopeless." The Ethiopian invasion, he reported dolefully, would commence any day; the sanctions under consideration at Geneva would prove futile. Austria had to align itself with Italy for self-preservation. It might have to leave the League altogether if Mussolini so decreed. The Duce, he added, was ready to come to terms with Hitler, even if it meant withdrawing from the Brenner.[91]

One by one the Austrian's forebodings came to pass. Writing to Phillips on 27 September, Messersmith again expressed confidence that Mussolini would ultimately "back down." A week later Italian troops moved into Ethiopia. The League immediately considered sanctions. Austria came under intense Italian pressure to bolt the debate, but stayed, only to join Albania and Hungary, the other Italian client-states, in a declaration of noncooperation when sanctions were voted. It was, Messersmith observed, "a reminder to the League that Austria owes its national life to Italy."[92]

Messersmith beheld civilization at a crossroads. He wanted to conserve Stresa as much as anyone, but making an example of a renegade Italy, he decided, would have still greater cautionary impact on Germany. He made the connection explicit. "If Mussolini succeeds in flouting the League and in having his way against almost entire world opinion by the application of force and intransigence," he declared, "then the League is dead and within a half year or less Nazi Germany will . . . proceed on a much more definite and dangerous path and have a much better chance of getting away with it." Only one thing could save the situation now: "Anglo-French cooperation which is so definite and far reaching and so clear to the whole world that there can be no mistaking it whatsoever." If this precipitated war, so be it. "As a lover of peace almost to the degree of being a pacifist," he wrote Phillips on 15 October, "it is my duty to tell you [that] I believe that it would be the greatest mistake for Europe and the world if it does not come to conflict now. . . . The greatest danger is that a face-saving formula may be arrived at. If, in order to avoid what . . . would be a very short war, and a comparatively bloodless one, a compromise is arrived at, a war a few years hence of a devastating character which will engulf Europe and involve the rest of the world, is certain."[93]

The compromise was attempted. Early December brought the bombshell revelation of the Anglo-French proposal to restore Stresa by handing Ethiopia over to Mussolini. Messersmith joined in the ensuing hue and cry over this Hoare-Laval plan, nearly exhausting his stock of apt clichés. It was "a sorry spectacle," "a great danger," "a rude shock," "a definite blow to British prestige, to the Empire, to the League, to collective security, and to peace." Of course it was not Europe's peace that he was concerned with. Hoare-Laval would have ended the Ethiopian conflict had Mussolini agreed, which, with second thoughts about the whole venture now that it was underway, he was tempted to do. Messersmith was quite prepared to write off Ethiopia and Europe in order to spare American democracy. Every time the confrontation with lawlessness was put off, he knew that the United States came a step closer to war itself.[94]

Still the picture was not all bleak. The days following Hoare-Laval gave Messersmith "new encouragement and hope." Public outrage had prompted a quick retraction by Britain and France, and the dismissal of both Hoare and Laval. Collective security had received a ringing popular endorsement that he believed the statesmen in London must heed. His British colleague Selby told him that London was in possession of information that Germany had already violated their naval agreement, which would presumably make Britain think twice before dealing with Hitler again. Inside the Foreign Office proponents of Anglo-German rapprochement were said to be losing ground to the likes of the permanent undersecretary, Sir Robert Vansittart, a Nazi-hater who urged rearmament and close cooperation with France. Messersmith rushed to the conclusion that "the iron ring around Germany is becoming stronger . . . with the realization that there is only one way of saving Europe from disaster—through the disappearance of the present regime."[95]

To make the regime disappear, Westerners closed their eyes. On 7 March 1936 German troops marched into the Rhineland, demilitarized under the terms of Versailles and the Locarno Pact of 1925. Messersmith excitedly fitted the facts into his framework. The Nazis' demons, he decided, had finally caught up with them. "The external pressure on Germany and the internal pressure of the economic and financial situation," he hypothesized on the 9th, had forced "a morale-raising adventure," a frontal assault on the European security system that would surely prove suicidal. It was a strained interpretation that attributed Nazi dynamism to weakness and desperation rather than to strength and Hitler's supreme confidence that he would meet no resistance over the Rhineland. It was an interpretation that even Messersmith clung to with difficulty as the days dragged on, as talk begat only more talk, as it became clear that Britain and, therefore, France were not going to move. Hitler had scored his greatest victory yet by again capitalizing on Europe's fear of war. With Britain scrambling to save face, "almost on her knees to Hitler 'to make a gesture'" for peace, begging him to come to Geneva to justify his actions—with all this, Messersmith asked disgustedly, "who can blame an increasing majority of the German people for believing that after all Germany is invincible and has a mission to carry through by the domination of Europe [?]"[96]

The Rhine exploit sent tremors through Central Europe. Messersmith reported that Austria was gripped with "a new sense of insecurity" born of the recognition that England and France, having acquiesced on the Rhine, were "even less likely to do anything" for it "if the next fait accompli is in this direction." So Hitler apparently intended. Papen, who had assuredly not been recalled, was since mid-1935 carrying out new orders from Berlin "to put Austro-German relations on a basis satisfactory to both sides, which should gradually lead to an Anschluss." With great fanfare it was announced that the Reich was at last prepared to normalize relations by way of a treaty.

Austria smelled a rat. For months Papen found Berger Waldenegg evasive and dilatory, when he could find him at all: their relationship, Messersmith reported on 23 August, had become a game of "hide-and-seek." But the changing complexion of Europe made such stand-offiishness increasingly untenable. Although the League's sanctions were not impeding the rape of Ethiopia, they were serving to estrange Mussolini from the West. In a long talk with Hitler's ambassador, Ulrich von Hassel, in January 1936, the Duce declared that Stresa was "dead and buried," that Germany's "benevolent neutrality" toward Italy had made it "possible to improve fundamentally the Italo-German relations, and to remove the last bone of contention, the Austrian problem." Austria, he agreed, might become "practically a satellite of Germany."[97]

Mussolini broke this devastating news to Schuschnigg during the semiannual Rome Protocols get-together in late March 1936. Messersmith, about to leave again for home, completely misread the situation. The Duce, he declared, had called the conclave "to show how important he was in the Danubian area," to demonstrate to the world that "at a time when all confidence in written agreements was gone, a proved friend was ready to assert his friendship and support" for Austria. Such friendship would be the death of the country. Mussolini was actually telling Schuschnigg that "in view of the general situation and the Italian commitment in Africa, he regarded an improvement of Austro-German relations as urgently necessary; Vienna should make direct contact with Berlin; this would be an effective extension of the Rome Protocols and offer the best possible international guarantee of Austria's independence."[98]

Returning on 13 June, Messersmith found Vienna abuzz with the impending rapprochement with Germany. With the cutoff of Italian subventions, the anti-German Heimwehr was crumbling. Starhemberg and the equally anti-German Berger Waldenegg were stripped of their portfolios. Schuschnigg opened talks with Papen, talks Messersmith was sure would fail. Mussolini, he wrote stubbornly to Phillips, although no longer "averse" to an Austro-German treaty, still supported Schuschnigg's "minimum conditions" regarding recognition and nonintervention—terms Messersmith believed "will be unacceptable to Germany."[99]

Explaining his failure of analysis is not hard. Messersmith simply refused to believe that Papen was capable of successful diplomacy. Moreover, he lacked inside informants. The expansive Papen might have kept him apprised of his negotiating progress himself had Messersmith not shunned him so assiduously. On the Austrian side, Berger Waldenegg remained a loyal friend from his exile as ambassador to Rome. But Messersmith's understanding of Nazi methods should have predicted the outcome. For three years he had been warning others that Hitler could sign anything because his signature meant nothing. Schuschnigg's "minimum conditions" posed no problem for Papen because any treaty was intended to be torn up at the opportune time anyway. By the end of June the agreement was in place. Austria bound itself to German foreign policy, to amnesty Austrian Nazis, and to provide the Pan Germanist "national opposition" with cabinet representation. Papen accommodatingly dropped other demands, such as for a veto over any restoration plan. Hitler and Mussolini bestowed their blessings. Not until 8 July, three days before the treaty was announced, did Messersmith quietly report that agreement was "very probable" in "ten days to two weeks."[100]

Caught unawares by the 11 July treaty, Messersmith was not slow in grasping its implications. "No one in Austria," he wrote Hull on the 12th, except her enemies, "are [sic] very enthusiastic about the agreement." He predicted that Austrian expectations of increased German trade and tourism would "be much disappointed": Germany would take Austrian raw materials only in barter for products that Austria did not need. Currency restrictions had long done away with the free-spending German sightseer. The treaty's benefits were illusory, and its dangers were manifest. Whatever the treaty provided or implied, Messersmith concluded, there had been "no change in Germany's ultimate objectives." The diplomatic consensus was that the pact actually brought Anschluss closer. Incurably subversive Nazi zealots were back on the streets. German newspapers again circulated legally, which, Messersmith observed, "will not be conducive to internal order here." Nazi sentiment inside Austria was now "bound to grow, for a good many people here will take the agreement to mean the beginning of the end despite this affirmation of Austrian independence."[101]

Schuschnigg, however, appeared determined to resist. In the weeks following the treaty Messersmith reported on his "valiant effort . . . to maintain real Austrian sovereignty." The two new cabinet appointees—Edmund Glaise Horstenau, minister without portfolio, and Dr. Guido Schmidt, state secretary in the Foreign Ministry—were indeed Pan Germanists, but not pro-Nazi. The chancellor retained full control over foreign policy, which he privately vowed to keep independent and neutral. Moreover, he made it clear that Nazi sedition would be resisted. In a mass rally in Vienna that turned violent, 700 party members were arrested and returned to prison. Messersmith applauded Schuschnigg's decisiveness. Hitler had secretly contributed to the calm. On 16 July he summoned Austrian Nazi leaders and ordered discipline. They could not be permitted to run amok, as Messersmith recognized, without destroying "the pact's intended effect on western Europe" and jeopardizing the nascent friendship with Italy.[102]

Thus, thanks to Schuschnigg's firmness and Hitler's wish to lie low, Austria enjoyed peace. How long this would last, Messersmith wrote Hamilton Fish Armstrong on 4 August, "it is difficult to say, for, as before, Austrian developments depend on developments outside." Nothing had changed. Despite near economic recovery, domestic tranquillity, and Schuschnigg's solid, if uninspired, leadership, the country's independence was not his to save. He quickly learned that those who could still help no longer deemed Austria worth saving. It had never been loved in the West, where it was an embarrassing reminder of postwar mistakes. Liberals had always deplored its quasi-autocracy, while many conservatives insisted that Austria and Germany were historically and racially destined to be one. With the German treaty, its remaining friends in the West virtually gave it up for lost.[103]

So too, apparently, Italy, notwithstanding Mussolini's continued assurances to the contrary. Historian Jürgen Gehl has observed that the 11 July agreement was "in fact more of a settlement of the differences between Germany and Italy than between Germany and Austria." Messersmith instantly recognized that the pact provided "the first basis for real active cooperation between Rome and Berlin," but insisted that no such cooperation would come to pass. Although ready to concede that Mussolini seemed to be "washing his hands of Austrian problems," Messersmith, in a 31 July letter to Hull, maintained that "Italy is not ready to desert the Western powers nor to throw her lot definitely with Germany." Even if current British and French overtures to Rome failed, the Hitler-Mussolini relationship, he assured Washington, could never last. The clash of interests and personalities would limit them to "surface cooperation." Hitler was a madman who had "tied Germany into a knot, which there is no untying"; the Duce was "still susceptible to reason and has some flexibility."[104]

Every development belied Messersmith's line. The outbreak of the Spanish civil war on 17 July and the Duce's entanglement with the Franco insurgents sped him into the German camp. The advent of the moderate left Popular Front in France drew the two Fascist powers together in the anti-Bolshevik cause. Western overtures were icily rebuffed. Consistent with his new orientation, Mussolini entrusted foreign policy to his young son-in-law, Galeazzo Ciano, who was only too eager to jettison Austria for an alliance with Berlin, which he

visited in October. Talks with Neurath, Göring, and Hitler left him
"completely overawed," as Messersmith put it, "with German military power and professions of German friendship." More momen-
tously, he reached agreement on the framework for an alliance—
what would become known, after a 1 November speech by Mussolini,
as the Rome-Berlin Axis.[105]

In contrast to the staged adulation he tasted in the German capital,
Ciano's reception in Vienna three weeks later was subdued. Messersmith reported that Schuschnigg "pulled out the stops" for him, but
from the Viennese, the hurt Italian grumbled, "never a salute, never
any applause, never a shout." He would have his revenge. The 11
July agreement was only weeks old when Hitler issued new demands
upon Austria, for currency and customs unification, a bigger role for
the Austrian Nazis, and a military pact, which envisaged the integration of the Austrian armed forces with those of the Reich. Ciano
relished denying Schuschnigg the support he needed to withstand
these pressures. The growing Spanish involvement, he informed his
hosts, precluded further Italian arms shipments. He suggested that
Austria turn to Germany instead. He then berated them for their
failures to quit Geneva and recognize Franco's government.[106]

Written off in the West and left in the lurch by Italy, Austria faced
Germany alone. In late November Schmidt paid a state visit to Berlin, and returned as overawed as Ciano. Messersmith reported "a
perceptible, if slow increase in German infiltration." Pro-German
diplomats began being brought home to fill high offices in Schmidt's
Foreign Ministry. The anti-Nazi Austrian envoy in Berlin, Stefan
Tauschitz, was recalled. Obviously, Messersmith wrote Edgar Ansel
Mowrer, Hitler's strategy was "to penetrate quietly and peacefully, . . .
undermining the position of this government so that it will be followed by a weaker one and eventually a [Nazi] one which will declare
the Anschluss."[107]

Despite his isolation, Schuschnigg continued to assert Austrian
sovereignty and to enjoy popular support. Internally the chancellor's
position remained "impregnable"; Messersmith credited rumors,
which again were unfounded, that Schuschnigg would soon purge
Schmidt and Glaise Horstenau. Nonetheless, these rumors may have
induced Schmidt to bargain hard during six weeks of trade negotiations with Papen. The result, Messersmith reported, was a commercial agreement "meagre and unsatisfactory" from the German standpoint. The Viennese gave the lie to German propaganda about the
great stifled yearning for Anschluss when the Führer's foreign minister visited in February 1937. Aside from a few "very feeble" demonstrations, involving, Messersmith estimated, perhaps 7,000 "mostly

boys and women," Austrians gave Neurath the cold shoulder. The Nazi press assailed Schuschnigg for "sabotaging" the 11 July agreement, but Neurath did not harp on the matter. Germany, Messersmith concluded, was unready to provoke another crisis.[108]

The way Messersmith had it, Germany literally could not afford one. Everything he was hearing about the Nazi economy suggested to him that the long-awaited breakdown was about to occur. He had been wrong before, of course. But, he protested to the State Department, he could not be blamed for making "a mistake which was made as well by the Nazi leaders themselves, for there is no one more surprised than they that they have been able to hold out as long as they have." In any case, he wrote hopefully and inaccurately to Hull on 30 January, "even those who have been giving the regime a still fairly long lease on life now see the end this year [1937]." He still placed credence in his German businessmen, who were reporting dwindling raw material stocks and "very unsatisfactory" progress toward laboratory substitutes. Some factories, he heard, had even had to shut down. The regime itself acknowledged the food shortages. One insider—Franz Hueber, a former Austrian minister of justice and Göring's brother-in-law—told Messersmith, who promptly passed the word to Washington, that Hitler, for some unspecified reason, was about to hand the chancellorship over to Göring, who was sure to adopt "a much more moderate program." Göring was in fact among the most ardent Anschluss immediatists in Hitler's inner circle.[109]

The apparent absence of a reliable ally also argued against Hitler's hazarding new foreign-policy dramatics. On 30 November Messersmith reported that Ciano's talks with Neurath had yielded "no binding agreements" (which, strictly speaking, was true), and asserted that, regarding Hitler and Mussolini, "each distrusts the other just as much as ever and that the basic opposition of their interests is just as great as ever." The much-ballyhooed Rome-Berlin Axis was "in reality very wobbly." Bogged down by guerrilla resistance in Ethiopia and the escalating Spanish conflict, Italy struck him as near economic exhaustion itself. William Phillips wrote him from Rome that Italians were entirely in the dark regarding the Spanish involvement—the troops having been told that they were going to Africa to subdue barbarians—and forecast trouble when the truth came out. Mussolini appeared to be losing his grip: "nervous and worried," "aging fast," and not to be relied upon in a crisis. In fact the Duce was finding refuge from his tribulations in dreams of omnipotence. Consultations with Berlin for the larger war against England he intended to wage went forward.[110]

6

Confident, then, that there was "not much prospect of the peace of Europe being disturbed by some overt act of Germany in the near future," Messersmith decided that he could safely take his accustomed spring leave. Besides, he wrote Hull, he did not want to disappoint his mother, now nearly blind, who "always looks forward to seeing me at this time of the year."[111]

The spring of 1937 ushered in a new Roosevelt administration and high anxiety throughout the federal service. Chiefs of diplomatic missions underwent their quadrennial rite of resignation. At minimum there would be many transfers. But not, apparently, for Messersmith. He heard through the grapevine that he was staying put in Vienna. That prospect, he wrote Phillips on 2 April, "pleases me very much, as I cannot conceive of my having a better post than this." Truly, the three years in Vienna had generally been happy ones for him and Marion. Certainly a transfer was likely to be to a non-European post, to a new setting and a new cast of characters.[112]

But there were posts he would have preferred, and one in particular. The action he was not getting enough of in Vienna would surely be his in Berlin. The German ambassadorship was the job he always coveted above all others and never obtained. In 1937, however, it looked ready to open up. Dodd was talking retirement. The State Department rejoiced at the prospect. Upon the resignation of the mortally ill Jesse Straus in August 1936, Moffat wished out loud that "it had been the Berlin Embassy rather than the Paris one which fell vacant." As far as Messersmith was concerned, Dodd had always seen things accurately enough, but lacked the requisite backbone. Their meeting on 4 April 1937, during his customary Berlin stopover, lent credence to the resignation rumors. Messersmith was shocked—and no doubt encouraged—by Dodd's deterioration. "Senility," he recalled, "had already set in." Dodd had become "an utterly ineffective and futile person . . . frustrated, bewildered, wandering in his expression and conversation, unable to concentrate adequately . . . no longer capable of reasoned thought and judgment."[113]

Dodd's days in office were clearly numbered, and Messersmith considered himself an heir possible if not apparent. In April 1936 Roosevelt, acting through an intermediary, had offered him the Moscow ambassadorship vacated by William Bullitt, who replaced Straus in Paris. The intermediary was Colonel Edward M. House, Democratic elder statesman and occasional Roosevelt confidant. Suspecting that Messersmith would decline the post, the president had decided to spare him the embarrassment of doing so directly. Roosevelt's hunch was correct. Messersmith was well informed on the rigors of Moscow. He feared for his stomach, like Kennan's. He did not know the language. Most of all, the luxury-loving Marion "would not stand in my way in accepting the post [but neither] would she go." Living without his wife, he conceded, "would be a great handicap." But the offer buoyed him. If Moscow in 1936, he reasoned, why not Berlin in 1937?[114]

The answer was twofold. The president preferred envoys capable of civil communication with their hosts. Bullitt had been transferred because after three frustrating years in Moscow his anti-Bolshevism had become all-consuming. Sending Messersmith to Berlin was sure to make the fur fly, to the possible detriment of American interests. Besides, the post was already spoken for. When Messersmith turned down Moscow, Roosevelt gave it to millionaire businessman Joseph E. Davies, with the promise of a transfer to Berlin within the year. Messersmith might have accepted Moscow on those terms with or without his wife. In any case, the State Department was pressing not his claim to Berlin but that of veteran career diplomat Hugh Gibson, languishing in Brazil since 1933. Unbeknown to Messersmith, who sailed from Hamburg on 7 April 1937, he was out of the running for Berlin.[115]

Messersmith's name had also come up in connection with another office. He had returned to Vienna from his 1935 leave to find, as he wrote Moffat, "that all sorts of rumors are current about me—mainly that I went home to arrange to get Carr's job as Assistant Secretary as he was to retire this fall! I need not tell you that I am happy in my job here . . . and certainly would not seek Carr's, who I hope will stay in the Department many years, for I consider he has done a great task and should be kept at it. How these rumors get started is too much for me."[116]

Messersmith's exasperation was sincere, but the encomium to Carr was not. Messersmith was less than a year in Vienna at the time, and unprepared for another move. The cost of living in Washington was another strike against it. But, as the months in Vienna dragged monotonously on, Washington started looking better and better to him. The year 1937 marked Carr's forty-fifth year in the State Department, the last thirteen as assistant secretary for administration. Without slighting his achievements—which had, after all, made it possible for a consul to become minister to Austria—Messersmith, as we have seen, had been dissatisfied with his leadership for years. He complained periodically about Carr's myriad failures: to recoup the budget cuts of the early 1930s, to promote consular-diplomatic interchangeability, to coordinate the bothersome commercial attachés.

When rumors of Carr's retirement revived in 1937, so did Messersmith's interest in his post.

Hoping for an offer of Carr's job or Dodd's, Messersmith, who arrived in Fleetwood in late April, requested an interview with the president. They met on the morning of 14 May. Neither possibility came up. Roosevelt gave him to believe that he was to return to Vienna. Two weeks later, just before he was due to sail, Messersmith called again. This time he came right to the point. "I have heard," he remembered saying to the president, "that I would be asked to serve in the Department." Was there anything to it? Roosevelt said no. He wanted Messersmith back in Austria because "the information that I was sending from there was so valuable and vital."[117]

Three days after his return to Vienna the telegram arrived. He was to return to Washington for consultation, after which "the President desires to appoint you as Assistant Secretary of State." In light of Roosevelt's assurances to the contrary, the news "came as probably the biggest surprise I have ever had. . . . we had just unpacked our trunks." Now they had to repack them, and quickly. The department, he explained to his colleague in Bucharest, "seems to want me at home as soon as possible." He booked passage from Hamburg for 13 July. This left a scant two weeks to wrap up their affairs and say their goodbyes, which were many after three years. Messersmith felt as though they were "leaving like a thief in the night." In any event, he wrote lightheartedly, "I shall try to see that our bills are paid."[118]

The Messersmiths departed on 11 July, after final talks with Miklas, Schuschnigg, and Schmidt. The chancellor was among the crowd of notables that gathered at the train station to see them off. It was by consensus a token of Austria's esteem.[119]

☆ **IV** ☆

Washington, D.C.
1937–1940

1

What brought Messersmith home was "one of the biggest shake-ups in years at the State Department." Since 1933 the New Deal lieutenants—Harry Hopkins, Henry Morgenthau, Jr., Henry Wallace, Harold Ickes, and others—had been clamoring, publicly and privately with Roosevelt, for a purge of the reactionary career diplomats who, in their view, held altogether too many key State Department policy positions and foreign missions. They were badly disappointed by the president's initial diplomatic appointments, which struck a rough balance between loyal Democratic amateurs and career professionals. But the domestic preoccupations of the first term kept the issue largely in the closet. The few foreign-policy initiatives that Roosevelt did undertake through 1936 almost invariably were conducted through informal channels and personal emissaries like William Bullitt and Hopkins. Relatively free of White House interference, the State Department, much to the New Dealers' annoyance, enjoyed considerable autonomy in conducting the nation's routine foreign affairs. In 1937, however, war clouds were gathering ominously over Europe and the Far East, and the condition of the diplomatic machine suddenly mattered very much. Sumner Welles's appointment as undersecretary of state in April was widely seen as a presidential mandate to reorganize and rehabilitate his department for the trials on the horizon. Heads looked ready to roll.[1]

The extent of Welles's mandate, however, is a matter of debate. Martin Weil, an engaging chronicler of these events, agrees that Welles was Roosevelt's handpicked hatchet man, charged with bringing the recalcitrant State Department into conformity with the tenor and philosophy of the administration. That such a thing did not happen, Weil concludes, bespeaks betrayal on Welles's part.

But Weil exaggerates Roosevelt's own hostility to the State Department and the Foreign Service, which is easy enough to do. Roosevelt liked to entertain people and tell them what they wanted to hear, and he was at his satirical best savaging diplomatic snootiness. In more sober moments, however, his actions, and occasionally his words, spoke differently. Overall, he wrote career diplomat Jefferson Caffery in 1935, he considered State "so vastly better" since Rogers and Moses-Linthicum that he felt "no great changes should take place." It was through thoroughgoing implementation of that watershed legislation that Roosevelt intended gradually to dislodge the ideological and social biases that he agreed were still objectionably overrepresented among America's senior diplomats. His differences with his domestic advisers on the issue were differences of means rather than ends. His solution to the problem was more professionalism, more merit promotions, and more Messersmiths; theirs was a general bloodletting that, the president recognized, would devastate morale in the ranks and set back the career principle to which he was committed. Practical considerations also argued against any wholesale purge. If sympathy for the New Deal became the standard of diplomatic loyalty, too few senior diplomats would be left in the field at the very time when the administration most needed their undeniable skills and connections.

It is fair to conclude, then, that Welles did precisely what Roosevelt wanted him to do, which was to lop off individuals judged guilty of egregious foppery and favoritism, or overt disloyalty to the administration's foreign policies. High on the hit list, for example, was Ray Atherton, counselor of the London embassy, a palpable dandy who had earned a reputation at his post as an "imitation Englishman." Others to be exiled included Robert Kelley, head of the anti-Soviet division of Eastern European affairs, and Edward L. Reed, in charge of the Mexican division. In Reed's case, hostility to the New Deal was fatal because it extended to the policies of Mexican President Lázaro Cárdenas, whom both Roosevelt and his ambassador in Mexico City, Josephus Daniels, regarded as a kindred spirit.[2]

Another marked man was Wilbur Carr. He had been permitted to stay on when the Democrats took over in 1933, but he was clearly on borrowed time. As early as November of that year Roosevelt contemplated naming him minister to Czechoslovakia, in the apparent hope that Carr, who had never seen service abroad, would choose to retire instead. In the end, Phillips persuaded Roosevelt that Carr was too much needed in Washington. He remained, but the joy went out of it for him. In June 1934 Roosevelt took him brutally to task for what he considered inadequate progress toward diplomatic-consular fusion.

Carr watched his cherished bureaucratic order come undone under Democratic patronage, depression budget cuts, and Roosevelt's administrative philosophy. To Carr's horror, Hull's senior subordinates were invited to bypass the secretary and come directly to the White House. Hull, whom Carr disgustedly characterized as "amazingly diffident" and "lacking in courage," not only did not object, but actually encouraged the practice so that he would have to deal with Roosevelt himself. True to his principles, Carr, according to his biographer, "never went to the President except in the regular channels through Hull." But Hull was not one to go the limit with Roosevelt in Carr's defense, as Phillips had done in 1933. By entrusting his fate to Hull, Carr effectively gave up his fight for himself, as he had long since given it up for reform.[3]

Operating behind the scenes, Welles displayed a nice flair for public relations in the execution. On 21 May Hull called in the press and read a statement announcing the merger of the Mexican and Latin American divisions into a new division of the American Republics, the first step, the secretary said, of a long-planned overhaul of the State Department in the interests of "modern efficiency." He planted the suggestion that the change was "revolutionary" by gratuitously denying it. Reed received a one-way ticket to Rome. A fortnight later came the announcement of the consolidation of the European divisions and Kelley's appointment as consul general in Istanbul. There followed a grabbag of transfers set in motion by the recall of the minister to Switzerland, Hugh R. Wilson, to become assistant secretary in Welles's stead. Well down the list was Atherton, "promoted" to the legation in Bulgaria. On 2 July a straightfaced Hull informed reporters that the department, in deference to Carr's "desire . . . to take a mission in the field," was sending him to Prague, thus assuring "the services of a tried official with just the right qualifications in one of the trouble spots of Europe." Carr's office, the secretary said with more candor, fell into good hands, for Messersmith, with his "considerable and varied experience in personnel and administrative matters," not to mention his knowledge of Europe, was "the most capable person in the service who is available for such an assignment." To cap the operation, the *New York Times Magazine* ran a puff piece by Harold B. Hinton, who covered the State Department for the *Times* Washington columnist Arthur Krock, Hull's dear friend. The article extolled the "revolution" that had transformed the department from "a more or less lumbering contraption" into a "disciplined organization geared to the new necessities" of foreign policy.[4]

It was a deft performance, duly applauded by most of the editorial writers who took notice of it. In his regular *Newsweek* column, Raymond Moley, whose own brief tenure as assistant secretary of state in 1933 gave him credibility in such matters, pronounced the shake-up "an event of firstrate importance to the peace of this country," and a blow against the "incompetence in our State Department and Foreign Service" that "invites embroilment in foreign wars." He particularly praised the Wilson and Messersmith appointments: "Both are the working type of professional diplomatist, easily distinguished from the many 'cookie-pushers' who flourish in the Service. Both are extremely well-informed on European affairs and will help infuse into the Department . . . a more sensitive awareness of what is going on across the Atlantic. Both are impatient with those men representing us abroad who are long on social graces and short on knowledge."[5]

Other commentators focused upon Carr's transfer, what it meant for him personally as well as for the organization that he had run for so long. They dismissed the official rationale, pointing out that Carr had not the least "desire" for Prague, and still fewer "qualifications": he knew no languages and, by his own admission, next to nothing about foreign policy. Rather, one journal revealed, his "'transfer' is really a demotion which FDR has promised Carr's critics for more than two years." The president had finally "turned an old war horse out to pasture," ridding the department of Carr's "tight bureaucratic control of the career service and his favoritism toward the 'white-spat boys' in the diplomatic hierarchy."[6]

Changes were predicted under Messersmith. As an outstanding product of the career system, he was the best advertisement the "new" State Department could offer up. The *Washington Post* sounded a common theme in hailing a "promotion . . . richly deserved" for a "brilliant career diplomat" whose skills "are frequently said to have been an important factor in the preservation of European peace." The *New York Times* cited his "intimate knowledge of the difficult questions of inter-departmental relationships [and] close acquaintance with the work and personnel of the foreign service." Moley confidently predicted that he would "slash red tape and increase the emphasis on merit (as opposed to family background) among career men."[7]

Messersmith's advent turned out to be the only silver lining for the New Dealers. Assessing the changes in toto, the *Times* rightly beheld "the latest proofs of the President's confidence in the capacity of the career men," or at least in the career principle. For all the ballyhoo about the "revolutionized" State Department, the diplomatic old guard did very well in 1937. Hugh Gibson, Jefferson Caffery, Butler Wright, and Leland Harrison all came out with choice posts. Hugh Wilson, whom Moley badly misjudged, assumed the critical "political"

George S. Messersmith, assistant secretary of state
Courtesy National Archives

assistant secretaryship. Moffat returned from Australia to head up the consolidated European division vacated by Dunn, who took on the no less powerful job of political adviser.

Drew Pearson sounded the alarm. His syndicated column was a frequent and pungent vehicle of New Deal outrage, of which there was plenty over this apparent sham of a shake-up. "The old Harvard clique" had triumphed once again, Pearson wrote on 28 July, and he accurately blamed neither Hull nor Welles but, rather, their "chief in the White House, Franklin Roosevelt, Harvard '04." Pearson found it nothing short of "amazing" that the president had decided to retain diplomats who "fit identically with the definition of 'economic royalist' against whom he preaches and who, furthermore, do not rate particularly high." And they were treacherous. "Several" prominent career men, Pearson charged, had "secretly cooperated" with William R. Castle, Harvard '02, undersecretary of state under Hoover and "ardent Republican, in the drive to elect [Alf] Landon" the year before. For reasons Pearson could not fathom, Roosevelt had wasted a golden opportunity to be rid of his enemies.[8]

The truth about this reorganization fell somewhere between the department's press releases and Pearson's laments. Clearly, policymaking responsibilities had merely shifted conservative hands. Latin Americanist Welles was to spearhead the bid for negotiations with the dictators. The anti-Soviet orientation found friends in Moffat, Dunn, and Wilson; Kelley's work would go on.

A potentially unsettling factor was the other new assistant secretary of state. Messersmith's discordant views on Germany and Russia were well known. The question was whether or not he would be able to make them felt from his new position. Carr had confined himself to administration of necessity as well as by preference. Keeping the department running was a full-time job, and never more so than in 1937. Additionally, Messersmith was reportedly to be charged with fleshing out the internal reorganization Welles had only started, which promised to be a major undertaking in itself. The myriad mundane duties of his office, then, seemed to preclude physically Messersmith's meddling in policy.[9]

But Messersmith was the equal of several Carrs, and he immediately began bringing in others as energetic as himself. G. Howland Shaw replaced Carr's close associate Thomas M. Wilson as chief of the division of personnel. "One of the most brilliant men in the State Department," Shaw was a refreshing anomaly to its critics: an independently wealthy Harvard graduate who led "an austere bachelor existence" and was "eager to abandon the snobbish standards of the Department." The division of Foreign Service buildings, mismanaged for years by Keith Merrill, an intimate of Mrs. Carr, went to Frederick Larkin, who had expertly handled similar work for the Treasury Department.[10]

Even Pearson admitted that these changes had done State "a world of good." But, with the advancement of the "white-spat boys," he wrote sadly, the shake-up "has undone all that it has done." What Pearson and his State Department nemeses both did not see was that Messersmith, even if confined to his office, had inherited the power to accomplish gradually what the New Dealers had wanted Roosevelt to do summarily. The decisions Messersmith would be making in his capacity as chairman of the boards of Personnel and of Examiners would affect the composition of the Foreign Service for years to come. As budget officer, with responsibility for appropriations, he had a chance to promote democratization by improving salaries and benefits. The diplomats and their critics were both correct: there had been no "revolution" at the State Department, and none was imminent. But Messersmith's thirty months in Washington were to see significant progress toward the unified, professional, more open Foreign Service that Roosevelt was determined to have.[11]

2

Such noble thoughts were far from Messersmith's mind on 22 July, when he and his wife landed in New York after a storm-tossed crossing. What was on his mind were several dismal prospects: the summer without her—she was to stay with relatives on Cape Cod and the Delaware shore—Washington at its sultriest, and a single bed at the Metropolitan Club until he had landed more permanent accommodations for them. And, now that the surprise and excitement of his new promotion had worn off, he was considerably miffed at the way the department had conveyed it. The telegram to him in Vienna had been a single sentence so peremptorily "phrased as to be an order" instead of an offer. It had left it to him to discover that it was Carr he was replacing rather than someone else. A fundamental question still unanswered was whether responsibilities as well as personnel were being shuffled—that is, whether anything had really been reorganized. If he was simply to take over Carr's machine without opportunity to help formulate European policy, in which he now considered himself the department's foremost expert, then he foresaw a very frustrating tenure in Washington.

His irritation and apprehensions were entirely justified. He probably did not know it, but at the very time that the State Department was ordering him home, delicate negotiations were going on concerning the appointment of his better-connected colleague, Hugh Wilson. Wilson had served in Washington during the 1920s, as an anticonsul chief of the personnel division, and so knew that it had little to commend itself over the lovely Swiss capital, his official home since 1927. He finally accepted his new assignment "as a sort of grim duty," but only after securing a promise from Roosevelt of "a more agreeable post later on." Messersmith had not even been given the option. It was a bad omen.[12]

Thus it was an out-of-sorts Messersmith who walked into Moffat's office at noon on Sunday, 25 July. Moffat commiserated with him over lunch, pointing out, however, that his "worries might be entirely dissipated after he had talked with the President and the Secretary." When Messersmith did—that afternoon with Hull, Monday morning with Roosevelt—he was enormously cheered. The president said he regretted having to recall him without warning, but "we have to prepare ourselves for the day to come. He said [Messersmith later related] that unfortunately there were too many people in Washington who felt that Europe was a good deal further off than it was, and the Orient even further. . . . In the Department of State there were too few who had any understanding of this situation." Messersmith would have his hands full, the president continued, with routine administrative duties and certain departmental reforms he wished him to carry out. But he expected Messersmith to attend policy meetings whenever possible, and to be at the ready with political advice on request.[13]

More reinforcement came the next day. He sat in on Carr's last oral examination for foreign service candidates. Carr had had definite preferences as to his successor, and Messersmith was not on his list. He rightly suspected him of involvement in the whispering campaign that discredited him with Roosevelt. Messersmith's "cocksureness" had long irritated him. But the examination together impressed him with Messersmith's "ability in sizing up personnel," and he told him so. Moffat observed that evening that Messersmith was "far more cheerful than he had been on Sunday."[14]

Messersmith's qualms dispelled, he dived in and found himself up to his neck. It required two separate State Department orders to list all his official duties, which included the "administration of the Department of State and the Foreign Service, with supervision of personnel and management matters, Departmental appropriations, consular affairs, passports, visas, Foreign Service buildings, and international conferences." With an authorized complement of 713 foreign service officers and more than 4,000 clerks assigned to the department in Washington and to 312 consular and diplomatic in-stallations over the globe, the service was a ponderous ship to pilot under the best circumstances. Convinced that the toughest tests lay ahead, Messersmith set immediately to put the service on an emer-gency footing. By the end of July the personnel division was at work compiling two new indexes: a card for every overseas post, noting special conditions and needs, and a card for every officer, setting down "specific capacities for specific kinds of work." Consultations with the political divisions on personnel matters got underway. To provide the systematic orientation that newly appointed envoys never had before, Messersmith implemented a practice he had long ad-mired in the British and French foreign services, requiring departing mission chiefs to leave detailed memoranda for their successors.[15]

It was a summer of innumerable small innovations, a summer of transition for Messersmith and the administration of the State De-partment. He filled out his staff. Ruth Shipley of the passport office became the only Carr holdover among the eight division heads re-porting to him. All the newcomers strained to learn on the job. Mes-sersmith quickly offset Vienna's sloth in overtime.[16]

State's budget request for the fiscal year ending 30 June 1939 was Messersmith's first order of business. The statistics assembled by budget assistant Charles B. Hosmer told the story almost as elo-quently as the privations they were causing. The department's cur-rent appropriation totaled $18.6 million—just what it was in fis-cal 1932. From that modest sum, some $4 million was earmarked for "international obligations"—American contributions to the Pan American Union and the Mexican-American Boundary Commission, for example—leaving only $14.2 million for operations. Anticipated revenues from passport and consular fees reduced the amount actu-ally drawn on the Treasury to $9.8 million—less than a third of 1 percent of the total federal budget, the least by far of any executive department.[17]

The case for more was never stronger. The emergencies in China and Spain were bringing out the best side of the Foreign Service. Americans evacuated from the war zones gave admiring accounts of officers' individual heroism and general aplomb under Fascist fire. Messersmith might have tried to turn the publicity to immediate ad-vantage. Instead, not wishing, perhaps, to arouse too much contro-versy on his first trip through the budgetary gauntlet, he asked for a very modest increase, some $570,000, in order to restore the service to its 1932 strength of 755 professional personnel, and to provide for some small salary and allowance hikes.[18]

Unfortunately for Messersmith, Roosevelt was in the midst of a shift in economic priorities. The depression emergency was declared over, and attention turned to reducing the public debt, which was seen as a threat to recovery. Across-the-board cuts were ordered in the executive departments. The State Department, one that had not benefited under the New Deal, was hardest hit in relative terms. Acting Budget Director Daniel W. Bell not only denied State its requested increase, but slashed an additional $3.3 million. Only after Messersmith appealed directly to Roosevelt, arguing that the proposed cut "takes lean meat and muscle from a Department in which there is no fat," did Bell relent, restoring $1.2 million, to a total of $16.6 million.[19]

Congress came next. Messersmith was not a complete stranger to Capitol Hill, but he might just as well have been. Ten years before, he had returned from Antwerp for a morning's discussion of the diamond-smuggling problem with the House Ways and Means Committee then revising the customs laws. That was the extent of his experience. On the bright side, the 75th Congress brought a change in chairmen on the House Appropriations Subcommittee. The ornery Coloradan Edward T. Taylor, who had contributed to Carr's miseries during his last years in Washington, yielded to the fair-minded Thomas S. McMillan of South Carolina.[20]

Hearings before McMillan's subcommittee opened on 8 December and lasted for eight grueling days. Messersmith came out whole, in fact, with several new admirers. In a September column, Drew Pearson had done an exposé on the Foreign Service buildings program with its cost overruns, the still uninhabited Bluecher Palace, and other small scandals. Republican committee members took up the attack. Messersmith admitted that the buildings program "was the one aspect of the Department's work of which we could not be proud." He promised "real progress." No funds would be requested for new projects while old ones were pending. He assured the panel that it would be kept fully apprised of his progress. They were "appreciative."[21]

In fact, H.R. 9544, reported to the House on 18 February 1938, granted State a few dollars more than Bell had called for. A speech by Representative Robert L. Bacon of New York, a member of McMillan's subcommittee, clinched passage. Hailing the Foreign Service as "one of the finest bodies of men who serve the United States Government in any capacity," he went on to eulogize J. Theodore Marriner, consul general in Beirut when struck down in December by an assassin's bullet, as an illustration of the "human element—men in gruelling conditions in far-off places, often in grave peril of their lives, obliged to make heavy sacrifices."[22]

Anticipating smooth sailing in the Senate and occupied on other fronts—particularly with Larkin on the buildings mess—Messersmith declined an invitation to come before Kenneth D. McKellar's Senate Appropriations Committee. That was a mistake, for McKellar's panel was quietly doing away with a provision of extreme importance to State. Under current rules, executive departments were permitted to apply up to 10 percent of any budget item to other purposes. State particularly needed this flexibility to cope with exchange fluctuations and overseas emergencies. But McKellar's committee, part of a budding congressional revolt against executive power, decided that the departments ought not to enjoy such freedom. When Messersmith chose not to testify, he gave up the chance to argue otherwise for State.

Not until H.R. 9544 reached the Senate floor did Messersmith see his mistake. He did mea culpas to majority leader Alben Barkley and to Key Pittman, chairman of the Foreign Relations Committee, begging them to work for restoration of the 10 percent allowance. When the bill came up for debate on 28 March, they rose to "exonerate" him of "negligence." Pittman explained that Messersmith, new on the job, "did not have a thorough knowledge of how the matter was [supposed to be] handled." McKellar went along, acknowledging that the department deserved consideration and "the highest praise for the modesty of . . . its requests for appropriations." The bill passed easily, and Roosevelt signed it into law on 27 April 1938.[23]

Messersmith certainly had nothing to celebrate. Most of the mandated $1.6 million in economies could be achieved through nonrecurring items in the current budget, but this was scant consolation in light of the urgent need for more. He was embarrassed at having nearly lost what little discretion he had in spending the pittance on which State was supposed to operate. But the indignity of it all revived his fighting spirit. "One of the things which I must accomplish during my present tour of duty," he vowed while the battle was going on, "is to get for this Department the appropriations which it needs for the proper conduct of its work." In State's case, poverty was self-perpetuating. Because "our appropriations are so small," he had discovered, "the Budget and the Congress can go into every item of our expenditure with a care which is obviously not possible in the case of a Department whose appropriations . . . contain single items almost as large as our whole appropriation." McMillan's panel had excoriated State for changing its typewriter ribbons too often. The War Department, with its $600 million budget, was not subjected to such minute scrutiny. In effect, Messersmith concluded, State was "penalized for good administration."

But, as he also appreciated, a more basic reason for the department's chronic impoverishment was the absence of an organized constituency to pressure Congress on its behalf. This was partly State's own doing. By long tradition it disdained the crush for place at the public trough. One critic denounced a "tacit understanding . . . between a Congress that begrudges money . . . and a State Department that doesn't want too much money for fear of losing its exclusiveness." State preferred conducting its affairs without Congress gazing over its shoulder. Dollars were sacrificed for privacy. Carr had kept close tabs on what money there was to prevent the men lacking outside income from starving. With his accountant's mentality, he then must have reasoned that asking Congress for more was an admission of failure to live within his means.[24]

This was one tradition Messersmith intended to break. Convinced that "we must get the right kind of sentiment behind the Department if we are to have the moral and financial support which is indispensable," he took to the stump "to bring the work and needs of the Department before our people." In four major speeches between November 1937 and February 1938, he hammered home the department's role as "the guardian of our peace." Spectacularly in Spain and the Far East, "quietly but effectively" everywhere else, dedicated men and women, he told his audiences, were "working many hours of the day untiringly" upholding the country's "vital interests." Those interests, he said in an oblique swipe at the isolationists, "lie beyond our shores in only a limited sense," for the "things which do happen daily in so many places intimately concern . . . every one of us." The department's ability to handle "the many details involved in [foreign] relations," he said, would ultimately determine "whether you and I will be able to live here at peace in this country."

It was therefore "only wise and prudent" that State receive "all the funds" it needed to discharge its responsibilities. At a time when the country was building battleships at $60 million a copy, he argued, it was absurd that the department charged with obviating their use should have to make do with less than the federal government contributed annually to the state agricultural colleges. The nation's "peace arm" had been reduced to penury. There was "an almost desperate need" for new personnel and equipment, for higher salaries and post allowances. "Almost every other country makes materially greater provision for representation, and our failure to provide adequate funds for this purpose is entirely out of line with our democratic ideals, in that it precludes certain officers with no private means . . . from accepting posts where the representation responsibilities are heavy," he declared in one of his public speeches. The American people could support the department's work with "a good conscience," knowing that "the return on the investment is unquestionable."[25]

Messersmith's speeches were favorably received. The *New York Times* praised one as "a useful corrective" to the notion that State was "a relatively unimportant accessory." Representative Bacon inserted them all into the *Congressional Record*. Civic groups launched letter-writing campaigns to Congress. From *The Nation's* Oswald Garrison Villard came an offer to form a national committee "to bring before all sections of our people through newspapers, periodicals, books [and] radio . . . adequate information concerning the work, policies, and needs" of the department. Messersmith was enthusiastic. Such a "pressure group . . . working for us as [others were doing] for the Army, the Navy, Commerce, etc.," was, in his view, exactly what State needed. He excitedly envisioned "a large nation-wide committee" with an executive board of eminent academics and businessmen. He compiled a list of prospects, and asked Villard to draft a statement of intent for their consideration.[26]

The plan got no further. The idea of outsiders like Villard making propaganda for the department was too much for Welles, who scotched the plan. Messersmith, still feeling "very definitely that [it] would be a very helpful and proper movement," had to ask Villard to call it off.[27]

Messersmith moved on to a key audience in his battle for support. Whether businessmen knew it or not, the politicization of world trade made them increasingly dependent upon diplomacy. He took this message to board rooms and convention halls at every opportunity: "It no longer makes any difference whether "A" in New York or Kansas City wishes to sell an article in Paris, and whether "B" in Paris is eager to buy it. Whether or not the sale is consummated depends entirely upon whether the laws of France and the myriad of regulations we have to deal with today will make that sale possible." Keeping trade channels open was "a matter of negotiations . . . between governments." The growth of American exports under Hull's trade-agreements program—up 60 percent with the sixteen nations that had signed trade treaties with the United States by 1937—attested to the department's success.[28]

Yet Messersmith acknowledged that State had a reputation for being "not deeply interested enough in the problems of American businessmen." Sometimes depicted as intimate partners in a rapacious dollar diplomacy, businessmen and diplomats seem on the whole to have barely tolerated each other's presence on those occasions when circumstances threw them together. Men who had, many of them, spurned lucrative business careers in favor of public service, the pre-Rogers diplomats typically, as we have seen, accorded a low priority to commercial and financial questions except in their larger geopolitical setting. There was, moreover, enough truth to their respective stereotypes—of businessmen as profit-mad Philistines, of diplomats as effete stuffed shirts no good for real work—to keep the stereotypes alive and their subjects apart. Ironically, Carr's pre-Rogers rapprochement with business, so critical to his success, was ultimately a casualty of it. As his reforms began bearing fruit, as fusion became a reality, the consuls lost their separate identity, and with it much of their reputation for hardheaded service.

The upshot was that State *had* lost business's support, to the extent it ever had it, and, what was worse, lost it to the commercial attachés. Decimated by the Economy Act of March 1933, the Bureau of Foreign and Domestic Commerce had hit bottom the following August when, under White House pressure, Secretary of Commerce Daniel Calhoun Roper signed a coordination agreement with William Phillips, acting secretary of state. The agreement required the attachés to report through diplomatic channels. But Roper immediately began to sabotage the agreement and rebuild his foreign service. He hinted that Hull's trade program would lose Commerce support unless coordination were scrapped, and he made "deliberate propaganda" suggesting that the emasculation of his service and the Great Depression were somehow cause and effect. He set up a high-powered Business Advisory Council, whose lobbying helped get his budget back. In the field the attachés became more brazenly intractable than ever, engaging in policy discussions "without the knowledge or consent" of mission chiefs, "refusing to accept orders," and, as Messersmith knew from Berlin and Vienna, resisting office consolidation. With a fine touch, Roper touted Commerce as a place where officials "sit around with their coats off, and . . . talk the businessman's language," in contrast to the "high hats" at the State Department. Business knew where to turn.[29]

Messersmith resolved to bring business back to State; the attachés would follow. Unification of the foreign services, Messersmith's "old dream," was an idea whose time had come. State had taken a rather indulgent view of Roper's resurgence, but by 1937 even the long-apathetic Carr was convinced that the commercial foreign service had gone too far and had to be stopped. For on 22 July Senator Royal S. Copeland of New York, anti-Roosevelt Democrat, chairman of the Commerce Committee, and great patron of the attachés, introduced a bill (S. 988) to provide his charges with the benefits of Rogers and Moses-Linthicum: commissions by class, automatic promotions, representation allowances, and a separate pension plan. The bill would put the commercial service on a permanent statutory basis, crushing Messersmith's dream forever.[30]

The State Department rose to the challenge. Carr, about to depart for Prague, fired off a memorandum to Welles, urging an appeal to Roosevelt. Copeland's bill, Carr wrote, was "definitely in conflict with the President's policy." That policy aimed to promote unity and administrative efficiency through reorganization of the executive branch, which a bill first introduced in January and now being readied for resubmission would authorize the president to do. Although Roosevelt was not saying publicly which agencies he intended to transfer or abolish, for obvious reasons, he had given the State Department to believe that the commercial foreign service would be among them. Copeland's bill, of course, threatened that goal. Moreover, Carr argued, S. 988 was inherently unsound. It provided a pension plan for the attachés based on "the very provisions that have placed the State Department's retirement fund in an insolvent condition"—a maximum contribution of 5 percent of salary, matched by the government. At that rate, the department's fund was running an actuarial deficit of nearly $5 million a year, and faced exhaustion by 1960. Carr suggested that Roosevelt explain to "his representatives in Congress" that Copeland would provide another 175 government employees with a false sense of security.[31]

But Roosevelt had bigger problems to contend with than civil-service pensions during the summer of 1937. His attempt to enlarge the Supreme Court had sparked a monumental congressional rebellion. CIO (Congress of Industrial Organizations) sit-down strikes in the steel and auto industries were being blamed on the New Deal's supposed softness on radicalism. In August the economy plunged, due in part to the cuts in federal spending. Harried by outsiders, Roosevelt had no time for quarrels within his official family.[32]

Messersmith and the State Department were thus on their own regarding S. 988. He toyed with the idea of actively lobbying against it in Congress, but Hosmer made a compelling case for noninvolvement. Such a lobby, he warned, would be misinterpreted as stemming from "a purely selfish desire on our part to prevent members of the Foreign Commercial Service from enjoying our benefits," and so was bound to fail. The net effect on the State Department would be to call attention to its own pension insolvency and impugn its motives. So, with the hope that S. 988 would either run aground on its own or be preempted by passage of the reorganization bill, Messersmith sensibly stayed away from the Hill.[33]

Where Messersmith felt he could help was with those whom a merger would most affect. He was delighted by what he heard from the half-dozen senior attachés he sounded out. To a man they agreed (privately, of course) that consolidation was overdue. Like the consuls before them, the attachés had long felt the sting of diplomatic condescension. For them, integration into the State Department would be a big step up in status. They also believed in unity as a professional good. "As long as the services of the two Departments remain apart," one wrote him, "there will be duplication, unnecessary expenditure, and an absence of that high type of service and assistance to which American business interests are entitled." Resistance could be expected, another warned, from "a few die-hards in the Bureau" and from Roper, but "if the Commercial men in the field felt that they would be fairly taken care of in any consolidation scheme they would be entirely for it."[34]

Messersmith also discovered an encouraging openmindedness on the part of business. In early November he attended the three-day annual convention of the National Foreign Trade Council (NFTC) in Cleveland. Previous conventions had witnessed "vicious attacks" by Commerce Department officials against State. This year Commerce had been shut out; Messersmith and Sayre, who had also been invited, had the floor to themselves. Sayre spoke on the mechanics of trade agreements, which Messersmith thought "went over very well." For himself he made it a point to be present at every session during the three days. "There was not a single speaker," he reported flatteringly to Hull when it was over, "who did not mention the trade agreements program in an approving fashion and who did not speak of the great service which you are rendering to our country."[35]

Messersmith addressed the assemblage on 3 November. He offered another plea for appropriations, tailored to his audience. The State Department he described was a model of efficiency that all American businessmen ought to be proud to call their own. In fact, he declared, no department was doing more to advance business interests abroad. Under Hull's leadership and the tide of political isolationism, State's work had become "preponderantly economic." The new orientation was evident in the service entrance examination, which stressed economics as never before; in the officers' training school, whose curriculum was being revised to include more trade-related subjects; and, of course, in the trade-agreements program, which had already produced such outstanding results. Messersmith asked for support in order to continue these efforts, to "make it more than ever your State Department."[36]

Business responded in kind. In late December Messersmith received a delegation from the NFTC led by their president, Eugene T. Thomas. They were "still under the excellent impression" created by his speech, which, they said, had "opened the eyes of a lot of people present to . . . what State was doing for them," and, conversely, to what the attachés were not. They said they were now aware of the confusion flowing from the present arrangement, and wished to go on record as favoring "further consolidation." Messersmith considered this "very significant," as the NFTC "until recently has been rather strongly supporting Commerce."[37]

This shift in support, however, had yet to make itself felt on Capitol Hill. The year 1937 was drawing to a close without action on Roosevelt's reorganization bill. Its prospects in 1938 were equally bleak. Democrats who had split with the administration over court-packing were ready to lead the fight against reorganization, which was being depicted as another presidential power grab. If it survived, mutilation by amendment was likely. At the same time, Roper was mobilizing his attachés and the Business Advisory Council in the fight for S. 988 and an impregnable commercial service.[38]

Without much that he could do, but needing to do something, Messersmith proposed an administrative stopgap. He suggested reviving the 1933 coordination agreement, which was practically void, but still on paper. The attachés might thus be brought to heel while their fate was being decided. Messersmith had always believed that "lack of direction and initiative by our own officers" was responsible for coordination's breakdown in the first place. He now took the initiative to provide the direction, in the form of a thirty-page circular instruction he proposed to distribute to American mission chiefs. It outlined the rules and principles that were supposed to be governing the attachés' conduct, called attention to practices in violation of those rules, and encouraged American diplomats to impose discipline.[39]

It was a bureaucratic declaration of war, a transparent attempt to steal a march on Congress with a dead letter. The cautious Hull refused to authorize its distribution until Messersmith had Roosevelt's approval. He tried, but did not get it. When they met at the White House on the afternoon of 1 February, Roosevelt was his most agreeable self, except with respect to the purpose of Messersmith's call. The reorganization bill, Roosevelt said, was at a critical stage; the State Department should not do anything to upset it.[40]

Messersmith collected himself—he was always somewhat overawed in Roosevelt's presence—and appealed in writing on the 10th. It was essential, he argued, "in these difficult and increasingly critical times that our establishments abroad should operate with the greatest effectiveness until your reorganization plan can bear fruit." Messersmith promised that the coordination memorandum would cause Roosevelt no grief with his cabinet; no department, he maintained innocently, could possibly object to a directive that "does not in any way change accepted and existing practice" but merely "clarifies the practice and brings it to the attention of the chiefs of mission."[41]

Roosevelt was not deceived. By late March Messersmith conceded that his stratagem had failed. Then came another setback. The reorganization bill had squeaked through the Senate, but House opposition could not be overcome. Congressmen who wished to restrict executive authority, protect pet bureaus, or inflict a defeat upon the president united against it. On 8 April the House voted it down, 204 to 196.[42]

For Messersmith it was a "disappointment" he could not safely linger upon. While the fight for reorganization was heating up, S. 988 had quietly passed the Senate and gone on to the House Commerce Committee. One exchange between Representative James Wadsworth, Jr., of New York and Dr. Alexander V. Dye, director of the Bureau of Foreign and Domestic Commerce, summed up the mood of the House hearing.

REP. WADSWORTH: Did you notice any profound reduction in our foreign commerce as a result of the [commercial service's 1933 budget] reduction?

DR. DYE: There was a profound change; but it would only be fair to say that there was a great depression at the time, which also reduced our commerce very much.

When this inquisition was over, the committee voted unanimously to report the bill intact to the House floor.[43]

In a memorandum to Welles marked "Urgent," Messersmith recommended an appeal to Roosevelt, alerting him to the dangers posed by the bill. If anything, the House version was worse than Copeland's, for it expanded the commercial service's scope to embrace "economic" as well as "commercial and industrial" matters. Messersmith considered this "a direct invitation . . . to engage in political reporting." In almost every particular—pensions, promotions, salary, allowances—the bill would place the attachés on par with State

Department officers and "perpetuate the present divided responsibility in certain aspects of our foreign relations."[44]

With House action imminent, Messersmith maneuvered for time. He asked Representative Samuel D. McReynolds, chairman of the Foreign Affairs Committee, to move for the return of S. 988 to the Commerce Committee, on the grounds that "it directly affects foreign policy and had not been brought to the attention of the State Department for possible amendments."[45]

Meanwhile Messersmith sought to persuade Roper to abandon his claim to "economic reporting." They met on 22 April, Messersmith arguing that "the line of demarcation betweeen economic and political reporting was a very narrow one." Roper professed to see the light and pledged to have the bill amended accordingly.[46]

Messersmith was also drawing up a rather more sweeping amendment to S. 988, one authorizing Roosevelt to consolidate the foreign services by executive order, accomplishing exactly what he had promised to do under the abortive reorganization bill. Welles, who had dropped off Messersmith's "Urgent" memorandum at the White House a few days earlier, returned on 26 April. Roosevelt apparently liked the idea of amending Copeland to death. After a 13 May cabinet meeting he took Hull and Roper aside and told them that "in view of the general situation and what we have to face," consolidation "should not await the reorganization bill," which he intended to modify and resubmit to the next Congress.[47]

With the president's go-ahead, Messersmith hit Capitol Hill. Meetings with Pittman and McReynolds produced a plan of action. They would move for the return of S. 988 to allow "amendments being considered by the president" to be heard. They agreed not to divulge the sweeping nature of those amendments until Hull met with Roper to try to arrange his cooperation.[48]

No sooner was it formulated than the plan fell apart. Far from cooperating, Roper threatened to resign if the president proceeded, and hinted as much to the press. On 14 May White House press secretary Stephen Early was obliged to issue a statement pooh-poohing a Hull-Roper feud. Roper followed with a terse public denial of his own: because "no conclusion has been reached" as to the disposition of the foreign commercial service, "no resignation is pending." In Congress the attachés' stalwarts vowed to fight any motion to recommit. Pittman and McReynolds declined the challenge.[49]

Messersmith frantically proposed another alternative. Consolidation through amendment to Moses-Linthicum rather than to S. 988, he argued, would bring it before the more tractable Foreign Relations committees. But it was late in the session, and Roosevelt, smarting from his recent defeats, had had his fill of legislative combat. He returned from a long Memorial Day weekend at Hyde Park having decided to pacify Roper and to let S. 988 run its course.[50] House passage was now a foregone conclusion. The bill came up on 6 June, and a half-dozen congressmen rose to rhapsodize over the attachés. B. Carroll Reece of Tennessee declared grandiloquently that "no group of employees has done so much toward extending the scope of American commerce abroad," and urged that the commercial service be "enlarged and extended." Luther Johnson of Texas attacked critics of a bill that "merely gives to the [attachés] the same rights and privileges that are given to men in the State Department who do exactly the same work." Robert Crosser of Ohio lamented that there were only eighty-nine commercial attachés in the field at present, "a very small number and I think it should be greater. Considering the valuable service they perform, I think it would be well to increase the personnel substantially." The bill carried by voice vote.[51]

Messersmith's last hope was Roosevelt's veto. Certainly, he wrote Hull and Welles on 9 June, a veto was in order. Roper had reneged on his promise to remove the "economic reporting" clause. The bill's salary and promotion schedules turned out to be even more attractive than State's, which "is from every point of view highly objectionable and dangerous to morale . . . unjust and obnoxious." To make a veto palatable, he suggested that Roosevelt cite the certain insolvency of the bill's pension plan. Instead of taking sides in the Hull-Roper feud, the president could pose as defender of the attachés' fringe benefits.[52]

Welles went to the White House that morning and returned with Roosevelt's agreement to kill the bill. Messersmith's draft veto message expressed the president's "hearty accord with legislation tending to bring all Government service to a common basis," but also his determination that "the whole subject of coordinating the work of several departments and agencies of the Government which relates to foreign service . . . be acted on comprehensively at the next session of Congress." Moreover, the "retirement system provided . . . will not provide a fund adequate to meet eventual requirements," and was "not therefore in the interests of the public or the personnel concerned." Roosevelt sent the message to the Senate on 10 June, as the 75th Congress was adjourning.[53]

Messersmith's sense of relief was palpable. Roosevelt, he wrote a colleague, was apparently "firm in his determination" for consolidation, which Messersmith saw happening "early next session."[54]

That was a trifle optimistic. Foreign service consolidation was not the kind of issue for which most politicians would incur great risk.

The opposition remained vocal and determined. But the president *was* on his side, firmly or not; and sooner or later, as Messersmith knew, that support would be decisive.

3

That prospect of legislative success scarcely eased Messersmith's deepening gloom about the state of the world. His first weeks in Washington had exploded any lingering illusions he may have had about the unhappy inevitability of American foreign policy. Appeasement, it was clear, was going to be played out, and isolationism taken to the last limit. That was what Americans were demanding and, coincidentally, what the State Department was working to achieve. In helping to cajole the revisionist powers to the conference table while disowning responsibility for the results, American diplomats were doing the clear majority will. The appeasers in Washington and London called themselves realists and, in the sense of what was practically possible, they were. There was nothing sinister or cynical in their attempts to head off war, nothing dishonorable in their appeals to reason and humanity.

What was Messersmith to do? He might have easily surrendered to the temptation to do nothing. He was already thoroughly overworked without also taking on a hopeless crusade against specious realism. He had no chance of persuading American diplomats to abandon their diplomatic efforts to save civilization from war and Bolshevism on the grounds that, in effect, it could not be done. He had no niche in the policy structure from which to advance this inadmissible view, no direct access to the cable traffic through which policy was transmitted, no authority to interject himself at all save for a casual mandate from a preoccupied president.

But if the odds and the opposition ever mattered to him, they no longer did. His tortured conscience drove him to protest. For a while longer he would entertain utopian fantasies of divine intervention—of Hitler, say, slipping in the shower—or of those economic laws that no longer looked so inexorable working their logic. But by now internal collapse was little more than a tired and transparent rationale for his moral opposition to the Nazi regime. Now, he recognized, there was only war, and if by shouting it out he brought the reckoning one day closer, that was enough. Eventually people would hear.

In the fall of 1937 there was at least the hint that some were hearing already. In Chicago on 6 October Roosevelt spoke out against the "epidemic of world lawlessness," suggesting that aggressors be "quarantined." Isolationist leaders howled, but there was much favorable comment as well. This response emboldened Roosevelt to endorse the League of Nations' condemnation of Japanese aggression in China, and to accept an invitation to Brussels, where further steps against Japan were to be considered. Roving ambassador Norman H. Davis, no appeaser, was named to head the United States delegation. And then, in December, Americans rallied impressively around the flag in anger over the sinking of the United States gunboat *Panay* by Japanese warplanes over the Yangtze River. Fascist aggression had hit home for the first time, prompting Washington to deliver its toughest talk yet.[55]

But the president's initiative faltered and public outrage died down, as would happen again and again. When it became clear that Roosevelt had nothing up his sleeve to stop aggression without resort to force, what enthusiasm there was for quarantines waned. Japan tendered profuse apologies and reparations for the *Panay* misfortune, salving American honor. Isolationists demanded that American ships get out of Chinese waters. And, perhaps most telling, Representative Louis Ludlow's two-year crusade for a constitutional amendment requiring a nationwide referendum before Congress could declare war finally gained enough supporters to force debate on its discharge from the House Judiciary Committee.[56]

The problem was that Roosevelt, however keen his appreciation of the Fascist menace, would go little or no further to meet it than public opinion permitted, which was not very far. The president's ego also led him astray sometimes. Welles encouraged him to think that the dictators could be assuaged, like Democratic ward bosses, through liberal application of his justly celebrated charm. Personal diplomacy, Messersmith recalled sadly, was "a sort of obsession" with Roosevelt. And there was the president's weakness for novel ideas in foreign as well as domestic policy. After telling reporters that his quarantine speech signaled a fresh search for "some way to peace," he was particularly receptive to the imaginative Welles, who brought in a proposal for a world conference "to secure general international agreement as to the fundamental norms of international conduct." Welles predicted that Germany and Italy, though probably not Japan, would subscribe to an agreement guaranteeing them access to raw materials. Concessions by the West, he concluded, would be necessary.[57]

On 11 October Messersmith handed Hull a long rebuttal, his first full analysis of the international situation since his return to Washington. He warned against the assumptions implicit in Welles's scheme in particular and appeasement in general. The world crisis, he argued, involved a "basic clash of ideologies" that no conference could resolve. The "three lawless states" stood for "the doctrine of force and of might and [of] an entirely different international morality . . . directly opposed to our concepts, basic ideals, and principles of action." A plan for world conquest was unfolding, orchestrated by the Hitler regime, which "is the main spring of the movement and the real power behind it."

> The maneuvers now in progress in the Far East, in Spain, and in the Mediterranean . . . are only steps along a long road which the dictators have fairly well surveyed and laid out. . . . [Their] final aim . . . is the disintegration of the British Empire, the consequent weakening of England in Europe and the opening of the way to attack on the United States . . . the richest and strongest country in the world. . . . It is really against the United States and England that the program is directed, for we are considered the only worthy antagonists and we have what they want.

The threat to the Americas, he insisted, was real and growing. This was no "idle supposition," but a fact drawn from "first-hand conversation with major leaders of the German Government, who . . . have made no secret of their intentions." "Hitler's own words" and the upsurge of Nazi espionage and sedition throughout the hemisphere left "no logical escape from the conclusion that the United States are the ultimate object of attack of the powers grouped in this new system of force and lawlessness." If unlikely to find fertile ground in North America, Goebbels's agents would doubtless fare better in Latin America, where, Messersmith observed, conditions were "already fairly propitious to receive a certain doctrine of force." Everything then hinged on how long the democracies would go on submitting to blackmail. So far the outlaws had achieved "a success that seems incredible" by arming "themselves to the teeth and brandishing their armaments before the world with the hope that through the threat of force . . . they may gain advantages contrary to international morality, right and decency." Their diplomacy was capitalizing on "the fear of war . . . which persists in the democratic states, and understandably so," to gain cheap victories. But if this trend continued, if "truth [kept] being ignored," "if too dangerous compromises continue to be made," "disintegration will proceed inexorably and to the point at which the peace of the world will definitely be endangered and catastrophic war the sole possible outcome."[58]

Hull read these words and caught fire. He had never been an isolationist. To internationalists like Henry Stimson he was indignantly denouncing the peace-at-any-price crowd's campaign for negotiations, "which he said could not have been better designed to aid the governments of Japan, Italy, and Germany than if they had been employed by those powers." Nazism had always horrified him, but, like so many others, he shrank from it. Messersmith's chilling vision stirred him to action. He took the memorandum to Roosevelt, to whom he attacked the Welles project as "illogical and impossible." The three bandit states, he argued, would "laugh" at the idea; "it would be fatal to lull the democracies into a feeling of tranquility through a peace congress at the very moment when their utmost efforts should actually be directed toward arming themselves for self-defense." This unaccustomed vehemence on Hull's part persuaded Roosevelt to back off the scheme, which he had probably not taken very seriously anyway. To justify his decision to those, like Welles, bound to be disappointed by it, he ordered Messersmith's memorandum circulated anonymously in the State Department. Roosevelt's thinking, Messersmith recalled, was that the piece "would have more effect and value if it did not appear to come from me . . . as there were so many who thought of me . . . as a warmonger and an alarmist." The memorandum was attributed to "a particularly well-informed observer." But the prose and the gist of the piece identified him as umistakably as if his name were in lights on every page. Welles appealed the decision, but the president had made up his mind—for now.[59]

A flush of optimism thus closed out Messersmith's 1937. Brussels produced no agreement on anti-Japanese sanctions, but it seemed auspicious that the United States had been present at all. At the same time, Anglo-American relations were warming up under the new Chamberlain government. Reciprocal trade talks were moving briskly ahead. Britain was rearming in earnest. "What I am hoping," Messersmith wrote a friend in December, "is that England and we can work out some common action and put up a stiff front, for I believe that that is still sufficient to save us."[60]

He even managed some enthusiasm for Roosevelt's choice to succeed Dodd in Berlin, concealing his disappointment at not getting the post himself and his real reservations about the appointee, his colleague Hugh Wilson. In a letter to Raymond Geist, the one person to whom he always found time to write these busy days, Messersmith accentuated the positive. The Wilson appointment, he wrote bravely, "is a very good one and in many respects I could not conceive of a better one. . . . That a career man should be sent to Berlin is, I think, a great achievement," and not only for the career. Sending Roosevelt's friend Davies as originally planned would have been misinterpreted as a friendly gesture to Berlin. As for Wilson, Messersmith thought him "a particularly well informed person . . . highly intelligent and considered." Under the circumstances, he decided, "in some ways it may be better that he should go than I. He will arouse less antagonism and, if he does not know the situation as well as I do, this may be counterbalanced by other factors." He could think of none offhand.[61]

But the isolationist resurgence early in the new year dashed any thoughts about Americans being ready to face international responsibility. "Our hands are tied," Messersmith wrote despairingly in February, by a "hysterical desire for peace" that was "encouraging the gangsters." The limits of his influence at the State Department also became clear. He and Joe Gray were badly outnumbered by "realists" in Hull's inner circle. Dunn, whom liberals regarded as "one of the most politically unenlightened men in the State Department," had become Hull's "surrogate son," his "closest friend and most trusted adviser." Even if Messersmith had nothing else to do, he could not compete against Hull's general diffidence on issues unrelated to his trade program. The peace congress controversy of October showed that Hull was occasionally responsive to moral suasion and always alert to opportunities to undercut his bête noire, Welles. But Messersmith could scarcely count on him to present the case against appeasement, either to his opposite-minded advisers or to Roosevelt, with regularity or conviction.[62]

When Messersmith's vigilance slackened, the self-proclaimed realists had the field to themselves. He was doing oral exams full time on 10 January when Welles, apparently inspired by William Bullitt, returned to the White House to resuscitate the plan that Messersmith and Hull had helped shoot down. Roosevelt now agreed to sponsor another world congress, this time with small nations drawing up codes of international conduct, which would be submitted to all nations for ratification. The idea, Welles explained, was to "lend support and impetus" to British and French efforts to arrive at "a practical understanding" with Germany and Italy "both on colonies and upon security." With Hitler and Mussolini co-opted, Welles reasoned, their support for Japan "will be very greatly weakened—at least to an extent sufficient to oblige Japan to make peace with China upon terms not inconsistent with the principles of the Nine Power Treaty" guaranteeing China's territorial integrity.[63]

This time Britain scotched Welles's plan. The Chamberlain government was pursuing a more direct line of appeasement. In November Lord Halifax, lord president of the privy council, had visited Berchtesgaden. He gave Hitler the welcome news that Britain was prepared to consider "possible alterations in the European order"—particularly regarding Danzig, Austria, and Czechoslovakia—in order to preserve peace. Chamberlain regarded the visit as "a great success" that had paved the way for the comprehensive settlement he sought. To that end, he wrote Roosevelt on 14 January, Britain was ready also to recognize the conquest of Ethiopia if the Italians gave "evidence of their desire to contribute to the restoration of confidence and friendly relations." The prime minister hoped that the president would "consider holding his hand for a short while" on the congress scheme and await the results of his talks with the Axis. Of course Roosevelt agreed.[64]

British policy, Alan Bullock observes, "amounted to an invitation to diplomatic blackmail which Hitler was not slow to exploit." Convinced that Britain and France would not fight, if indeed he ever doubted it, Hitler now resolved to do the Anschluss. On 12 February 1938 Schuschnigg came to Berchtesgaden to discuss problems arising under the July 1936 treaty. Instead he was subjected to one of Hitler's most memorable tirades. A livid Führer insisted that Austria lift all bans on Nazi activity, parole all imprisoned Nazis, and appoint the Nazi Arthur Seyss-Inquart minister of the interior (with control over the police). It was made clear that if Schuschnigg refused, German troops would march. By the 16th, with no real choice, Austria had complied with German terms. London and Paris, assuming the crisis was over, congratulated Schuschnigg for his good sense.[65]

It was really the beginning of Austria's last chapter, as Messersmith recognized. When by the 18th he had not been asked to comment on a situation he knew as well as any American, he volunteered his depressing thoughts in a long memorandum to Hull and Welles. He held out no hope for Schuschnigg. If the Austrian resisted—and Messersmith believed he would—he was "likely to meet the same fate as Dollfuss." "Rapid absorption" of Austria into the Reich would shortly follow. The July 1936 agreement had been ruthlessly and unilaterally abrogated, which ought to "convince a certain group in England which has been fostering such agreements, how utterly futile and fatal is any idea . . . that they can make lasting and binding agreements with Germany under present conditions." Yet, incredibly, it seemed that "English policy is more than ever oriented toward such agreements." The next would surely involve Czechoslovakia. Messersmith doubted that the Czech president, Eduard Beneš, could "hold on . . . for more than four or five months" without Western support. The annexation of the two Danubian states would give Germany much of the "raw materials and agricultural products which now make it impossible for her to make war." And, he repeated, the gangster states intended to take that war to the Western hemisphere, where they had "definite objectives."[66]

Messersmith's Austrian scenario developed in due course. By the end of February Nazi subversion had become intolerable; and Schuschnigg, in a last attempt to save his country, adopted a desperate expedient. Seeking finally to disprove Hitler's contention that a majority of Austrians favored Anschluss, he called a plebiscite for 13 March, the question being whether Austria should remain "free and independent, German and Christian." That was Hitler's cue to mobilize. Seeking suitable pretext, he pressed a series of impossible demands upon Vienna. President Miklas finally capitulated, but it was too late. At daybreak, Saturday, 12 March, the German Eighth Army crossed the border. After lunch came Hitler himself. Heinrich Himmler had arrived in Vienna the night before to supervise the arrests, including Schuschnigg's. On 13 March Austria was declared a province of the Reich. Britain and France filed perfunctory protests. The Anschluss was history.[67]

Messersmith mourned for the Austria that had been home and for the Austrians he had called friends, the poor people already undergoing the stark horrors of German occupation. The widely reported hounding of Jews and leftists, the murders and suicides, the systematic plundering were all reminiscent of Germany in the spring of 1933, but worse; after all, Messersmith wrote bitterly to United States minister John F. Montgomery in Budapest, the Nazis "have made great progress in the meantime . . . in the refinement of cruelty." For his part, Montgomery was "very happy that you and Mrs. Messersmith were not in Vienna when all this took place. I think having passed through it in Berlin must be enough to last you a lifetime, and that it would be incredible to have to endure it twice." This time he would be spared the pain of watching mass suffering and Austria being looted bare. The Germans' first order of business was to move Austrian bullion reserves to Berlin and to plunder the warehouses. Austrian civil servants were discharged; German bureaucrats took over the government. "Has there ever been," Messersmith cried out, "the rape of a country more complete? For years, Austria has been . . . struggling to build up her economic situation and now her people are to be impoverished" for the sake of the Nazi war machine. Little more was heard from him about a German economic collapse.[68]

The Anschluss created all sorts of headaches at the State Department. American minister John C. Wiley was accredited to a government that no longer existed. The status of his legation had to be decided. So too the status of Austrian passports, Austrian visa quotas, Austrian accounts in American banks, and Austrian bonds, $25 million worth, in American hands.[69]

Now that the problems were procedural rather than political, they became Messersmith's. He put them off for a time, torn, as Moffat noted, between a conviction "that we should not recognize the new situation" and the appreciation "that there are many steps which must be taken as a practical matter which will involve a recognition of this change." Practicality prevailed. Wiley's legation became a consulate general reporting through the Berlin embassy. In State Department operations, too, Austria became a German province, its people German citizens, its wealth German property. The department's demand that Berlin honor Austria's bonded debt was ignored. Messersmith's only consolation was that the Nazis gained no entrée into the American market through their new province: on 6 April Roosevelt revoked Austria's most-favored-nation privileges.[70]

Another practical problem involved human lives. Desperate Jews by the hundreds milled about Wiley's establishment day and night in search of visas and escape from Nazi persecution. Reports of their plight moved Welles to propose that Roosevelt call yet another conference. On 22 March invitations went out to thirty-three governments to meet in a cooperative effort to aid German and Austrian refugees. Meanwhile Roosevelt assembled an advisory committee comprising leaders of private philanthropic and religious organizations, who were to explore possibilities for resettlement.[71]

The committee's search for refugee havens was quickly complicated by internecine conflicts, particularly between the leading Jewish groups. The American Jewish Committee—old, elitist, given to private persuasion—was locked in a long feud with the more militant American Jewish Congress, organizer of the 1933 anti-German boycott, which drew more of its strength from the rank-and-file of American Jewry. By mid-April the squabbling had reached the boiling point; and Messersmith, the "Jews' man" in the State Department, was despatched to New York on a peacemaking mission.[72] He went under duress. When it came to the refugee problem, his logic was hardheaded and hardhearted. He had already decided that the unfortunates trapped in the vise of Nazi barbarism could not be saved, not without jeopardizing human rights everywhere. He could never divorce the refugee problem from its source. He was convinced that the Germans intended "to use the refugee problem as a lever to get us to enter into trade talks" or otherwise assist their economy, to enhance their ability to make war. Bargaining with Hitler over refugees, he maintained, was as futile and as dangerous as over trade. Already the Poles were demanding that any opportunity given Germany to be rid of its Jews ought to be extended to themselves. Humanitarianism was encouraging brutality.[73]

And, assuming that Hitler delivered up his hostages, who would take them? Certainly not the United States, not if Messersmith had his way. Half a world away from their suffering, he viewed the Jews of Greater Germany less as innocent victims than as unwitting agents of Nazi subversion, with the potential to disrupt social harmony and economic recovery in the United States. Their plight had already sparked calls for liberalization of American immigration law, a movement Messersmith frantically and almost singlehandedly squelched. In New York he gravely told Jewish leaders that the "temper of Congress" was such that "if the issue of revision came up," the laws would be tightened rather than relaxed. He worried out loud about a nativist backlash with unhappy consequences for American Jews. They agreed that the times were unpropitious for revision. Messersmith reported this decision back to the six Jewish congressmen with whom he met on 17 April.[74]

Messersmith's assessment of the public mood was probably on the mark. *Fortune* magazine's July poll showed that 68 percent of Americans favored retention of the present quotas. Previous attempts at liberalization had in fact elicited more restrictive proposals. But he seems to have been as unnerved by the possibility that liberalization would succeed as fail. He feared an avalanche of people he wished to keep out. Their attitude irritated him. Every day, he wrote Wiley, brought him "rude shocks" in the form of "some of the most extraordinary letters from professors and others who seem to be very resentful that we are not giving them on a golden platter a position which native-born Americans would be glad to get at the end of a long and hard fought career." Other visa-seekers had the gall to write him criticizing American immigration policy and to dilate on "how we ought to run things here." Fortunately, as far as he was concerned, the present regulations would serve to exclude most of these ingrates. Messersmith was "glad to say that this country still belongs to the native-born American," and expressed the hope "that the ideals of our native-born may continue to control."[75]

The world refugee conference, which opened in July at the French resort town Evian-les-Bains, showcased world restrictionism and once more undermined Germany's moral isolation. Hitler scored a major propaganda victory when the conference broke up after nine days of speeches explaining why no nation present except Holland and Denmark could accept more Jews. The Nazi press had a field day; Evian, one paper crowed, served to "justify Germany's policy against Jewry." Evian's single positive accomplishment, the formation of an Intergovernmental Committee on Refugees (IGC), caused Messersmith further distress, for its mission was to engage Berlin in negotiations. He would "have counselled against its formation," but his counsel, again, had not been solicited. The IGC, under the direction of George Rublee, an American international lawyer, proceeded, with Roosevelt's blessings, to try establishing contact with the Germans.[76]

This latest invitation to extortion evoked no immediate response from Berlin. Hitler had bigger fish to fry in mid-1938. Austria had hardly been digested when plans to crush Czechoslovakia were set in motion. In April the Czech Nazi leader, Konrad Henlein, demanded autonomy for the Sudetenland, home of the German minority. Hitler planned to march when Beneš refused, as he was sure to do. The West's devotion to appeasement, however, surprised even the Führer. France had a military pact with the Czechs, but also a new government headed by Edouard Daladier, who was only too willing to jettison his commitments in order to avoid war. As Halifax had made explicit, Britain was perfectly prepared to sacrifice Czechoslovakia in order to obtain a comprehensive European settlement. Thus London and Paris urged Beneš to give way, suggesting strongly that they would not fight to save a government that denied "justice" to its German minority.[77]

After a long, tense summer of negotiations, Beneš accepted most of Henlein's demands. In response the Nazis staged riots in the Sudetenland, using their suppression as an excuse to break off talks. In a 12 September speech Hitler vowed to stop the "annihilation" of the German minority. The next day Messersmith sat down with Hull and Moffat to make preparations for the European war that now seemed certain.[78]

Their preparations proved premature. In conferences with Hitler at Berchtesgaden, Chamberlain proposed that Germany occupy the Sudetenland in stages. Mussolini, whose grandiose vision of general war bore no relation to his ability to fight one, urged Hitler to accept. France promised to compel Czech acquiescence.[79]

At the State Department, Messersmith for the first time took part in discussions over how the United States might assist the cause of peace. In that context, his apparent contribution, that Washington issue a "definite threat . . . that we could not be indifferent if the Germans provoked hostilities" was, as Moffat wrote impatiently, "obviously out of the question." Instead, Moffat and the like-minded assistant secretary, Adolf A. Berle, who had replaced Hugh Wilson in February, drafted a general appeal for peace, which went out to the German, English, French, and Czech heads of state over Roosevelt's signature a little after 1 A.M. on 26 September. At 10 o'clock that evening Messersmith phoned the president with his translation of the Führer's response. It was the usual litany of wrongs inflicted upon the Sudeten Germans, Hitler blaming the Czechs in advance should hostilities ensue. Messersmith did not fail to add his criticism of the administration's whole approach, which, as he told Roosevelt, "was quite useless and only created a wrong understanding of our position and . . . did not help things at all. I realized the good intentions which the President had had, but [Hitler and Mussolini] were not men . . . with whom one could deal in the manner the President had intended."[80]

Immediate developments, however, suggested quite the opposite. On 28 September Hitler invited Chamberlain, Daladier, and Mussolini to Munich. Yet of all the considerations that led Hitler to accept negotiations, Roosevelt's pleas were probably the least significant. The Führer was much more impressed by the partial mobilization of Britain and France; by the arguments of his generals, to which Goebbels and Göring also subscribed, warning of German vulnerability in the west; by the evident apathy of the German people; and by the entreaties of Mussolini, whose acceptance of the Anschluss had won him Hitler's undying gratitude. In the end the Führer fell back on the tactics that had served him so well since 1933. He took the Sudetenland as a gift, his concession to peace. The rest of Czechoslovakia would come when the time was ripe.[81]

News of the Munich conference "was greeted abroad much as was the armistice of 1918," Berle wrote in his diary. "The 'break'!" he exulted. "Thank God." The next morning, the day of the conference, Messersmith set forth rather different sentiments in another unsolicited memorandum to Hull. "Needless to say," he forced from himself, "I shared the general relief upon hearing the news [that] . . . hostilities was [sic] to be avoided by . . . the meeting at Munich today." But "optimism and relief" had to be "seriously tempered by fears" of a "cynical sell-out of principle" that would "put Germany in a position to carry through successfully the war which she intends to fight and which she is not in a position to wage successfully now." Munich could only conclude "arrangements to ward off immediate hostilities"; "no four powers can sit down and settle in a few days the general problems which are disturbing the world." Unfortunately permanent peace was "impossible until there is a regime of law and order in Germany," one "which has respect for the rights of others . . . and which is not aimed at world domination." Moreover it was unrealistic "to assume that with the gaining of its now-proclaimed objectives in Czechoslovakia, Germany will be satisfied as far as her territorial objectives are concerned." What remained of the Czech state after Munich would soon go the way of Austria. Nor would it stop there: "the Monroe Doctrine," Messersmith warned again, "is just as much of an irritant to the present German Government as the maintenance of the Czech State."[82]

Nothing that Messersmith or anyone else could say could dampen the euphoria over the avoidance of war. Chamberlain, guilty in Messersmith's eyes of "one of the most disastrous things carried through in history by a British statesman," returned from Munich to a hero's welcome. When Winston Churchill rose in the House of Commons to denounce Munich as "a total unmitigated defeat," the catcalls nearly drowned him out. It did not take long, however, for disillusionment to come. German troops poured into the Sudeten occupation zone, creating an ominous backdrop to new German demands upon Prague. With every bellicose speech, it became clearer that Hitler had no more intention of abiding by Munich than by previous agreements. In the United States elation gave way to anger at those who had betrayed the poor Czechs. On 11 October Roosevelt called for a $300 million increase in military spending and received widespread editorial support. Perhaps, Messersmith decided, it had required a debacle like Munich to "shock . . . the public conscience" to the Nazi danger and the bankruptcy of appeasement.[83]

Anti-German feeling burst its bounds with the events of 10 November. At 2 A.M. the Kristallnacht pogrom began, an orchestrated "spontaneous" reaction to the assassination of a German diplomat in Paris by a Jewish youth. An American correspondent in Berlin described "a wave of destruction, looting and incendiarism unparalleled in Germany since the Thirty Years War." When the orgy was over, some 200 synagogues had been burned, 800 shops destroyed, 7,500 plundered, and more than 20,000 Jews arrested.

World response showed that repeated outrages had not entirely dulled its conscience. The American press rose in condemnation. Protest rallies in most large American cities produced piles of petitions demanding retaliation.[84]

It was Messersmith's cue to move. On 14 November he drew up a long memorandum urging Hull to "consider recommending strongly to the President that Ambassador Wilson be ordered home immediately 'for consultation.'" All the lies from Berlin did not change the fact

that the wholesale arrests, plundering, pillaging and terrorizing of innocent men and women throughout Germany in the last days were due to the orders of the German Government. . . . Of all the many acts of the present German Government against

innocent and defenseless people, these last are the culmination
. . . irresponsible and mad acts that our government cannot pass
unnoticed.

We have throughout our history let it be known where we
stand on matters of principle and the decencies. . . . Whenever
such acts in the past have been committed, or permitted by Governments . . . we have spoken and acted. . . . When a country
which vaunts its civilization as superior commits in cold blood
. . . acts worse than those we have in the past dealt with vigor-
ously, the time has come . . . for us to take action beyond mere
condemnation.

Recalling Wilson was sure to meet with "general and enthusiastic approval throughout the country." The American people were "waiting
for something of this kind"; if the administration disappointed them,
it ran "the grave risk of losing the leadership of opinion . . . at a time
when this leadership is all important in our most vital interests." A
recall, he promised, would have an "excellent" effect on Germany. "It
will give heart to the right-thinking people there who are in the majority, if impotent. It will give the German Government food for
thought. It will not stop action against Jews and Catholics, but it will
stem the orgy." Nor would American interests in Germany suffer
with Wilson gone. "We shall be just as well off with the remaining
representation there, which can amply take care of all of our problems so far as it is possible to care for them. . . . It can have no ap-
preciable effect on our commercial relations, for Germany is only
buying from us what she has to buy and will continue to do so."
Moreover, Britain and France might be inspired by the American
example to stand firm in their own dealings with Germany. As for
Wilson, he could be "kept in the Department usefully until such time
as the President and you [Hull] may believe it desirable for him to
return to Berlin."[85]

Some of Messersmith's reasons for wanting Wilson withdrawn he
kept to himself. He would have recommended the recall regardless
of who the American ambassador was, but the fact that it was Wilson
was sweet incentive. The furor over Kristallnacht was not only an
opportunity to show Germany and the world that, as Messersmith
put it, "there is going to be no Munich for us," but also to remove—
he hoped permanently—an envoy who was working toward one.[86]

The two had had words just before Wilson departed for his new
post in January 1938. Wilson promised to play up the good side of
Nazi Germany; Messersmith told him there was no such thing. Messersmith concluded that Wilson "misunderstands Nazi psychology,"

but trusted this would change with a few months on the scene. Wilson, he wrote Raymond Geist of his new chief, "is a good man"; he would soon "see things in their right perspective."[87]

Wilson's perspective did not change. The independently wealthy ambassador quickly irked Messersmith with insistent complaints about the inadequacy of his $3,000-a-year housing allowance. "If it costs him more to get a house," Messersmith wrote testily to Geist, "he will just be in the same boat that a good many of us have been in for a long time." More worrisome was the implication that Wilson intended to lead an active social life, as though German-American relations were perfectly normal. Messersmith appreciated that an ambassador "must do the right thing and establish contacts," but for American diplomats in Germany "the time for lavish entertaining is over." "I do not believe," he continued acidly, "we should fall all over ourselves being nice" to Nazis "when in a year or so they may force us into a war with them." Wilson should be content with modest accommodations. Messersmith did not share Geist's satisfaction in finding Wilson "a fine large villa" in suburban Grünewald for only $2,000 over the department's allowance.[88]

By the fall of 1938 all of Messersmith's initial misgivings had been confirmed. He seethed at hearing from Geist about the ambassador's parties, like the October soiree for Göring and an overawed visitor, American aviator Charles A. Lindbergh.[89]

Worse still was Wilson's official attitude. From the first he was inordinately impressed by Hitlerite Germany. Nazism appealed to this ardent anti-Communist. In letters to Hull and Roosevelt, Wilson wrote glowingly of the German economic miracle. While the democracies struggled their way out of the depression, "boom conditions" prevailed in the Reich. Nazi pageantry had pacified the working class. At his first interview with Hitler, Wilson expressed pleasure at meeting the "man who has pulled his people from moral and economic despair into the state of pride and evident prosperity they now enjoyed."[90]

Convinced that the West should be learning from Germany rather than fighting it, Wilson did everything in his power to make appeasement work. He sympathized with German claims on the Sudetenland, a question he regarded as having "two sides . . . and not only the Czech side." In May he suggested to Washington that Carr should more emphatically press the necessary concessions upon Beneš. In June he assured Hitler's new foreign minister, Joachim von Ribbentrop, that he would spare no effort to prevent American entry into any European war. He denounced the "Jewish controlled press" in America for its "hymn of hatred" against Germany. Munich took a load off his mind; the agreement, he wrote in relief, had opened the way to "a better Europe."[91]

Moreover, and almost as disturbing to Messersmith, Wilson was industriously assisting George Rublee in enticing Berlin into refugee negotiations. Wilson's motives were clear enough: a solution to the "Jewish problem," he told Walther Funk, Hitler's economics minister, would serve to "banish the hatred in which Germany was held abroad" and remove what Wilson viewed as a prime obstacle to harmonious German-American relations. Messersmith knew how right he was. His greatest fear was that under Wilson's entreaties, the Germans would recognize it, too.[92]

Wilson set the tone for his establishment, leading his subordinates down the same accommodationist path. After four years of Dodd's cantankerous idiosyncrasies, Berlin embassy staffers had taken fast to their charming new chief. A particular closeness developed between Wilson, who knew a good man when he saw one, and Raymond Geist, which rankled Messersmith to his bones. Assuming that his mentor would be only too delighted to learn how smoothly things were running after the transition to Wilson, Geist provided Messersmith with all the galling details. Wilson and his wife, Geist reported happily, were treating him "almost as a member of the family." Wilson recommended him for promotion to first secretary. Geist assured Messersmith that he had "not changed my attitude an iota" about nazism, but confessed that Wilson's friendships in German officialdom had facilitated his protection work. He also wished the refugee negotiations success, though more for humanitarian than political reasons.[93]

As the most open and enthusiastic exponent of the policy Messersmith was impelled to fight, Wilson became the focus of his frustrations. "It pains me a great deal to say that I have been a good deal disappointed with the Ambassador's attitude," he wrote on 7 November to Geist, thus putting him in the middle of their feud. "He seems to be quite condoning all that Germany has done." Wilson was not the only American envoy in Europe whitewashing Hitler. Joseph P. Kennedy, the financier and former Securities and Exchange Commission chairman who had replaced the deceased Robert Bingham in London, was also making himself obnoxious to Messersmith by promoting a Nazi peace. The difference, in his mind, was that Wilson was "a career man, and we should be able to depend upon him for the definite presentation of our point of view, and we cannot expect from him the vagaries of a free-lance like Kennedy." Of course, Wilson was closer to the department's view than Messersmith, who was speaking only for himself. That was one more painful reality he chose to suppress.[94]

All this is background to Messersmith's Kristallnacht memorandum to Hull. The secretary responded with unusual celerity, conferring with his top advisers that morning. No minute of the meeting has been found, but Hull's memoirs suggest a split decision to recommend Wilson's recall to Roosevelt. It was argued that the ambassador was needed in Berlin "to keep in close contact with the aims and acts of the German Government and to give weight to any representations we needed to make." More to the point, a Wilson recall would be a setback in the "realists'" campaign for negotiations. But public outrage over Kristallnacht needed to be stilled; and opponents of the recall probably calculated that Wilson could be returned to Berlin when the excitement died down. That afternoon, therefore, Hull saw Roosevelt, who signed the order summoning him home. The next day, 15 November, the president announced the move to the press. To the bland statement prepared for the occasion by the State Department, Roosevelt added that he "could scarcely believe that such things [i.e., the pogrom] could occur in a twentieth century civilization." Hitler retaliated by recalling Ambassador Hans Heinrich Dieckhoff from Washington. Neither envoy was to return.[95]

Messersmith reveled in this success and the prospect of greater ones to come. Public opinion was finally catching up to him. He noted with satisfaction that many newspapers were criticizing Wilson for having been "too sympathetic to the Nazis." Anti-Nazi opinion, he assured a Belgian friend, was bound to grow, so Wilson would not be returning "in anything like the near future." Messersmith intended to see to that.[96]

Some benefits that Messersmith anticipated from the recall did not materialize. It did not divert attention from the victims of Kristallnacht. He had hoped that the Rublee mission would collapse with Wilson gone. It did not. Indeed, the recall elicited wide public approval partly because it was not a break in relations and thus did not foreclose refugee and other negotiations with Germany. At his 15 November press conference Roosevelt had emphasized that the work of the IGC was going forward even as the American ambassador was being withdrawn.[97]

In December Rublee's overtures brought a positive response from Berlin. After the 10 November orgy, the Nazis felt the need to do some appeasing of their own. With Hitler's approval, Schacht delivered a new proposal to Rublee in London. One hundred fifty thousand Jewish wage earners would be permitted to leave Germany over a three-year period, their dependents to follow. The asking price was 1.5 billion marks—roughly a quarter of the wealth estimated to remain in Jewish hands. That sum was to go into a trust account administered by Berlin, to serve as collateral for foreign loans to finance German exports. Rublee listened in silence and passed Schacht's proposal to Washington.[98]

It was a plan worthy of Messersmith's purest scorn, "the most cynical thing," he wrote Geist, "which could be conceived of, and utterly unacceptable." Sure enough, the Germans were trying to use the refugees as "pawns" in "breaking down our whole trading program," to bail themselves out of their persistent exchange problems. Hitler expected "the decent countries" not only to take his surplus population off his hands, but also to "pay . . . Germany very liberally for the privilege." Surely Roosevelt would now see that there was "no way to buy off this Government in Berlin except complete abject surrender," and order Rublee to close shop. That would crush some hopes, but there was no alternative. Messersmith was convinced that the Jews' suffering would unfortunately continue "no matter what may be done by Jews and others outside" as long as the Nazis remained in power. There was only one solution: "the reestablishment of decent government and . . . decent treatment of people at home."[99]

But Roosevelt and the State Department were ready to negotiate. Although the idea of bartering "human misery for increased exports" revolted Welles (Hull was attending the Pan American Conference in Lima), Rublee was authorized to stay at it. The scene shifted to Berlin, where, on 18 January 1939, agreement was reached. The governments of the Dominican Republic and the Philippines signaled their willingness to admit refugees. Believing that he had achieved his mission, Rublee relinquished his post to Sir Herbert Emerson, who was to work out the details.[100]

Messersmith remained skeptical, with good cause. The halfhearted participation of non-German Jewish leaders reinforced Emerson's innate lassitude. The immense practical problems of resettlement were compounded by the addition of 350,000 Czech Jews (after March 1939) and 3.3 million Polish Jews (after September 1939) to the refugee pool. The Germans, moreover, were determined to extract the last advantage from their hostages before letting them go. Yet it remains that they wished them gone, resorting to the Final Solution—extermination—only after the possibilities for emigration had been exhausted. By doing nothing to open the doors, by refusing to bend to save lives, Messersmith upheld the worst "native American ideals."[101]

While Rublee was negotiating in Berlin, plans were afoot to send him assistance, in the person of Hugh Wilson. Wilson had given Roosevelt's summons a conveniently literal reading, leaving his wife behind in Berlin to underscore his expectation of returning. His reception in Washington suggested that she would not be without him for long. Welles ordered him to keep abreast of German developments and to hold himself in readiness to return on fast notice. Wilson lived out of his suitcases.[102]

The new year 1939, however, found him restless in Washington, with only his colleagues to console him. The attitude in the department was that the United States had made its point, that Wilson belonged back in Berlin to restore "ambassadorial authority and emphasis" to German-American relations. He could not have agreed more. Britain and France were both on record as favoring his return in the interests of "reconciliation." In talks with the British ambassador, Sir Ronald Lindsay, Welles linked Wilson's disposition to German behavior—which, in early 1939, struck some as decidedly improved. The Schacht-Rublee discussions were then making progress. In late December the German chargé d'affaires, Hans Thomsen, had informed Welles that Berlin was lifting restrictions that had prevented Americans from collecting the bequests of deceased German relatives, suggesting that Germany might be willing to abandon discrimination in other areas. It seemed unreasonable to prevent Wilson from returning to explore the possibility.[103]

Reasonable or not, Messersmith did his best to keep Wilson home. In memoranda to Hull, Welles, Dunn, and Moffat, he warned against "surface indications" of a German desire "to improve the status of its relationships with this country." It was just another cynical shift in tactics. He cited recent speeches by Goebbels and Göring implying that "only the Jews and the Jewish problem stand in the way" of better bilateral relations, speeches designed to "stir up anti-Semitic feeling in this country," "to make it appear that the Jews are responsible for the attitude of this government." And he established the context of the concession on the transfer of legacies: Welles's threat, issued just prior to Dieckhoff's departure, to seek congressional authorization for retaliatory measures sure to hurt exchange-poor Germany much more than its restrictions had cost Americans.[104]

It was more proof that the "present Government in Germany understands only one language: . . . that of force and direct action." That was why, Messersmith wrote Hull and Welles on 15 February 1939, it was "definitely inadvisable" for Wilson to return. It would "be misconstrued . . . as a distinct retreat by the President . . . and widely exploited in Germany." It would be "demoralizing and disorienting" to American opinion, "which has crystallized along such sound lines." If firmness had had some "restraining influence" on Germany and a "heartening influence on other countries" like Czechoslovakia, why change course? Messersmith simply saw no compelling reason to send Wilson back. "Our interests in Berlin are well-provided for" by Geist and the experienced chargé, Prentiss Gilbert. "We are not losing anything by the Ambassador not being there," he concluded, quickly adding that "this does not imply anything derogatory to the person of the Ambassador."[105]

His arguments again made little impression. Perhaps Wilson was simply more persuasive. He and Welles went back together to the prewar diplomatic service. Moffat and Dunn and Davis were old friends of his. They were sympathetic to his laments about his wife, stranded in Berlin. And there was the promise of restored, possibly expanded, communications with Germany if he returned. In any case, by March the State Department, with Messersmith a lone holdout, was prepared to recommend to Roosevelt that Wilson be sent back. On 13 March, according to Moffat, his return was "virtually . . . decided upon."[106]

Hitler changed these plans. On 15 March German troops occupied Prague, trampling the Munich accord and the whole pretense of German self-determination. The State Department's top officials gathered that afternoon. The scheme to return Wilson was "completely abandoned." The debate centered instead on further sanctions against Germany. Messersmith, "his eyes aglow," called for an immediate break in relations. Norman Davis concurred. But Moffat, Dunn, and Berle advised restraint and, as usual, they prevailed. On 17 March the United States publicly condemned the German aggression, continued to deal conspicuously with Czech representatives in Washington, and imposed countervailing duties, long sought by Treasury Secretary Morgenthau, on subsidized German exports.[107]

Although all this fell considerably short of the break Messersmith advocated, it was Washington's strongest message yet to Berlin. And Wilson's status had been resolved to his satisfaction. On 20 March the ambassador called his wife home. Five months later, when Molotov and Ribbentrop signed their nonaggression pact, Wilson, his faith shattered, seemed finally resigned to not returning. But hope sprang eternal, or, in Wilson's case, until the undeclared war of 1940–41 made the outcome unmistakably obvious even to him.[108]

For many Communist as well as Nazi sympathizers, the Molotov-Ribbentrop Pact was the final, bitter disillusionment. Such a rapprochement, however, was almost implicit in Messersmith's analysis of European power politics. He was one American not taken entirely by surprise when it happened. In light of his longstanding contention that for both Hitler and Stalin ideology was merely a tool in the service of national interests, they were not such far-fetched bedfellows after all. Nor, he believed, had their coming to terms done more than postpone the confrontation between them that he still considered inevitable. Stalin had only done what Schuschnigg and Beneš had tried to do before him when they, like him, were spurned and abandoned by the West. Their desperate attempts to buy time against the German threat had not saved them. Time alone would tell whether Stalin and Russia would have any better success.[109]

The invasion of Czechoslovakia was a turning point in prewar diplomacy. Thereafter, Hitler's warlike intentions were taken all but for granted in Washington and London. For people like Messersmith and the Briton Vansittart, who had known the same frustration, a long intellectual exile was coming to an end. And yet, they themselves had had little to do with their redemption. Their governments finally responded not to the force of their logic, but to Hitler's faits accomplis. Indeed, although the trampling of Munich dealt appeasement a critical setback, its underlying assumptions lived on. Even after September 1939 and the outbreak of the war for which Messersmith had been praying for years, he was kept awake at night by concern that the "realists" would induce Roosevelt to accept Berlin's invitation to mediate. As Messersmith departed for a new post in 1940, Sumner Welles's peace mission to Europe was in the works. In connection with this initiative, it was rumored that the United States was planning to appoint a new ambassador to Germany. Hugh Wilson volunteered his services to Roosevelt. Messersmith took up his pen—or dictaphone—again in protest. And once more, German aggression—this time against Denmark and Norway—not his objections, killed the scheme.[110]

In 1953, retired from government service and preparing to write his memoirs, Messersmith reviewed the literature that had begun to appear on American diplomacy before World War II. He found to his ineffable delight that he was "really the only one of our diplomats . . . who escaped adverse criticism." In indicting the appeasers, history had vindicated him, one of the few whose hands were clean.[111]

One of the episodes Messersmith went on to recall in those memoirs involved his former colleague Moffat. Despite sometimes heated disagreements during their tenure together in Washington, the two officials were friends. Frequently, Messersmith recalled, Moffat stopped by his office in the evening before heading home. The conversation invariably turned to the world crisis. "George," he has Moffat saying at one point, "I wonder whether you know what you are doing. You are helping us to get into this war which is coming on." Messersmith wearily explained that Hitler and democracy could not coexist. "But what a horrible thing [war] is," Moffat is supposed to have responded. "How can we think of it?" When the European fighting began, Moffat was disconsolate and short tempered. "Now, George," he snapped, "you are satisfied." Messersmith continued: "I said, 'Pierrepont, you are a very just man; you have never said a more unjust thing and I am sure that you realize it.' Tears came to his eyes and he begged forgiveness. . . . 'You have been right all the time [he said] and of course, I knew that you were right. I just could not face it.'"[112]

Messersmith obviously relished, and possibly embellished, the tale. But he was entitled to gloat—not only because events proved him right and the appeasers wrong, but for what he endured in sticking to his convictions. Frustration was a large part of the physical exhaustion he was increasingly suffering. Messersmith was learning the limits of his energy as well as of his influence in Washington. "For the first time in my life," he confessed to Geist, "I cannot altogether keep pace with what I have to do," despite eighty-hour work weeks. The few diversions he used to allow himself and most personal correspondence went by the board. By the time he got home at night—home was a fine old Georgetown estate—it was usually past 8 P.M., and he was too worn out to go out. "Being as fond as I am of my fellow human beings," he wrote a friend, "I miss this very much." Marion missed it more. She compensated by filling the house with guests. Messersmith would join them for late dinner and then retire to the study to review papers in quiet reflection.[113]

This burden was largely self-imposed, but not entirely. Others were not holding up their end of the load. Of the department's top people, Hull was not deeply involved in daily operations, due to his frequent need for rest. Counselor R. Walton Moore celebrated his eightieth birthday in 1939. Assistant Secretary Berle, vaguely charged "with such duties as may be assigned to him by the Secretary of State," was getting few such assignments. Hull and his associates regarded Berle as another Raymond Moley, a neophyte on secret mission from the White House, and treated him accordingly. Berle found his official duties "anything but heavy," leaving him ample time for his manifold outside activities. With Berle ostracized, and Hull and Moore frequently incapacitated, a disproportionate burden fell on Welles and Messersmith, both of whom, Moffat observed, wound up "working far harder than they should."[114]

By the summer of 1938 Messersmith was showing the strain. Moffat noted in June that he was "looking desperately tired and if he does not let up soon he will be threatened by a breakdown." From Berlin, Ray Geist admonished him to take care. With this prompting, he and Marion left in June 1938 for the quiet of her brother's log cabin near Yarmouth on Cape Cod. By mid-July he was back to resume the battles against appeasement and for departmental reform.[115]

4

At least Messersmith had the satisfaction of a successful legislative program. The deteriorating European situation, Roosevelt's return to deficit spending, and, very possibly, Messersmith's own efforts to publicize the department's needs, helped him to secure the first real increase in its appropriation over predepression levels. The Sudeten crisis was raging on 15 September, when he appeared before Acting Budget Director Bell with the department's requests for fiscal 1940: $20.4 million, up 20 percent over the current figure. He asked for boosts in virtually every category of expenditure, and for the biggest expansion of foreign service personnel—264 new officers and clerks —since 1919. In his statement Messersmith depicted a State Department that had husbanded every dollar, instituted every efficiency, met every challenge, and simply needed more if it were to fulfill the "real needs of our Government for the conduct of our foreign relations which perhaps at no time have been more vital to our fundamental interests." He called attention to the "difficult and threatening" developments abroad, and the fact that "it is the budget of the Department which has the principal responsibility for the maintenance of peace so far as any Government agency can have any influence on its preservation." Scrimping now was unthinkable. Bell allowed two-thirds of the requested increase.[116]

In congressional hearings beginning 12 April 1939, Messersmith reported progress in the problem areas that the Appropriations Subcommittee had focused upon the year before. Inefficiency at State, he declared, had been eliminated; with his reorganization, the department's machinery was "perfected." He had promised to clean up the buildings program, and had kept his word. Projects underway in Ciudad Trujillo, Port-au-Prince, Helsinki, and elsewhere were all on schedule and under budget. He took special pride in telling the panel that as of 1 April all permanent representatives of the United States in Berlin were operating out of the refurbished Bluecher Palace. Geist had arranged with the German government for a very favorable rate of exchange, so that the job, budgeted at $200,000, had been completed for under $56,000. It was another example of the federal government's senior and most frugal department being meticulous with the taxpayers' money. "We are perfectly content to be the Cinderella of our Government," he said in closing remarks.

But even Cinderella required sustenance. That was all he was asking for the State Department.[117]

On 18 May McMillan reported the bill. While disallowing some requests, as for a State Department motor pool, his committee let stand increases totaling over $1.3 million. One hundred twenty new positions were approved. The lawmaker paid "tribute . . . to the character of the administration of this Department," from which, he assured his colleagues, "we are truly 'getting our money's worth.'" The budget finally passed by both houses and signed by the president amounted to $18.5 million, a 12 percent increase. Messersmith had a valid claim to more. But the 1940 appropriation sufficed to repair much of the damage wrought by years of austerity. He could depart Washington confident that the State Department had the wherewithal for the challenges ahead.[118]

He could also rest assured that foreign service officers and their spouses were provided for in retirement. In July 1938, after exhaustive studies, recommendations for changes in the pension plan were put into legislation. H.R. 3655, amending Moses-Linthicum, was not one of the glamour issues before the 76th Congress; it passed without ceremony in April 1939. Buried within it, however, in section 3, were provisions so favorable to the service that in explaining it to the field, Moffat confided, Messersmith had "to understate the advantages to prevent an attack in the Senate." Knowingly or not, the legislators had committed the government to picking up the deficits in the department's fund, while expanding benefits—to include widows, for example—and holding the mandatory contribution to 5 percent of salary.[119]

But co-option of the attachés was most on Messersmith's mind. During the summer of 1938 he prepared for battle with Daniel Roper. Messersmith discovered why the commercial service had never published a *Biographical Register* like the State Department's when he compiled one himself. With an average 3.4 years of business experience—mostly clerical—the attachés looked pretty bad by comparison. Their qualifications, as Messersmith had suspected all along, were primarily political. In a memorandum to Hull, he concluded "that practically all appointments and transfers in the Foreign Commercial Service are dictated by certain political personages." He presented his findings to business leaders in a bid for support. He worked to assuage the attachés' concern for their jobs with the promise of prestige and opportunity in the unified Foreign Service.[120]

On 7 September he handed Hull a seventy-five-page plan for consolidation along with a proposed amendment to Moses-Linthicum embodying it. The agricultural attachés would be absorbed, too. In compensation, Commerce and Agriculture would gain representation on the Foreign Service boards of Examiners and of Personnel, and permanent liaison officers would ensure that requests for foreign information were transmitted through State to the field; the secretaries of State, Agriculture, and Commerce would consult periodically.

Messersmith guaranteed "broad support" for this plan. Having long assumed it was advantageous to have "two competing services in the field," trade associations now saw "that this policy was a mistake" and "have informed me that they are prepared to change this attitude." "But for a few [congressmen] who will resist the erosion of patronage," legislative approval, he told Hull, was a sure thing. Secretary of Agriculture Henry A. Wallace had already expressed his approval in principle. Top officials of the commercial service and most of the attachés were heartily, if as yet only privately, in accord. There would undoubtedly be "narrow bureaucratic opposition" from Roper and his closest associates, but Messersmith urged that this not deter a move so very vital both to trade promotion and to the administration of foreign policy.[121]

While Messersmith's memorandum made the rounds, Commerce was mobilizing to resist. On 6 October Roper and Assistant Secretary of Commerce Richard C. Patterson met with their Business Advisory Council, urging an all-out fight against consolidation, which, they claimed, would "greatly weaken" government assistance to business. The group responded with a resolution to that effect to Roosevelt. Messersmith's contacts on the NFTC reported "organized opposition" to a contemplated endorsement of the merger. Patterson prepared a "Brief for the Retention of the Foreign Commercial Service," and distributed it to the press and other interested parties.[122]

Messersmith fought back. The evening of 8 October found him in New York, pleading his case over dinner with representatives of Roper's advisory council. In early November he was back for three days, buttonholing delegates to the NFTC's twenty-fifth annual convention. It quickly became clear that he had underestimated the opposition. Loyalty to Roper and the attachés, anti–State Department prejudice, and hostility to consolidation ran deeper than he had thought. Messersmith argued that 85 percent of the foreign information delivered by Commerce was actually collected by State; that its officers were generally superior to the attachés; that the present duplicative arrangement was one no good businessman would tolerate in his own firm. But many persisted in viewing the merger as just "another blow" against business by the New Deal.[123]

This opposition apparently registered on Roosevelt, who had a modified reorganization bill ready for the upcoming 76th Congress. The White House had made a key concession: whereas specific reorganizations would have required only the president's say-so under the aegis of the abortive bill, the new version made such plans subject to legislative veto. The lessons of 1937 and the charge of executive tyranny had evidently cut deep. What Roosevelt now feared was that a combination of vested interests would defeat reorganization again. If any one contemplated shift, like foreign service unification, jeopardized the larger bill, Roosevelt was prepared to jettison it, too. Messersmith, who had assumed that the president was "firm in his determination" for the merger, learned in early November that he was now "undecided on the matter."[124]

Messersmith's memorandum helped persuade him. By 18 November all of State's top officers had been able to comment upon it, and all agreed it was "an unanswerable argument for consolidation." Messersmith suggested that the president get a copy to peruse during his week at Warm Springs, Georgia, in early December.[125]

Roosevelt took the memorandum with him and returned determined to see the merger through, though not via Moses-Linthicum. The whole idea behind reorganization was to deal with such things systematically rather than piecemeal. It seemed pointless for the State Department to go it alone while reorganization was in the works.[126]

Messersmith tried being sly. He advised Welles to warn Roosevelt of "mounting opposition" to consolidation that might indeed "jeopardize . . . the larger bill." For the sake of the latter, he suggested that consolidation be spun off. What had become of the "broad support" he cited in September he did not say. His real concern, of course, was exactly the opposite: that reorganization would fail again and drag consolidation down with it, as before. Roosevelt's new measure, he worried, would "undoubtedly be a controversial measure and will undoubtedly be under discussion for some time before it is passed," if it passed.[127]

None of this mattered in the least to Daniel Roper, who was the loser either way. He and Hull, adversaries of late, shared the same status, or lack of it, in the administration. Roper, recalled Rexford Tugwell, "might as well not have existed" in Roosevelt's inner mind. Hull fell into the same category. He may have known it better than Roper, who committed the cardinal mistake Hull always avoided. By taking a stand against the merger, Roper placed temptation in the president's path. Having threatened to resign last time, Roper had no honorable choice but to resign when he was now overruled. Resign he did on 15 December.[128]

The fact was that the president was now delighted to see him gone. The likelihood that a decision for consolidation would lead to Roper's resignation may have actually helped Roosevelt make the decision. Roper did not figure in his future plans; Harry Hopkins did. In late 1938, at one of the lowest ebbs of his presidency, a weary Roosevelt was looking longingly to 1940, when he might hand over his burdens to a successor, which he hoped would be Hopkins. But Hopkins had a reputation for being among the most radical New Dealers, at a time when public opinion was shifting decidedly to the right. To help him broaden his support in preparation for that race, Roosevelt promised to appoint him secretary of commerce when the office became vacant. Ten days after Roper resigned, Hopkins was sworn in.[129]

With Roper's departure and constant prodding from Messersmith, consolidation proceeded rapidly. Hopkins needed the prodding at first. Unregenerate advisers like Patterson and Dr. Dye argued that submission would erode the new secretary's credibility with business and set back his political ambitions. And he was unhappy about ceding a piece of his inheritance. But his own soundings convinced him that business opposition would not be serious. Messersmith arranged for Hopkins's friends Averell Harriman and Josephus Daniels to tell him they supported the merger. And, of course, the president wished it. In early February, then, Hopkins and Messersmith sat down to begin ironing out the details.[130]

Meanwhile reorganization was wending its way through Congress. Messersmith need not have feared for the bill. It passed the House on 8 March, after three days of debate; the Senate followed suit. Roosevelt signed the measure on 3 April 1939.[131]

State, Commerce, and Agriculture accelerated their negotiations. On 13 April Messersmith saw Roosevelt, who ordered him and Hopkins "to get together in a room, throw the key out of the window and come out with an agreement which could be submitted to him." The next evening, after a long day with McMillan's subcommittee, Messersmith concluded his negotiations with Hopkins's designee. Wallace came around a week later. On the morning of 25 April Wallace, Hull, and Hopkins gathered to initial the final plan.[132]

Messersmith was leaving nothing to chance. Within twenty-four hours dozens of letters had gone out to business leaders and newspaper editors, explaining the plan, asking for a suspension of criticism or a favorable editorial. Several editors obliged, more, perhaps, as one wrote him back, out of "regard for yourself than from a careful study of the subject matter." He then hit Congress, only to find himself preaching to the nearly converted. Michigan Republican Arthur

Vandenberg assured him that most senators viewed consolidation as "one of those things which should have been done a long time ago." Senate approval on 12 May enacted the merger.[133]

It was the signal achievement of Messersmith's career, "the biggest thing," he boasted to a colleague, "since the Rogers Act." It was not quite that big. Consolidation of the foreign services broke no new ground. It simply advanced Rogers's vision of unity. But it was a long stride indeed in that direction. By confirming State Department jurisdiction over trade promotion abroad, a scholar concludes, co-option of the foreign commercial service was "the most important development of specialization in the period" 1924 to 1939. It ended three decades of conflict, confusion, and duplication in American foreign policy. When, on 1 July 1939, 114 commercial and agricultural attachés received commissions as foreign service officers, the State Department gained exclusive charge of the nation's permanent civilian representation abroad. It also gained, at a fell swoop, 114 additional foreign service lines—more than had been added over the previous fifteen years. This expansion, which helped the department to meet its manpower needs during the war, may have been no less significant an accomplishment.[134]

Despite what he had told McMillan's subcommittee, Messersmith had no illusions that the department's administration was "perfected." Although more convinced than ever that "we have on the whole the best Foreign Service organization of any government," he still saw room for improvement. As the State-Commerce-Agriculture Committee started to work out their new relationship, Messersmith undertook a new project, compiling studies of foreign service practices of other nations. He hoped to pick up an idea or two.[135]

5

But he had already achieved his administrative goals in Washington. The machinery had been tuned for the challenges he knew lay ahead. Actual preparations for war began during the Czech crisis, when Messersmith and Nathaniel P. Davis, chief of the division of Foreign Service administration, laid plans for a special division to handle wartime whereabouts and relief cases, repatriation of Americans and protection of their property, liaison to the Red Cross, and so forth. On 29 March 1939 war-zone missions were instructed to ready similar special sections of their own. Negotiations with the navy and private steamship lines produced a detailed evacuation plan, the State Department to advance money for fares to stranded

Americans on a promissory-note basis. In mid-August, as the Polish crisis built, Messersmith, Welles, and other top officials reviewed procedures with counterparts from the War, Navy, Justice, and Treasury departments. Over the next two weeks Messersmith attended to final details, for example, instructing American diplomatic missions to paint on their roofs the letters "U.S.A." seven feet high by one foot wide, "in chrome yellow on a black background," to guide away attacking aircraft.[136]

At 2:50 A.M., 1 September 1939, a starting date Messersmith had predicted, Ambassador Anthony Drexel Biddle in Warsaw telephoned Roosevelt to report the German invasion. Twenty minutes later confirmation arrived from Bullitt in Paris, and Roosevelt ordered the machinery activated. At 4 A.M. Messersmith, Berle, Welles, and Hull gathered in the secretary's office, the various division chiefs drifting in as the discussion progressed. The order establishing the special division was promulgated the next morning. On 2 September Breckinridge Long, Roosevelt's envoy to Italy from 1933 to 1936, returned to head it up, with Hugh Wilson as his assistant and a staff of twelve foreign service officers.[137]

Despite the preparations and resources of the new division, problems arose that further tested Messersmith's stamina and ability to improvise. At least 100,000 Americans who had shrugged off the department's warnings and continued their European summer holidays now clamored for passage home. The evacuation effort got off to a rocky start, through no fault of Messersmith's or Long's. Some of the maritime unions tried to extort premium wages, large bonuses, paid-up life insurance policies, and other sweeteners; it required the threat of a court order to force them to sign on crews. There was obduracy from certain American mission chiefs to contend with, and open insubordination from Bullitt in Paris. With German bombs expected to fall on the French capital any day, Messersmith frantically arranged to move the embassy to Touraine, to the south. Budgetary restraints hampered him. And he had to put up with nagging from the Department of Commerce, which wanted its commodity reports from Europe on time, war or no.[138]

Messersmith eventually prevailed. By the end of September 20,000 berths were available to take Americans home. By then, in fact, the main problem was persuading them to return at all. Panic had subsided in western Europe. With the conquest of Poland, talk of a negotiated settlement filled the air. Far from requiring sanctuary, the diplomats returned to center stage.[139]

At the State Department, too, the crisis lost its edge, and Messersmith found time to catch his breath. For over a year he had been working at a pace that, Moffat was sure, "if he does not moderate it, will kill him." Messersmith was too careful for anything so dire to happen. He had managed before to get away for serious rest when he felt in danger of being overwhelmed. There had been a week in New York in December 1938 set aside for sleep and theatergoing, and he and Marion "trying to get to know each other again." They had several extended holidays at the Cape Cod cabin. Moreover, he had received significant relief from the department in two able executive assistants.[140]

But it was someone else's turn. His understanding with the president was that he was to return to the field upon completion of his administrative reforms. Thus, consolidation of the attachés was for Messersmith not just the fulfillment of a longstanding conviction, but also his ticket out of Washington. So he had thought. The war emergency upset everything. His domestic and social life, meager to begin with, threatened to disappear altogether. Messersmith tried to make light of Marion's resentment and concern. "My wife," he reported to John Montgomery, "continues to threaten me with divorce if I am not able to spend more time at home, but I am trying to persuade her that it would be difficult to find someone who is really on the whole nicer than I am to live with!" Of course that was precisely her point; she wanted more of him. He was undoubtedly joking about divorce, but the strain on their relationship was no laughing matter.[141]

Thus, when the crisis abated at the State Department, Messersmith apparently petitioned for his transfer. A suitable spot soon presented itself. On 4 December 1939 Roosevelt's third ambassador to Cuba, J. Butler Wright, whose path had crossed Messersmith's over Prague, died suddenly at his post. Messersmith would have accepted most any offer, but he leaped at Cuba. Havana afforded extraordinary opportunity for influence—as much as any American embassy—at a tropical pace. Messersmith expected interesting but not terribly taxing work. He could "do a real job" without overexerting himself. Moreover, Cuba's proximity to home would presumably enable him to keep track of the European and administrative "problems which have absorbed me in recent years."[142]

Eminently satisfied, Messersmith hastened to tie loose ends, brush up his Spanish, and cram for the Cuban assignment. Any second thoughts about leaving vanished when he learned that his office was going to Breck Long, "one of the finest men I know, and if I could have selected my own successor I could not have chosen one in whom I have more confidence." By the end of January Messersmith had relinquished most of his duties. But he did not clear his desk until

Saturday before the Wednesday, 28 February 1940, that he and Marion boarded the SS *Oriente* in New York, Havana-bound. The press was on hand at the pier, and the *New York Times* ran his full-length portrait on page seven the following morning. Ever jaunty, stick in hand, a white carnation in his lapel—recent affectations—he was obviously happy to be returning to the field and escape from the job Long soon called "terrible" and Dean Acheson later described as "a perfect hell." The department had had its tribulations, to be sure. But Messersmith's worst problems were of his own making. He could have contented himself with daily administration and reform. He could have stayed out of policy controversies; he could have stopped provoking them. He did not, because he was Messersmith.[143]

☆ **V** ☆

Havana
1940–1942

There was to be little leisure for Messersmith in Havana, where he and his wife landed on 2 March 1940. The ranking embassy officer, First Secretary Willard Beaulac, made the mistake of greeting his new chief with a friendly warning about the local heat, which Messersmith, ever on guard against slackers, interpreted as a veiled suggestion that he relax his fabled work habits accordingly. In the unlikely event that that was Beaulac's scheme, Messersmith made him regret it. Washington, he snapped back, had been "much hotter than Havana," but good public servants overlooked such things. By May, he saw Beaulac's point. But the tropics, even at its sweltering worst, proved no match for the Messersmith conscience. "It keeps you working," scolded Breck Long, "when you ought to be playing." There was no finer place to play than Havana, Shangri-la for North American hedonists. Messersmith's only weakness was for the cigars, which he chewed to a pulp at his desk.[1]

As always, he was preoccupied with his mission. Roosevelt's previous envoys had found Cuban stability elusive, and the interventionist habit hard to break. The first of them, Sumner Welles, arrived in 1933 to an island in violent rebellion against dictator Gerardo Machado. Welles quickly arranged his ouster and replacement by the pliant Carlos Manuel de Cespedes. Three weeks later Cespedes was himself deposed in favor of the liberal nationalist Ramón Grau St. Martin. Welles took this as a personal challenge. At his frantic urging, United States warships and a battery of marines were despatched to Cuban waters. Washington refused to recognize Grau's government. The combination of North American hostility and the world depression proved too much for Grau, who was driven into exile. A series of weak civilian governments ensued. The real power on the island was increasingly behind the scenes, in the person of the army chief of staff, Colonel Fulgencio Batista, backed by the American ambassador, Jefferson Caffery, who succeeded Welles in late 1933 and carried on in his activist spirit. While the civilian government debated itself into irrelevance, Caffery and Batista, individually and as a team, came to control Cuba's destiny.[2]

Batista's advent opened a new era in Cuban-American relations. The Cuban army left the barracks to relieve the United States of police duty, for the sake of stability consistent with Good Neighborly nonintervention. Washington recognized the transition in 1934, when it abrogated the infamous Platt Amendment, its interventionist carte blanche, and honored Cuba with the first of Hull's reciprocal trade agreements. The duty on sugar, far and away its most important export, was cut 40 percent. Cuba enjoyed three years of relative prosperity as a result. But the 1938 crop was a disaster and the economy crashed. The threat of renewed unrest brought the State Department to a better appreciation of the fragility of Cuba's monoculture and the need for more diversified development. A program took shape in Washington that envisaged Eximbank loans and modifications in the trade agreement in order to open the mainland market to more Cuban products. J. Butler Wright, who had replaced the controversial Caffery in the 1937 shake-up, was charged with promoting this program in Havana.[3]

It was the Good Neighbor at its most enlightened. Although the United States stood to increase its already vast influence over the Cuban economy in the short term, State's program also promised eventually to reduce the island's dependence on sugar and American imports. As such, it would have been a significant concession to Cuban sovereignty and a major contribution to long-term stability.

But Washington could not resist a quid pro quo. When a Cuban trade delegation visited in early 1938, now Undersecretary Welles set stiff preconditions for American assistance. He insisted, first of all, that Cuba make permanent its Decree-Law 522. This gave American sugar interests control over the island's Sugar Stabilization Board, which set production quotas. Next, Welles said, Cuba would have to overhaul its corruption-ridden Treasury and Internal Revenue departments, and balance its budget. And it would have to settle with the American holders of some $85 million in Cuban public-works bonds. Grau had defaulted on these issues in 1933. While Cuba was flirting with national bankruptcy, the State Department had resisted the bondholders' demands to help them collect. Although hardly surfeited with cash, Cuba, in the department's view, was now sufficiently solvent to address its obligations.[4]

Cuba fell compliantly into line. In February 1938 the country floated bonds to retire all but $15 million of the public-works debt.

Wright pressed gently for liquidation of the balance. So did Welles, more emphatically, in Washington talks with Batista in November 1938. The result was an agreement with the remaining bondholders, subject to ratification by the Cuban Senate. Two days after Batista's departure, Welles announced that talks would soon begin on a supplementary Cuban-American trade agreement. Two Columbia University taxation experts were sent to troubleshoot Cuba's internal revenue system. The Eximbank president, Warren L. Pierson, toured the island with the Cuban secretary of public works examining proposals for new projects.[5]

Wright made the Good Neighbor a political reality as well. As a rule, he operated through regular channels at the Cuban State Department and the office of the civilian president, Federico Laredo Bru, rather than at rendezvous with Batista, which had been Caffery's practice. The charming and gregarious Wright trumpeted the "cooperation between equals" theme in his many speeches all over the island.[6]

Cubans professed to be appreciative, but they demonstrated it in a strange way. When American pressure eased, progress on the State Department's preconditions came to a dead halt. The Cuban Senate displayed no disposition whatsoever to take up the bondholders' relief bill. It was business as usual—corrupt—for Cuba's tax collectors, as the American suggestions for reform were politely ignored. Welles complained repeatedly to Cuban Ambassador Pedro Martínez Fraga, but his promises of "rapid action" on all fronts proved entirely worthless. In July 1939 the United States threatened to break off the trade talks unless Cuba mended its ways. Meanwhile the vicissitudes of the sugar market were playing extraordinary havoc with the island economy. Depressed throughout most of 1939, prices soared at the outbreak of war in Europe, plummeted when Roosevelt suspended sugar quotas (thereby raising Cuba's duty from .9 to 1.5 cents per pound), and revived in December, when the quotas were restored and a stopgap supplementary trade agreement was signed.[7]

Economic instability translated into victory for the anti-Batista parties in the November 1939 elections for a constituent assembly, which was to draft a new constitution and schedule general elections. In a field of eleven, the Cuban Revolutionary Party, better known as the Auténticos, came out on top. That was the party of Grau, whose triumphant return from four years abroad made him the odds-on favorite for president. The United States now had reason to fear a radical new Cuban constitution and a hostile new Cuban chief of state. On 6 December Batista resigned from the army and declared his candidacy, but many were predicting a Batista coup unless Batista's electoral prospects improved.[8]

Wright's sudden death on 4 December had no discernable impact on this situation, which was to his credit. A Batista-Grau agreement to a 14 July election day cleared the air somewhat. Cubans seemed almost disappointed when Messersmith arrived and made no attempt to impose a political settlement. Despite Wright's twenty-seven months of aloofness, Cubans had been conditioned over four decades to count on American intervention when they got themselves into trouble. From the moment Messersmith set foot on Cuban soil, politicians hounded him for his endorsement. The former president, Mario Menocal, who led the third largest bloc of delegates to the constituent assembly, called on him to inquire as to whom the United States wished him to support for president.[9]

Messersmith told Menocal and the others exactly what he was saying in public: that the United States was entirely impartial and would "not intervene in any way directly or indirectly in the electoral situation." But the politicians paid him no mind. They took for granted, he wrote Breck Long in amazement, "that we say this for public consumption, but, in fact, try to run the show from the inside." When these same politicians returned to the campaign trail alluding to their new "connections" at the American embassy, Messersmith learned yet another fact of Cuban political life: "everything which [the American ambassador] says or does is used or misused to serve personal interests when it can be done."[10]

He thus exercised "great care" in his initial approaches to the government. Economic relations were still hung up over the $15 million outstanding to American bondholders. As far as the State Department was concerned, Cuba's whole good faith and credit rode on passage of the settlement bill. Messersmith did not relish having "to begin my stay here by being a bill collector," but, as he told Laredo Bru and the secretary of state, Miguel Angel Campa, on 15 March, the claims themselves were secondary. Economic development required "the maintenance and re-establishment of Cuban credit and the confidence of the American business community here and in the United States." Cuba, Messersmith said, had a splendid opportunity to show potential investors that it took its obligations seriously.[11]

The trouble was that he was speaking to the wrong people. Laredo Bru and Campa were "thoroughly understanding," but they were very lame ducks. With great effort the president did manage to get the settlement bill moved up on the Senate calendar. On the scheduled day, however, that august body failed to raise a quorum, even though, wrote Messersmith indignantly, "there were sufficient Senators in the lobby" to do so. Messersmith finally spoke to Batista, who got to the heart of the problem. It was a sad fact, the Cuban said, but the senators expected to be bribed, and were quite prepared to watch the island's credit sink until they were taken care of. Batista said that he personally deplored this, but recommended that the American creditors pay up, so that Cuban-American cooperation" could proceed. When Messersmith indignantly replied that such a thing was unthinkable, Batista smoothly agreed that there was a fine line between realism and cynicism, adding that he welcomed the ambassador's support for his own anticorruption drive.[12]

Messersmith wanted to believe him. But the weeks wore on with still no sign of legislative action. "For a dictator," he wrote suspiciously of Batista on 19 April, "he is proceeding with unusual caution and restraint" in trying to get action out of his senators. At first Messersmith was inclined to attribute Batista's behavior to campaign politics. Although aligned with Grau in the constituent assembly, Menocal, after Messersmith sent him away, had gone out and made his best deal, endorsing Batista for president. Batista stalwarts were complaining about the high price in patronage promised for Menocal's support; and the candidate, Messersmith hypothesized generously, probably concluded that it was no time to start depriving his senators of their graft as well. But by summer, with the settlement no nearer, Messersmith stopped making excuses for him, depicting Batista as the arch corruptionist rather than the pragmatic reformer. The legislators, he was finally convinced, were obeying, not defying, their leader in holding the settlement bill for ransom.[13]

He also informed the State Department that venality and demagoguery were running riot at the constituent assembly, in session since 9 February. Messersmith's own expectation—hope—of a conservative new constitution was bitterly disappointed. Instead, the assembly, with Grau presiding, turned out a string of provisions Messersmith sourly judged "worse than anything Soviet Russia produced at its worst." Articles proscribing large land holdings, restricting land ownership by foreigners and creditors' rights, all threatened, in his irritated opinion, to make Lázaro Cárdenas's Mexico "seem like a paradise for capital" by comparison. Worse was to come. In late May the assembly took up the last item on its agenda: a measure suspending service on private debts until 1942 and forever thereafter except when sugar prices were abnormally high. Assembly leaders did not fail to include special immunities for themselves.[14]

The proposed moratorium caused consternation up north. A committee of New York bankers threatened to "remonstrate" with Cuba personally unless the State Department did so for them. To many concerned Americans the moratorium looked like a deliberate Cuban provocation.

On orders from Washington, Messersmith spoke to Laredo Bru and Batista on 28 May. Emphasizing that he was not making representations, but simply "friendly observations based on our deep interest in Cuban credit," Messersmith warned against alienating American capital when Europe was at war and incapable of filling the fiscal void. As before, Laredo Bru was sympathetic but powerless; and Batista, notwithstanding his pledge of assistance, was sure to "do nothing," Messersmith predicted, "in spite of all that I have tried to convey to him" because the moratorium was something "he has been advocating constantly."[15]

At 3 A.M. on 29 May, the assembly, by a vote of 49 to 7, adopted the moratorium. Messersmith was "unhappy," but he had done everything within his power short of "direct involvement." First Secretary Beaulac, on the other hand, believed that a strong response was now necessary to dispel the "theory which is widely held in the Cuban Government that the United States is so anxious not to have trouble with Cuba, for the sake of inter-American solidarity, that it will accept almost any affront rather than openly protest." He urged retaliation, suggesting renunciation of the reciprocal trade agreement.[16]

Messersmith passed the idea along to Washington unenthusiastically. He pointed out that the trade agreement was worth a lot more in dollars to the United States than to Cuba, and advised Washington not to ignore its immediate self-interest. Moreover, he warned, unilateral abrogation would be interpreted in Cuba and the rest of the Americas as a return to the "Big Stick." If the United States was serious about Cubans taking charge of their own destiny, he wrote on 1 June, it would have to forebear Cuban mistakes. At least the island republic was finally getting a constitution that, upon sober study, seemed not quite so bad as Messersmith had originally thought. It included basic safeguards for property and contracts—no small achievement given the anticapitalist atmosphere of the assembly. Nor had the delegates discriminated: 12,000 small Cuban creditors, not American bankers, he observed, promised to be hardest hit by the moratorium.[17]

Accordingly, Washington turned the other cheek. The failure of the settlement bill and the 1940 constitution were obstacles to economic cooperation, but Messersmith and the State Department wished to avoid crises, not start them. Beaulac's analysis was on the mark. Cubans had come to learn that they could act with unprecedented impunity toward the United States provided that they played along regarding hemispheric security. This Cuba was unquestionably doing. In May the State Department had engaged the American Republics individually in defense discussions. Ambassador Martínez Fraga could not have been more forthcoming. In June an American military mission arrived in Havana for secret exploratory talks with Laredo Bru, Batista, and Colonel José Pedraza, the new army chief of staff. Messersmith reported that the talks "went even better than . . . expected," ending in "complete agreement in principle on all points raised." The details were to be worked out in staff conferences set for August.[18]

Military cooperation bought Cuba the continued indulgence of the United States in the political and economic spheres, which, in Washington's view, the islanders were exploiting to the hilt. Beaulac's contention was that such crass reciprocity was "not a healthy basis for future cooperation." He argued that the United States could not let the Cubans, ninety miles from the mainland, simply mishandle their affairs. Cuban cooperation would be meaningless if the country went to pieces internally.[19]

This was persuasive. But Messersmith was not yet ready to abandon the policy of hands-off, a policy that suited his current mood. Within a few weeks after his arrival he could agree with Beaulac on at least one point beyond the climate: Cuban politicians, he concluded, were more self-serving and pettifogging than even the worst of the Nazis. Very well, he wrote Long, "but they will find"—as the Nazis had—"that it is a very difficult thing to wear me down."[20]

Yet they did wear him down, in spirit if not in body. The immorality and incompetence in public affairs that made Beaulac fighting mad made the still unseasoned Messersmith recoil in disgust. His reports to Washington were as exhaustive as ever during his first months in Cuba, but they betrayed his unhappiness with where he was and a longing to be out and back into what he called "the big picture." Despite occasional infusions of departmental gossip from friends like Long, he still felt "very far away from things." More and more his thoughts centered on the future after what he hoped would be a very brief "interlude" in Havana. In the meantime he wrote a friend with a twinge of self-pity that he was doing his best to bear up under the demoralizing circumstances. "Were it not that the defense of the Americas is so vital to us and that Cuba is in some respects a key country in this picture," he confessed, "I would be very unhappy indeed being here [rather than] in the front trenches."[21]

If this was malaise, the fall of France and the Low Countries snapped Messersmith out of it. A German attack on the Dutch,

French, and British colonies in the Western hemisphere became a live possibility. Berlin denied any such intentions, which told Messersmith that the danger was real. The "Monroe Doctrine," he wrote Hull, as he had been writing him for years, "has always made them see red." Now Germany was poised to challenge for control of the New World, just as Göring had vowed to him in 1933. "We are already at war," Messersmith excitedly wrote Long on 26 June, "because Germany is at war with us." Nazi aggression had placed him where he wanted to be: in the "front trenches" of the battle for civilization.[22]

In long, impassioned, even panicky "Observations" to the State Department dated 3 June, Messersmith pronounced the hemispheric situation "critical." Militarily "not a single one [of the republics] is in a position to defend itself." The security implications of government corruption seem to have suddenly dawned on him: politicians throughout the hemisphere were ready to "jump aboard the German bandwagon" for the right price. Ethnic Germans and Italians, an especially influential minority in Argentina, Chile, and Brazil, would need no bribes. Messersmith feared that in order to get Gibraltar back, Franco would join the Axis and take Latin opinion with him. As it was, the myth of German invincibility was gaining ground. Hitler's diplomats and propaganda were energetically extolling the opportunities presented by the enlarged German market, a siren song for the impoverished Latins.[23]

Moreover, Messersmith was "not optimistic" about conditions inside his own bailiwick. Cuban opinion seemed dedicated to solidarity with the democracies, but fifth columnists were a problem. "There are people here," he declared, "who are potentially excellent Nazis, and the Germans know who they are and are in touch with them." The crumbling economy furnished a favorable medium for sedition. The loss of European markets hit hard. Credit was drying up due to the moratorium. Government revenues plunged, as imports from the United States, which entered at lower duty, substituted for those from Asia and Europe. Rumors had government workers going unpaid. Those in a position to fill their own pockets hastened to do so before the source gave out.[24]

What was worse, these political thieves were, according to Messersmith, taking cues from Batista, who would "be elected or at least in some way become President of Cuba" when the polls closed on 14 July. The ambassador was sure this spelled trouble for the United States. Batista had been an obstinate "ruler from behind the scenes," and Messersmith surmised that "he will be much more difficult to deal with once he is President." Although he professed "great friend-

ship" for the United States, "basically I do not believe that he likes us
or ever will." Most American-owned businesses were resisting his demands for campaign contributions, "very properly refusing to be
shaken down," but "I think we can take it for granted that this will
not make him feel any better towards American interests." Forced to
dip increasingly into his already "sizeable" ill-gotten personal fortune, Batista was betting that as president he would be "in a better
position than ever to recoup" at American expense. The governing
principle of a Batista administration, Messersmith forecast, would be
to "try to get as much out of us as he can" in exchange for continued
Cuban military cooperation.[25]

Messersmith did what he could to reverse these ominous trends.
Convinced that German inroads owed largely to ignorance of "the
physical, moral, economic, and religious bondage which Fascist regi-
mentation imposes," he undertook in several well-publicized speeches
to set the record straight. He particularly cautioned against Nazi economic blandishments, and exhorted his colleagues in other American capitals to do the same. The Latins had to be reminded that
the United States was their "only solvent customer"; that German
promises "cannot be fulfilled"; that any nation "allowing itself to be
tempted" would find "economic slavery [which] will rapidly turn itself into political slavery."[26]

But Messersmith considered talk "worthless" without active United
States leadership. "We must make our strength known," he counseled
the State Department, "and impress it constantly upon the American
Republics." "Appropriate arrangements to support their economies"
were imperative. The hemispheric cartel under discussion in Washington, designed to supervise the joint marketing of major exports,
won his vocal approval.[27]

In the meantime, the republics had to be organized and armed.
The American foreign ministers were not scheduled to meet again
until December, in Havana, but there was provision for advancing
that date in an emergency. This option, he wrote Hull on 15 June,
should be "promptly" invoked to get the Latins "committed in principle unequivocally to all the action which is involved in inter-American cooperation, which must now enter the military phase." In a conference setting, under peer pressure, no Latin republic, Messersmith
believed, not even contrary Argentina, "could stand out from mutu-
ally agreeing to military aid to the others and from accepting all
kinds of military aid from us." Two days later, American mission
chiefs in the hemisphere were instructed to propose holding the Havana foreign ministers conference at "the first possible moment."
This turned out to be 21 July.[28]

Even as Messersmith entered into marathon negotiations with the Cuban State Department and representatives of the Pan American Union over the Havana agenda, the hemispheric situation continued to deteriorate. In a 10 June speech Brazilian dictator Getulio Vargas had ridiculed "the sterile demagogy of political democracy," calling upon "virile people to comprehend the new epoch." A regular purchaser of German arms, Vargas was reported to be actively pursuing expanded trade with the Reich. Yet, by the end of June, the idea of the American-sponsored cartel had been all but abandoned at the insistence of the incurable free-trader Hull. Argentina was its normal recalcitrant self. In accepting its invitation to Havana, Buenos Aires made it clear that it would not be party to resolutions compromising its neutrality. As some of Argentina's neighbors were expected to follow its lead, this did not bode well for the conference.[29]

Messersmith advised "fighting fire with fire." The Latins had to be warned that the United States much preferred their cooperation, but would act unilaterally and ruthlessly in self-defense. "This is a struggle for existence," he wrote Laurence Duggan, chief of the division of American Republics, "which may necessitate a return to the Big Stick"; Washington must reserve the right to intervene wherever hemispheric security was endangered. If any American government chose to consort with Berlin, "we have got to see that such a Government does not live." Merely threatening to boycott Brazilian coffee, he trusted, would bring Vargas to his senses.[30]

And it was time to stop coddling Cuba. Sounding very much like Beaulac a month earlier, Messersmith urged "a stronger and firmer stand here" to disabuse local politicians of the conviction that they "can get away with anything." Their "new alibi" for not taking up the settlement bill was maddeningly typical: because the Havana conference was supposed to assemble in the Senate chambers, the senators had no place to meet. Now "we will be told very solemnly that the Congress will settle the obligations matter as soon as the Conference is over." Smugly confident in American credulity and concern for Cuban stability, Batista was openly predicting that economic assistance was on its way nonetheless. "He is playing with us," Messersmith fumed, "and what is worse, he feels that he is getting away with it." Unless "we stick by our guns," refusing even to discuss the question of aid until Cuba did its part, "we can look forward to continued blackmail of our Government and of the United States interests here." The State Department assured him that it was not contemplating softening its stand.[31]

There followed slow but definite improvement in the Cuban and the larger hemispheric pictures. On 14 July Cubans went to the polls.

As predicted, Batista emerged the victor. Although this produced no joy in Washington, the near absence of violence and electoral chicanery was a comfort. A week later the Havana conference opened. Hull, with Messersmith serving as his personal assistant, managed in the end to secure Argentine assent to the conference's final act and convention. In this the republics unanimously endorsed the no-transfer principle of the Monroe Doctrine, and authorized preemptive intervention by the United States. It was a major diplomatic coup and a great personal triumph for Hull.[32]

On 30 July, the day before the conference adjourned, Hull, accompanied by Messersmith, paid a courtesy call on Laredo Bru, whose term was up in October. Hull thanked the Cuban president for his efforts on behalf of the settlement bill, emphasizing how vital it was for "orderly and stable governments," particularly governments seeking financial assistance, to meet their obligations.[33]

The message got through to Batista. On the threshold of presidential power, he was already preoccupied with retaining it. Some observers were giving him no more than six months in which to turn the economy around before Cubans took the situation into their own hands. Because there could be no recovery without United States economic aid, nothing further was to be gained, and much was to be lost, by holding the settlement bill hostage. Self-survival, Messersmith noted on 8 August, had "forced [Batista] into a position of giving [it] his full approval."[34]

The politicians, however, proved obdurate. Batista enjoined them to act, but, Messersmith reported on 15 August, "these hungry members of Congress are frankly saying that for many of them it is their last chance, and that they are poor people and must be paid for voting for this bill!" Claiming to be at his wits' end, Batista enlisted Messersmith to help spread the word that there would be no payoffs. The ambassador invited the solons to the American embassy in small groups for drinks. After a low-keyed plea for the debt settlement, he steered the conversation to the international situation. The congressmen, he wrote later, appreciated being spoken to "as though they were statesmen." On 4 September, with only two dissenting votes, the Cuban Senate passed the bill.[35]

The next day Messersmith sailed home for talks at the State Department. When Beaulac reported the signing of the settlement bill, Cuba was formally invited to send a mission to Washington to "deal comprehensively with United States–Cuban economic relations." The agenda mapped out over two years earlier—agricultural diversification, revisions in the trade agreement, and Eximbank financing for a "moderate and largely self-liquidating" public works program—was dusted off.[36]

Cuba grabbed the invitation. But the four-man mission that arrived on 5 October had its own agenda. Their leader, Martínez Fraga (an active grafter, according to Messersmith) had gained Batista's confidence and kept his Washington post by telling Batista what he wanted to hear: that the United States was "eager and over-eager to lend money to Cuba and that Cuba could have any sum she wanted for the asking," no strings attached. Without stopping to confirm this with Messersmith, Batista decided that $50 million was a nice, round figure, and had got his Senate to authorize a loan in that amount. On 14 October Martínez Fraga handed Welles the details of Cuba's request. Ten of the $50 million was intended to defray Cuba's current budget deficit and shortfalls anticipated in the coming fiscal year. The rest was earmarked for a congeries of Batista pet projects: hospitals, roads, and the purchase of land for a national park.[37]

Back in Havana for Batista's inauguration, Messersmith recommended outright rejection of the Cuban proposal. To do otherwise, he wrote Welles, would be a "betrayal of Cuba, . . . our own taxpayers, . . . and our interests." Cuba, he charged, had a budget deficit only because the politicians had looted the treasury for campaign funds and pork-barrel projects; a loan to cover the shortfall was sure to "stimulate increased and even more irresponsible spending." The proposed "public works" amounted to installments on Batista's political debts, projects with "vast potential" for fraud. Among them was a partially completed tuberculosis hospital, construction of which had been forced to a halt by the "disappearance" of half the allocated funds. The road projects, ostensibly for the island's defenses, were meant to enhance the value of certain real estate. Other personages stood to profit handsomely in transactions for the national park. Messersmith thought it "interesting that even supporters of the Government express fear of the misuse which would be made of money which we might give to Cuba without what they call adequate safeguards." Patriotic Cubans, people who yearned for honest government, "are hoping that we will not let them down."[38]

Messersmith's stand made the "hungry" politicians frantic, and none more than Martínez Fraga, who continued to report pie-in-the-sky progress in his loan negotiations. Messersmith's outspoken opposition was Havana's first indication that all was not well in Washington. Martínez Fraga apparently tried to have him recalled for unspecified "insolence," as though Messersmith were the only obstacle to his success. When on 4 December Welles formally presented the

American response, Martínez Fraga's fortunes and Cuban dreams of vast new largesse came crashing down. Categorically rejecting the Cuban request, Welles demanded an immediate 10 percent budget cut, administrative reforms, new agricultural studies, and extension of Decree-Law 522. When Cuba met these conditions, Welles said, the Eximbank was prepared to consider up to $10 million in agricultural credits and closely supervised public works. In an "acrimonious" 9 December telephone conversation with his ambassador, Batista expressed "dissatisfaction and disappointment" with these results, Messersmith reported. Martínez Fraga tendered his resignation, and it was accepted.[39]

A week later, Batista's secretary of state, José M. Cortina, sought to make a fresh start. In talks with Messersmith, he admitted that the Cuban government had operated under certain misconceptions concerning American attitudes, which he blamed on Martínez Fraga. He promised an improvement in the new Cuban ambassador to Washington, Aurelio F. Concheso, and begged for American economic aid. Diversification and public works were essential to the island's economic future, Cortina said, but the current sugar crisis demanded immediate remediation. The loss of world markets had forced the sugar board to limit 1941 production to 2 million tons, which would mean mass layoffs in the fields and mills. Eximbank financing for an additional 500,000 tons, he continued, would stabilize the situation and consolidate Batista's position. Only with popular support, he added, could Batista proceed with the sure-to-be-bitter battle against official corruption.[40]

Messersmith was sympathetic. He had objected to Martínez Fraga's $50 million loan primarily because little of that money, he knew, would reach the average Cuban. He differentiated between the politicians' proposals and "our doing something to aid the Cuban people." Additional sugar financing fell into the latter category, for, as he told Washington, it "would go almost entirely into the payment of wages," averting "economic disaster for Cuba" and certain political unrest. The local Communists had gained legal status for having backed candidate Batista, and were already using it to undermine him and pro-Allied feeling, "making a lot of trouble here," Messersmith reported, "exploiting the rural laborers and the poorer people of the cities," who figured to get poorer still without outside relief. More than ever, Batista needed "propping up" to survive, and Messersmith now considered his survival a matter of prime importance to the United States. Not that, in the ambassador's eyes, the presidency had transformed Batista overnight into any paragon of strength, judgment, or rectitude. Politics, not the island's problems, remained his chief preoccupation. To Messersmith's disgust, Batista had appointed cabinet officers "with no real regard for their particular competence for their jobs." Cubans had the idea that they had elected themselves a caudillo, but the Batista the ambassador knew was "a timid man [who] feels himself insecure."[41]

In Messersmith's judgment, though, there were sufficient offsetting positives. As before, Cuban military cooperation was complete. September staff talks had committed the Cuban government to "full use" of its territory for hemispheric defense. And the law of averages came into play: at least two cabinet members, as it turned out, could be counted upon to talk sense to Batista. One was Carlos Saladrigas, a conservative lawyer now prime minister; the other was Cortina, "highly intelligent and friendly to the United States," who was encouraging Batista to crack down on Nazis and Communists. Cortina insisted that Batista's government could not submit to the State Department's preconditions for assistance and "hope to live," and Messersmith believed him. He agreed to present Cuba's case for sugar financing personally in Washington and to convey Cortina's "categorical assurances" that all of the administrative reforms the department desired would be promptly implemented as soon as Batista could safely do so.[42]

In Washington on 8 January 1941, Messersmith advised the State Department to accept these assurances and to provide Cuba with immediate sugar relief and a general commitment on long-term aid. If the sugar emergency worsened, he argued, Batista's government "may well fall, and we will see it replaced by no better a one," and perhaps a worse one. The fact was that "this is the first constitutional Government which Cuba has had for seven years"; Batista's overthrow would be a severe setback for democracy and hemispheric stability. Those extra sugars, he trusted, would undoubtedly not go to waste. In the meantime, Cuban purchasing power and an $80-million-a-year market for American exports would be protected.[43]

Messersmith brought quick—if, for Cuba, mixed—results. He returned to the island on 14 January carrying an Eximbank offer to finance 400,000 additional tons at $3.25 per hundred-pound bag, interest to be fixed at 3.6 percent and secured by a six-cent-per-bag production tax. The bank, against Messersmith's advice, insisted on renewal in advance of Decree-Law 522. The Cuban government, Beaulac reported, "exhibited an extraordinary sensitiveness" on that point; Cortina "deeply regretted" the bank's refusal to finance the entire requested 500,000 tons; the growers grumbled over the offered price; a six-cent tax had already been earmarked by the Cuban treasury for other needs. Still, Cuba's immediate problem was being resolved, and for this, Cortina told Messersmith, he was "deeply appreciative." After a little haggling, the bank even agreed to increase the purchase price to $4 a bag. A struggle between large and small growers for representation on the sugar board delayed action on the authorizing legislation, but Messersmith, "working intensely" with Cortina and Saladrigas, finally prevailed. The bill Batista signed on 21 March was, as Messersmith noted with satisfaction, "a sound measure with practically no extraneous provisions in it, and no one was bought off and no special interest groups were satisfied to secure [its] passage." Messersmith considered the measure "a milestone on a road which we are endeavoring solidly to construct."[44]

But, as he made clear to Cortina, Eximbank development aid was contingent on Cuba's "cleaning house." By late January, Messersmith could report real progress in that direction. His appetite whetted by American sugar aid, Batista declared war—selectively—on official corruption and mismanagement. He singled out the armed forces, where there was plenty of both; but more because he feared Colonel Pedraza as a rival, possibly out to subordinate him as he, Batista, had subordinated Laredo Bru. Messersmith applauded Batista's dismissal of corrupt officers and his cuts in the military budget. He did not notice the army-Batista showdown in the making.[45]

For Pedraza the last straw was Batista's firing of his friend, the chief of the national police, Colonel Bernardo García. One scholar reconstructs the record to show that García was fired when implicated in an illegal lottery scheme. Messersmith's despatches tell a different story: that García's mistake was protesting *Batista's* involvement in the lotteries.

In any case, the die was now cast in the Batista-Pedraza feud, as both sides spurned Messersmith's offer to mediate. For the first three days of February, he recalled in his memoirs, Batista was "practically a prisoner in the Palace." On the 3rd Messersmith reported "a real danger of revolution which may or may not involve civic strife." But Pedraza did not move, and Batista seized the initiative. At 4 A.M. on the 4th, he left the presidential palace and drove to the main barracks at nearby Camp Columbia to make a dramatic personal appeal to the troops. While Pedraza slept at home in Havana, the army was submitting to its commander in chief. Messersmith was awakened by a message from Batista assuring him that the situation was under control, asking him to arrange flights to Miami and exile for Pedraza and two associates. Batista was back in the capital by mid-morning. He looked "utterly fatigued" at his 11 A.M. meeting with Messersmith, but satisfaction also registered, for, as he told the ambassador, the insurrection had been put down with the loss of exactly one drop of blood: Batista had pricked his own thumb on a button wire.[46]

"On the whole," Messersmith wrote Welles the next day, "it was one of the most interesting . . . series of events I have passed through." The department invited him to withdraw and consolidate the six cables sent during the crisis, but he refused, not wanting to "give the historian later a wrong impression of the degree and promptness with which we had informed the Department."[47]

Most of all, Messersmith acquired new respect for Batista, who had "gained tremendously in stature" in Cuban eyes and his own. Batista had displayed a self-confidence and courage that Messersmith never imagined he possessed, not only in subduing the rebels, but also in sparing their lives. In the ensuing weeks, Messersmith's estimation of him rose still higher. Batista's anticorruption campaign expanded into the civilian sector, and before long Messersmith was reporting a clear improvement in public administration. A customs house reorganization was expected to raise $1 million a year in additional revenue. Seven million dollars in new taxes were levied. A special presidential commission was set up to study fiscal reform and to review the budget. In contrast to the dragged-out battle for the public-works settlement, a bill providing compensation to the American owners of expropriated land sailed through the Senate. Without hesitation, without even attempting to bargain, Cuba granted permission to the United States Navy to enlarge the Guantánamo facility and to conduct maneuvers on Cuban soil. Cortina told Messersmith that Cuba was preparing to raise 300,000 troops for an American war effort, and that Batista had ordered all officers to learn English. A measure outlawing the Communist party was being drawn up. Effective anti-Fascist decrees had already taken effect. In suppressing Axis propaganda and apprehending Axis agents, Messersmith concluded on 25 February, Cuba was "going further . . . than any other American Republic . . . further even than ourselves." After a year to the day in Havana, he could "safely say that on the whole we have good reason to be satisfied with developments in Cuba."[48]

Considering what had been, this was no small understatement. The year 1940 had been a critical and eventful one in the two countries' relations. The new constitution and Batista's unsullied election had set the stage for constructive diplomacy. Martínez Fraga's removal advanced Cuban-American understanding. Batista had been somewhat sobered by his high office.

And Messersmith had made an important contribution. Once he had adjusted to the way Cubans did business and began taking a personal interest in his mission, he became a tireless fighter for the American program. Now it was he who was wearing down the local politicians rather than the reverse. In the process, in achieving the public-works settlement and the sugar authorization act, political nonintervention became almost a dead letter. Pausing to ask himself "how I can be so occupied in this little country," Messersmith decided that it was hard getting "things done in the interest of both countries without giving the appearance of our meddling in internal affairs." Appearances were all that mattered anymore. From 1937 until the spring of 1940 the United States had gradually returned Cuban sovereignty to Cuba in exchange for Cuban military cooperation. What the Cubans did with their sovereignty after being without it for so long was predictably discomfiting to Washington. Faced with Cuba apparently coming apart at the seams just when the European war seemed ready to engulf the Western hemisphere, the United States resorted once more to imposing its own discipline. With the State Department's tacit approval, Messersmith began playing a more active role in the Cuban picture, taking advantage of Cuba's basic dependence upon the United States. Even during the time of political laissez-faire, Cuba had not been allowed to forget its economic vulnerability. But after Batista's election, the pressure was applied more forcefully and more successfully. Finding that American aid was not his for the asking, as Martínez Fraga had led him to believe, Batista, hungry for himself and for his country, simply submitted to American demands in order to get what he wanted. Cuba obediently passed the public-works settlement, renewed Decree-Law 522, and undertook various administrative reforms that pleased the United States and, not incidentally, helped Batista consolidate his power. He may have loved Americans no more than before, but he had learned to do a convincing impersonation of the loyal ally.[49]

He certainly convinced Messersmith, who in April 1941 proudly certified to Roosevelt and the State Department that Cuba's behavior was such as "to warrant our proceeding without delay" with an Eximbank development program. Home for consultation, he "appeared satisfied" with the decision to recommend a $25 million credit for public works and agricultural diversification. Eximbank approval, he reported on 8 May, was "deeply appreciated by this friendly people who feel themselves bound to us by unseverable ties."[50]

Having aimed "to make Cuba as little as possible a source of preoccupation to us at home," Messersmith soon had reason to feel that he had perhaps succeeded too well. Cuba seemed forgotten once solidly in tow. The economic aid program was exasperatingly slow getting started. The State Department, without shame, discovered new financial claims against Cuba to be settled first; the Eximbank officials needed in Havana to draw up the contracts and approve the initial projects were scattered all over the hemisphere on more pressing assignments. Other American actions seemed positively calculated to harm Cuba economically and to bruise Cuban feelings. In Washington the Senate passed the O'Mahoney bill, raising duties on imported sugar. At the same time, the United States Navy, with new Caribbean bases to supply, withdrew the liner *Oriente* and her refrigerated cargo hold from the New York–Havana service, throttling tourism and a promising export trade in perishable produce. To add insult to injury, the War Department ignored Havana's military overtures and steadily opposed arms transfers to Cuba under the Lend-Lease Act of 11 March 1941.[51]

After doing everything to deserve Washington's consideration and cash, Cubans were resentful, and Messersmith was on their side. As always, he spoke up. "I do not want to make myself a nuisance," he wrote, doing just that, in his second letter in a week to the Eximbank president Pierson, begging his presence in Havana. In letters to his State Department superiors, Messersmith blew off steam at the War Department's "incompetence." He objected to State's "alleged [financial] claims," which were "dubious" and beneath the embassy's dignity. Pressing them, he warned, "would tend seriously to prejudice our moral position in Cuba." On 5 June he informed Hull that the *Oriente* withdrawal and the O'Mahoney Act had aroused "grave fears and resentment . . . in other American republics as well as here," furnishing "food for attacks to all the unreasonable elements." "Single acts of this kind," he reminded Welles in two separate letters that very same day, "can go far towards causing infinite harm [to] our whole good neighbor program . . . and our own defense." He urged some "gesture of reassurance" to Havana.[52]

He got it. The State Department agreed to drop the financial claims. At Hull's urging, the administration rallied to secure House rejection of the O'Mahoney measure. Cuban-American military cooperation perked up. Lend-lease talks got underway in Washington. On 7 November Ambassador Concheso signed an agreement providing Cuba with $7.2 million in military materiel. The navy bestirred itself to get on with the Guantánamo negotiations. Batista's longstanding offer of air bases finally found takers: in July Welles got together with Army Chief of Staff George C. Marshall and Navy Chief of Operations Harold R. Stark to review potential Cuban sites.[53]

Best of all, on 12 June Pierson arrived with his team of experts. At noon the next day, in what Messersmith described as a "simple and appropriate" public ceremony at the presidential palace, Pierson signed the sugar contracts. The $25 million development credit was all the talk at the embassy dinner that evening and at meetings the following day. Pierson delivered a homily on morality in public administration, urging Cubans to choose projects that made economic as well as political sense. Pierson's advisers stayed behind to continue negotiating with Cuban counterparts.[54]

With the loan program on track, attention turned to a related issue, long-deferred revisions in the Cuban-American trade agreement. Because the United States had now committed $25 million to Cuban economic renewal, the islanders reasonably assumed that Washington would grant the tariff concessions its own experts deemed vital to the program's success.[55]

As always, sugar topped the Cubans' list. With rising freight charges and labor costs, Cuban sugar was pricing itself out of the American market. To restore its competitiveness, Cuba requested a 17 percent reduction—from .90 cent per pound to .75—in American duties. Cuba sought stability through a permanent minimum quota, in effect a guaranteed share of the American market. To avert what he called "the greatest crisis . . . in the history" of the Cuban cigar industry, Cortina petitioned for a minimum annual quota of 20 million cigars duty-free. Moreover, he claimed that Cuba's fledgling cattle industry faced "ruin" unless the United States provided an immediate outlet for Cuban beef that could not be consumed domestically "due to the bad economic condition of the country."[56]

On 27 September the State Department responded, and Cuba got a shock. The American counterproposals included the .75 cent sugar duty but no permanent quota; a reduction in the beef duty but no emergency quota; and reductions in tobacco duties but no concession on cigars. In return the United States wanted concessions on thirty-nine items ranging from razor blades to packing crates. Some of Washington's demands were especially irksome. Before 1937 most of Cuba's rice, its basic foodstuff, came from the Far East. By 1941, 90 percent of it came in from the United States at half the duty. The difference was $1 million a year to the Cuban treasury. The United States now wanted still lower duties and a permanent quota to protect its exporters from the inevitable revival of Asian competition. It wanted a concession on tires and inner tubes just when two new Cuban rubber factories were going into operation. It wanted a concession on cigarettes despite the admitted plight of the island's tobacco industry.[57]

In October Washington added yet another condition inimical to the diversified development it was supposedly sponsoring. Whatever the point in demanding tariff reductions on products soon to be rationed, vital strategic considerations underlay the bid to purchase Cuba's entire 1942 sugar crop. Sugar was one of many essential goods now being stockpiled for war by Secretary of Commerce Jesse H. Jones's Reconstruction Finance Corporation and subsidiary agencies in cooperation with the State Department. Back in Havana after two months of vacationing on the Delaware shore, Messersmith was instructed to propose the purchase to Cortina, emphasizing what "a splendid opportunity [it] was for the Cuban Government and the sugar industry to implement their assurances of cooperation." If this was not persuasive enough, he was to make clear that the trade agreement talks, "although separate, are in fact closely related to the purchase proposal"—that is, that Cuba would receive tariff concessions only to the extent that it cooperated on the sugar sale.[58]

Based on experience, Cuba was well advised to approach the sale with caution. Similar transactions with the United States during World War I had burned Cuba badly. Selling at a fixed, discount price in return for a guaranteed market, Cubans had then resentfully watched Washington turn around to resell the sugar abroad at a profit. Meanwhile, soaring import prices were snuffing out a brief boom. Worse still was a prolonged postwar depression, as the overstimulated sugar industry suffered a precipitous drop in demand.[59]

Cubans wanted safeguards this time around, and Messersmith urged that Cuba get them. The United States, he wrote Hull on 27 October, needed the sugar, but "we must keep in mind the problems we are creating for Cuba" in fostering expansion and disrupting diversification. Cuba would therefore insist on a multiyear contract and, above all, the permanent quota already rejected by the State Department. As such a quota would help cushion the inevitable postwar contraction, Messersmith concluded, "it is the equitable thing for us to do." Cortina was talking in terms of pegging the purchase price to the cost of Cuba's vital imports. Messersmith was "strongly impressed by the reasonableness of this point of view." And Cuba's proposal that resale profits, if any, be divided equally struck him as "eminently fair."[60]

Because Washington paid him no heed, the talks that opened there on 12 November foundered fast. Convinced that Cuba had to sell, the American negotiators were surprised when the Cubans insisted on their price and the safeguards Messersmith advocated. The Americans accused the Cubans of being "unreasonable." On 26 November they returned to Havana for "reflection."[61]

Two developments broke the logjam. The first week in December,

Washington yielded to the major Cuban demands. It granted the division of profits and minimum sugar quota, and came up with an acceptable money offer: 2.65 cents per pound for the entire 1942 crop, less domestic needs and 65,000 tons for export elsewhere.[62]

Tentative agreement was thus in place when Pearl Harbor blew up. First thing Monday morning, 8 December 1941, Cortina told Messersmith formally that his government viewed Japan's attack "as an attack against Cuba and as against every one of the American states." Batista volunteered Cuba's "absolute and decided cooperation . . . and solidarity." The island government promptly declared war on the Axis, even though, as Messersmith reminded State, "Cuba is practically defenseless and open to attack." More materially, Batista squelched suggestions that Cuba try to renegotiate the sugar deal to take advantage of the loss of Philippine production. He told the growers, Messersmith later revealed, that the agreement was "a matter of cooperation, and that the sale would be carried through even if it takes the Army to make sugar deliveries."[63]

Messersmith recommended that Washington reciprocate with trade concessions. The supplementary treaty negotiations were going badly, he wrote bluntly to Welles on 8 December, because of the department's unrealistic demands on "articles which I had hoped we had forgotten and some of which present real difficulties for the Cubans." In his opinion Cuba had "good and adequate reason" to resent and reject any tobacco quid pro quo. On yet another new American stipulation, raising duties on Cuban salt, Batista was adamant; he would do nothing that exacerbated the poverty of the salt miners of his native Oriente Province, who had cared for him as an orphan. And it was "unreasonable to ask for a concession on an article [rice] which they are practically exclusively importing from us." Persisting in bargaining "purely on a commercial give and take basis" would "introduce an element of uncertainty, distrust, and complete disillusionment in our relationships with Cuba, which I believe will cause us in the end great trouble and more loss than to Cuba."[64]

The State Department came back with a somewhat better offer, and Cuba accepted. Washington agreed not to increase the salt tariff, and withdrew its demand for a rice quota. Yet the final concession was still Cuba's to make. The permanent sugar quota, its precondition for the purchase deal, came under fire on Capitol Hill. Rather than "risk offending members of Congress and perhaps jeopardize Cuba's future position," the department suggested, in place of the offending provision, an exchange of notes committing Roosevelt to "doing [his] best" to prevent reductions in Cuba's quota. Cortina reluctantly assented. On 23 December he and Messersmith signed the second Cuban-American supplementary trade agreement. This paved the way for conclusion of the purchase of the 1942 crop four weeks later.[65]

That done, it was appropriate that Messersmith now depart for a new post. Roosevelt had called back in November with word of his appointment to succeed Josephus Daniels as ambassador to Mexico. Messersmith had expressed the usual mixed feelings: pride in a promotion to what "some believe is the most important and most difficult diplomatic post we now have"; regret at leaving Cuba, "where my life has been as happy as life can be anywhere . . . and the work so pleasant."[66]

No such ambivalence was evident among the Cubans, who, as he wrote Hull on 28 November, were "naturally very upset" by the news. "They are quite personal and somewhat temperamental in their dealings, and I think they have become accustomed to me and view with a good deal of concern the change involved." They needed time to adjust, and he did not want to leave in the middle of trade and sugar negotiations. The department agreed to a delay in his departure because there was "nothing very pressing at the moment" on the Mexican-American calendar.[67]

Ratification of the sugar purchase thus brought Messersmith's Cuban mission to a close. In twenty-one fruitful months, he wrote proudly to Welles, "every outstanding and long-pending matter in our relationships with Cuba" had been resolved. It had required "infinite pains and effort, but the results have been more than worthwhile." On every front, Cuban cooperation was "wholehearted and complete." "I do not believe," he assured Spruille Braden, his designated successor, "you could begin your work under more favorable auspices."[68]

Cuba gave him an impressive and heartfelt farewell. When he rose to speak at the 23 January sugar industry dinner, the ovation, reported one guest, "practically shook down the lighthouse tower at Morro Castle." Another highlight was Batista's 5 February banquet. Instead of the expected toast, the Cuban president delivered an emotional fifteen-minute tribute to, as Messersmith put it, "our country and me." In their final private talk, Batista expressed "great satisfaction" with the state of bilateral relations, "which he could not conceive as being better." He also "had unusually generous things to say about me . . . which I will not go into."[69]

Another Cuban politician had Messersmith's measure. Senator José Casanova had sparred with him over the public-works settlement and collaborated frequently with him since. Casanova's remarks at the sugar dinner noted the evolution of Messersmith's Cuban experience. "When he learned all about us," said Casanova, "he decided to help us." Indeed, the more Messersmith had learned, the better he understood how deeply troubled Cuba really was. He had come to see its desperate need for economic development, and championed that cause in Washington with all his accustomed vigor. From 1941 on, he advised his superiors to adopt "an enlightened and long range view" in these matters. Responding retrospectively to critics of the State Department's ill-fated Cuban policy, he recalled his own very real efforts to put "the Cuban economy on a sounder basis."[70]

Yet, as he departed for Mexico, Cuba was still more dependent upon sugar and American imports than on the day he arrived. The wartime boom was already underway; the 1942 crop, sold in advance, would total 3.8 million tons, the largest since 1930. Diversification did not stand a chance. The $25 million Eximbank credit, which had incited such high hopes, faced uncertain prospects. Everyone knew that the American defense effort would take precedence over modernization of the Havana waterworks (one of the contemplated Eximbank projects) for scarce construction materials. By July 1944 the Eximbank had spent only $3 million. According to Batista's enemies, most of that sum wound up in his Swiss accounts.[71]

Messersmith had helped Cuba get the best possible terms in its commercial bargaining with the United States. But the established relationships, which benefited many Americans and many fewer Cubans, were strengthened during his tenure in Havana. That, he often protested to Washington, was precisely what he aimed to do. "I am not a special pleader for Cuba," he once wrote in its behalf to Hull. "I am a special pleader for only one country, and that is our own." In 1940 and 1941 the United States had especially high strategic and commercial stakes in the Cuban status quo. State Department policies were therefore designed to consolidate American influence, not to withdraw it. The $25 million "development" credit, ostensibly to make Cuba more self-sufficient, became a pay-off to Batista, who had proved his worth. The State Department paid lip service to diversification while demanding tariff concessions designed to inhibit it.[72]

The better Messersmith knew Cuba, the harder he questioned these policies and the harder he worked to mitigate them. Even so, his most notable success was in carrying out the department's program, not moderating it. Welles congratulated him for having "established the authority of the Embassy." But his conscience, which kept him working rather than playing, would not let him savor Welles's and others' praise. He was passing on to Braden a "slate very largely clean of current problems," but also, as he was aware, a slate of fundamental social and economic problems still festering. From Washington's standpoint the Cuban situation in February 1942 could hardly be better. Messersmith was not deceived. "We are," he wrote Welles late that year, "sitting on a volcano in Cuba."[73]

Mexico City
1942–1946

1

Messersmith's plan was to sail directly west to Mexico on the morning of 7 February. But German submarines were suddenly sighted in Cuban waters, and his naval attaché ventured the improbable suggestion that they were lying in wait to abduct him from his ship. Messersmith took the threat (and himself) too seriously. "As public enemy number two or three of the Nazis in the United States," he told the State Department over the phone early that morning, he felt that "some spectacular action" on the high seas was a distinct possibility. For himself, he said, he wanted nothing more than another chance to browbeat Nazis, even as their prisoner, but not at the risk of jeopardizing fellow passengers. So, with State's approval, the embassy announced an indefinite delay in his departure. Two days later he slipped out almost unnoticed, catching a flight to Miami, where he rejoined Marion and her mother, now a spry eighty-two, for the long rail trip to Laredo, Texas, and connections to the Mexican capital.[1]

This circuitous route took its toll on him. He arrived weary from lack of sleep, his bones still rattling from the ride south over Mexico's ramshackle national rails. He began a painful adjustment to the thin air at 8,000 feet. Then he found the embassy residence in disrepair and unfit for habitation, forcing him and his party temporarily into a hotel. His stomach quickly succumbed to the cuisine.[2]

The situation at the chancery gave Messersmith more cause for upset. Unlike the neurotic Dodd in Berlin, the genial Daniels had enjoyed the finest relations with his staff. But, similarly weak in organizational ethic, he had run a lax ship by Messersmith's strict standards. Of course, Messersmith wrote Welles, Daniels had had "the best intentions," but he actually did "a good deal to impede good administrative practice rather than facilitate it." Daniels was so beloved partly because he allowed his subordinates extraordinary latitude in doing their daily duties. But the need for closer coordination among the twenty-nine United States consular offices in the country and for less spontaneity inside the embassy was plain even to them. Messersmith took one look and pronounced a stern verdict: Daniels's, he wrote Raymond Geist, was "the most sadly neglected of any [embassy] I have yet seen."[3]

All Daniels *had* done, in his modest and irregular way, was to help steer Mexican-American relations off a collision course onto a historic road of cooperation. His mission had coincided with a resurgence of Mexican revolutionary fervor. Beginning in 1934 President Lázaro Cárdenas attacked the Catholic Church, confiscated and redistributed land, and championed industrial workers, especially the employees of the American-owned oil companies. When the companies ignored a government-decreed wage and benefit increase, Cárdenas, on 18 March 1938, nationalized their assets. Mexicans celebrated in the streets. Washington and Wall Street found common cause in ending their rejoicing. Cárdenas felt the screws, economic and diplomatic. The companies organized a boycott of Mexican oil. The new government monopoly, Petroleos Mexicanos (Pemex), soon found itself unable to obtain vital replacement machinery and tanker transportation. Lurid oil-company propaganda warned prospective tourists that their own property would be no safer on Mexican roads and streets. The United States Treasury Department declared a moratorium on Mexican silver purchases. The State Department ordered Daniels to deliver a blunt protest and then to return to Washington. A break in relations seemed imminent.[4]

Daniels prevented that break by sitting on his instructions long enough for tempers to cool and the national interest to reassert itself. On 1 April Roosevelt told reporters that the Good Neighbor policy would not be sacrificed to save the oil men. Over the months American pressure began to have decidedly undesirable consequences, as Mexico found eager customers for its oil in Germany, Italy, and Japan. At the State Department nervous thoughts turned increasingly to the possibility of a cash settlement to the crisis. But the companies insisted upon the full restoration of their property rights, and nothing less. Time, they believed, was on their side, in the inexorable decline of Mexican production and revenues under Pemex and in the 1940 presidential elections, from which they anticipated new chief executives more friendly to their interests both north and south of the border. They were doubly disappointed, for Cárdenas's handpicked successor, General Manuel Ávila Camacho, won easily over a more conservative opponent. In his inaugural address, before a

crowd of dignitaries including United States Vice President Henry A.
Wallace representing Roosevelt, Camacho pledged to "make relations
between the United States and Mexico better than they have ever
been before." As foreign minister, he appointed Ezequiel Padilla, a
New York- and Paris-educated lawyer and an unbounded admirer of
the United States—and so not a popular choice among Mexicans.
Camacho was obviously determined to make good on his inaugural
pledge, whatever the political risks.[5]

The oil men, as Daniels kept reminding Washington, remained
inflexible obstacles to rapprochement. But their time was running
out. By the middle of 1941 Hull and Welles, who could not stand
each other personally but who agreed on policy at least as often as
not, were at the end of their patience. In a spirit of conciliation born
of the impending national emergency, the State Department, urged
along by Daniels and Roosevelt, sat down with the Mexicans to resolve their differences. On 19 November 1941 a comprehensive settlement was reached. It called for the creation of a joint commission
to decide for the companies what they would get in compensation.
Mexico pledged $40 million in advance to satisfy other American
claims. The United States in turn extended a $95 million package of
economic aid—in effect, as the *New York Times* observed sourly, "furnishing Mexico with the funds to pay for the properties it had expro-
priated." Wall Street winced and the companies shrieked betrayal.[6]

For Mexican-American relations, however, the agreement was
gold. The two countries became official friends and unofficial allies.
Camacho had already taken sides in the world crisis. In January 1941
Mexico made a major sacrifice in ending oil sales to Japan, a ban
soon broadened to embrace other strategic raw materials and the
other Axis powers. In a July agreement the United States promised
to purchase Mexico's entire exportable mineral output. Mexico im-
pounded some Axis property—including much-needed oil tankers—
and dismantled a largely inconsequential Nazi apparatus.

With the comprehensive settlement and Pearl Harbor, Mexican-
American military cooperation raced ahead. Padilla's condemnation
of the Japanese attack was swift and emphatic, and his paean to Pan
Americanism at the Rio conference in January 1942 was positively
inspirational. Mexico broke diplomatic relations with the Axis, and
interned some Axis nationals. Preparations to repel an anticipated
Japanese invasion of the west coast commenced under now General
Cárdenas and the American West Coast commander, General John
L. De Witt. A Joint Defense Commission (JDC) institutionalized this
cooperation. Lend-lease negotiations were well underway. The oil-
property evaluators, Morris L. Cooke for the United States and

Manuel J. Zevada for Mexico, approached an agreement. Every day seemed to bring another cultural or economic mission from Washington. The pace was marvelous. Historically no nation had more reason to hate the United States and to side with its enemies. During Word War I, in the wake of Vera Cruz, the Pershing mission, and the Zimmermann telegram, several thousand American troops were lost to the Allies doing guard duty along the uneasy Mexican border. Before World War II was three months old, Mexico, although not yet a belligerent, had become a pillar of hemispheric solidarity.[7]

This was Daniels's brilliant legacy, and Messersmith was properly appreciative. "No one," he assured Welles, "could begin his work under more favorable auspices than I am beginning mine here." He merged smoothly, if lightheadedly, into official life. Having to greet after-hours callers in his hotel suite hindered him initially, but his Cuban colleagues graciously extended him the use of their good offices and homes. His first "intimate contact" with Camacho took place on the golf course adjoining the president's Cuernavaca retreat. With Padilla and the interior minister, Miguel Alemán Valdes, they made a convivial foursome. Messersmith remembered "four husky caddies" "keeping score" in a manner that inevitably corresponded to the hierarchy of power: the president first, then the ambassador, then the foreign minister. The pretense amused Messersmith greatly. Certainly it lowered his handicap. Everything was simpatico, especially with Padilla. The suave, conservative foreign minister had got on famously with Daniels, the homespun "shirt-sleeve diplomat"; with Messersmith, who looked and sounded the part, relations would be even better. After nine years in the country, Daniels still spoke almost no Spanish; Messersmith's command of the language would grant him access to a Mexico that Daniels, for all his good will, could never know.[8]

These and other contrasts to his popular predecessor went on display on 24 February, Mexican Flag Day, when Messersmith presented his credentials. In public remarks likely calculated to calm Mexican apprehensions about North American career ambassadors, he dedicated himself to tolerance and understanding à la Daniels. Warm words for Mexico's incumbent administration were pro forma, but his tribute to Cárdenas's "program of social betterment" was definitely not the State Department talking. Several local editorial writers called approving attention to his concluding pledge to work for a Mexico "strong, happy, and free."[9]

And he meant every word of it. For Messersmith as for many others, Pearl Harbor had been both a shock and a relief. "Japan could have done us no better service," he wrote a few days thereafter, "for nothing could have consolidated opinion more than this." Finally the doubts and debates were behind; with American might, the Fascist scourge would be destroyed, probably soon. He did not think that "Japanese resistance will last very long," and saw in Hitler's first Russian winter "the beginning of the disintegration of German power." Sadly misinformed about Axis strength and American readiness, he thought it "at least possible that the war will be ended in a year."[10]

The sickening string of early setbacks for the United States, notably in the Pacific theater, shattered these illusions. In South America there was renewed speculation that the Axis might enjoy the final triumph after all. In lieu of good news from the battlefields, Messersmith could respond only with heartfelt words that at least made his listeners want to believe. On 14 February he assured Mexican journalists that although the road to victory would be "long and hard," the democracies, with their superior resources and moral purpose, would indeed prevail. In the United States, he declared, "we are transforming our industries and our social life to create the most powerful war machine in the world." The Axis could never match the forces upholding eternal verities: that, as he told another Mexican audience with unaccustomed eloquence, "man is essentially noble; that his soul does possess dignity; and that man without freedom is more degraded than a slave in the galley."[11]

For the democracies, these ideals entailed responsibilities beyond crushing their enemies. Once the war was underway Messersmith began to gaze beyond. On 14 April, Pan American Day, as Japanese armies swept through Burma and Java, he told a Mexican symposium that "the problems of the peace after the victory is achieved may . . . be even greater than those of the war." The Atlantic Charter promised a richer life for all people, not just those liberated from Axis chains. A new "world organization" would be needed to ensure that the "peace and security will not again be threatened.[12] But he was confident that these challenges would be met. For one thing, he believed that the United States was finally ready to assume the mantle of world leadership. "Everybody realizes that isolationism is dead," he told a convention of foreign service officers. So too, he trusted, was appeasement. He hated to say it, he said anyway to a dinner audience, but "the peoples of the democracies have no one but themselves to blame" for their present tribulations. Had the lawless nations been met when their true colors became clear, he reminded everyone, the sacrifices so far and those still to come could have been avoided. That lesson, he mused, would perhaps be better learned in the cauldron of war.[13]

That was not the only good that Messersmith thought would come of all the suffering. Participation in the anti-Axis crusade laid a foundation for postwar cooperation especially critical to Messersmith where he was. Already, he exulted to Henry Wallace, who kept a close watch on matters Mexican, "the war has enabled us to make more progress in our relationships with this neighbor than fifty years of peace." Here was an opportunity to consolidate Daniels's gains, for the United States and Mexico to work together for a common cause in a spirit of respect and harmony. Moreover, Camacho was almost exactly of the same mind. "We have in the President of Mexico," Messersmith excitedly wrote Hull, "a man who is thoroughly convinced of the necessity for the closest cooperation during and after the war, and [he repeated for emphasis] he envisages this collaboration continuing in the political and economic field after the war. He is a man deep and firm in his convictions and he has been a tower of strength for us here. He is a man who in his personal life is clean and honest and fine."[14] He was also a believer in free enterprise and capitalist development for his country, under whom private investment enjoyed "a freedom which seemed only a short time ago impossible." And Padilla, who was "very close" to the president, was carrying out his policies with "courage and clear convictions." It was indeed "a great fortune for Mexico and for all of us in the Americas" that Mexico was in such hands.[15]

But Messersmith was not overlooking the flaws in this promising picture. Foremost was the fact that the government's enthusiasm for collaboration seemed practically limited to itself. Camacho, he observed on 24 March, was "far ahead of the people" in his pro-Americanism, and Padilla had virtually no "strength . . . among the masses." Mexican public opinion was overwhelmingly "apathetic" to the war, "which has not touched them much." Most Mexicans favored neutrality for their country. No matter what Camacho said or did, the ambassador explained to Hull, "there remains the historical background, particularly among the masses," where there was, to put it mildly, "no love for us." A century of rancor could not be expunged overnight. Mexicans were confused by the shift away from traditional friends Spain and Italy, toward age-old tormentors Britain and the United States. Incorrigible Yankee-baiters like leftist labor leader Vicente Lombardo Toledano saw to it that bitter memories lived on. The Catholic Church, though much reduced by the Mexican revolution, remained the most potent force in Mexican life, and, Messersmith wrote Henry Wallace, "it is an extraordinary thing how, among the lower clergy and even among the laity . . . there persists this idea that Hitler and his cohorts are the protectors of the Catholic Church and of religion."[16]

And there was General Lázaro Cárdenas. A United States Navy intelligence report of 26 March quoted him as assuring his country-men that Mexico's armed forces stood prepared to "repell any at-tempt at invasion, whether such enemy force came from the west . . . *or from the north* [original italics]." That bespoke the mood of his talks with General De Witt, which were already in deep trouble. In late May he created an incident by intercepting an American military team sent to reconnoiter Baja California for suspected Japanese air-fields. Navy intelligence concluded that the former president was "at least as hostile as ever" to the United States. Secretary of War Henry Stimson thought that Cárdenas might actually be "in touch with the Japs."[17]

Messersmith and Cárdenas saw each other fairly regularly during his tenure in Mexico. But it was not an intimate association. Given their backgrounds, the kind of open relationship Messersmith was to enjoy with Padilla and the president could not be had with him. But Messersmith came to know him well enough after only a few months in the country to know that he was "no Nazi and no sworn enemy of the United States." Cárdenas, he understood, spoke for the masses deeply skeptical of Camacho's contentions that friendship with the United States could be consistent with Mexican honor and sover-eignty; that American power, long Mexico's curse, might now become an asset to its economy and armed forces; that participation in the war would be materially and morally uplifting. Mexicans, and Cár-denas, demanded proof. For them, cooperation with the United States was on probation, a fact of which Messersmith became acutely, even obsessively, conscious. In 1946, when Camacho's single six-year term was up, Mexicans would pass judgment in choosing his succes-sor. So if the war was an opportunity, it was also a challenge—the biggest one Messersmith believed he had ever faced.[18]

Messersmith's perception of the precariousness of good relations so full of promise governed his four years in Mexico. That was why he was so ambivalent about its 30 May declaration of war. Rather than plotting to abduct American diplomats, German U-boats were preying on merchant shipping in the Gulf of Mexico, among other places. On 14 May one of the confiscated Italian oil tankers, now the *Portrero del Llano*, plying between Tampico and New York, was sunk off the Florida coast. Five Mexican crew members perished. Yet Mexican outrage was surprisingly muted. Almost 60 percent of those polled in the capital on 20 May opposed a declaration of war. Hence the Camacho government limited itself to verbal protest to Berlin.[19]

Even this went too far for many Mexicans, while not going nearly far enough to satisfy opinion north of the border. Americans in 1942 were intolerant of ambiguity: either Mexico was in the war as an ally or out as an enemy. Messersmith continually argued in response that Mexican belligerency would be worse than worthless, that it would invite Axis reprisals against what amounted to America's own soft underbelly. The best thing Mexico could do for the Allied cause, in his view, would be to retain its present benignly neutral status and wait for its own public opinion to catch up.[20]

The same arguments applied after 14 May, but Messersmith recognized that for better or worse, Mexican belligerency was now inevitable. "No answer which the Germans can make [to Padilla's protest] can . . . satisfy the national honor," he observed on 20 May. Germany delivered its answer two days later, a torpedo amidships the *Faja de Oro*, another tanker, claiming seven more lives. Soldier-at-heart Camacho, who was following the war news from map rooms set up at home, would no longer be denied. On 28 May an extraordinary session of Congress assembled to hear the president's war message. The legislature approved by a 53 to 0 vote. The *New York Times*, stalwart of the oil men, hailed a "new era in Mexican history." Many glasses were lifted to the common cause in diplomatic circles.[21]

But there was no place for complacency in Mexican-American relations. While the official festivities went on, the rumormongers were grinding out plausible new lies in public. One theory making the local rounds had the United States sinking the tankers. Another current rumor was that Camacho had declared war only after the United States threatened to occupy Mexico if he did not. Mexican-American friendship obviously had a long way to go. Messersmith would spend much of his next four years admonishing Americans in Mexico and at home not to take that friendship for granted, lecturing them in the new etiquette. To be sure, Mexico sought material assistance, but what it expected first and foremost could not be bought. Mexico, he lectured Assistant Secretary of State Dean Acheson and, in time, every senior official in the department, "expects and demands respect which she believes due her, as a sovereign state, of her good faith and intentions." Mexicans were understandably touchy about their much trod-upon national honor, especially in dealing with its number one abuser. Americans, moreover, would have to unlearn their condescending habits and curb their mercenary and missionary impulses. And, for trusting the United States with so much reason not to, the Mexican government expected implicit trust in return. "We must give faith and credit to her acts . . . and put confidence in her officials," always mindful that "there is a past . . . which people here are trying to forget, which could easily be pushed into the foreground."²²

2

Unfortunately, many interested Americans were indifferent to the history, fragility, and ground rules of the new relationship. American military men proved to be the worst offenders. They insulted their counterparts on the Joint Defense Commission and in the field by insisting that American units carry out sea and air patrols from Mexican bases. Mexicans maintained that with the hardware promised by Washington, their newly reorganized 52,000-man army could and should assume such responsibilities. They would welcome American troops into Mexico in an emergency—but only then. Messersmith felt "we should be more pleased than otherwise that it is their desire to make every effort on their own"; the government had "to actually do something" in order to "awaken full consciousness among the Mexican people of the war and their interest therein."²³

These considerations carried no weight with a War Department convinced that the defense of Mexico was too important to be entrusted to Mexicans. The Baja mission, which led to the border imbroglio with Cárdenas, was typical: "ill-timed, ill-advised, and unnecessary," Messersmith complained; the Mexicans had only recently completed their own thorough, fruitless search for the supposed Japanese airfields that, as the Americans soon sheepishly agreed, did not exist. The Mexican government had pocketed its pride, and did so again when the United States requested bases in the Yucatán for antisubmarine operations. An obviously irritated Padilla assented, but for one month only, until American aircraft were delivered to enable Mexico to take over the task. Messersmith suggested to Washington that a month might just suffice if Mexicans trained in the air alongside American pilots; the planes could then be turned over to Mexico. On those terms, the army lost interest. Then it ordered the dismissal of key Mexican personnel employed by Pan American Airways, on the grounds that they were security risks—a "marked show of lack of confidence," Messersmith sputtered to Welles, "so dangerous that we cannot even think of it." The order was rescinded.²⁴

Despite occasional blow-ups and persistent mutual wariness, Mexican and American officers accomplished some things together in 1942. A protracted negotiation over the installation and command of radar stations in Baja was finally resolved; by the end of July three such posts were operational, manned by Americans in civilian garb. A month later the Mexican army took charge. A similar compromise provided upgraded air-ground communications, long needed by Americans flying the Mexican route (under an earlier agreement) to the Canal Zone. Construction of three military airstrips began when it was agreed to defer consideration of the rules governing their use. Field relations improved dramatically when Camacho promoted Cárdenas to the cabinet as defense minister. By 16 September, Mexican Independence Day, enough lend-lease equipment—armored and other vehicles and especially aircraft—had been delivered to mount an impressive public display. The heads of the American section of the JDC, General Stanley D. Embick and Admiral Alfred W. Johnson, were on hand for the occasion. Embick was taken ill, but Johnson was with Messersmith in Camacho's box to view what the ambassador described to Welles the next day as "the finest military spectacle [ever] staged in Mexico. One could tell how proud the officers and men were of this equipment, and there was every evidence that they had known how to organize and use it. I think if there has been any doubt as to the justification for such shipments, yesterday's show was ample justification. An army needs tools and without tools it cannot work nor have spirit." Mexican generals were "very voluble in their expressions" of gratitude.[25]

Privately, however, bickering and bad blood still reigned. Messersmith played social director for the Johnson-Embick mission, hoping through contact with Mexico and its people to promote understanding of its negotiating position. He brought the top officers together at an embassy banquet on 18 September, and Cárdenas even dropped his customary scowl, becoming "very affable and cordial." The president of the republic arrived, uninvited but welcome, and Johnson and Embick took Camacho aside after dinner for chit-chat on strategy, to the latter's delight. Messersmith felt that "if the only result we got out of this mission . . . was to have had this dinner, it was well worthwhile."[26]

This entertainment had, however, provided only an evening's respite to an otherwise unproductive United States mission to Mexico. Embick and Johnson had come expecting to gain liberalization of base-use restrictions and other concessions, and returned home empty-handed and frustrated. In a 12 December letter to Messersmith, Johnson denounced Mexico as the least cooperative of the American Republics aside from still-neutral Argentina and Chile. He could not forgive Mexican "unwilling[ness] to permit United States forces to operate" on its territory. The Mexicans, he suggested, were primarily interested in cashing in on lend-lease. The wholehearted cooperation of, say, the Cubans was entirely absent among them. Thus, Johnson concluded, Mexican-American military collaboration "cannot be said to be entirely satisfactory."[27]

As Messersmith pointed out in response, Johnson ignored the whole "history of controversy" between the two nations. Mexico, he reminded him, was "the only American Republic from which we have taken territory and with which, in fact, we have been at war." The continued "occasional" maltreatment of Mexicans in the United States rubbed salt into century-old wounds. Mexico was not Brazil. That it was cooperating to the present extent was "extraordinary." All Latin nations were seeking American arms; Mexico "should be commended for trying to build up her armed forces, to aid in hemispheric defense." And it was "entirely justified" in rejecting American troops on its soil until its own were found wanting. The notion that "it is our troops that have the sole responsibility and are solely capable of defending Mexican territory," he observed brutally, was "our own complex . . . to overcome."[28]

But no words could do what months of intimate contact had failed to do. What saved Mexican-American military relations from worsening was the improving strategic picture, which rendered Mexican assistance increasingly superfluous. The Japanese invasion of Baja looked more and more like a figment of overwrought post-7 December imaginations, especially that of General De Witt. By 1943 JDC meetings centered on the abandonment of the same joint projects that the United States had just months earlier fought tooth-and-nail to get started.[29]

On the civilian side, Messersmith finally took charge. But for him personally, in ways he did not immediately comprehend, the cost would be great. No sooner had he departed Washington in 1940 than the rationalized Foreign Service he left behind began to come undone. The war brought forth a bevy of new United States government agencies with business abroad. In August 1940, after the fall of France, an independent Office of the Coordinator of Inter-American Affairs (OCIAA) was created over State Department opposition. With a broad mandate to promote hemispheric solidarity and security, and a first year's budget of $3.5 million (to $60 million by 1943), Coordinator Nelson A. Rockefeller flooded the Americas with news and propaganda and money and his own people. Soon OCIAA agents calling themselves "cultural attachés" or "special assistants to the ambassador" were setting up shop throughout the hemisphere.[30]

From Cuba, Messersmith urged American diplomats to resist. Accept Rockefeller's amateur emissaries, he warned prophetically, and "there will be no limit to the number of men who will be sent out on these special details." He was writing while one of Rockefeller's "me-

*Surface cooperation. George S. Messersmith, ambassador to Mexico, with
Coordinator of Inter-American Affairs Nelson A. Rockefeller*
Courtesy National Archives

dia experts" was in Havana supposedly reporting on public opinion,
but "the poor fellow is . . . utterly incompetent to begin with," and so
was pestering the embassy to do his research for him. Washington
had asked for an evaluation of his performance, and Messersmith
intended to tell all and to demand a veto over new personnel assignments. He hoped that his colleagues would be equally frank.[31]

Harassed in Havana and in other Latin American capitals with
strong United States ambassadors, Rockefeller availed himself of
Daniels's hospitality and the vacuum after his departure to entrench
himself in Mexico. Messersmith arrived to discover that the OCIAA
had "succeeded in going further here than I believe anywhere else in
the Americas." It would go no further. "Our friend Mr. Rockefeller
means well," he wrote the like-minded Spruille Braden in Havana,
but good intentions and cash were no substitute for diplomatic skill
and understanding. In Messersmith's jaundiced view, Rockefeller's

projects fell into one of two categories: worthy ones, like artistic exchanges, being bungled in the execution, and unworthy ones, like his Hollywood movie stars on tour, that smacked of cultural imperialism, insulted Latin intelligence, and probably converted not a single soul to the Allied cause. On the bright side, Messersmith accurately foresaw "a hell of a time" awaiting Rockefeller when next he had to go before Congress to justify his prodigious expenditures. Until then, "we must see to it that these projects are kept in line. . . . The Coordinator's Office is here today and maybe gone tomorrow." The damage it did would fall to the State Department to repair.[32]

"Absolutely determined," as he put it, to stop the coordinator's minions from trampling "the delicate flower" of Mexican-American relations, Messersmith, on his own authority, gradually took over most of the coordinator's Mexican operations. Rockefeller complained to the State Department, which had finally acquiesced to his well-financed presence. But their joint protests were to no avail. When Messersmith reportedly "blew off in a two-hour harangue against the Coordinator's Office" at a conference of United States consular officials in Mexico, Duggan, the liaison man, sent him a stern reprimand that had no apparent impact on him whatsoever.[33] The only one he was taking orders from, he informed the coordinator's men and later would-be interlopers, was Roosevelt, and, one of them later recalled, "in this he did not exclude Hull and Welles." When he got no orders to desist from Roosevelt, Messersmith continued to enforce his vision, which he increasingly believed was also the president's vision, of the Good Neighbor in Mexico. In conversations with Padilla and Camacho he made it a point to emphasize the damage he believed uncoordinated Americans were doing, or were capable of doing, to bilateral relations. Rockefeller's operatives increasingly found themselves either working through the embassy or losing access to the Mexican government. In July Messersmith formed a volunteer committee of resident Americans to monitor local opinion, on which basis he secured the transfer of the OCIAA agent in Mexico for that purpose. In a wing of the embassy residence he had converted into "a little theater with a bar and comfortable seats," his committee held advance screenings of Rockefeller's cinematic propaganda. By 1943 the embassy had taken over the distribution of all OCIAA publicity materials—and was withholding materials it deemed unsuitable.[34]

Visitors to his embassy in 1942 were instantly reminded that a war was in progress, though they may not have appreciated its bureaucratic dimension.[35] Messersmith's establishment, the *Christian Science Monitor* told its readers back home, was "the busiest spot in Mexico."

Workmen scurried about, enlarging and sprucing up the physical plant. Inside, Messersmith drilled his troops. He insisted upon "complete unity of action, coordination, and exchange. I said that I would not tolerate anything less, and if any officer stationed here was not willing to conform he would have to go home." Some who did not fit in were transferred out. But for every man who left, it seemed as though two arrived to take his place. By 1943 the professional staff exceeded 250, the most of any American embassy in the world.[36]

In July 1942 Messersmith implemented a sweeping internal reorganization. Expanded cultural and information sections optimistically anticipated the coordinator's demise. The core of the new configuration, however, was an economic unit of eight separate sections and a staff of sixty housed in their own six-story building. It reflected the economic thrust of Mexican-American relations during the war. Mexico's assigned role was that of supplier of strategic raw materials. Minerals, rubber, oils (fuel and edible), and chemicals—these items would be the stuff and substance of wartime relations, and the tangible test of Mexican-American cooperation.

With Messersmith's arrival, the embassy became an increasingly active partner in the government's procurement program. The Commerce Department's Reconstruction Finance Corporation (RFC) was in charge, but the RFC representatives he dealt with in Mexico welcomed the embassy's preferred assistance. Dr. Alan Bateman, a Canadian-born Yale professor of mineralogy, had arrived in January 1942 representing the Metals Reserve Company, an RFC subsidiary, to negotiate a new master contract for the purchase of Mexican ores. Messersmith, always leery of specialists, had only praise for Bateman. The scientist's "competence, discretion, and judgment," and close ties to the embassy, paid off. On 29 April he signed an agreement with the Mexican interior and labor ministries that attested to his diplomatic as well as technical talent. The United States agreed to pay liberally for all the lead, zinc, copper, feldspar, antimony, mercury, manganese, and tungsten that Mexico could produce; the miners union, a party to the agreement, made concessions on working conditions and job tenure. The Camacho government pledged not to raise producer or export taxes. The RFC promised to assist in securing vital machinery, raw materials, and consumer goods in order to absorb the expected avalanche of dollars and so hold down inflation. Bateman, Messersmith wrote admiringly, has "done a very fine job in a very fine way."[37]

His colleague Floyd D. Ransom represented the Rubber Reserve Company, another RFC satellite. A longtime resident businessman, Ransom was everything Messersmith considered important: "upright

[and] constructive . . . speaks Spanish like a native . . . skillful, tact-ful, and understanding." In March, and in close touch with the em-bassy, he commenced rubber negotiations parallel to Bateman's. Mexico's acceptance of limits on domestic consumption presaged early agreement.[38]

Meanwhile the State Department was busy promoting economic cooperation. In late March Padilla visited Washington, had an audi-ence with Roosevelt, and signed an agreement with Welles supple-menting the November general settlement. The United States prom-ised to underwrite two industrial projects—a steel mill and a refinery to produce high-octane aviation fuel—"as soon as the needed equip-ment becomes available." Negotiations for a reciprocal trade agree-ment got underway. On 19 April the two countries exchanged notes accepting the Cooke-Zevada compensation recommendations.[39]

Messersmith cheered State's efforts to rehabilitate capitalism in Mexico and assert its authority over foreign economic policy. He ob-jected, however, to making supply commitments that could not be kept. Indeed, Welles informed him confidentially that material short-ages meant a delay of at least two years, "possibly even longer," in getting the high octane plant underway. Padilla had been told as much, but had insisted on a commitment for public consumption at home. Messersmith regretted this for two reasons. Aside from the disillusionment the delay would inevitably cause, other projects were, in his view, much more critical to Mexico and to the war effort. With the shortage of oceangoing shipping, the whole procurement pro-gram rested precariously on Mexico's sagging roads and rails. Bate-man's report had concluded flatly that the Mexican national railways were "inadequate to handle the expected ore and metals transporta-tion." A third of the locomotives were laid up for lack of spare parts, mechanics, and repair facilities. Crumbling track caused an aver-age of one accident per hour. In April Messersmith welcomed an OCIAA-sponsored railroad mission, charged with investigating the situation. He was pleased to report his daily meetings with Major Howard G. Hill, the chief engineer.[40]

This tidy arrangement soon faced a mortal threat. An executive order dated 13 April 1942 transferred responsibility for foreign pro-curement and preclusive buying from RFC to a new Board of Eco-nomic Warfare (BEW), under Vice President Wallace. The BEW was authorized to engage in direct negotiations with foreign govern-ments to meet its mandate.[41]

Cordell Hull and Commerce Secretary Jesse Jones were the clear victims of this bureaucratic bombshell. For them, a Hull subordinate recalled, the order of 13 April was "a painful, bitter, and humiliating defeat." It was a setback felt through the ranks, and no one felt it more than Messersmith, who was "sick at the stomach" on hearing the news. The president who had brought the attachés into the State Department had signed an order, he wrote in bewildered anger, "practically put[ting] it out of business." Messersmith could only assume that "the President had not been informed of the full implications and extent of this Executive Order when it had been presented to him." He was correct. Hull had been vacationing in Florida when the order was promulgated, but he returned with a vengeance on 20 April. At a 1 May press conference, with Hull at his side, Roosevelt reaffirmed the State Department's "complete charge of the nation's foreign relations," and promised further clarification of the BEW's role.[42]

A relieved Messersmith was "infinitely happy." He had been spared a painful duty. "I had definitely made up my mind," he wrote Geist, "that if this order was carried through . . . I would go home and tell the President and Hull and Welles that I could not continue to assume the responsibility of a post in the field." Roosevelt's 1 May pronouncement and the "Clarification and Interpretation" issued three weeks later withdrew the BEW's authority to conduct government-to-government negotiations, and placed BEW personnel in the field under the supervision of the diplomatic mission chiefs.[43]

Messersmith intended to enforce his jurisdiction. The BEW's "wings have been clipped," he noted, "but if not able to fly, [it] will be able to peck and annoy." It retained its province over procurement, and Wallace's executive director, Milo Perkins, continued to move aggressively into resource-rich Mexico. By June he had six men in the country assigned to rubber production alone, doing work, Messersmith complained, "which has already been done or which is underway in [Ransom's] competent hands." Then he was informed that a new BEW minerals mission was on its way, headed by a Colonel McCoy, who, according to embassy evidence, was personally interested in some of the mines he was scheduled to inspect. McCoy was the last straw. The Mexicans, Messersmith wrote Washington, want to "deal with one man and one organization here, and with the Embassy," and the Mexicans agreed that Floyd Ransom should be that man. Ransom was summoned home for consultation, and made a good impression on Wallace and Perkins. In late June they agreed that all technical personnel would report through him and the embassy.[44]

This modus vivendi with the BEW, coupled with the embassy reorganization, satisfied Messersmith that he had "probably as ideal a setup as we can have." A busy and productive summer and autumn 1942 for Mexican-American economic relations was the result. Ransom met regularly with Messersmith and the embassy economic counselor, Thomas Lockett. Procurement contracts with individual producers were signed almost daily, stimulating the Mexican economy. Embassy supervision helped stop the McCoys of the world from selfishly exploiting the BEW's ardor and naïveté. "The crooks and the 'coyotes,'" Messersmith wrote to the State Department's Phillip Bonsal, "have been routed." Although some American money went into exploration and experimentation, operating mines and reopened dormant mines got the lion's share of Washington's minerals business.[45]

3

Interest in other Mexican resources created new complications. As the oil expropriation controversy wound down, the United States, at the worst possible moment, began paying the piper. The State Department and the oil companies had failed to cripple Pemex, but substantial damage had been done while Mexicans taught themselves how to run, and how not to run, an oil industry. Desperately short of capital, vexed by labor troubles and corruption, Pemex in its first four years barely kept pumping. Exploration virtually stopped. In 1942 crude production hit bottom at under 35 million barrels, compared to 193 million in 1921. Only the payroll grew. Maintenance had slipped so badly that there was real danger of "complete failure or disastrous accidents."[46]

In July 1942 the formidable American wartime petroleum bureaucracy swung into action. A half-dozen concerned agencies were represented on the Foreign Petroleum Policy Committee (FPPC), but the driving force was the Petroleum Administrator for War (PAW), Secretary of the Interior Harold Ickes. In its preliminary report, FPPC declared a state of emergency in Mexican oil. Pemex officials were invited to Washington to arrange for urgently needed repair materials and replacement parts. FPPC also proposed to despatch a team of experts to conduct a "rapid field survey," to determine how most expeditiously to increase Mexican output. On 23 August a PAW mission headed by the eminent petroleum geologist Everette L. De Golyer arrived in the Mexican capital, with instructions to work through the embassy.[47]

De Golyer confirmed the urgent need for American assistance. The future of Mexican oil, however, was moot and very much on American minds. Much more than for strategic minerals, postwar considerations determined American wartime petroleum policy. Concern over dwindling domestic reserves and increasing dependence on foreign suppliers had been voiced by Americans as early as 1919. Soaring consumption since 1940 converted many of the skeptics. By mid-1942 negotiations were underway around the world to ensure long-term American access to foreign oil. With Mexico's propinquity and vast potential reserves, it naturally figured prominently in Washington's thoughts. The question was one of means. Mexico had no cash and, after the 1938 nationalization, no credit, and so no imminent prospect of developing its reserves by itself. For Americans, it followed that the necessary sums—at least $150 million to start—would have to come from the United States.[48]

At this point the consensus broke down. One of wartime Washington's hottest internal quarrels centered on whether the development of foreign petroleum should be a job for private or public enterprise. On one side, Bull Moose Progressive Ickes stood foursquare against the oil barons. He had been among the least dismayed Americans over Cárdenas's 1938 expropriation coup, and the ensuing crisis in bilateral relations convinced him that the oil companies and the State Department were in unholy alliance. With the idea of circumventing both and getting back into Mexico, he went so far in February 1942 as to propose that the United States government try to purchase the nationalized properties. This scheme, inherently insulting to the Mexicans, earned a swift and deserved presidential rebuff.[49]

Ickes's hostility to private development made allowances for political cronies. Edwin W. Pauley, president of the Fortuna Petroleum Corporation of California, was the administration's oil man, treasurer of the Democratic National Committee, bearer of the impressive title "special representative of the president on petroleum." He showed up in Mexico in March 1942 with a contract calling for the construction by his own syndicate of the high-octane plant under discussion between Padilla and Welles in Washington. He proposed to supplement an Eximbank loan with as much as $30 million of his own, and to use his influence to arrange priority shipment of machinery. This munificence carried a heavy price tag. Pauley would get the first option on the refinery's entire exportable output in perpetuity, plus 10 percent off the top for himself. His annual profit would be in the neighborhood of $1.5 million. The Mexicans balked at these numbers. When they did, Pauley threatened to pull strings to cut off critical American exports unless they signed.[50]

Unaware of either Pauley's verbal blackmail or, as he later admitted, the terms of his contract, Ickes supported the project. He correctly suspected the State Department of engaging in its own blackmail over the refinery. Hull and Welles intended to use wartime aid to Pemex as a lever to bring back private capital. This was consistent with the State Department's whole global emphasis on free enterprise and free trade. But the single-mindedness with which those objectives were pursued in connection with Mexican petroleum suggests that the oil companies' cries of anguish and charges of sell-out in November 1941 had found their mark. Hull and Welles now saw a chance to recover lost face, taking advantage of Mexico's desire for assistance to pry open the door slammed shut in 1938.[51]

August 1942, with the Pemex mission in Washington and De Golyer headed south, was deemed a "singularly propitious moment" for Messersmith to seek "clarifications" from Camacho on Mexican petroleum policy. He was instructed to make clear that wartime aid to Pemex would be tied to a "comprehensive program" providing for long-term development as well as increased emergency output.[52]

Messersmith delivered the message against his better judgment. On one basic point Ickes and the State Department agreed: South American oil reserves were, as one Ickes aide put it, "more important to the United States than to the countries that have them." Against this attitude, Messersmith's broader conception of self-interest shines. He agreed that the United States needed the oil, but more than that he felt it needed stable southern neighbors, and that required their economic development. Messersmith viewed Mexican petroleum in terms of its phenomenal potential in that regard. He saw the development funds coming from a combination of public and private sources—the Eximbank underwriting equipment and materials, but the Mexicans having to raise high-risk exploration capital elsewhere. Doing this would require "sound changes" in Cárdenas's petroleum law, which now barred foreigners from contracting with Pemex. Mexico, he held, should then negotiate long-term exploration and operating contracts—not concessions—with American companies (and not necessarily the expelled companies) on "equitable" terms.[53]

Camacho himself seemed receptive. His message to Roosevelt upon the Cooke-Zevada oil compensation agreement had stressed his government's "desire to grant ample guarantees to the participation of private capital, national or foreign, in the exploitation and development of the material resources of this Republic." Camacho was losing patience with Pemex's growing pains. But, as Messersmith recognized, he was not in a position to act. It may have been a "singularly propitious moment" for Hull and Welles, but their initiative put the Mexican leader in a difficult spot. The symbolic importance of the oil nationalization—18 March had become a Mexican national holiday—had failed to register upon Washington. Camacho was already suspect for his pro-Americanism, and he now had Cárdenas to contend with in the cabinet, standing guard over his presidential legacy. Messersmith pointed to "a very decided change" for the better in Mexican public opinion toward the United States, but felt it was too soon to subject that opinion to the emotional stress of the petroleum issue. Camacho, "wise, prudent, and cautious," thought so, too.[54]

But the State Department insisted that Messersmith continue to seek "clarifications," which finally arrived the first week of 1943. Speaking for the government, Padilla said that "they did not see the possibility of the participation of foreign, and of course American capital, except in the foreign marketing of Mexican oil." He indicated, however, that this verdict might not be irrevocable, and expressed the hope that emergency aid to Pemex not be delayed.[55]

Messersmith hoped so too, but he joined the Mexicans and the State Department in denouncing the Pauley plan. Not all "the crooks and the 'coyotes'" had been routed, after all. Worried by Pauley's threats, Camacho showed his plan to Messersmith, who remembered reading "the most one-sided contract that I have ever seen." He advised Camacho not to sign "under any circumstances," and not to fear for Mexico's vital imports.[56]

In January 1943 Pauley stalked into Messersmith's office to inform him that the contract was going to be signed. Messersmith disagreed. Pauley insisted. The ambassador said no. "No voice was raised." "Well," the oil man rejoined, "perhaps the next time I come in here and sit in this chair, there will be someone else sitting in your chair." Messersmith "smiled, and said, 'Mr. Pauley, I am equally convinced that [if that happens] someone else will say exactly what I have said.'" They rose, shook hands, and Pauley left, "completely sure of himself."[57]

Pauley had outsmarted himself. Roosevelt did not care who built the refinery, just that someone did. Ickes had embraced Pauley principally from frustration with State Department obstructionism. The State Department attacked Pauley because he was Ickes's man; because, as Hull had written the president on 27 November, his scheme "suggested a type of exploitation which might invite a repetition of earlier difficulties"; and, not least, because Mexico had not yet offered the right "clarifications" on the readmission of private capital. In February 1943 Roosevelt rejected State's quid pro quo. He could not "see the relationship between this immediate need [for high-octane fuel] and 'the clarification of general [Mexican] petroleum policy'" that Hull and Welles sought. Under White House pressure, State seems to have saved face through the expendable Pauley. The refinery went forward without him. On 19 March 1943 a Pemex team arrived in Washington, where the financial details were arranged. A reputable American consulting firm was hired to do the designs. Roosevelt stepped in to speed clearance of the machinery. Even so, the project was not completed until 1945, too late for the war effort.[58]

Interests meshed better in tapping Mexico's human resources. Even during the depression 1930s, western American farmers clamored for more *braceros* and fewer immigration restrictions. With Pearl Harbor and the accelerated manpower drain, these calls became more insistent and more credible. In April 1942 another interdepartmental committee formed in Washington to study an urgent request from sugar-beet growers for 8,000 Mexican farm workers. By June the committee had prepared a farm-labor master plan for presentation to Mexico, which Messersmith was directed to do.[59]

The Mexicans were cool to the idea. Padilla's undersecretary, Jaime Torres Bodet, observed gently that "Mexican labor had gone to the United States before and the results had not been too good." During World War I thousands of *braceros* had been recruited directly by American farmers and then dumped into the depressed postwar farm economy to fend for themselves. Their plight turned into a scandal for the Mexican government, which was ultimately forced to underwrite a wholesale repatriation. To ensure that this would never happen again, the Mexicans had passed protective legislation to which Washington's new proposal would have to conform. Moreover, Mexico wanted confirmation that the American wartime labor shortage existed in fact, not solely in the imaginations of farmers intent upon holding down wages. Such studies would be involved and time-consuming, but, Padilla told Messersmith, the workers' welfare had to come first.[60]

Padilla got no argument from the ambassador, who shared Mexican misgivings about the *bracero* business. Personally he suspected that "the alleged labor shortage" flowed more from greed than need. "Some of our people at home," he complained to ex-farmer Henry Wallace, "still think that Mexican labor can be brought in like cattle and exploited." Washington's proposal offered safeguards that he feared would prove unenforceable. Many of the migrants would encounter a side of the United States that was better left hidden for the sake of bilateral relations. Where Jim Crow laws were in effect, they applied to Mexicans as well as Negroes. The inevitable incidents would play into the hands of professional anti-Americans like Toledano, who were already warning darkly of North American plots to waylay Mexicans for cannon fodder. From Messersmith's perspective, the American labor initiative posed more risk than it was worth.[61]

Messersmith half hoped that Camacho would see the matter in the same light. But the Mexican took his country's belligerency seriously, even if most of his people did not, and hoped that a labor program would rouse them from their apathy. Besides, there were farm skills to be acquired and wages to be remitted home. Negotiators for the United States Department of Agriculture, who arrived in July, yielded to Mexican demands for tougher protective guarantees. The agreement signed on 4 August stipulated that the United States government, not individual farmers, contract for the workers' services; certification of need and farmers' compliance with the established standards for wages and working conditions fell to Washington to enforce.[62]

Under close embassy supervision, officers of the Farm Security Administration began signing on *braceros*. In late September the first contingent crossed the border, waving American flags, chanting "Viva la Roosevelt," searching in vain for the expected welcoming party. Instead they were hustled along by stone-faced American immigration and customs agents. This slight came to Roosevelt's attention, however, and he sent a warm belated greeting to the Mexican "soldiers in the battle of production," promising them "a more just compensation as well as a higher standard of living than you have enjoyed before."[63]

Indeed, the cash inducements—a thirty-cent-per-hour minimum wage and $3-a-day subsistence in the event of unemployment—attracted would-be *braceros* to Mexico City faster than they could be processed. By 1943 the backlog exceeded 4,000, a small army for the Camacho government to house and feed and police. The need-certification requirement was suspended, which speeded up recruitment and threw a new burden onto the already overtaxed Mexican railways. A critical shortage of day coaches elicited suggestions that *braceros* be moved north in boxcars—political dynamite. Messersmith did "not want the suggestion to come from any source within our Government."[64]

The *bracero* bottleneck, then, had basically become a transportation problem. As all concerned acknowledged, Mexico's decrepit national rail lines remained the weak link in the two countries' whole wartime cooperation program. But bureaucratic conflict in Washington over what the United States ought to do to help and what, if anything, could be asked of Mexico in return, had prevented Major Hill's recommendations from being acted upon. Because Hill had said many unkind things about the caliber of the Mexican management, the OCIAA and the BEW insisted that the Mexicans be required to accept an American-supervised reform program as a condition of American cash. Messersmith agreed that reforms were in order, but not through a patently coercive quid pro quo, not when the United States had, as he put it, a "selfish interest" in keeping the Mexican rails running at any cost.[65]

The railroad plan finally agreed to in November without preconditions was a war measure, prompted less by concern for Mexico's present or future economic health than by fear of the dire consequences of further delay that Messersmith constantly expanded upon. Seven and a half million dollars was appropriated for the program. A team of crack American railway executives and technicians was assembled and sent south. Repairs began at once around the clock on the key Laredo-to-Mexico-City line which had dealt Messersmith that bruising welcome back in February. The rest of the system received attention in turn.[66]

As the threat of actual collapse receded, Messersmith began to discuss the rail situation in terms of Mexico's future. As he told reporters in March 1943, the two were inextricably related. "From an efficient railroad system," he predicted, "Mexico will obtain her industrial and economic impetus, not only in the present war period, but also after the war." But the mission's patchwork did not an efficient system make. For Mexico to fulfill its economic promise, the very real organizational problems besetting the Mexican lines would have to be addressed. The National Railways, like Pemex, suffered from an excess of politics and politicians where experienced managers should have been. Featherbedding was rampant among the workers, who took orders from union leaders rather than their supervisors. The American mission's recommendations for change in those practices were perhaps too fundamental and far-reaching to have a chance for acceptance. But its work was eventually to bear important fruit, especially in upgrading railroad maintenance and worker training.[67]

In November 1942, just after the exchange of notes covering the railroad program, Messersmith moved to head off a resurgent BEW. Its first offensive stymied, that agency, he charged, was now trying to "take over the control of our foreign relations . . . via the backdoor." Procurement chief Floyd Ransom was suddenly inundated by BEW "assistants, so termed," in what Messersmith took to be an effort "to undermine and isolate him."[68] Moreover, BEW agents were now actively promoting their superiors' social philosophy. Wallace and Milo Perkins liked to think of themselves as embattled keepers of the Progressive flame abroad. Having decided to do good for foreign workers engaged on BEW projects, they started wielding their considerable economic power to that end. Latins wishing to do business with the BEW were thus obliged to meet elaborate codes for workers' housing, sanitation, health care, job safety, accident compensation, union representation, and more. Although the BEW pledged to obey "all laws of the country of origin, so far as they affect labor relations," its standards were to apply "regardless of the actual provisions" of that local law. Wallace and Perkins were determined to prevent employers from hiding behind the repressive laws in force in many American Republics.[69]

Of course, it was not this simple. Coercion, even in what looked like a good cause, was still coercion. The history of United States–Latin relations was replete with episodes of deeply resented Yankee intervention for the Latins' supposed benefit. Nowhere were the BEW's intrusions less warranted than in Mexico, which, as Messersmith pointed out, had "the most advanced social legislation of any country in Latin America." The BEW was apparently oblivious to the headaches its labor standards caused Camacho, who had to contend with demands for equality from the vast majority of Mexican workers not covered by BEW contracts.[70]

The contrast in tone between Messersmith's protests to Wallace and to the State Department is striking. Because in trying to expand the scope of its activities the BEW was only doing what Messersmith would have undoubtedly tried to do himself under the same circumstances, and because its chief was still the vice-president of the United States, he was calm and respectful to Wallace. Mexico, he explained, was on its way to becoming America's number one supplier of strategic materials. It had "not been an easy task" because there were so "many enemies of the United States here." He had succeeded only by dealing with Mexico "on the basis of full equality and complete understanding," and that meant respecting its laws. Unfortunately, "some of our people at home . . . sometimes feel that we can do things in other countries just as we do them at home." That was a fallacy with unlimited potential to harm the procurement program for which Wallace was accountable.[71]

Partly for effect, partly from genuine pique, Messersmith was the very antithesis of reason with the State Department. He laid the blame for its bureaucratic decline since 1940—for the loss of the advantage he had bequeathed it—at its own door, and particularly that of Duggan, the man in charge of relations with Wallace and Rockefeller relative to Latin America. As far as Messersmith and colleagues like Braden in Havana and Caffery in Rio were concerned, those relations remained all too cordial. Writing on 24 November, Messersmith was good enough to give Duggan a choice: either he put his foot down against amateurs running rampant in the field, or "I would have to resign. We are in a war and I am willing to do my part, but no agency of our Government . . . can destroy our position. . . . This is strong language, but I mean it." He went on to assure Duggan that he was not "desperate or disturbed"; Duggan may have drawn that conclusion himself before Messersmith suggested it to him.[72]

In any case, Duggan ignored this ham-handed ultimatum. Messersmith was soon informed that BEW agents were not only not going to be withdrawn, but that new economic "special assistants" were on their way. Messersmith turned to Wallace, inviting him to send someone to survey Mexican procurement and then to decide for himself whether or not a "special assistant" was really necessary. December brought the BEW assistant director, Hector Lazo. Lazo and his aides, a relieved Messersmith wrote Braden, "found our arrangement working so well here that they agreed that the appointment of a 'special assistant' in Mexico City was not necessary."[73]

Sensing the upper hand, Messersmith determined to settle the issue for good. On 15 January he left for Washington, meeting with Wallace twelve days later. Wallace's problem was that the embassy had largely usurped the BEW's functions in Mexico and was performing them all satisfactorily. Thinking of Mexico, Wallace admitted privately that "some of our men had not fully understood how to go about the job of working in a foreign country." Although he accused Messersmith of "thinking more about bureaucratic rights than . . . of getting the job done," statistics on present and projected Mexican production showed that the job was getting done nevertheless. During their conversation, Messersmith unkindly pointed out what Wallace wished to forget, that problem areas like the rubber program were precisely the areas in which the BEW had been most active. He went on to attack the labor clauses as "interference in the internal affairs of the country," arguing that "we had no mandate whatever . . . to establish certain social or labor standards in other countries through the operation of our procurement and development program."[74]

Messersmith's contemporary and retrospective accounts recall two Wallaces: respectively, "keen[ly] interest[ed]" or "cold and difficult." Wallace's diary entry characterizes the encounter with him as "very satisfactory," which suggests, at least, the absence of open animosity. The conversation seems to have turned rapidly to the question of procurement priorities for the coming year. Those priorities were achieved on Messersmith's terms. When Messersmith returned to

Mexico, BEW labor clauses were replaced by a provision stating un-qualifiedly that "buyer and seller will agree to abide by all pertinent provisions of the Mexican labor and social laws."[75]

In July 1943 Wallace's ongoing feud with Jesse Jones and the RFC spilled into the open. An annoyed Roosevelt then abolished Wallace's agency, transferring its responsibilities to a new Office of Economic Warfare. By that time the BEW had ceased to play an important independent role in Mexico. Wallace neither forgave nor forgot Messersmith's contribution to his downfall. A voluminous correspondence between them came to an abrupt halt. Messersmith asserted in his memoirs that Wallace "undertook a really definite effort to get me removed"; he was proud of having foiled a "fanatic," a "danger" to his country. Wallace delivered the crueler cut. Writing in his diary in August 1945, he recalled his admiration for Messersmith's stand against nazism in the 1930s. Since then Wallace had become con-vinced that "he is spiritually a Nazi himself, or at any rate a narrow-minded martinet with a 19th century outlook." The not uncommon irony was that these two willful men were fighting for like ideals and never recognized it.[76]

4

After the showdown with Wallace, Messersmith's 2 February 1943 conference at the White House was almost anticlimactic. From it, however, emerged plans full of symbolic and tangible importance for Mexican-American relations. Camacho had often expressed his ad-miration for Roosevelt in Messersmith's presence. The two presi-dents, of course, had never met. So, when Roosevelt now happened to mention an upcoming presidential inspection tour of military in-stallations in the south and southwest, Messersmith proposed adding on an exchange of visits with Camacho. Roosevelt was enthusiastic, with one condition: "George," he remembered Roosevelt saying, "the big boy will have to go to see the smaller boy first"; their introduction should take place on Mexican soil. That would be a first for an American president, and the first meeting between United States and Mexican heads of state on either's soil since William H. Taft met Porfirio Díaz in 1909. Messersmith suggested that they meet at Mon-terrey, site of a new American-assisted industrial complex. Camacho could then return the visit in Texas.[77]

When Messersmith informed Camacho of Roosevelt's intentions, the Mexican president's "face was really luminous." Messersmith and Padilla waded into the details. A Secret Service agent was spirited in to make tight wartime security arrangements. Not until 15 April, five days before Roosevelt's scheduled arrival, did rumors of a visit appear in the press. On the 17th, still in secrecy, Camacho and his entourage boarded the train that took them to a siding five miles outside Monterrey. Messersmith and Padilla continued on, meeting Roosevelt's train at the border. At 4:03 P.M., 20 April, as scheduled, the Mexican president and Señora Camacho climbed into Roosevelt's car. Roosevelt struggled to his feet to greet them, revealing as he rose the current *Time* magazine cover on the seat of his chair. That cover bore the portrait of Manuel Ávila Camacho. Messersmith and other onlookers gasped at the unfortunate symbolism. But the Mexican president broke the tension with a joke, to Messersmith's eternal relief.[78]

Nothing more marred the occasion. Mrs. Roosevelt created a small stir by holding forth on the touchy subject of racial injustice in America and its impact upon Mexicans there. But the others refused to let these unpleasantries disturb the festive mood. Encouraged by their government, thousands of Mexicans turned out on short notice for a glimpse of the two presidents waving from open cars. Girls in folk costumes showered the procession with flowers and confetti. A military parade followed, featuring infantry "in perfect order" and motorized units on their new American trucks. At the state banquet that evening Roosevelt and Camacho saluted the war effort, the Good Neighbor policy, and each other in prepared addresses broadcast to their people. The next day, 21 April, the two presidents traveled to Corpus Christi for brief private talks and good-byes. It marked the happy culmination of an era ill-begotten 107 years before to the day, when Sam Houston won Texas its independence at San Jacinto.[79]

Camacho's train lurched home without two of its original passengers. Messersmith and Padilla opted for a more private return trip. They drove south together in high spirits, meandering through the provinces, which Messersmith had not had much chance to see. The local color sustained their exhilaration over what they had helped bring about at Monterrey. From North Carolina Josephus Daniels spoke for all advocates of Mexican-American friendship in pronouncing the presidential visits "a consummation of the Good Neighbor policy." Messersmith, for his part, was ecstatic at what he learned upon his return to the capital. "The general reaction," he concluded, "was magnificent . . . no event in Mexican history has made so profound an impression on so great a mass of the Mexican people."[80]

An infusion of good feelings was never more needed. Roosevelt's visit had coincided with rising anti-Americanism in Mexico, the subject of that embarrassing *Time* cover story. The enemies of collaboration were making dangerous headway agitating Mexico's wartime economic woes, which were being blamed, with some justice, on the United States. Inflation in 1943 was a near-universal affliction that struck Mexico particularly hard due to the volume of its exports and the inadequacy of its price controls and anti-hoarding laws. Food prices had gone through the roof as farmers abandoned their corn and beans to fill lucrative procurement contracts for oilseed. In early 1943 inflation was running 13 percent per month. Mexicans found themselves with swollen profits and pay envelopes and frustratingly few manufactures to buy. The government expressed fear of social disorder or at least lagging production. On the eve of Messersmith's departure for Monterrey, Finance Minister Eduardo Suárez had come begging relief. Messersmith explained Washington's policy of allocation equality, pointed out the privations all Americans were enduring, and urged Mexico to tighten controls, raise taxes, and sell bonds to relieve the inflationary pressures.[81]

The two presidents had taken up these concerns. Camacho sought increased capital, as well as consumer products. He showed Roosevelt what amounted to a master plan for Mexican development: a long list of industrial, agricultural, and social-welfare projects requiring American materials and machinery. The upshot, announced simultaneously in Washington and Mexico City on 29 April, was the formation of a Joint Economic Commission to study Mexico's problems and establish a framework for intergovernmental cooperation.[82]

Messersmith invested the commission with his aspirations for Mexican-American relations. "In the economic field," he told an audience in August 1943, "there are no two countries in the Americas whose industry and agriculture can be so closely and intimately helpful to each other, and so thoroughly complement each other, with almost a complete lack of any clash of interest." The United States needed Mexico now and, contrary to some thinking, he believed it would need Mexico more than ever in the future. The thought that haunted him and many others in 1943 was that the economic depression that had given rise to this war would return with the peace. But to Messersmith, the way to a prosperous postwar was clear: develop and distribute the vast potential wealth of countries like Mexico; provide the means to satisfy the crying needs of its 21 million souls, he argued, and American farms and factories would thrive. "Mexico," he wrote Welles on 3 June, "will never be a completely satisfactory neighbor until . . . the present wide gap between our standards of living is reduced." He saw the joint commission as a signal step in that direction. Its report, released on 2 July 1943, proposed a forty-one project agenda and a new Mexican-American Industrial Commission to oversee the program. To Messersmith's intense satisfaction, the two countries were now committed to joint development of Mexico's resources and industrial base.[83]

Unfortunately, as before, Messersmith found that good Mexican-American relations were not everyone's top priority at home. Roosevelt had promised Camacho an investigation of the allocations situation. Coordinator Rockefeller arrived in late May bearing a report showing how well Mexico was faring under the current system. He supplied, as the *New York Times* put it, a "much-needed explanation" why no additional exports were possible. To soften the blow, Rockefeller offered a $2.5 million public health program. Commendable on its face, the coordinator's gift was a relative insult. Brazil was the recent recipient of a $5 million grant, as was Chile, which had not broken with the Axis until January 1943.[84]

Messersmith protested. If the OCIAA could not scrape together at least as much for Mexico's health program as for Chile's, he snapped, "we had better forget about the whole thing." He acknowledged that "we have done . . . quite well by Mexico in the way of materials"—almost twice as much per capita as for Brazil—but statistics did not calm Mexican discontent. "We cannot approach the question of materials," he admonished Welles, "with the idea that we have been prodigal with Mexico and that therefore she should be very happy." American policy proved that the squeaky wheel got the grease. Camacho's critics were muttering that Mexico would be treated more generously, like Chile, were she less cooperative. Allocations equality, Messersmith argued, was a nice phrase, but limited resources had to go where they meant most. He was "not making a case for Mexico. I am making a case for ourselves." Preferential treatment for the southern neighbor, he promised, would be amply repaid later on.[85]

His entreaties produced no modification of American allocation policy, no infusion of consumer goods, no new money for public health. By September the corn shortage had grown to crisis proportions, and again Mexico and Messersmith met frustration at the hands of Washington's wartime bureaucracy. The Department of Agriculture rejected Mexico's urgent request for 25,000 tons of corn on grounds that none was to be had either from government warehouses or from the free market. Starving Mexicans were gratuitously advised to tighten their belts.[86]

On 23 September, in what was a major departure for him, Messersmith appealed directly to Roosevelt. He did so for two reasons. First, the Mexican visit and Messersmith's vision of a model partnership seem to have caught Roosevelt's imagination. He had enjoyed easy rapport with Camacho and, as he later wrote his ambassador, "developed a high regard for [Camacho's] sound statesmanship [and] progressive and practical policies." That camaraderie encouraged Messersmith to call upon the White House in late September in order to help friend Camacho avert famine among his people.[87]

Second, the person Messersmith would otherwise have turned to at the State Department was no longer there. On 16 August 1943 Undersecretary of State Sumner Welles resigned in order to prevent a public scandal from breaking loose over certain homosexual entanglements he was alleged to have had. His loss, as historian Irwin F. Gellman has observed, was a grievous one for Latin America. Messersmith had relied upon Welles's informed and sympathetic advocacy for the hemisphere. His successor, Edward R. Stettinius, Jr., a former executive at General Motors and U.S. Steel, was an amiable sort rather than a force for policy.[88]

Without Welles to help him, Messersmith increasingly looked to Roosevelt as an ally against his own intractable bureaucracy. The concerned agencies, he wrote the president, were insensitive to how "really serious" the Mexican corn shortage was. "If Mexico cannot get some corn, it will have serious repercussions in the economic and political life of this country where, fortunately, there is more order than had prevailed here for many years. . . . The whole program of the Mexican Government will be endangered . . . if corn cannot be got to meet the needs of the great mass of the Mexican people." Mexico's whole constitutional system might be jeopardized. "You know what can happen when people get hungry and you know that such things can happen more easily in Mexico than in some other places." The war effort could ill afford food riots south of the border.[89]

Messersmith's appeal worked wonders. Roosevelt ordered an investigation and emergency food shipments. At his direction, a complex deal was worked out between the concerned agencies and the Mexican government under which corn was exchanged for vegetable meal (oil seed residue), a tolerable animal feed. On 13 October Assistant Secretary Berle informed Mexico City that 5,000 tons of corn, the first of five installments, was moving south.[90]

With this impressive display of presidential muscle behind him, Messersmith redoubled his efforts on behalf of his and Roosevelt's Mexican program. Again the obstacle sat in Washington. On 25 October he was notified that Donald Nelson's War Production Board was about to rule unfavorably on the Mexican-American Industrial Commission's agenda. Materials for its projects would be subtracted

from Mexico's current allocation. The commission would thus be reduced to competing for export priorities against critical immediate
needs.

This decision secretly pleased most concerned parties in Washington. To people like Duggan and Rockefeller, hemispheric unity was
the overriding imperative. They worried about the impact of the
Mexican-American commission on their nineteen other Latin clients
and foresaw a negotiating nightmare in nineteen new demands for
equality. The State Department, then, was relieved by Nelson's decision, which stripped the Mexican-American agreement of all but
symbolic meaning.[91]

Messersmith, on the other hand, was livid. Nelson's decision con-
tradicted the understanding he had witnessed between the two presidents at Monterrey that "something special" was to be done during
the war to aid Mexican development materially. The present commission and its predecessor had operated on that assumption. Was he
now supposed to tell the Mexicans that it had all been a big mistake?
He appreciated that, as Nelson had explained, the "armed forces
must come first," but what were he and Camacho supposed to make
of reports that supplies were being diverted to rebuild reconquered
Europe, southern Italy, for instance? "Our first duty," he lectured
Stettinius, "is to our friends and not to our enemies."[92]

If, for whatever reason, the United States declined to assist Mexican development, others, he assured Washington, would fill the
void. The Russians in particular had become busier all over Latin
America. In 1943 they sent Constantin Oumansky to Mexico City as
ambassador to Mexico and the Central American republics. Messersmith knew him well. Oumansky had come to Washington as Soviet
embassy counselor in 1938 and immediately set to undermine his
superior, Ambassador Alexander Troyanovsky. Within six months
Troyanovsky had been recalled, and Oumansky promoted to his office. In record time he managed to alienate official Washington.
Hull came to consider him "one of the most difficult foreign diplomats with whom we ever had to deal . . . insulting in his manner
and speech." Dean Acheson soon decided that Oumansky "cultivated
boorishness as a method of showing [his] contempt for the capitalist
world." Whatever his motives, Hull and Welles eventually refused to
receive him. The disagreeable duty, yet another, fell to Assistant Secretary of State Messersmith. As usual, he pulled no punches. "I don't
think you can go any lower," he told Oumansky; he would either
mind his manners or be totally isolated in Washington. Presumably
chastened, Oumansky behaved like a perfect gentleman in their subsequent contact, which even attained a degree of warmth. Messer-

smith chalked up another success for undiplomatic tough talk. More likely, he was only getting his just desserts for having been a lonely friend of Soviet-American cooperation during the 1930s. In the same sense, Hull and Welles had got their due, too.[93]

In any case, in 1943 there was evidence that Oumansky was on a trouble-making mission to Mexico to stir up anti-Americanism and establish a base for Soviet operations in the hemisphere. He made quick contact with local leftists, like Lombardo Toledano, and frequent disparaging public comments about the United States and its failure to open a second front. He wooed Cárdenas with wondrous accounts of Soviet heroism and productivity. Russia, he promised the Mexican, would take care of its friends in the postwar; all the machinery and equipment Mexico needed would become available just as soon as the Red Army had finished destroying German power in Europe. He promised to see if some farm machinery might be spared for Mexico at once.[94]

In his own conversations with Cárdenas, Messersmith predicted that Oumansky would be unable to deliver on his promises. Western Russia, he pointed out, was presently scorched earth; the mammoth rebuilding job would require every scrap of steel and mortar the Russians could lay hands on. Not for years would materials be available for export. When those Soviet tractors arrived, Messersmith asked to be informed so that he could inform Washington, where the Soviets were pleading for just such machinery under lend-lease. ·Only the United States, he maintained, would be capable of fulfilling Mexico's postwar needs, and, he added, "I was not saying this egotistically or as an American, but that it just seemed sound judgment."[95]

Messersmith drew quite a different picture for Washington. First, he tried to allay the rampant concerns about Oumansky, who, he agreed, was up to no good—that was in his nature—but who, he insisted, was a waning relic of an old-line conspiratorial Bolshevism that no longer characterized the Soviet state or its diplomacy. Messersmith was convinced that "Communism in the full sense did not exist any longer in Russia." In May 1943 the Comintern was dissolved, which he took as further evidence of Russia's friendly intentions toward its allies. He noted the nationalistic flavor of Stalin's appeals to his people. Whatever they were fighting the Germans so valiantly for, Messersmith concluded, "it was not for the Communism of Lenin and Trotsky." Rather than fomenting confrontation or revolution, he felt that the Russians "will be more and more inclined to work with us" to preserve the hard-fought peace. There would be occasional disputes between friends, as over the second front, but he was confident that "understanding and collaboration" between their two nations would triumph over all, including Oumansky's impulsive machinations.[96]

The same pragmatic Russian nationalism told him—or so he told Washington—that Russia would become an economic competitor a lot sooner than he had suggested to Cárdenas. If the Soviets approached their rebuilding with "the same zeal which is now being put into the war effort," Russian industry and agriculture would soon be back on their feet. There would be help, moreover, from friends and enemies. "As surely as the sun will rise tomorrow," he wrote Phllip Bonsal, the Russians will "use anything they can pull out of Germany in the way of technical assistance and material to help them in the reconstruction." With Russia, then, soon to become "a friendly competitor" for hemispheric markets and influence, it was vital that the United States "build up the economies of our friends." That was why Messersmith was "so interested in the Joint Mexican-American [Com]mission for Economic Cooperation."[97]

He was playing a Russian card on Washington, and its apparent effectiveness in this instance would encourage him to play it again, for higher stakes, later on. But other factors were at least as important in overturning Nelson's allocation decision. Messersmith went to Washington to press the cause. After conferring with Roosevelt on 27 January 1944, he met with Nelson, Hull, and other officials to deliver the president's directive that materials for the Joint Industrial Commission's projects fall outside normal allocations. Roosevelt had also asked Messersmith to emphasize "the importance which he had laid to the work of this Commssion and [to] . . . other agencies of our Government collaborating with it." Nelson promised "the most favorable treatment" consistent with "the exigencies of war." Fortunately war production was finally meeting demand. The Joint Industrial Commission hastened to prepare detailed materials estimates for the War Production Board to work into planning. In a 31 March cover letter to Nelson, Hull urged adoption of the commission's twenty-one-project 1944 program, with one major reservation. The State Department, he explained, had not completed its evaluation of the program's economic impact. He was endorsing the program because "failure to make substantial progress during 1944 towards the realization of this program might have unfortunate political consequences . . . [for] Mexican-American relations." Necessary modifications could come later.[98]

Fear of Soviet penetration, gratitude to Camacho, obeisance to Roosevelt, and Messersmith's usual relentlessness do not entirely explain the bureaucracy's sudden support for the commission. The "unfortunate consequences" Hull mentioned bore directly upon an obscure Mexican decree of 18 December 1943, a decree that hit Hull and his commercial advisers like a thunderbolt reminiscent of the petroleum nationalization. The decree provided for "sweeping upward revisions" in Mexican tariffs on some 700 items. Perceiving a precedent-setting challenge to postwar free trade, the department set grimly to its annulment. To the Mexican ambassador, Francisco Castillo Nájera, it expressed its "deep concern." On 15 January Economic Counselor Lockett, on orders from Washington, confronted Eduardo Suárez, who tried to defend the tariff hikes as revenue-raising, anti-inflation measures. When Lockett presented a personal appeal for time from Messersmith, still in Washington, Suárez agreed to wait thirty days before effecting the decree.[99]

But the State Department would not rest until the dastardly decree had been dropped altogether. Hull furnished the embassy chargé d'affaires, Herbert Bursley, with debating points to puncture Suárez's defense and force him to admit and recant his protectionism. Bursley was also authorized to promise reinvigorated support for increased allocations if Mexico did Washington's wishes. Messersmith, who returned to the Mexican capital on 10 February, got Mexico's answer the next day. He reported that Padilla "was as much disturbed [by the decree] as we were . . . [and] was of the opinion that there should be no increase in rates whatever, and that the decree as a whole should be made ineffective." On 17 February Camacho did just that, over Suárez's bitter protests. Then Hull, quid pro quo, interceded with Nelson on the commission's behalf.[100]

As previously noted, this support was qualified. The basic contradiction in American policy toward the developing world that had surfaced during Messersmith's stay in Cuba now intruded itself into the Mexican picture. Washington professed to favor balanced growth for its neighbors, but remained implacably hostile to the tariffs needed by infant industry to weather American competition. Thus, in evaluating the industrial commission's projects individually, Hull and his advisers rejected those that "conflicted with our commercial policy"—that is, projects that would require tariff protection.[101]

Messersmith spotlighted the inconsistency. "We are living in a changing world," he observed, and from a front-row seat; for he saw Mexico in the forefront of southern nations poised to leap into the twentieth century. Having achieved political stability, "the country is going to settle down to developing her resources. . . and her internal life in general." The United States had a chance through the Joint Industrial Commission to play the instrumental role in both countries' interests. But Messersmith was convinced that "the industrialization of Mexico will go forward whether we help it or not," and, he now recognized, not always along complementary lines. The fact was that "industries of a competitive character . . . have already been established in Mexico and will be established in the future and quite rapidly. They will need some tariff protection"—protection no Mexican government, not even one as friendly as Camacho's, could fail to provide.[102]

This prophecy was shortly borne out. A new Mexican decree dated 15 April 1944 authorized the imposition of import controls. State Department free-traders yelped, invoking the trade agreement, threatening reprisals and representations. Upon Messersmith's protest, Suárez agreed to notify Washington before implementing the decree, but would go no further. That the Mexicans were about "to protect some phases of their national economy," Messersmith warned, was a reality to which Washington had better adjust. "If we are not prepared to do this," he added, "then our efforts in aiding these weaker economies are largely in vain."[103]

In Washington there were proposals to retaliate by withdrawing from the Joint Industrial Commission, with which the State Department had been unhappy from the start. Rumors of an American pull-out persisted even as the sanitized 1944 program got underway. Finding the idea of withdrawal "incredible [and] astounding," Messersmith vowed to fight. "I may be getting older," he roared to the State Department's trade division chief, Harry Hawkins, a likely suspect, "but I am not getting tired and there are some things for which I will struggle to the last ditch when I know that they are in the interests of my country." The commission, child of Monterrey and Corpus Christi, could not "be sabotaged by narrow thinking in the Department." For himself, "there is no one more convinced of the soundness of [Hull's] trade policies," but "we must keep in account the legitimate aspirations of other sovereign countries . . . to improve their own well-being and standards of living" through industrialization.[104]

Hull assured him that there was "no serious discussion in the Department with reference to withdrawal from the Commission." It carried on until January 1945. By then all the equipment required for the 1944 program had been licensed and much of it delivered. The first project, a tomato-canning plant in Sonora, neared completion. With the relaxation of American export controls, materials were increasingly available on the open market. So, by an exchange of letters between Roosevelt and Camacho, the commission adjourned sine die.[105]

In its final report, the commission congratulated itself for having "contributed substantially to the economic development of Mexico." This was true. But the commission's record and subsequent American policies showed that the realities Messersmith hammered home had not all sunk in. The commission's projects, however laudable, were mainly of the noncompetitive variety, with heavy emphasis on tourism, export agriculture, and domestic aviation. The State Department never ceased combating Mexico's attempts to protect its industries. The Mexicans did what they had to do. By the end of 1945 restrictions had been imposed on almost a hundred imports, and the list was growing. Time and again, Washington ordered formal protests. Messersmith steadfastly resisted, arguing for accommodation and quiet discussions with Suárez. And he won a significant, if temporary, rollback in restrictions, even though—or perhaps because—he had "the most complete sympathy" for Mexican protectionism.[106]

Nor had the State Department abandoned its efforts to bring back the American oil companies. In November 1943 Messersmith was instructed to find out whether the Mexicans had reconsidered their opposition to private participation and, if not, to talk them into it. Perhaps recalling Messersmith's reluctance, the department appealed to his patriotism, expressing its "confiden[ce] that the personal attention which it knows you will give this matter will produce the results so necessary to the future welfare of this country."[107]

But Messersmith had always envisioned a cooperative relationship between the American oil industry and the Mexican government. He despaired of Pemex ineptitude, which deprived Mexico of revenues so critical to its development. "Until 1945," one student agrees, "Pemex would have been judged a failure by almost any test." But the Mexican political climate remained inhospitable to change, and Messersmith advised against pressing the issue as long as it was. The shadow of Cárdenas loomed large over Camacho and Padilla. The rapid bureaucratization of Pemex had created a powerful vested interest from which they shrank.[108]

Messersmith was therefore surprised when, during a conversation early in January 1944, Cárdenas said he would be open to "constructive changes" in his petroleum law. It seemed to be the State Department's break. With Camacho's blessings, Messersmith flew home to discuss the matter. He arrived in Washington on 10 January. A car and driver from the Mexican embassy were waiting for him at the airport, an unprecedented courtesy that turned into disappointment. He was driven directly to the embassy to be handed a message from Camacho, regretfully withdrawing Mexico's assent.[109]

What had happened? When Messersmith returned to Mexico,

a "visibly embarrassed" Camacho explained that Cárdenas had resumed his opposition to change. Messages from Ambassador Castillo Nájera in Washington had given him good reason to change his
mind. Petroleum Administrator Ickes was reportedly hinting that the
Roosevelt government was prepared to finance Pemex's exploration
and production program. There would be no need for private capital. Not surprisingly, the Mexicans chose to investigate the possibility.
Until they had, an agreement to the contrary was impossible.[110]

There the matter remained until July. On the 6th, Padilla arrived
in Washington for an official visit. The trip had been Messersmith's
idea, partly to prevent Mexico and the hemisphere from being totally eclipsed by D-Day and its aftermath. He also had Padilla's future
in mind. Mexicans were already busily maneuvering in anticipation
of their presidential elections some two years off, and Messersmith
hoped that a Washington visit, his first in over two years, would enhance Padilla's stature as a statesman both at home and abroad. And
he had another motive. In the course of Padilla's scheduled discussions with Roosevelt, Hull, and other officials, Messersmith expected
that the rumors of major United States assistance to Pemex would be
finally laid to rest, enabling negotiations with potential private devel-
opers to go forward.[111]

Things did not quite work out this way. Padilla made a splendid
impression in Washington during his ten-day stay, highlighted by tea
and talks at the White House. The visit, Messersmith reported when
Padilla had returned home, had "deepened the bonds of friendship
which he already has had for us and for this reason alone [it] has
been worthwhile for our two countries."[112] In fact it may have done
Padilla, who was already too close to the United States for many
Mexicans' comfort, more harm than good. As for the oil-loan question, Padilla had indeed discussed it with Roosevelt, only to emerge
more convinced than ever that a big loan was in the offing. Roosevelt
had sent him to Ickes, who naturally did nothing to discourage him.
Hull learned all this from Padilla during their talk on 12 July.[113]

The news of this "fly in the ointment" made for one of Messersmith's "few sleepless nights" so far in Mexico. For the first time in its
history, Mexico was a net importer of petroleum in 1944, and would
remain so until 1949. The confusion in Washington, he feared, "will
merely . . . delay any progress" toward Mexican regeneration. As for
the source of what he was sure had been a misunderstanding, Messersmith recalled Roosevelt speaking about joint development of
a Mexican oil field as an American military reserve. Under that
scheme the United States would pay all costs—estimated at under $4
million—build and fill storage tanks, and then turn a producing field

over to Mexico. Messersmith suspected that the president, "who has so much on his mind these days may . . . have confused this limited idea with the broad question."[114]

That was just what had happened, as Roosevelt made plain in a 19 July memorandum to Hull. Although Messersmith explained what had happened to Padilla, the Mexican was ordered to lodge a formal request for negotiations based on his understanding of his Washington discussions. With Ickes continuing to promote the big-loan idea, a definitive presidential ruling was needed. The pressures of the war, the planning for the peace, the campaign for the fourth term, and a three-week post-election holiday at Warm Springs, Georgia, delayed the matter until December 1944. Messersmith flew home for what proved to be his last face-to-face encounter with Roosevelt. They had not seen each other since January, and Messersmith recalled being "shocked beyond measure by the change in his appearance." His judgment and phenomenal mastery of detail seemed unimpaired, however. Messersmith was vastly relieved to hear him say that a large loan for exploration "was out of the question and not to be considered and that he would not consider it"; Messersmith should continue working toward the strategic reserve and "equitable arrangements" between the Mexican government and the American companies. Roosevelt ordered him to inform Ickes, who subjected him to an hour-long harangue on oil-company evils. Padilla, whom Messersmith saw on 3 January 1945, was much more understanding.[115]

5

After clarifying his Mexican oil policy, Roosevelt turned to another topic much on his visiting envoy's mind. Messersmith's stars all pointed to an imminent change of posts. His sixtieth birthday back in October 1943 had passed almost unnoticed, but not so his thirtieth anniversary in the Foreign Service, 27 July 1944. It was "a day filled with a good deal of emotion" for him. "You know I am not a sentimental person," he wrote Hull, who had sent a nice note; but for this occasion he made an exception. Camacho called him in to congratulate him, and Padilla, whom Messersmith admired as much as any foreign statesman he had ever known, scaled new heights of eloquence in his tribute. Joe Gray, himself going on ten years as Hull's assistant, one of those who knew Messersmith longest, also knew him best. "I don't know of anyone," he wrote his former chief, "who has labored so hard and earnestly in season and out for the establishment and maintenance of high principles, sound progressive ideas, and the inculcation of a spirit of sober endeavor. . . . To me you will always remain the symbol of the finest tradition in the Service."[116]

He was not even remotely ready for retirement, however. His old surgical stomach needed minor repairs, but otherwise his physique, carefully monitored and maintained, gave no complaint. His zest was undiminished, his "passion for justice" as strong as ever. As the war entered its final year, Messersmith looked forward to "at least several more opportunities for usefulness" in putting the world back together. "I am hoping," he wrote Hull, "that at the appropriate time my background in the European picture may be utilized."[117]

Rumors to that very effect, or at least that he was not long for Mexico, had already cropped up. One report he heard had the current ambassador to Chile, Claude Bowers, replacing him in Mexico City when he moved on to Europe. Messersmith thoughtfully passed the report on to Hull, with the opinion that Bowers would make an unhappy choice. The workload in Mexico, he explained, was such that the historian-diplomat would find no time for his scholarship.[118]

While he prepared to close out this phase of his personal and professional life, major changes were taking place at Roosevelt's State Department, starting at the top. Tired of the responsibility and sick of his alienation from the White House, which had become almost total, Hull was ready to resign in 1944. Messersmith was his last scheduled appointment on what turned out to be his last actual day on the job, 2 October 1944. Roosevelt begged him to reconsider, and actually meant it, but Hull would only agree to wait until after election day to make his decision public. Though forewarned, Messersmith grieved on 27 November, when the announcement came. "Words fail me today," he wrote Hull. A record twelve years as secretary of state came to an end. Messersmith's relationship with him of even longer standing continued on. Hull was one person—Roosevelt not excluded—for whom Messersmith never had a harsh word. In Hull Messersmith always believed he had a kindred idealistic spirit. Life would be different and more difficult for him with Hull gone.[119]

Hull had over the years assembled a staff that suited his own peculiar and extensive needs, a structure largely dismantled upon his departure. Roosevelt and Hopkins, who would carry out the demolition, first took up the question of his successor. Messersmith later heard that someone—it may have been Hopkins himself—suggested him for Hull's job. According to his source, Roosevelt had blithely dismissed the idea on ethnic grounds: "Well, what with Messersmith and Eisenhower, people would wonder whom we were at war with!"[120]

More serious considerations were actually involved here. No modern career diplomat had ever served as secretary of state; but then again, no president had ever served a third term, either. So it was not simply for lack of precedent that Roosevelt ruled him out. Determined to succeed where Woodrow Wilson had failed in 1919, Roosevelt wanted a salesman for his peace arrangements heading the State Department. When Hull retired, Roosevelt sought the next best thing. Even in absentia, Hull figured prominently in the choice of his replacement. Henry Wallace, one supposed front-runner, and Sumner Welles, probably the president's personal choice, were disqualified out of concern for Hull's tender feelings and still formidable influence with Congress. Undersecretary Stettinius finally got the job because he was acceptable to Hull, because in important respects he was the nearest thing Roosevelt had to Hull. Like his predecessor, Stettinius was cast from the Harding mold, at least to the eye. Without Hull's connections, Stettinius nevertheless made friends fast, as attested by his quick Senate confirmation. His specialty was public relations, not foreign relations, but that fitted the bill. In Stettinius, Roosevelt got exactly what he wanted: a handsome figurehead and a "good clerk."[121]

That was not Messersmith. In any case, he figured in Roosevelt's plans in a manner much more to his liking. He would get his chance to upbraid Germans again, as the United States' top civilian official after the Reich fell, a collapse that looked imminent in November 1944. Messersmith had all the right ideas on Germany as far as Roosevelt was concerned, ideas that, as in the 1930s, put him at odds with orthodoxy at the State Department. Tracing Hitlerism to the punitive features of Versailles, the department's German planners in 1944 envisaged a lenient peace, one that would hasten recovery, foster democratic institutions, and, again, serve as a bulwark against possible Soviet expansion.[122]

Messersmith's thinking on the Hitler phenomenon had not changed appreciably, either. Since 1933 he had characterized nazism as a form of mental illness, and he continued to do so. But he had long ceased to view the German people as its innocent victims. They had yielded too unprotestingly to evil, had too eagerly abetted what Messersmith considered the greatest crime in history. Witnessing their craven submission had been among the "most disillusioning experiences" of his life. He believed that the German national character, which had caused the world such grief, would require thoroughgoing long-term rehabilitation—"six months or more" of military government, followed by "perhaps two generations" of civilian controls and reeducation before Germany would be ready to rejoin the family of nations. "We must be hard and stern and definite," he counseled, ". . . if we wish to avoid another war."[123]

Roosevelt was using much the same language. "We have got to be tough with Germany," he declared in August 1944, "and I mean the German people, not just the Nazis." At his September conference with British Prime Minister Churchill at Quebec, Roosevelt advanced Henry Morgenthau's plan to partition and deindustrialize Germany, reducing it to a loose confederation of agrarian states incapable of ever again threatening the peace. Although he later disowned that plan, Roosevelt continued to think in terms of a Carthaginian peace.[124]

The like-minded and experienced Messersmith looked just right to head up the occupation. In reorganizing the State Department, Hopkins and Stettinius assumed that Messersmith would quit Mexico early in 1945 in preparation for Germany. Hopkins offered Mexico to Breck Long, who was being swept out with the rest of Hull's assistant secretaries. But Long declined, citing the altitude and his lack of Spanish, and retired instead. Stettinius looked into the possibility of moving Spruille Braden from Cuba to Mexico.[125]

But for the identity of his successor, everything seemed in place when Messersmith departed Mexico for his December 1944 petroleum talk with Roosevelt. The *New York Times* reported approvingly that he was coming home primarily to discuss the German assignment. "He speaks German and knows the genesis of the Nazi movement and the psychology and problems of the German people. In addition to his diplomatic experience, he is considered an able organizer and administrator," vital skills in setting up a new German government.[126]

Roosevelt did not disappoint him. On "his own initiative," Messersmith later stressed, he confirmed that he would eventually be going to Germany. But the Germans were not cooperating. Three days earlier, on 16 December, the optimistic forecasts and the four American divisions guarding a seventy-five-mile stretch of woods east of Bastogne, Belgium, buckled under a massive German counteroffensive. Americans stopped planning their victory celebrations and returned to the grind of combat and production. Bringing Messersmith home to work on the occupation details when Allied lines were in danger of being breached was surely putting the cart before the horse. The president therefore instructed him to return to Mexico "to clear things up before it would be necessary for me to go to Europe."[127]

That was fine with Messersmith, for there was important clearing up to do. Uppermost was the forthcoming and, in his view, long overdue Mexico City meeting of the American foreign ministers, the first such gathering since Rio in 1942. By 1945 Rio's glow of shared purpose and common sacrifice was but a fond memory. The old habits of North American neglect were reasserting themselves. The Latins had looked on resentfully as the big powers, in the old colonial manner, sat down without them at Dumbarton Oaks in the summer of 1944, and laid the groundwork for the postwar world. At Mexico City the Latins would make their voices heard. They also had economic anxieties about the postwar world to take up: declining markets for their raw materials, access to capital goods, and foreign competition to their budding industries.[128]

Ironically, the single most pressing issue facing the hemisphere did not appear on the official agenda. Getting the United States to agree to discuss the Argentine question at all had been difficult enough. By mid-1944, however, the failure of Washington's wartime policy toward the hemispheric maverick was obvious even to those responsible for it. After almost three years of United States economic and diplomatic sanctions, the nationalists in Buenos Aires were stronger than ever. When in January 1944 President General Pedro Ramírez bowed to the extent of breaking relations with Germany and Japan, he was himself overthrown by a new clique headed by General Edelmiro Farrell and Colonel Juan D. Perón. Hull's call for the hemisphere to unite in isolating the new regime evoked a disheartening silence especially pronounced among Argentina's neighbors, who were properly wary of its vengeance. Undaunted, the State Department in June raised the stakes, recalling Ambassador Norman Armour from Buenos Aires. Nervous speculation ran through Latin capitals as to what Washington's next step might be.[129]

It was primarily to defuse this explosive situation that Ezequiel Padilla proposed to hold a conference where the republics might air their economic concerns and thresh out the conditions under which Argentina might be readmitted to the inter-American fold. Messersmith urged Washington to avail itself of the chance to extricate itself from its increasingly untenable Argentine position. Few people, he wrote the department on 7 August 1944, least of all Padilla, approved of Argentine misconduct, but regardless of "how badly the Argentine regime is behaving . . . [the Latins] do not like to see the Argentine lambasted too much and they do not like us to do it." The unilateral hard line, he cabled Hull courageously, was creating sympathy for the Argentine underdog and undermining confidence in the Good Neighbor policy.[130]

But Hull could not bring himself to abandon his Argentine policy, a policy maligned at home for, if anything, not being tough enough. In his waning days, he played more and more to posterity. By refusing to compromise with Argentine "fascism," he hoped to expunge the stigma of compromise with German fascism during the 1930s. Still more important to him was the fledgling United Nations Organization, to which he was devoting himself with a zeal surpassed only by his ongoing efforts for reciprocal trade agreements. Both of his overriding objectives—the quarantine of Argentina and the internationalization of postwar security—seemed jeopardized by Padilla's initiative on behalf of regional solidarity and autonomy. The State Department therefore acknowledged its receipt and hoped the idea would go away.[131]

It did not. Aiming to relieve its isolation, the Farrell government appealed to the Pan American Union for a hearing on its status. Padilla renewed his call for a general conference. Backed into a corner, Washington finally assented to the latter on condition that Buenos Aires be excluded. After intensive negotiations between Padilla and Messersmith, invitations to the Inter-American Conference on Problems of Peace and War, scheduled for February 1945, went out to all the republics save Argentina. It was agreed that the Farrell government might speak its piece at the end, when the conferees took up the last item on the agenda, reworded at American insistence (and over Messersmith's objections) to read "Other Matters of General and Immediate Concern" instead of "Argentina."[132]

What the United States might do, or not do, at a conference it was attending under duress was now very properly Messersmith's prime concern. If the thinking current at State controlled American behavior at the conference, it was indeed doomed to failure. In Washington, the European-oriented economic planners prepared to combat Latin protectionism and to finesse the expected demands for loans and export priorities. The political planners, especially Leo Pasvolsky and Harley Notter, who had helped shape Hull's outlook, also had Stettinius's ear, and they warned the new secretary, as they had warned Hull, against furnishing the British and the Russians with further pretext to establish exclusive regional blocs of their own. Moreover, Mexico City was expected to see embarrassing proposals for a hemispheric defense pact independent of the projected United Nations Security Council, as well as demands for modifications in the Dumbarton Oaks formula in order to give more power to small nations. It was suggested in the State Department that Stettinius beg off Mexico City altogether—he could cite his prior commitment to accompany Roosevelt to the Big Three conclave at Yalta, which was expected to run well into February—or to limit his attendance at Mexico to one of the projected two weeks.[133]

Messersmith argued passionately and cogently that hemispheric unity was not only consistent with United States security, but actually indispensable to it. The Grand Alliance was showing deep signs of strain by 1945. Both Russia and England were openly flouting the Atlantic Charter principles of free trade and self-determination. Eastern Europe was rapidly being reduced to a Soviet vassal. The British were clinging tenaciously to the empire. Churchill's policies in reconquered Italy and Greece were overtly hostile to their progressive elements. As the war against Hitlerism drew to a close, Messersmith was profoundly saddened to think that a new chapter in the struggle against colonialism, British and Russian, might only be beginning.[134]

British and Soviet agents were also at work in the Western hemisphere. By mid-1944 Messersmith was reporting a "definite increase" in leftist agitation in Mexico. Padilla came under intensified and increasingly vulgar attack for his ties to the United States. Behind it all Messersmith saw the malign hand of Oumansky, operating through Lombardo Toledano and his Mexican Workers Confederation. Soon there was what he considered conclusive evidence that what he had earlier discounted had been true all along: Oumansky's local machinations were part of a larger and more diabolical scheme of Soviet subversion. Early in 1945 Oumansky demanded that Mexico provide him with a private flight to Costa Rica, where he was to present his credentials. On the morning of 25 January the plane crashed on takeoff from Mexico City, killing all aboard. From the wreckage was recovered Oumansky's briefcase, which turned out to contain 200 U.S. $1,000 bills—money Messersmith was sure was earmarked "to suborn Government officials or labor leaders in Costa Rica or some of these other Central American countries."[135]

At the same time, British imperialism was entrenching itself in Argentina. While paying lip service to Hull's policies, London was privately exploiting the Washington-Buenos Aires rift. Arms and markets and consumer products withheld by the United States were furnished by the British, together with assurances that Argentine neutrality toward Britain's enemies need not prejudice bilateral relations. As a result, under United States sanctions, Argentina boasted some of South America's best-stocked shops, while loyal allies like Mexico went without. London claimed innocently to be interested only in Argentine hides and beef for the cold, hungry British people. But the Royal Air Force bases reportedly being planned suggested otherwise.[136]

Messersmith, still burning over the way Sir John Simon crawled to

Berlin in March 1935, echoed Hull's outrage at Whitehall's latest duplicity. If the British thought they could carve out a South American
sphere of influence under Argentine cover, "they are utterly wrong.
Nothing could be more stupid." It looked to him like Munich all over
again, with London courting an iniquitous regime for selfish advantage. "One would think," he seethed, "that people learn, but it seems
that they do not. [The British] really think that they can keep the
Argentine as a spear head for their trade and to maintain their investments." He hoped that Roosevelt would "put the screws" to Churchill at Yalta.[137]

If the United States intended to uphold its principles against their
enemies, the inter-American system would have to be strengthened,
and, Messersmith maintained, Mexico City was the place to do it. He
urged Stettinius to attend the entire conference. "I know that you
have these major problems in the world picture which are requiring
your attention every day, but . . . we have got to have this American
picture in shape or our hand in the world picture will be immensely
weakened." A united hemisphere committed to political and economic liberalism would be essential to counter British and Russian
blocs at the United Nations. Those two powers would evidently be
promoting quite different principles. Unlike them, he wrote "Ed"
Stettinius,

> . . . we are not interested in establishing a closed economy in
> this hemisphere. We are planning an American picture in which
> certain political principles and ideals and certain economic
> practices will control because all of these states believe in them
> and that is something to which Great Britain and Russia cannot
> object. We are planning to keep the markets of this hemisphere
> open to all. Russia and Great Britain are planning economies
> which will be open only to those whom they choose to admit.
> The Latins are deeply conscious of this. For this reason the at-
> mosphere for establishing real American unity and cooperation
> is better than it has been at any time.[138]

Whether Mexico City actually fulfilled this promise depended, in
Messersmith's view, on Washington's posture on the economic issues.
"We can secure the reaffirmation of liberal trade policies at the coming conference," he wrote on 13 February, "but if nothing further is
offered by way of a program, it will cause the keenest disillusionment." Once they liquidated their war-swollen dollar balances, the
Latins would need loans, "just as much as we needed them some
sixty to seventy years back and when we got them from Europe."
They would need technical assistance. Finally, although prepared to

pledge allegiance to the State Department's trade principles, the Latins hoped for pragmatism in their application. Unless Washington could offer an alternative route to stability, Messersmith held, it should not condemn preferences and protectionism categorically. "Hence our thinking must be less adamant" to show the Latins that Washington valued their well-being more than ideological orthodoxy.[139]

Messersmith had ample opportunity to urge these views upon members of the American delegation. On 19 February he welcomed the first of them, his new immediate superior. Nelson Rockefeller's appointment as assistant secretary of state for Latin affairs turned the tables on his former diplomatic adversaries. But Rockefeller was too much the gentleman and diplomat himself, and too devoted to the hemisphere, to allow old grudges to spoil good working relations with his envoys in the field. With Adolf Berle, now ambassador to Brazil and another United States delegate, he was already on good terms from their Washington days together. Stettinius and his retinue arrived on the afternoon of 20 February, to stay for the duration. The Democratic chairman of the Senate Foreign Relations Committee, Tom Connally, and the ranking Republican, Warren Austin of Vermont, were delayed until the conference was already underway.[140]

Padilla's rousing welcoming address marked the end of months of preparations for Messersmith and his staff. He was to remain in the background while the delegates deliberated. He saw inconspicuously to the Americans' comfort, putting up a number of them at the embassy residence. He arranged Stettinius's afternoon press briefings at the embassy theater, where he got his first chance to watch the new secretary in action. To Roosevelt he praised Stettinius's "extraordinarily constructive leadership." The truth, which shocked him, was that Stettinius was "completely beyond his depth." Berle recorded similar astonishment at his chief's "cheerful ignorance."[141] Fortunately, Stettinius did have the good sense to delegate all the real authority to men more knowledgeable than himself. That was partly why when the Chapultepec Conference (named after the historic castle where the plenary sessions took place) adjourned on 8 March, "a general feeling of alleviation and good will among the delegates" (as the American communiqué put it) prevailed.[142] Resolutions had been passed calling for continued wartime cooperation and, soon to become a dominant issue, the removal of remaining Axis influences and interests. The Pan American Union's mandate was expanded. Regional autonomy received recognition at the expense of United Nations supremacy—not to the extent, perhaps, the Latins wished, but enough to cause Pasvolsky and other internationalists considerable anguish. The United States promised to commend to its allies at the upcoming San Francisco conference a set of "comments and suggestions" for modifications in the Dumbarton Oaks proposals, which the Latins endorsed in advance. And they emerged feeling more secure in their borders. The Final Act of Chapultepec laid the groundwork for a postwar hemispheric defense pact. The southernmost nations particularly rested easier with the thought of a military deterrent to Argentine aggression that, they believed, another achievement of Chapultepec had made still less likely. At Rockefeller's initiative, the United States renounced its undeclared war against Buenos Aires, joining the other republics in inviting Argentina back into the family once it had subscribed to the Chapultepec resolutions and declared war on the Axis. On 27 March Argentina did just that. Two weeks later the American Republics simultaneously extended recognition. Spruille Braden was named Washington's ambassador to Buenos Aires. The hemisphere, it seemed, was again of a piece.[143]

Judging by the results, Stettinius and company had apparently heeded Messersmith's preconference pleas for flexibility on the economic issues. The Final Act included a number of resolutions embodying a decidedly nondoctrinaire brand of economic liberalism. One called for reductions in tariff barriers, but not at the expense of "high levels of living and sound development of [national] economies." Domestic and foreign capital were to be treated equally, "except when the investment of the latter would be contrary to the . . . public interest." Industrial development was given special emphasis. That state enterprise and controls, also anathema to the State Department, might be necessary for stability was also acknowledged.[144]

The road to these resolutions, however, had been tortuous. The positions initially staked out by the United States delegation represented another rebuff to Messersmith and Latin aspirations. In his 27 February speech, Will Clayton, assistant secretary of state for economic affairs, had delivered a ringing attack on economic nationalism in all its varieties. He asked the Latins to forgo temporarily industrialization, warned of continuing shortages of capital goods until Europe had been rebuilt, and urged the Latins to support a Europe-first policy as the best way of restoring their market for raw materials. From the Latin standpoint, the single encouraging aspect of Clayton's speech was his announcement that the Eximbank was again ready to consider requests for loans for "sound" (i.e., noncompetitive) development projects.[145]

Although Stettinius thought the speech generally made "an excellent impression," he also admitted that it evoked "some disappointment" from the Latins. That was an understatement. One Latin commentator suggested that Clayton had plagiarized "a good speech made by Theodore Roosevelt before 1910." Fearing open rebellion, the American delegates on the economic committees agreed to drop some of the resolutions incorporating Clayton's points and to modify others to satisfy Latin concerns.[146]

Gratified by the Chapultepec economic resolutions but mindful of the pressures that had shaped them, Messersmith was justifiably concerned about their implementation. Even if Stettinius and Clayton had been truly converted to the Chapultepec principles, which he doubted, there was still a generally hostile State Department bureaucracy to contend with. Messersmith had all he could do just to see to Mexican needs. Camacho had broached a large Eximbank loan for highway construction, railroad improvements, and rural electrification back in December 1944, and Messersmith had taken it up with Roosevelt and the State Department during his trip that month to Washington. Warren Pierson attended Chapultepec as an adviser, at which time he discussed the matter with Eduardo Suárez. On 29 March 1945 the Eximbank tentatively approved a $45 million loan, making over $90 million in total credits outstanding. Notwithstanding the Chapultepec resolutions, Washington continued to battle economic nationalism wherever it reared its head in Latin America, and Messersmith continued to argue for understanding. If understanding was unattainable, he would settle for economic aid.[147]

6

With the conclusion of Chapultepec, Messersmith reached the final item on his Mexican checklist, the one whose resolution, he promised Stettinius, would deliver "the last blow to all of the Doubting Thomases here." A treaty signed on 3 February 1944 had resolved a century-old dispute over the control and apportionment of three international rivers: the Colorado, the Tijuana, and the Rio Grande. The seven Colorado-basin states had been the main stumbling block. To encourage growth, they had plundered the Colorado's waters, leaving less and less downstream for Mexico. The completion of the Hoover Dam system in 1940, which diverted still more of the Colorado, was a boon for California's Imperial Valley and cities like San Diego but ruinous for Camacho's agricultural expansion program in Baja. Mexican growers were forced to buy from California the water that according to international law was rightfully Mexico's to begin with.[148]

The California bonanza contained the kernel of a solution for Mexico. The other basin states grew jealous of California's windfall and increasingly sympathetic to a treaty providing federal supervision of facilities currently operated by Sacramento. With this support and Roosevelt's, American and Mexican negotiators, who had resumed talking in early 1942, made rapid progress. Their treaty called for 1.5 million acre-feet of Colorado water annually for Mexico, with lesser amounts of Rio Grande and Tijuana water going to the United States. Administrative machinery was set up. A State Department officer who had helped draft the treaty modestly described it as "the most important of its kind in the history of the world." Both sides appeared satisfied.[149]

The treaty immediately ran into trouble on Capitol Hill, however. The entire state of California, it seemed, rose in well-organized wrath. On the Senate Foreign Relations Committee, the seventy-eight-year-old Hiram W. Johnson vowed to defeat the treaty as his "swan song in public life," the White House congressional liaison reported. California Governor Earl Warren and former President Hoover were scheduled to testify against it. Republicans had already seized on the issue for the coming elections. On 26 April the Democratic leadership, on order from Roosevelt, moved to postpone hearings until after November.[150]

Prospects looked much brighter in the 79th Congress. Johnson was back, but, afflicted by advancing senility and a throat condition that made speaking difficult, he was a shell of his old irreconcilable self. Roosevelt pledged to Camacho to do "all I can" to see the treaty through. Messersmith urged the State Department to give it the "positive publicity" it deserved and to expose the "entirely selfish" character of the opposition. So much rode on the issue, he wrote Nelson Rockefeller. The treaty was "a test of the degree to which we are able to conduct our foreign relations in a way that is effective in the interests of our country as a whole." Ratification would be "an important event in the history of the Americas," "an outstanding example of how a long-standing and difficult problem can be solved in an equitable manner when there is a spirit of understanding." Failure to ratify would "play into the hands of those who are not our friends in Mexico."[151]

Taking his own advice, Messersmith wrote Eugene Meyer, editor-publisher of the *Washington Post*, requesting "one of your excellent editorials" on the water treaty. He summarized Mexico's magnificent contribution to the Allied cause. Mexico had furnished nearly a billion dollars worth of strategic minerals alone; and, "although [it] was a seller's market, it is to the eternal credit of Mexico that she did not attempt to use this advantage to get prices for these materials which were not entirely fair." Under the *bracero* program, which had been expanded in April 1943 to provide industrial as well as agricultural workers, 200,000 Mexicans had already seen service in the United States. And its most glorious contribution was still to come. Eighteen months in the formation and training, the Mexican 201st Fighter Squadron, 300 of its best pilots and support personnel, was about to embark for combat in the skies over the Philippines. For so staunch an ally, simple justice concerning the international rivers could no longer be denied.[152]

Yet, for Messersmith the water treaty was more than a matter of diplomatic credibility, more than a gratuity for wartime cooperation, more than a gesture of support for Camacho and Padilla. Mexico needed the water to grow and prosper. The country needed it above all because, as he wrote Meyer, "twelve of her twenty-one million people live on a desperately low standard of living which has got to be improved" for their sake and that of the American way of life. When they joined the war, Mexicans were among the world's hungriest people, consuming fewer calories per capita than even the Chinese. And the situation had worsened during the war, what with inflation and the procurement-related food shortages Messersmith had worked to alleviate. The Camacho government's program "to bring about greater production . . . in order to improve the people's nutritional standard" required a fair share of Colorado water. It deserved the full support of the United States.[153]

Messersmith got his *Post* editorial. The nation's newspapers were overwhelmingly supportive. The State Department did its part, too. Assistant Secretary Acheson testified before a much friendlier Foreign Relations committee. The Californians continued the fight, but admitted themselves that it was lost. The sparsely-attended floor debate was winding down on 12 April 1945. Shortly before 5 P.M., Vice President Harry S. Truman adjourned the body for the day, and headed back to his office. There was an urgent message waiting for him, summoning him to the White House.[154]

A telephone call from Hull brought word of Roosevelt's death to the embassy in Mexico City. Messersmith was "simply overwhelmed," as he wrote Stettinius the next morning. "There is no way in which I can express my feelings and my grief. The President had honored me with his friendship and his confidence since 1933. I knew that the burden of the work which fell on him was increasingly taking its toll. I knew that he was not so well but had the feeling that he had been getting somewhat better. The news came as a shock from which I have not been able to recover." He and Roosevelt had never collabo-

rated more closely than during the Mexican years. His death deprived Messersmith of the power to move the otherwise immovable
obstacles to the special relationship for which they had been working
together.[155]

Mexicans understood how grievous a loss that was. Roosevelt's
passing, the embassy reported, "has caused greater grief in Mexico
than that of the passing of any Mexican in generations." A three-day
period of mourning was declared, unprecedented for a foreigner.
Camacho "frequently had to brush away a tear" when he and Messersmith exchanged condolences. "The world," the Mexican declared,
"had lost the greatest man it had produced in centuries."[156]

When he had composed himself, Messersmith undertook to calm
Mexicans about the future. In a radio address on the 14th, he assured them of what he only hoped was true, that "there will be no
change" in American hemispheric policy; that President Truman was
"a man of sound, considered judgment, of wisdom and great industry." Mexicans and Latins generally were comforted by the new president's early declaration that "to the Good Neighbor Policy of which
[Roosevelt] was the author, I wholeheartedly subscribe."[157]

Messersmith was as worried about his own future with Roosevelt
gone. He was not alone in that regard. But he made the mistake of
calling early attention to himself. "It is not improbable," he wrote
Truman clumsily on 17 April, "that the late President Roosevelt may
have discussed with you the plans which he had for utilizing my services in Europe as our principal civilian representative when the first
stages of the purely military government in the defeated countries is
over." Truman, with whom Roosevelt had discussed next to nothing,
may have found a bit of grim humor in this. In any case, Messersmith's ostensible purpose for writing was to advise that he remain in
Mexico "a little longer"; the loss of his honorable self on the heels of
the loss of Truman's beloved predecessor might be too much for the
Mexicans to bear.[158]

We can only speculate on how Truman reacted to this transparent
piece of self-interest. Certainly, coming as it did a week after he took
office, with the weight of the whole world on his shoulders, it could
not have been much appreciated. Their relationship was off to a bad
start. It would get worse, without Messersmith knowing it. Like Roosevelt, Truman came in with a low opinion of the career diplomats,
and left thinking even less of them. In good democratic fashion he
enjoyed skewering the striped-pants "smart boys" hopelessly out of
touch with grassroots America. Messersmith was not as smart as
some, but he had supreme confidence in his own opinions. He came
off as a decided know-it-all to Truman, whose one candid reference

to him, on his daily appointment sheet for 29 September, noted that Messersmith had called at 11:45 A.M. "to tell me how to run the govt."[159]

Yet Truman gave no hint of irritation in his written response to Messersmith's inherently irritating plea for Germany. Far from it. Messersmith got back a gracious invitation to pay Truman a visit when next he was in Washington. He had been planning such a trip for some months, to have those stomach repairs tended to. With the water treaty out of the way—it had passed the Senate on 18 April— and Truman's words of encouragement, he made his reservations at the Bethesda Naval Hospital. Arriving in Washington, he checked in first at the White House, for his first meeting with Truman. It was 10 A.M., 5 May. Messersmith recalled the president's saying first that "our good friend [Roosevelt] has frequently spoken to me about you. I know how much he appreciated your work . . . and valued your judgment." Someone was not telling the truth. Truman went on to request Messersmith's assistance in his "difficult task," and another chance to talk after he left the hospital. Messersmith "gathered, though [Truman] did not specifically say so, that he intends to discuss some phases of the Central European situation."[160]

Eight days at Bethesda left Messersmith feeling "very much better than I have for years" physically, and refreshed in spirit from contact with fellow patient Cordell Hull. After completing his recuperation in the country, he returned expectantly to the White House on 1 June. Sure enough, Truman said that "he was thinking very much in the same terms as the late President Roosevelt . . . that when we switch over from purely Allied military control [Germany had surrendered on 8 May] to Allied civilian control . . . he might have to use me there in a very responsible capacity." When this transition might take place, however, Truman could not predict. So he wanted Messersmith to continue on in Mexico, as "he did not know of any one who could do the job [there] better for the present than I." That was as close as he came to the German assignment, which did not materialize until 1949. In the interim, disagreement over the future of the former Reich helped to precipitate and inflame the Cold War. By the time John J. McCloy was named American high commissioner to oversee the new Bonn government, Messersmith was two years a private citizen.[161]

He returned to Mexico on 6 June 1945 to one of the bitterest disappointments of his life. That day Miguel Alemán Valdes resigned as interior minister and declared his candidacy for the July 1946 presidential election. With the support of the official Mexican Revolutionary party and the endorsement of Camacho, Cárdenas, and

Lombardo Toledano, Alemán was virtually assured of victory. Padilla, who had been quietly testing the waters and organizing his supporters, found himself out of the running before the campaign had even begun. Taking Camacho's decision as a vote of no confidence, Padilla on 9 July resigned his portfolio, ordered his workers to stop, and retired to his Cuernavaca home.[162]

"It is all a great tragedy," Messersmith wrote Hull on 31 July. "We have lost [in Padilla] the strongest champion for the principles for which we stand, not only in the Americas, but in the world." Messersmith could do nothing for him; in fact, he may have done too much already. Their intimate friendship and the near-perfect correlation of their views became liabilities for Padilla, who, to his everlasting credit, refused to resort to anti-Yankee polemics in order to rebut the charges of subservience to Washington.

Now there was Alemán, intelligent enough, but "a rather weak man" with "very little knowledge of . . . international relationships," who "has promised everything to everybody and he will owe his election in a large degree to elements which are not friendly to us." For three years Messersmith had given his all to vindicate the policy of collaboration with the United States. With Alemán, he concluded disconsolately, "all the circumstances seem to point to a step backward for Mexico rather than accelerated, steady, and continued progress in her social and political development."[163]

With no illusions about the outcome, Padilla changed his mind and made it a race, offering himself as a sacrificial lamb in the name of democracy and a choice for Mexican voters come election day. The campaign got underway in earnest in December. By Mexican standards it was a model of decorum, at least on the part of the candidates. Their supporters were less restrained. In a 16 December speech, Toledano claimed that American firms were smuggling arms to various right-wing groups in preparation for a coup that would place a "pro-United States Quisling"—Padilla—in power. Ominously, Radio Moscow broadcast the charges, which Toledano, when called to account, could not substantiate. This did not stop him from issuing new charges, accusing Messersmith of "campaigning" for Padilla, demanding his recall and replacement "by a proven partisan of democracy and of the Good Neighbor Policy."[164]

Messersmith turned the other cheek. Because of his relationship with Padilla, he was keeping a low profile even for him. The Mexican press and government came to his defense. Camacho announced that "Mexico has never had a more sincere friend in the American Embassy." The capital's La Prensa, second in circulation, called Tole-

dano's arms-smuggling charge "political blackmail." On 22 December
the government formally dismissed all allegations of American interference. Local opinion was that Toledano's prestige had taken "a serious blow."[165] That was a setback not only for him personally. As was
acknowledged by Mexicans from Alemán down, Toledano spoke for
Moscow—Oumansky's successor, as it were. Mischief-making by the
Mexican Communists was symptomatic of the decay in United States–
Soviet relations generally. The year 1946 brought fresh evidence of
totalitarian expansionism again on the march. With confrontation in
Iran, the failure to hold promised elections in Eastern Europe, Russian vetoes in the United Nations, and the collapse of negotiations
over Germany, a sickening chill had settled over East-West relations.
Talk of World War III filtered through the world's capitals while the
toll of recent combat was still being tallied.[166]

"It is a sorry spectacle that we have to witness today," Messersmith
wrote Claude Bowers in February, "and if I were not so profoundly
convinced of the necessity for struggling for the good, and its inevitable triumph, I would be a very disillusioned man indeed." He *was*
disillusioned, much as were all Americans who knew little more than
what the newsreels had told them about inter-Allied solidarity. But,
having viewed Hitler and Stalin as fraternal twins since the 1930s,
Messersmith was perhaps less surprised than most by Soviet misbe-
havior in 1946. The Hitler-Stalin analogy began to exercise an increasingly powerful hold over him. But the analogy was flawed, and
he knew it and took comfort in it. In the 1930s Hitler faced a depressed and divided world. In 1946 war-ravaged Russia faced the
United States at the pinnacle of its military and economic power, with
overwhelming conventional superiority, an atomic monopoly, and the
apparent will to use it all to consolidate "the triumph of good."[167]

For the showdown that Messersmith now considered inevitable
and, increasingly, necessary, hemispheric solidarity would have to be
consolidated first. That meant, among other things, getting on with
the American foreign ministers' meeting to draw up the hemispheric
defense pact conceived at Chapultepec. Originally scheduled for October 1945 at Rio, the meeting had been indefintely postponed while
Washington sorted out its feelings toward Argentina. Over bitter Soviet opposition and their own ambivalence, the American delegates
to San Francisco had, in accordance with the Chapultepec formula,
secured a United Nations seat for Argentina. The military rulers in
Buenos Aires did little to make that chore less onerous. Ambassador
Spruille Braden had arrived in May 1945 to discover what he reported was a police state in which Axis interests operated unmo-

lested. Braden tried to prevail upon the Farrell-Perón regime to expel its Nazis, while simultaneously inciting that regime's overthrow. These objectives proved quite incompatible.[168]

Most North Americans, however, applauded Braden's crusade. Messersmith was among them. The Argentine failure to respond in good faith to the olive branch proferred at Mexico City angered him. Seating the Farrell clique in the United Nations when constitutional guarantees in Argentina were still suspended and Axis agents reportedly had the run of the country was "damnable," he wrote Braden, who of course could not have agreed more. "There can be no temporizing with Governments of this kind." Braden's and Washington's assumption that a cowed Argentine majority needed and welcomed outside assistance in toppling a hated regime seemed plausible. Writing in September to Hull, who was well pleased by the return to the hard line he had pursued in office, Messersmith expressed confidence that "this [Argentine] regime cannot last for more than a few months longer."[169]

Messersmith could no more will away Juan Perón than Adolf Hitler. On 14 December 1945 Perón resigned his posts in the government and declared himself a candidate for the presidency in elections to take place 24 February. The army promised a clean contest. Washington was skeptical, but foresaw such a resounding victory for the opposition candidate, Dr. José Tamborini, that the military would not dare try to steal it. Braden, inevitably persona non grata, kept up the pressure from a new post, assistant secretary for Latin affairs, replacing the accommodationist Rockefeller. Twelve days before the Argentine election, Braden released the *Blue Book*, documents hastily compiled to prove "Argentine-Nazi complicity" supposedly masterminded by Perón. Intended to discredit him in Argentine eyes, the *Blue Book* made him a hero instead. Even the anti-Peronists were aghast at this thinly veiled intervention. Perón, whose domestic support exceeded the State Department's original estimates by a wide margin, was quick to capitalize on its blunder. "The question of the hour is this," he bellowed to an excited crowd on 13 February: "Braden or Perón." In what the American embassy conceded was "unquestionably [the] fairest [election] in Argentine history," Perón and his ticket won a smashing victory.[170]

Braden and the State Department were publicly defiant. The United States promptly proclaimed its refusal to enter into a hemispheric defense pact with "fascist" Perón. But American unity and world tensions argued for accommodation. Argentines had voted freely; the Latins were becoming impatient with the Rio delay; an isolated Argentina might be driven into Russian arms. So Camacho argued in a 14 March talk with Messersmith. In response, he duly restated Washington's official position, but, as he told Braden, he was now inclined to agree with Camacho that the Good Neighborly precedent and the security of the Americas required the establishment of relations with popular-choice Perón.[171]

Messersmith had no inkling of how importantly he was to figure in the effort. Spring was in the Mexico City air on the morning of 1 April 1946. Messersmith walked briskly across the flowered courtyard separating the embassy residence from the chancery, just as he had done almost every morning for four years. Despite international tensions and the local electoral ferment, "I felt very much at peace with the world and very happy. I was very busy, I was working too hard, [and] I was injuring my health, but I had an interesting task, and I was enjoying it, and felt that I was doing something worthwhile." The war's end had brought some change in his duties, but no more leisure. In October 1945 he had become doyen of the Mexico City diplomatic corps, with all the attendant ceremonial responsibilities. He settled some old scores. Robert Jackson, chief American prosecutor at the Nuremberg war-crime trials, invited him to come to testify. Messersmith declined—"not due to any personal considerations," he explained to Hull, "for I did not hesitate to stand up to these people when they were in power, so I would certainly not have any personal reserves to appear against them when they are on trial." With too much to do in Mexico, he contented himself with a thirty-page affadavit to Jackson, recounting his conversations with Göring in Berlin and what he knew of Papen's exploits in Austria.[172]

Mexico, of course, was Messersmith's first concern. Important work still remained to be done in 1946. At his insistence, the sensitive negotiations to readmit private capital to the petroleum industry had been suspended, so that it would not become a campaign issue. It had required his best efforts just to prevent the Mexican standard of living from getting any worse. The European orientation of Washington's evolving postwar policies reflected his failure so far to win Mexico the priority treatment he believed was due his country's most important neighbor. Nor had he secured more than grudging tolerance for Mexican industrialization, which nonetheless surged ahead. Yet under his firm hand, Mexican-American friendship had come through it all, and that was a great achievement. That Alemán was not Padilla proved to be a blessing in disguise; for he was to practice a less ostentatious brand of pro-Americanism more congenial to his people.[173]

So Messersmith could well be content on that beautiful 1 April morning. With no European post in sight, he had quite happily re-

signed himself to concluding his career with a few more years in
Mexico. As he approached his office, he heard the telephone ring.
"All at once," he wrote later, "it came over me that every time I had
this feeling of self-satisfaction, that something usually happened." He
was suddenly filled with "foreboding that [the phone call] was not
something good." At the other end was Truman's secretary of state,
James F. Byrnes, asking him to go to Buenos Aires as ambassador,
"to bring the Argentine government and Perón into line. It had
been suggested that I was the only person to do it." He had many
good reasons to refuse, and he cited them all in the course of their
hour-long conversation: he abhorred the limelight, dreaded having to
move, and wanted to finish up in Mexico. Byrnes was insistent. Messersmith promised to get back to him after discussing it with his wife.

He returned home. "What a difference between my feelings when
I came over to the office just an hour before and when I crossed the
garden again to the house!" He woke up Marion with the news. He
never forgot her response. "What is the use of talking about it," he
recalled her saying bitterly. "You know that you will go. The chances
are that it will ruin you. They will tell you that they are going to
support you on a given policy and then they will pull the rug from
under you. It will be the biggest mistake you ever made. . . . But you
have made up your mind to go because I know how you feel about
the situation in Latin America and . . . the Argentine and how necessary it is to bring her into the picture. . . . I will go and help you, but
I think it is all wrong." So encouraged, he phoned Byrnes with his
conditional acceptance. The secretary promised to appoint a career
diplomat as his successor in Mexico. He also agreed to try to get
Messersmith more money. Buenos Aires was relatively as expensive
as it had been in 1928, and Messersmith was no more inhibited by
pride where his wallet was concerned. Finally, Byrnes agreed that
"when there had been a settlement of the differences . . . between
[the United States and Argentina], he should be assigned to some
other post."[174]

The announcement evoked enthusiastic approval throughout
Latin America. Coupled with the easing of export restrictions on
Argentina and Byrnes's statement on 8 April, expressing a conditional readiness to proceed with Rio, it was clear that "a major reori-
entation of [American] policy [toward Argentina] is in progress." The
apparent decision to reverse the Hull-Braden hard line, said Mexico
City's *Mañana*, "merits the loud and enthusiastic response of the
whole continent." *Excelsior* regretted losing Messersmith, "but we are
glad that he has been named to the Argentine Government, because
we are sure, beforehand, that the skill and diplomatic tact of Mr.

Messersmith will accomplish in Argentina what they did in Cuba and Mexico, the creation and strengthening of ties of friendship and reciprocity . . . [and] may scatter the last clouds that might darken [hemispheric] relations."[175]

That Mexico's loss was a gain for all the Americas was the gist of the "literally hundreds" of farewell messages he received from Mexicans ordinary and not. Camacho handed him an official letter of appreciation, a "historic document" never given before to a foreign diplomat. As usual, Messersmith kept his head amid the encomiums. "All that concerns your country," he wrote in response to Padilla's tearful goodbye, "has interested me tremendously because I see so many forces at work which can do so much for the benefit of the great number of the Mexican people." He was, a local radio commentator told his listeners, "the true diplomat of democracy."[176]

☆ **VII** ☆

Buenos Aires

1946 – 1947

Judging by editorial opinion in the United States, the Latins were woefully mistaken about what it was that Messersmith was going to Argentina to do. The North American press was almost as one in insisting that rapprochement with President-elect Juan Perón take place on American terms or not at all. The *Philadelphia Inquirer*, for example, praised the Truman administration for taking a "realistic step toward solidarity in the Americas," but hastened to condemn the "Argentine Government's brand of totalitarianism" and demanded that Perón "make plain to the world his friendship for the United States." The *Christian Science Monitor* envisaged no relaxation of the Hull-Braden hard line, which it believed had "helped to put heart into democratic forces in Argentina" and the fear of God into Perón. *U.S. News* wished the new ambassador a successful "mission against fascism," noting his peculiar qualifications for the job: "He knows and hates Nazism from deep and intimate study, and is quick to recognize its manifestations. . . . Argentines who congratulate themselves that American policy toward their country has softened apparently have not taken into consideration the characteristics of the instrument of that policy, Mr. Messersmith." *Time* also endeavored to dampen any jubilation in Buenos Aires. It observed that Messersmith was blessed with "an uncanny nose that can smell an s.o.b. as far as the wind can carry the scent." Maintaining that "there has been no basic change in U.S. policy," *Time* warned Argentina that "Messersmith is Braden's man. And Perón might remember Messersmith's 'uncanny nose.'"[1]

Those who hoped to drive Perón to his knees and those who would close ranks with him alike welcomed Messersmith's appointment to Buenos Aires, which was no small point in its favor. For although United States public opinion generally thrilled at the thought of him cutting Perón down to size, as he had done with German Nazis, American, like Latin, proponents of reconciliation with Argentina saw Messersmith's more recent record of Good Neighborly successes as proof positive that the Truman administration was finally moving earnestly in their direction. United States military planners were especially heartened by the apparent breakthrough. Early on they had perceived the common struggle against the Axis as an opportunity to forge a standing *Festung Americana*, so that last-minute improvisations would not be necessary the next time that the hemisphere was threatened from without. Intensive bilateral and interagency talks to that end had commenced in 1943, and three years later, in the spring of 1946, the enabling legislation was ready for submission to Congress. The Inter-American Military Cooperation Act proposed to train, arm, and integrate Latin military establishments—that is, to implement the Rio pact, being held up, however, by the Argentine impasse. While Rio was in abeyance, the Pentagon nervously noted that Washington's rivals for influence and the Latin arms business, including the Russians, were working methodically to exploit the vacuum, to separate the Latins from their wartime loyalties and their accumulated hard currency; and the Latins, despairing of Rio, were beginning to show a live interest in their solicitations. The chance to standardize and consolidate the hemisphere's armed forces seemed to be slipping away.[2]

But the emerging Cold War was throwing a new light on the situation, lending an urgency to hemispheric relations in much the same way that the impending showdown with fascism had driven the Good Neighbor policy a decade before. At his acrimonious October 1945 confirmation hearings, Braden got a blunt indoctrination in the new global perspective on the hemisphere. Anti-Soviet inquisitors like Senator Arthur Vandenberg warned him to call off the war against Argentina for the sake of bigger confrontations ahead. Neither these strong words nor the mounting evidence that Vandenberg and his colleagues were justified in their Soviet apprehensions made the least impression on Braden. By April 1946, in the wake of his *Blue Book* ineptitudes, the senators had had enough. On the 7th, Tom Connally, Walter George (D–Georgia) and Wallace White (R–Maine) met secretly with Byrnes at Blair House. They demanded detente with Perón, and threatened "some vigorous statements in the Senate" were it not forthcoming. Drew Pearson revealed that the lawmakers "paid tribute" to Braden—"only the tribute was not of the kind he would appreciate. They kicked him verbally all over the lot." The next day, 8 April, Byrnes issued the ambiguous public statement that became the definitive formulation of American policy toward Argentina. The "road would be open to . . . the negotiation and signature

A turn in policy toward Argentina? The White House, 11 April 1946.
President Truman, Secretary of State Byrnes, and the new ambassador to
Buenos Aires
Courtesy National Archives

of a [Rio] mutual defense pact," the secretary declared, upon "un-equivocal and sustained performance" by Buenos Aires in rooting out "Axis influence." Washington, he emphasized, would be looking for "deeds and not merely promises."[3]

No matter how Byrnes conditioned it, no matter what construction was placed on Messersmith's appointment, the administration had clearly edged, albeit under duress, toward Perón. Braden's absence from an 11 April White House conference between "his man" Messersmith, home for consultation, and Truman and Byrnes seemed to confirm his eclipse. But, cautioned Arthur Schlesinger, Jr., in *Fortune* (August 1946), "it is impossible to write him off the books." Spruille Braden was a man driven at whatever he did, one not to be underestimated. Born in Elkhorn, Montana, in 1894, Braden followed in the footsteps of his illustrious father, the mining engineer who developed Chile's famed copper lode, El Teniente. After graduation from Yale, young Braden set off for Latin America to make his fortune. In the course of his travels he acquired a blueblooded Chilean wife, fluency in Spanish, and a reputation for bulldog tenacity. But the

Wall Street crash ruined him financially and left him searching for a new line of work. Braden was a Republican to the core; but if his Latin expertise alone was not enough to earn him the embassy in his wife's Santiago, his first choice, it did get him a spot on the United States delegation to the 1933 Montevideo conference, where he distinguished himself. He then served as chief American negotiator at the talks that ultimately settled the bloody Chaco War between Paraguay and Bolivia. Ambassadorships to Bogotá, Havana, and Buenos Aires came to him in quick succession.[4]

Aside from his father, Braden's hero was Roosevelt—Theodore, not Franklin. Braden, all 275 well-packed pounds of him, led the vigorous life, on the job and off. An All-American in water polo at Yale, a lifelong boxing enthusiast who almost to the end loved few things more than climbing into the ring himself, Braden had little use for the New Deal, home of intellectuals he considered soft and policies he considered softheaded. In his whole public career, he decided when it was over, the only thing he ever regretted doing was speaking out at Montevideo in defense of Roosevelt's renunciation of the gold standard. Fortunately for his conscience and his diplomatic career, his duties rarely called on him to pass judgment on New Deal economics.[5]

He was even less sympathetic to the administration's foreign policies. To him, the Good Neighbor was a weak-kneed abdication of the virile Roosevelt's active commitment to the civilization of South America. The end always justified the means for Braden. Hence Ambassador Braden brandished the big stick with anachronistic abandon. In Colombia, in what even a sympathetic scholar concedes was "Yankee imperialism," Braden used his influence with American advertisers and newsprint suppliers to silence local journalistic critics of pro-American President Eduardo Santos. In Cuba Braden got up a first-class feud with Batista and turned it into a public spectacle—a harbinger of things to come. By the time he was moved to Argentina in 1945, after repeated Cuban attempts to have him recalled, the two sides were barely on speaking terms.[6]

To his Argentine mission Braden brought his usual lust for combat, buttressed by, as the British ambassador, Sir David Kelly, put it, "the fixed idea that he had been elected by Providence to overthrow the Farrell-Perón regime." Ultimately Braden's failing in Argentina was less his meddling in the country's domestic politics, egregious and counterproductive though it was, than his hotheaded misreading of the Peronist phenomenon in the context of Argentine history. To Braden, Perón was simply another Fascist gangster intent upon aggression against his neighbors. Understandably, Braden did not take kindly to the idea of Washington's furnishing him with arms, arguing that Perón's signature on a Rio pact would be worth about as much as Hitler's at Munich.[7]

But Perón was hardly the "megalomaniac fascist" of Braden's fantasies. It was clear to the few dispassionate observers at the time, and to most scholars today, that the Argentine was an ambitious pragmatist leading a popular movement inspired by, if anything, the Labour-socialist revolution in Britain rather than continental fascism. Beginning in October 1943, when he made himself secretary of labor in the Ramírez government, Perón tapped the long-smoldering discontent of the masses against the big industrialists and the landowning oligarchy that had dominated the nation since independence. By the end of 1945, Argentina, which had been perhaps the most socially backward of all the American Republics, had become among the most advanced, courtesy of Perón, "Argentina's number one worker." Old-age and disability insurance, low-cost housing, health benefits, paid vacations, and wage increases were enacted. Labor's share of the national income shot up. Unions were established where they had never been permitted. All told, it was one of the most rapid and thoroughgoing upheavals in hemispheric history.[8]

Like Roosevelt's New Deal, to which Peronists were wont to compare their movement, it provoked violent resistance from the elite it aimed to displace. Perón was only the most adroit Argentine among those on both sides who manipulated Braden in the course of their struggle for power. Braden's portrait of Perón as a brutal tyrant despised by the masses was surely a comfort to the beleaguered oligarchs, whose only hope was that foreign support would offset the popular support they lacked in their war against the Peronist-labor insurgency.[9] Yet one leans to the conclusion that Braden was not so much deceived as he was the deceiver—that he understood full well what Peronism was all about, and aimed to help crush it by making it out to be something it was not. Braden's association with the John Birch Society after he left government service brought into the open a longstanding hostility to organized labor. As for Perón himself, as distinct from the forces he led, Braden's hatred bordered on the pathological. Nothing the Argentine people could say at the polls or elsewhere could convince him otherwise. Twice he and Perón had nearly come physically to blows; Perón, a former army boxing instructor, would have made a worthy opponent for him. Braden was still swinging when he left Argentina in September 1945. In a final press conference, he urged Argentines to armed resistance, assuring them without the slightest authority to do so that the United States would aid and recognize "any revolutionary government" that surfaced to challenge Perón. If "the light and power [were] crippled enough," he suggested helpfully to reporters, "that might turn the trick and get rid of that guy."[10]

As assistant secretary of state, as we have seen, Braden defied his Senate interrogators to continue his crusade against Perón, from a distance. Only his tactics changed. The *Blue Book*, with its hair-raising intrigues, was designed as much for effect upon Americans as Argentines, and was vastly more successful in the former regard. In the United States, people were already thoroughly conditioned to believe the worst about Argentina generally and the military government that spawned Perón particularly. What had gone on in Argentina during the war was contemptible enough from the American standpoint without the concerted efforts of the United States press corps in Buenos Aires to make the situation look even more ominous than it was. Since 1942, Arnaldo Cortesi of the *New York Times*, Joseph Newman of the *New York Herald-Tribune*, Virginia Prewett of the *Chicago Sun* syndicate, and Ray Joseph of *PM*, among others, had drawn and overdrawn a lurid and undifferentiated picture of Nazis, imported and homegrown, in control in Argentina. The reporters dismissed as blatant propaganda the claim that Peronism was a genuinely popular movment.

What motivated them to carry out what one congressional critic justly characterized as an "outrageous smear campaign" against Perón and his predecessors is an important, if ultimately unanswerable, question. The unhappy history of United States–Argentine relations, which cast a self-perpetuating cloud over all who worked under it, was a fundamental factor. The journalists themselves faced anti-Peronist peer pressures from each other and from their colleagues on venerable Argentine establishment dailies like *La Prensa*. The pressure of deadlines always favored superficiality: it was much less taxing intellectually to harp on Perón's early admiration for Mussolini—overlooking, of course, the fact that he was in quite respectable company in that regard—than to dissect the complexities of him and his movement. And there were the temptations of self-interest in sensationalism, to which the Argentine situation so lent itself.[11]

In Braden, whose own views on Argentina were formed long before he set foot in the country, the reporters had found an ally even more committed to their cause than they were. In his despatches from Buenos Aires, the ambassador gave prominent notice to his own role in foiling the government's extraordinarily clumsy attempts, born more of frustration than intent, to muzzle the American journalists. They were profuse in expressing their gratitude in print, and their editors enthusiastically carried on Braden's fight in their pages after he returned home. His *Blue Book* allegations received all the credence and coverage of proved facts. By 1946, however, public cracks in Braden's anti-Argentine front began to show. Independent journalists, drawn to the purported spectacle of a new Hitler fastening himself on his people, came away writing that a gigantic hoax was being put over on American opinion. Perón's election put Braden clearly on the defensive, which he countered with a good offense. In a remarkable polemic he probably intended to be read as a statement of administration policy—for he at no point denied that he was speaking in his official capacity—he undertook to rally his followers. The usually responsible—except, like others, where Argentina was concerned—*Atlantic Monthly* ran his essay "The Germans in Argentina" under his byline in its April 1946 issue. Far from regretting his *Blue Book* intervention, Braden intimated that even tougher sanctions might lie ahead; for, as he described it, Argentina under Perón represented an immediate threat to American security: "With the defeat of Germany Argentina remains under the bare dictatorship of uniformed men who drink at the same fountain where drank Hitler, Mussolini, and Franco. As long as the people of Argentine live under the heel of this dictatorship . . . none of us can sleep soundly nights. Either the idea of the rights of man triumphed or it was defeated. Either the Hemisphere is united or it is broken. There is no room anywhere for middle ground."[12]

This was the government to which Messersmith was appointed to come to terms. While the American press was shaking its collective fist at Perón, the newly appointed ambassador was home quietly clearing off Mexican leftovers and consulting with everyone but Braden on Argentina. He was impressed by the new mood of the executive establishment. The bureaucratic rivalries and backbiting of the Roosevelt years seemed to have given way to good fellowhip and agreeableness under Truman. All of the officials with whom Messersmith dealt, from the president down, evinced a heartening desire to oblige. His wife's apprehensions could not have looked more unfounded. At his urging, Secretary of Agriculture Clinton Anderson approved restoration of 200,000 bushels of wheat cut earlier from Mexico's monthly allocation. Truman approved Messersmith's and Braden's recommendation that the current ambassador to Bolivia, Walter Thurston, replace him in Mexico City—no small achievement considering the long list of politicos hankering after the post. Messersmith saw General Eisenhower, who promised to put an army plane at his disposal for the move to Argentina. During their 11 April conference, Byrnes and Truman assured him that he would "come out whole" financially, though, with compensation set by law,

they could not yet say how. And they pledged "complete and unquali-
fied support" and "complete freedom in the way I would proceed to
get the right things done" in Argentina. The "right things," he told
them, were to resist pressure from the Pentagon and Capitol Hill
for Rio at any price, and to insist upon good-faith compliance with
Chapultepec from Perón. Byrnes promised to "speak definitely and
concretely to Braden as to what had been decided upon."[13]

That was one conversation that never took place. Byrnes had no
taste for a confrontation, especially an unnecessary one, with the
pugnacious Braden. The 8 April "deeds not promises" pronouncement and Messersmith's appointment had for the time being pacified
the Senate and the military; and Byrnes apparently feared that the
well-connected Braden, who had threatened to resign over the Blair
House meeting with Connally and company, would carry out that
threat now if pressed. That was something that Byrnes could not
afford. His always awkward relationship with Truman, who held the
office Byrnes thought should be his, was increasingly strained these
days, and the secretary was under growing fire for "babying" the
Soviets. In April 1946 Byrnes needed whatever domestic support
that Braden's continued presence provided.[14]

Whether Braden had any intention of making good his resignation
threat is another question. Although Perón's electoral victory had
dealt a sharp blow to his credibility, Braden still held a strong hand in
Washington. With Byrnes almost continually abroad negotiating the
European peace treaties and Truman preoccupied with the reconver-
sion economy and domestic politics, Braden retained effective control over hemispheric policy. From Buenos Aires Messersmith was to
address his communications to Truman and Byrnes, but theirs would
be a sporadic involvement with his mission. It would soon sink in
that he was dealing with Braden and his chief lieutenants, Dr. Carl
Spaeth, Ellis Briggs, and Thomas C. Mann, men who were all unal-
terably opposed to normalization of relations with Perón's Argentina and the Rio pact: the very things Messersmith was sent to accomplish.

The one official in a position to rein in Braden was the undersecretary, Acheson. He later regretted not doing so. Although he recalled
that his "disillusion" with Braden was "well advanced" by this time,
Acheson consistently took his side against Messersmith. One did not
have to agree with the way Braden went about things to share his
misgivings, as Acheson did, about supplying Perón with arms. An old
grudge against Messersmith also affected Acheson. He was one of
the many officials Messersmith had antagonized during the war for
the sake of good relations with Mexico and embassy autonomy. In

1942 he and Acheson had several nasty rows over BEW activities. In 1946 it had fallen to Acheson to convey the news of the cut in Mexico's wheat quota. Embassy economic counselor Merwin L. Bohan, who happened to be in the ambassador's office at the time, overheard one end of a violent argument, which ended with Messersmith shouting into the phone, "Now listen, Dean, you know a lot of things about a lot of things, but you don't know a damn thing about wheat." Acheson did not forget.[15]

It was only the president's confidence that Messersmith cared about, support he assumed he had when he departed Washington in April for three final weeks in Mexico City before proceeding directly to Buenos Aires. That the assurances he had got in Washington seemed to be forgotten once he was safely abroad was an annoyance, but one to which he was by now accustomed. It took several blunt, even insulting missives home to budge the bureaucracy to arrange the promised Mexican wheat deliveries. His personal financial aid turned out to be a waiver of the weight limits on the shipment of his baggage—a far cry from the $20,000 subsidy that, no doubt unbeknown to him, Braden had received in 1945. Then the army decided that it could not fly him and his party to Buenos Aires after all—regulations, it explained. Messersmith was relegated to commercial airliner via Miami and Rio, without Marion or their faithful servants, who arrived later by boat.[16]

The last leg of his journey made him curse the army. Heavy rain forced the closing of Buenos Aires's Morón airfield, stranding his flight from Rio. After circling the city for more than an hour, the plane finally skidded down and discharged its weary passengers shortly before midnight, 22 May 1946. Two military officers stepped forward to greet him on behalf of Perón. "Tell the Colonel," Messersmith replied, "that I appreciate his *saludos* and hope to see him soon."[17]

Thus commenced what Cortesi's replacement from the *New York Times*, Frank Kluckhohn—another change that augured well—declared was "perhaps the most difficult Latin American mission . . . since Dwight W. Morrow was sent to Mexico by President Coolidge to find a way out of an impasse as stubborn as this one." The analogy was apt. In both cases new envoys were supposed to undo a predecessor's mischief. Both missions were saddled by hostile public opinion at home. Morrow and Messersmith both walked into furnaces of defiant anti-Yankee nationalism. The Argentines had rejected Byrnes's 8 April formula; their position was that their Chapultepec commitments had already been met. Farrell's lame-duck foreign minister, Juan I. Cooke, demanded publicly that Washington drop the noncompliance charge. The arrival of a Soviet trade delegation suggested that Perón was hedging his bets in case negotiations with the United States fell through.[18]

At the same time the Argentine president-elect was signaling his willingness to meet Washington at least halfway. With his electoral triumph over American opposition, Perón, according to Argentine scholars Paz and Ferrari, now aimed to consolidate his position as "the champion of anti-Yankeeism in the continent." If "deeds" Byrnes and Braden wanted, deeds they would get. The state of siege in effect almost continuously since Pearl Harbor was lifted, and civil liberties restored. April saw the latest in a series of well-publicized "humanitarian" gestures to alleviate the European food shortage: increases in the wheat subsidy to spur production, Sunday shutdown of food markets, and a voluntary rationing program. Argentina issued a stamp bearing Roosevelt's portrait on the first anniversary of his death. With the cooperation of the British and American embassies, Axis remnants were being rooted out. The United States chargé d'affaires, John Moors Cabot, certified that "more or less adequate action" had been taken against all but nine of 122 identified German agents, that "there were no Axis periodicals in Argentina at present," and that "all dangerous German institutions, other than schools, are believed to be closed and inoperative at the present time."[19]

Messersmith's warm welcome also argued for optimism. The Stars and Stripes flew conspicuously over many buildings along the route from the embassy residence on the Avenida Alvear to the Casa Rosada downtown, where he presented his credentials his very first morning in the country, 23 May. The Argentines, he explained to Byrnes, wanted to be done with the formalities so that substantive talks could begin forthwith. It was "an expression of interest . . . in my mission and at least a friendly gesture which you may be sure did not go unnoticed here."[20]

That night, also at Perón's initiative, their intimate conversations began at the home of a mutual friend. Perón, who had obviously done his homework, said all the right things. He expressed his admiration for the United States and regret for Argentina's past errors, and his determination to set things aright, to compose the family quarrel that had, he said, too long disrupted the harmony of the Americas. With his inauguration less than a fortnight away, he shared his dreams for his country, for uplifting the *descamisados*, the "shirtless ones" whom he and Señora Eva Duarte Perón had adopted as their own. But, he emphasized, fiscal and constitutional scruples would be observed at all times. He said that his heart went out to Europe's hungry, that he would do more for them but for Washington's freeze on $644 million in Argentine assets that prevented the purchase of vehicles and spare parts needed to move food from the interior. And, especially heartening for Messersmith, Perón kept relating the imperatives of hemispheric unity, social justice, and European recovery to the intensifying Cold War with Russia, which Perón said he feared would soon turn hot. If it did, he promised that Argentina would be on the "right side." He revealed that diplomatic relations with Moscow, broken since November 1918, were about to be restored, but noted that Argentina was almost alone among its American sisters, including, of course, the United States, in not having done so long ago. At no time, the ambassador stressed in his report of the conversation, did Perón "endeavor [to] use the Russian efforts here as [an] indirect means [of] applying pressure on us."[21]

Altogether it was almost enough to sweep the new envoy off his feet. The Messersmiths resumed fond relations of their own with friends not seen since they left for Berlin in 1930. Local society, or at least the Peronist element of it, was alive with preinaugural festivities. Marion was happily in her element. The embassy staff, accustomed to Braden's state of war, reveled in the government's sudden solicitude for their comfort and convenience.

The glow lingered. On 15 June Messersmith presented his preliminary findings in a rambling, excited, 10,000-word letter to Byrnes (copies to Truman, Acheson, and Braden). Conditions, he announced, were ripe to break the current logjam and unite the hemisphere more solidly than ever before, and to do so "with decorum and without sacrifice of principle." The fact was that "mistakes have been made on both sides." Another letter of the same date, marked "Personal for the Secretary Only," expressed Messersmith's incredulity at learning the extent of Braden's ambassadorial indiscretions. In any case, although Braden "did make mistakes . . . they were all made in good faith and he was acting with the approval of the Department," whose Argentine policy was floundering long before Braden arrived on the scene. The key now, Messersmith advised, was "to forget the past" and work for the cooperative future at hand. He was convinced that the Argentines, long oriented to Europe, were ready to become good members of the American community, more eager to give their "wholehearted and loyal collaboration . . . in the political, economic, social and defense field[s] . . . than they have been at any time in a century." With his sense of the moment, Messersmith perceived a historic and timely opportunity to make Pan Americanism complete.[22]

But "a major agreement on pending matters of compliance," he agreed, would have to come first. Although he concluded that Argentina had already surpassed countries like Uruguay and Brazil in eliminating enemy interests, the "unequivocal and sustained performance" "very properly" demanded by Byrnes was still lacking. Part of the problem, Messersmith explained, was that the accused Axis persons and property were finding refuge in the anti-Peronist courts, which were vacating deportation and expropriation orders on the grounds that the Argentine Congress, suspended with the state of siege, had obviously not ratified the Chapultepec and San Francisco pacts as prescribed by the constitution. Congress was soon to convene, and Foreign Minister Juan Atilio Bramuglia assured him that the pacts would be taken up at once and passed by the end of June. The government would then have clear authority to move toward compliance. If it did, Messersmith thought that the Rio meeting might take place as early as "October or November of this year."

As far as he was concerned, that would not be a moment too soon. Calling the world situation "dismal," he expressed concern that an isolated Argentina was leaving an "exposed flank" to Soviet subversion. Perón's neighbors were even more concerned about the Argentine threat, worries that Messersmith did not entirely discount. The dream of an Argentine-led southern bloc, he found, still fired the national imagination. He doubted whether Perón himself had "abandoned . . . [his] thoughts in that direction" despite his emphatic assurances that he had. How that squared with Perón's supposedly sincere desire to be one among many Messersmith did not say. He was almost certain, however, that Argentina posed no immediate expansionist threat. Perón, he predicted, "would have too much to do in the next few years" domestically to pursue an adventuristic foreign policy. Messersmith saw just such domestic considerations behind his modest arms shopping list—in this case, the need to satisfy his army's insistence on parity with traditional rival Brazil, a major beneficiary of lend-lease. But it was precisely to guard against the possibility that Messersmith was wrong—that Perón might indeed be planning to use the arms secured from the United States or elsewhere against his neighbors—that he and the Latins considered a Rio mutual defense pact including Argentina to be so vital.

Messersmith offered one more argument for accommodation. He depicted Perón as an earnest, impressionable amateur whose first months in office would go far in shaping his political personality. One thing was certain: "if Perón cannot have good friends, he will have bad ones," and that was true internationally as well as domestically. Continued rebuffs from Washington, Messersmith warned, would serve only to play into the hands of those of Perón's advisers who wished to keep the Argentine-American feud alive.[23]

No one gainsaid this analysis, not to his face. Specifically, he recommended that Washington lift the freeze of Argentine assets, and it
was done. Despite obstinate jurists and inexperienced administra-
tors, Perón's government was able to report anti-Fascist progress with
gratifying regularity. All but two of fifty-five German and Japanese
schools were shut down. Messersmith met regularly with Bramuglia,
"an honest and very intelligent man," to go over their list of targeted
Axis firms and persons. The stumbling block, again, was the law,
under which forty aliens had just been released from detention.
Messersmith praised the government's "admirable" devotion to due
process. In a talk with him on 24 June, Perón pledged "constant
personal attention" to compliance matters. Two days later, in his
opening address to the Argentine Congress, Perón outlined a foreign
policy based on "peace and fulfillment of international promises." In
keeping with the first objective, he proposed cuts in the military budget. As for the second, he submitted the acts of Chapultepec and San
Francisco for ratification. Congress took time out from its delibera-
tions on 4 July to pass a resolution congratulating the United States
on its Independence Day.[24]

That afternoon Messersmith delivered his maiden public speech
as ambassador to the American Society of the River Plate. In remarks cleared with the State Department, he expressed his happiness
"again to serve in this great country and to labor in strengthening the
bonds which must unite Argentina and the United States as they
unite every one of the American Republics." He then collapsed quietly into his chair. Fortunately the newly appointed ambassador to
Washington, Dr. Oscar Ivanissevich, one of the country's leading di-
agnosticians, was also on the dais and noticed him suffering. He
rushed the patient home and began treatment for the gastritis that
was to keep Messersmith bedridden for three critical weeks.[25]

Messersmith tried passing off this attack as merely another in a
long series of painful reminders that he was after all only flesh and
blood. Certainly, he wrote a friend when he was feeling somewhat
better, it was not the first time that his "overapplication" to duty
felled him.[26] But this time was different. Thirty-six hours before the
onset of his illness a telegram had arrived from the State Department
with all the impact of a punch to the solar plexus. It was the opening
salvo in Braden's counterattack, fired off over Acheson's signature.
It had been brewing since Messersmith's April stay in Washington,
when he and Braden met each other for the very first time. They
had been strangers only in the personal sense, however. Since 1941,
as fellow regional specialists, they had followed each other's careers
with live interest. Braden's success in denazifying Colombia led Mes-

sersmith to endorse him, or so he later claimed, as his successor in Havana. In his poisonous memoirs, Braden blasted Messersmith's Cuban record, but he sang a different tune at the time. "So great is my admiration for you," he wrote him sycophantically in October 1942, "both as my predecessor here and in general, so closely do our views seem to coincide . . . [that] I am emboldened to suggest that we drop the more formal means of address. I would consider it a great honor if you would call me by my first name and were I able to reciprocate in kind." They would be calling each other other names before long.[27]

In these early years they vied with each other in a friendly competition to thwart the BEW and the Rockefeller office in the field. "George is one up on me," Braden noted enviously in a margin of a Messersmith letter exulting over the cancellation of the "special economic assistant" in Mexico City. But Braden was no slouch in these matters. He was "impossible to work with," the BEW's Morris Rosenthal decided in retrospect; Messersmith could at least be reasoned with.[28]

From this high point of common purpose, their ways began to part. Messersmith, who always shunned publicity, frowned on Braden's bumptious public diplomacy in Cuba and then in Argentina. In keeping with the anti-Argentine spirit of 1945, as we saw in the preceding chapter, he initially counted himself among Braden's legion of admirers in his war against Argentine "fascism."[29] But for Messersmith as for so many others, Perón's election and the Cold War shattered the rationale behind Washington's hard line. In a letter dated 16 March 1946, a letter that he admitted was "very difficult for me to write," Messersmith frankly told Braden that he could no longer count on his support, suggesting that Braden rethink his own position in light of the new realities. Braden pretended not to notice. In the ensuing State Department discussions, he later claimed, he backed Messersmith for Buenos Aires because he had "always professed agreement with my Argentine policies"—implying, of course, that Messersmith went on to betray his trust. But the appointment of an ambassador to Argentina of any persuasion was a bitter defeat for Braden. Of all people, Messersmith, who had watched Hugh Wilson set off in 1938 to negotiate with Hitler, would have understood.[30]

So there was already considerable bad blood between them when they met for the first time in Braden's office, and considerably more by the time their talk was over. Messersmith was cordial but remote in a way that convinced the sensitive Braden, probably with good cause, that he was being patronized, much as a condemned man. Braden apparently tried to draw him out on the subject of his White

House talks on the 11th, but Messersmith was politely evasive. Braden fumed.[31]

Shortly after Messersmith left to finish up in Mexico, the two of them again locked horns, this time over a shipload of prized Brazilian zebu breeding bulls en route to Mexico. Former Brazilian President Getulio Vargas had a large personal financial stake in the venture. The problem was that his Rio Grande do Sul, where the bulls originated, was on the United States Department of Agriculture's (USDA's) list of suspected hotbeds of the dread hoof-and-mouth disease. According to a 1930 sanitary treaty, the United States and Mexico were obliged to quarantine livestock imported from any such region on pain of embargo. Mexico, however, lacked approved quarantine facilities. Camacho's Agriculture Ministry proposed adoption of an expedient used for a previous zebu shipment six months earlier. A temporary quarantine station had been set up on Sacrificios Island, eleven miles off Vera Cruz. After sixty days the cattle had come ashore with no ill effects. Messersmith recommended that Washington go along once more, with the proviso that Mexico would be expected to have permanent facilities in the future.[32]

The USDA refused to budge. Messersmith was ordered to tell Mexico to reject the bulls or suffer a ruinous border closing. And Brazil, for whom it had become a matter of national pride, refused to turn the ship back, vowing instead to slaughter the cattle and dump them overboard, and to film the whole bloody spectacle for exhibition back home. Relations among three major American nations hung in the balance.[33]

On the morning of 7 May, with the Brazilian freighter and her bovine cargo riding anchor in stormy seas off Vera Cruz, running out of food and water, Messersmith telephoned Braden, in Washington, urging him to appeal. But, Braden cabled back later in the day, Agriculture was "adamant that [the] risk involved [is] too great to waive strict adherence [to] treaty terms."[34]

Messersmith should have given up the issue at this point. Instead he lashed back with the special wrath he reserved for the State Department when he decided it was permitting other government agencies to make foreign policy. In letters and despatches virtually guaranteed to offend their readers, he attacked the USDA decision and everyone associated with it, and threatened to resign unless it were rescinded. Duggan and Welles and Acheson had heard him blow off like this before, but for Braden it was a new and, judging by his marginalia, infuriating experience.[35]

Meanwhile the Mexican government was landing the bulls on Sacrificios anyway. Washington drew the reasonable conclusion that

Messersmith had presented its objections with insufficient emphasis. On 28 May, with Messersmith six days in Buenos Aires, a quarantine on cattle imports—not the threatened border closing—was imposed on Mexico. The United States–Mexican Agricultural Commission met in July to address the question. American veterinarians arrived on Sacrificios to inspect the herds, and pronounced them fit for transfer to the mainland. In October, with the domestic meat shortage and upcoming congressional elections in mind, Truman lifted the quarantine.[36]

Other than as an irritant in the already strained Messersmith-Braden relationship, none of this would have mattered much. But as it turned out, the cattle *were* infected, and the contagion soon overspread Mexico. The border was sealed off on 27 December. With American financial and technical assistance, the situation was finally brought under control, but, Braden chortled libelously in his memoirs, "not before Messersmith's insubordination had cost American taxpayers considerably more than one hundred million dollars."[37]

But for Braden, Messersmith's cardinal sin was his soon evident willingness to wipe the slate clean with Perón. In an 11 July letter to Claude Bowers that somehow fell into Braden's hands, Messersmith urged that Argentina be given "a chance to perform." "Good God," Braden blurted into the margin. "What have we been doing since 1942." Obviously "performance" meant two different things to them. The issue boiled down to whether Argentina was to be judged by the same standard as its Latin sisters, who had had the good sense to declare war on the Axis while there still *was* an Axis. Braden was, rather, thinking in terms of the Perón government being forced to do prolonged penance for Argentina's recent and historic transgressions. Messersmith was falling for Perón's smooth talk and token compliance; Braden determined to stop him.[38]

The 2 July telegram that help land Messersmith in bed was a terse attack on Perón and Argentine "excuses" for noncompliance. It warned that Washington would accept nothing less than full and complete "performance."[39]

In a ten-page "Dear George" letter dated 10 July, Braden expanded on these themes, taking on Messersmith's analysis point by point. He was sorry to say that Messersmith was wrong: all the mistakes, he insisted, were on the Argentine side, unforgivable mistakes likely to be repeated if forgotten. He reminded Messersmith of Argentine obstructionism at the 1942 Rio conference. "We would do well to remember—not out of malice, but because history has a way of repeating itself—that these were our darkest hours." Perón, he maintained, could not but obey the imperatives that had "always conditioned Argentine foreign policy": bringing "adjacent states into its orbit" and challenging the United States for hemispheric leadership. Such hubris, in Braden's view, was too deeply ingrained for any quick fix. "An enduring solution," he concluded, "can only come slowly with the development of democracy and a sense of international responsiblity." In the meantime, the Monroe Doctrine and the United Nations charter would safeguard the security of the Americas until conditions were right for Rio.[40]

Moreover, Braden was suddenly writing with as strong a claim to Truman's confidence as Messersmith himself. For not only had Byrnes never told him "what had been decided upon" at the White House in April, Truman on the very morning Braden wrote his letter had given him to believe that the decision had gone in his favor. "Spruille," Truman said (according to columnists Robert Allen and William Shannon, who undoubtedly got the story from Braden), "I want you to know that I'm one hundred per cent behind you. I'll back you all the way." In Braden's account he excitedly rushed back to the State Department only to have the wind knocked out of his sails by Acheson, who advised him not to take Truman's enthusiasm too literally. Braden recalled being "shocked" at the thought that the president might not be as good as his spoken word.[41] But it could not have been a revelation to him that this latest swing back to a hard line on Argentina, if that was what it was, was probably not the last. Well aware that Truman's support might be withdrawn as unexpectedly as it had been bestowed, Braden artfully undertook to get it in writing. On 12 July he submitted a long memorandum to Truman setting forth the case against Perón that he had delivered orally two days before. On page twenty-eight he offered three "alternatives of procedure." "A" and "B" amounted to dropping everything to embrace Perón. Choice "C," Braden's recommendation, called for "strict adherence to Secretary Byrnes' statement of April 8 that there must be deeds and not merely promises before we will sign a military treaty and deliver arms to the Argentine." Truman circled "C" and affixed his initials. Braden then sent the whole damning memorandum to Messersmith, with a cover letter saying pointedly how "delighted [he was] by this splendid support from the very top."[42]

That was not all. While Messersmith was down, leading American newspapers, which had been relatively reticent on the subject since April, returned to the offensive against Argentina. Frank Kluckhohn picked up where Cortesi left off, contrasting American "concessions" to recent Argentine actions, like the court-ordered release of accused Nazis, "undesirable from the U.S. point of view," and questioned whether Argentina was serious about "obtaining agreement on any but its own terms." On 21 July, two days after Perón issued his "strongest pro-U.S. statement yet," pledging to fight at its side in the "next war," the *Washington Post* informed him editorially that the United States would not play his "sucker. Our dignity, let alone our interests and the interests of the hemisphere, forbid any such truckling to President Perón or anybody else." Perón's 10 July courtesy call to Messersmith's sickbed, with its implication of untoward chumminess, was widely reported at home. Quoting an unnamed "State Department official," the *Post* assured its readers that Argentina would be forced to "quash Nazism" in advance of any deal. And the *Times* chimed in, applauding State for refusing "to sacrifice principles on the altar of expediency."[43]

Then, on 7 August, Messersmith's embassy counselor, Charles R. Burrows, returned from home leave with an extraordinary message to him from Dr. Spaeth, Braden's special assistant. Burrows said he had been directed to remind Messersmith that when Nelson Rockefeller tried to "appease" Argentina in 1945, the "openly and strongly expressed disapproval" of the *New York Times* and the *Washington Post* had "blown him through the roof" of the State Department. Burrows continued, "Mr. Spaeth then described in some detail the happy relations which Mr. Braden enjoys with the press in general and with the more important radio commentators in the United States. According to Mr. Spaeth, Mr. Braden sees regularly, at least once a week, some seven or eight of these commentators." Spaeth made it clear that Braden intended to use these connections to combat reconciliation with Perón. "He said that Mr. Braden feels so strongly that the issue is a basic one to American foreign policy that he will never resign quietly but that he will carry the fight to the press and the radio." That, Spaeth added, would be "extremely unfortunate" for all concerned. "Mr. Spaeth said he does not know what ambitions Ambassador Messersmith has, but believes that perhaps the Ambassador would like to be 'Civil Governor' of Germany. In this connection he stated his opinion to the effect that it would be very unfortunate if the Ambassador, justly or not, should become labelled in the public eye as an 'appeaser.' So endeth the message."[44]

Assuming, as Messersmith did, that Spaeth was indeed delivering a message from his boss, we can only guess at Braden's motives. If he or anyone else expected Messersmith to yield to such rank blackmail, they did not know him. Of course, Byrnes *had* promised him a future after Argentina, and Truman had indeed indicated that Germany would be the place. But, as Messersmith wrote scornfully to Byrnes, when "threats are made that unless I do this or that thing, my career may be ruined and future usefulness destroyed, it leaves me cold, and Dr. Spaeth and whoever else may have been behind this conversation which Spaeth had with Burrows, know little about me and the springs of action which I have been, I believe, guided by in my service for our Government." It does Braden more credit to conclude that he aimed to do what he finally accomplished, which was to provoke a still unwell Messersmith into a series of increasingly intemperate responses, sending the issue into the public arena, where Braden knew he held the advantage.[45]

The ambiguity of the administration's Argentine policy gave Braden a base from which to hold up détente with Perón almost indefinitely. For "strict compliance" could be construed to require the arrest and deportation of every last individual cited in the *Blue Book* before Rio could go forward. By mid-August Perón was already complaining that too much was being asked of Argentina. When he and Messersmith sat down for private talks after the embassy dinner for the departing Ambassador Ivannisevich on the 9th, Perón poured out his dismay and bewilderment over the continued vituperations of the United States press and Washington's failure to reciprocate his own friendly gestures. Argentines, he said, himself included, were beginning to wonder whether anything they did would be enough to satisfy the United States. Extreme nationalists in his Senate, he pointed out, were blocking ratification of Chapultepec and San Francisco with the argument that "even if the Argentine ratified these acts . . . that we would continue to bring up new requirements for compliance."

Messersmith brushed this aside. "I said to the President that we must not pay any attention to these newspaper articles and that the important thing was to get ahead with the matter of ratification." Argentina's United Nations seat would not truly be its until it had. It was useless, he said, to discuss how much action against enemy firms and persons would be sufficient until the government had the legal authority to act against them. But Messersmith's private opinion was that when "most" of the identified firms and persons had been dealt with, "I was sure that my Government would consider this as adequate compliance."[46]

His "Government" thought otherwise. He was admonished by telegram to refrain from further discussion on the "measure of performance which would be regarded as satisfactory." The next day, 16 August, Messersmith could contain himself no longer, firing off to Truman, Byrnes, and Acheson packets containing a lengthy critique of Braden's 12 July memorandum to the president, Burrows's account of the Spaeth conversation, and the rest of the evidence to date that "Braden is opposed to any reasonable solution of the Argentine problem and that he wishes to impose conditions of compliance which go far beyond the action taken by the other American Republics." Braden, he charged, was placing a personal vendetta ahead of the national interest, and this could not be countenanced. "My own feeling is that Mr. Braden has so permitted his passions to continue to control his attitudes that he has never been able to see this Argentine picture in all of its proper perspective." Certainly his conduct as ambassador had left a residue of resentment toward the United States, a legacy that was a "tremendous handicap" for Messersmith to overcome. He was sacrificing his stomach to do it, he said, and the atmosphere was improving. That improvement apparently distressed Braden, and so he or "some sources in the State Department" were inspiring "tendentious articles in the press at home which are unduly critical or skeptical with regard to the intentions of the Argentine Government," defaming Perón in order to nip the budding rapprochement. As for himself, he wrote Acheson, "I am pretty much fed up with some of this stuff that is being given out that I am 'selling out,' etc. I am just as much attached to principle as I think any of us are, and I think I have shown it over a long period of years and by the personal sacrifices which I have made." He vowed to "immediately resign this mission" and go "home to the Mayo Clinic for observation and treatment" unless the sniping stopped.[47]

Messersmith's timing was unfortunate. His rebuttal found Byrnes in Paris with the foreign ministers and Truman cruising the Potomac on his first presidential vacation. Acheson was about to leave for vacation as well when Messersmith's complaints came to his attention. Irritation was written all over his reply. He said he would tell Braden that there was suspicion of attacks emanating from his office, but was convinced in advance that "Braden is a wholly honorable man and would not be capable of participating in or permitting such conduct." Acheson agreed that Spaeth's remarks had been "both foolish and wrong," but could not accept "that Braden either authorized or knew about such a conversation." In any case, Spaeth had just left the department to return to his teaching post at the Stanford University law school. And as far as Acheson was concerned, it was just "borrowing trouble" to dwell on the apparent divergence over what constituted compliance when everyone agreed that Argentina was nowhere near that point. At the proper time a decision would be made, and not "by Braden or me but by the Secretary and the President." In the meantime, he wrote, Messersmith could count on "our full support" and rest assured that neither "Braden [n]or anyone else in the Department is undermining you publicly or privately."[48]

The day before Acheson penned these words, Henry Wallace, last of the cabinet New Dealers, soon to be ex-secretary of commerce for publicly criticizing Truman's Russian policies, a long-time hardliner on Argentina and, of course, no friend of Messersmith's, reported having "a very interesting lunch with Spruille Braden." Braden was on a mission of character assassination. As an appetizer he told Wallace "the story of why Messersmith had been shifted from Mexico to Argentina." "It seems [Wallace wrote in his diary] that Messersmith had had a very close personal relationship with Padilla, and had refused to see Alemán. Messersmith, in fact, had more or less backed Padilla in the election. After Alemán was elected it was more or less necessary, therefore, to shift Messersmith."[49]

This was more or less a lie, as Braden knew. The story originated with one William Prescott Allen, publisher of the *Laredo* [Texas] *Times*, whose brother-in-law, one Phillip Kazen, never forgave Messersmith for scotching his appointment as BEW "special economic assistant" in 1942. Kazen had ties to Lombardo Toledano, who, it will be recalled, in early 1946 publicly accused Messersmith of campaigning for Padilla, until he was repudiated by Camacho. The *Laredo Times* crusade culminated in a 23 January 1946 editorial alleging vaguely that Messersmith had snubbed Alemán in 1942, and so had "jeopardized the feeling between Alemán and our government." Denouncing "Messersmith imperialism," Allen telegraphed Truman demanding his recall. Answering for the president, Braden expressed full confidence in the ambassador. But he did not forget the charge.[50]

Wallace was now hungry for more, and Braden was happy to oblige. Four days before Messersmith left Mexico for Argentina, he had delivered a farewell speech at an American colony banquet in his honor. Then, saying that he was speaking off the record, he offered extemporaneous remarks on the world situation. The next day, 12 May, on page twenty-eight of the *New York Times*, there appeared the headline "Messersmith Sees Soviet Aggression; Retiring Envoy to Mexico Holds Russian Policy Similar to Hitler's of 1933–1938." Actually, as *Times* correspondent Camille Cianfarra acknowledged, he "did not specifically name the Soviet Union" in characterizing the current situation as an "armed truce." But his import was clear.[51]

The day before Braden's lunch with Wallace—and what may have prompted it—another article appeared. The 27 August Communist *Daily Worker* ran the banner headline "U.S. Envoy Woos Argentina for Anti-Soviet War," flanked by portraits of Perón and Messersmith. Noting that Byrnes was just then in Paris, "hotly denying . . . that responsible Americans were speaking of the inevitability of war between the U.S. and the USSR," the *Worker*'s copyrighted story had

Messersmith doing just that three weeks earlier in a speech before the American Legion post in Buenos Aires. Bringing the article to Wallace's attention, Braden vouched for its veracity, citing Messersmith's Mexican speech in the same vein. Wallace fervently agreed that such talk was "criminal."[52]

The *Worker* story sparked recriminations of the sort depressingly routine in mid-1946. *Pravda* took notice, predictably denouncing the alleged speech as one "worthy of a political gangster." Ordered by Washington to respond, Messersmith heatedly proclaimed himself the victim of a vicious Communist misrepresentation, and his Legionaire audience went on record to the same effect. Acting Secretary of State Will Clayton passed their denials on to the press on 3 September.[53]

Whether or not Messersmith said what he was quoted as saying at the time and place he was supposed to have spoken, the views were his, as he freely admitted in a 3 September letter to Braden. Actually his thinking was even more belligerent and, to his mind, more realistic. By this time most of the State Department's European experts had also abandoned their wartime belief in peaceful coexistence with Russia, which they now judged an irremediably aggressive threat to Western values. But few had the courage to draw the logical if horrifying conclusion from their convictions. To meet the perceived threat of Soviet global expanionism, backed within five years, according to State Department experts, by an atomic bomb, they embraced what would be called containment—an essentially static and acquiescent concept, which, at its most optimistic, held out a frail hope of a long-term "mellowing" of Soviet power.[54]

For all of the attention analysts have devoted to United States–Soviet postwar relations, this gulf between what American diplomats believed to be true about Russia and the steps they proposed to meet it has never been seriously addressed. In his prize-winning study of thirty American career diplomats between 1933 and 1947, Hugh De Santis asserts that his subjects "perceived Moscow's aims in three discrete ways, each of which called forth different foreign-policy paradigms." By 1946, two of those images, which envisioned cooperation, were dead. The third, "ideological confrontation," requiring an "ideological counteroffensive" by the United States, took hold. But there was a fourth possible scenario: what De Santis calls "realistic confrontation, the advancement of Soviet interests by means of military expansion," whose logical response was "retaliatory confrontation." This, however, "was not seriously considered by professional diplomats." War, De Santis suggests, was repugnant to their liberal-internationalist values; it also foreclosed diplomatic options and opportunities for diplomatic influence. In sum, professional egotism, a recurrence of their 1930s failure of nerve, and a resignation to what they believed was politically impossible led De Santis's subjects to ignore the substantial evidence that national interest, rather than ideology, was the driving force behind Stalinist expansionism. That, of course, had been Messersmith's contention since 1935. And the Nazi experience had further convinced him that diplomacy was futile in dealing with the implacable evil that he—and the State Department—believed the Soviet state embodied. A limited military action in 1933 would have spared the world the ordeal of total war. Given the current imbalance of power, a preemptive strike against Stalin in 1945 promised similar dividends. But, as Messersmith assured Braden, "whatever my personal views" on the subject, "I would certainly not express them in a speech. . . . I have too great a sense of responsibility for that."[55]

Why he expressed those sensitive views to Braden, the one person most likely to use them against him, is unclear. Perhaps he was trying to establish some common ground from which to reconcile their Argentine differences. To know anything about Braden was to take his anti-Communism for granted. In a talk with Wallace in November 1945, Braden had been so full of rancor toward Russia that Wallace privately voiced regret at having supported his nomination as assistant secretary of state. But hostility to Perón conditioned Braden's whole world outlook; and his case against Rio required minimization of the Soviet threat. So he could disingenuously assure Wallace over lunch in August 1946 that he did not "look on Russia as the same kind of menace as Germany," that the Soviets were behaving erratically only because they were "scared to death" by rhetoric like Messersmith's.[56]

Braden's desperate conspiracies could only buy time. In the larger picture, he and the developing feud with Messersmith were irrelevant. Whatever assurances Truman had given them, however Truman hedged and backtracked, Braden's fate had actually been decided back in April, when the focus of American policy shifted from Perón's person to his "deeds." The initiative had thereby passed to the Argentine leader to decide how far he wished to go to secure Washington's arms and good graces. In fact, by early 1947 haughty Argentina had fulfilled its inter-American obligations to the surprise and satisfaction of all save Braden and his followers. In the end, the State Department's pretext for the continued postponement of Rio narrowed to the handful of accused Nazis who had eluded capture and fled into the vast Argentine hinterland. In Latin eyes, Perón won points for effort; Washington lost them for pettiness.

A critical break came on 30 August 1946. The struggle for ratification of the acts of Chapultepec and San Francisco witnessed noisy nationalistic street demonstrations, threats on Perón's life, demands for "reservations" to safeguard sovereignty, and much political maneuvering and attempted horsetrading. In private talks, Messersmith tried to sway Senate irreconcilables like Diego Molinari, known as "the Argentine Henry Cabot Lodge." But it was Perón's fight and his victory. With ratification, Messersmith had no doubt whatsoever about Argentina's "determination . . . to collaborate more closely in the American picture and with us." Ratification cleared the way for action against enemy firms, and by the end of September the sixty-nine "most important" were in the process of liquidation. The residency law, which protected aliens from arbitrary deportation, still obstructed the government in that area, but vigorous prosecution had begun to bear fruit: thirty-five enemy aliens already deported, with papers against forty-three others, "really the principle ones," Messersmith wrote, being drawn up.[57]

All of this rolled off the irreconcilables in Washington. Ratifying the two pacts whose benefits Argentina had been enjoying for over a year, shot back Thomas Mann, was the least Perón could do. Although new instructions to the embassy dated 25 September conceded that "perfect performance should not . . . be expected or required," attached was a long list of *Blue Book* persons and firms against which unspecified action would be required. The State Department continued to grind out intransigent policy statements. Messersmith was irked no end when Braden's 12 July memorandum, the one innocently approved by Truman, was distributed to all mission chiefs in the hemisphere for their guidance. Messersmith's critique and ratification of the pacts had made no impression on Washington whatsoever.[58]

Now certain that Braden would stop at nothing to undermine him, Messersmith began to retaliate with increasingly desperate measures of his own. In language that sometimes bordered on the hysterical, he expatiated on the dire consequences of Braden's obstructionism for United States global and hemispheric interests. He put Washington on alarming notice that its economic, military, and political rivals were beginning to fill the Argentine void. He reported a "tremendous effort" by the Russians to sow internal discord and anti-Americanism through their local party apparatus and new diplomatic mission. Fortunately, Perón "wants nothing whatever to do with Communism," but, Messersmith argued, he could not remain isolated and impassive to American hostility and his legitimate arms requests. Nor, he warned, were the Russians alone in cultivating him. Agents of the Swedish Bofors and Czech Skoda firms were on the scene and active, and Messersmith painstakingly reported their every move. He called attention to secret arms overtures by Britons, in defiance of their government's just concluded Gentleman's Agreement with Washington to honor the American embargo. In case Washington missed the point, Messersmith made it explicit: the clock was running out on the administration's arms standardization plan.[59]

The British were also making commercial inroads. Not only that, Messersmith was assisting them. In July a trade delegation headed by Sir Wilfred Eady arrived in Buenos Aires to negotiate the necessary adjustments in Anglo-Argentine economic relations. For its food shipments since 1939 Argentina had accumulated credits totaling £150 million now blocked in British accounts. Argentina demanded their release, with interest, with a view to their conversion into dollars for the purchase of manufactures only the United States could presently supply. "Argentinization" of the economy was a key Peronist theme, and there were proposals that some of the frozen sterling go to repatriate the British-owned railroads. The Argentines also sought higher prices—100 percent higher—and fixed quotas for their beef.[60]

Within a month the Eady mission was on the verge of collapse. The chief Argentine negotiator, Miguel Miranda, president of the just nationalized Central Bank, was a "rude and crude" businessman (Messersmith's words) with a confirmed aversion to Britons and Americans alike. Taking every opportunity to rub Eady's nose in Britain's economic plight, he insisted that the sterling assets be freed-up first; then the talks could proceed. Fearing a run on their reserves by a long line of creditors, the British refused. Eady and his colleagues packed their bags.[61]

Messersmith stepped in. It was Sunday dinner with Perón, 1 September. When the Argentine leader had finished dilating on one of his favorite themes, the Communist threat, Messersmith observed that he could do something constructive about it. Emphasizing that he was speaking unofficially, he urged Perón to start negotiating with Britain, for Argentine's sake and the free world's. He said that he appreciated the preoccupation with the immobilized sterling, but that the real issue was British recovery, to which mercantile Argentina could hardly be indifferent. He reminded Perón of all of Washington's sacrifices—most recently in the form of a $3.75 billion credit—to see Britain through its economic difficulties. He appealed finally to Argentine magnanimity and international responsibility.[62]

The next day Perón issued new instructions to Miranda and ordered Bramuglia into the talks. The British ambassador, Sir Reginald

Leeper, secured concessions from his government. On the 17th, in a dramatic turnaround, agreement was reached. All but a fraction of the assets were to remain frozen, except for the purpose of redeeming British investments. The railroads were to come under mixed ownership, with total capital equal to the lines' market value—about £90 million—plus a £32 million contribution from the Argentine government for improvements. The British stockholders—the former owners—were guaranteed a minimum 4 percent return on investment, Argentina reserving the right to acquire their shares at par. Britain agreed to purchase 80 percent of the country's exportable beef, at only 7 percent over the 1945 price. Negotiations for a new trade agreement were planned. Perón sealed the bargain with a "Christmas gift" to Britain: three shiploads of sorely needed beef.[63]

Both sides had yielded enough to be vulnerable to charges of having yielded too much. But because Argentina's bargaining position was much the stronger to begin with, Perón's critics probably had the better case. A *Washington Post* editorial was only half right in describing the Miranda-Eady agreement as "a blow to Britain." Although the railroad plan dealt gently with British investors, their days were clearly numbered. Another outpost of the informal empire was soon to fall. But Britain's vital interests, if not its ego, had been safeguarded. In a world of shortages, the British had secured their meat supplies and scored a big victory on its price. The agreement paved the way for a revival of British exports. And the majority of the sterling balances were preserved, at least for the present.[64]

Both sides generously acknowledged—too generously, on Eady's part—that the agreement would not have been possible without Messersmith's help. Bramuglia told him privately that his intercession with Perón had been decisive. The British, on the other hand, thanked him formally, which served, perhaps intentionally, to implicate him openly in an agreement that he and the British both knew would cause considerable consternation at the State Department.[65] For Miranda-Eady not only made Perón again look the statesman and Braden again the liar in that regard, it was also distinctly prejudicial to American commercial interests in Argentina. Messersmith was quick to point out that the British now had a chance to gain "undue influence" in the Argentine market. In *The Limits of Power*, historians Joyce and Gabriel Kolko aver that "Messersmith saw the Anglo-American rivalry as perhaps the central diplomatic issue in Latin America," but here he was clearly aiding the British "rival" as a means of bringing pressure on Washington for rapprochement with Perón. "There is plenty of room for both of us," Messersmith smoothly assured Acheson, referring to Britain, "but a proper equilibrium must be maintained in Argentina. That required normal United States–Argentine relations.[66]

But Messersmith failed to reckon with his government's postwar economic might, as well as its readiness to use it for worthy political ends, like Perón's isolation. Messersmith's scheme was nullified through nullification of the treaty on which it was based. Treasury Department experts found Miranda-Eady in technical violation of Britain's big American loan, which, among other things, bound Britain to make the pound freely convertible into dollars. Miranda-Eady, however, permitted Argentina to further draw down its frozen sterling to finance any deficit that might develop in its sterling balance of payments—an obvious ploy to promote British exports. Pressed by Washington, the British argued coyly that because Argentina was and would probably remain a net sterling creditor, the provision was unlikely to come into play. But the Americans were adamant. Miranda-Eady was permanently shelved.[67]

Messersmith was going to inexcusable lengths to make his point: that American interests in Argentina were in jeopardy—partly his own deliberate doing—and would remain so as long as a refractory Braden remained in office poisoning relations. Braden, he sorrowfully wrote Truman on 12 October, "will never . . . collaborate fully in this American picture and isn't inclined to collaborate adequately with you and the Secretary and with me. That, of course," he added charitably, "is an understandable situation." Braden could have accommodated himself to the revised policy in a "broad and statesmanlike way," but he had apparently "utterly forgotten his responsibilities as an Assistant Secretary of State." With breathtaking presumptuousness, Messersmith ventured only "one solution and that is for him to leave."[68]

But the solution that Messersmith had no business proposing was no solution at all for a Truman administration nervously awaiting its first real test at the polls. The outlook was encouraging only for Republicans. After thirteen years of Democratic congresses, the voters were ready for a change. The Democrats themselves were bitterly divided. Liberal unhappiness with Truman's style and policies had turned into a full-fledged rebellion over the dismissal of Wallace. With his liberal connections, Braden was at least temporarily indispensable, an advantage he hastened to exploit. Throughout October "persistent reports," probably of his own manufacture, had him resigning "if the current moderate attitude toward Argentina was not stiffened." Byrnes, just returned from Paris, was again caught in the middle: Vandenberg and Connally clamoring for Rio; Acheson and Braden and their supporters contending that the United States must not embrace another "reactionary" regime. At his 22 October press conference, the beleaguered Byrnes refused comment on rumors of a pre-election "showdown" over Argentina, taking refuge under the "deeds not words" obfuscation. He did not dispute, however, that some softening of the official line toward Perón had in fact taken place.[69]

A week later—five days before elections—Byrnes all but closed the door to normalization. He told the press that Braden enjoyed his and Truman's "full confidence," and added some gratuitous insults of Perón for good measure. For in the meantime word had come of Perón's proposed Five Year Plan, a package of twenty-seven laws that aimed to transform Argentine society and the Argentine economy. The Perón government committed itself to full employment without inflation. The plan envisaged public investments totaling $1.5 billion to develop the nation's natural resources and industry. Large sums were earmarked for public health and transportation projects, applied research, and immigration and settlement.[70]

Cool observers sized up the plan for what it was: a giant step toward a mixed economy and Perón's "third position" between capitalism and socialism. To his enemies in the United States, the Five Year Plan, with its totalitarian connotations, was a declaration of war. The anti-Argentine press was quick to seize upon this "Hitler-style" plan as "proof" of Perón's intention to build "a powerful expanding war machine."[71]

Too quickly, Messersmith leaped to Perón's defense. He too had been uneasy with the plan's scope and worried about its impact on the private sector and on foreign opinion. But Perón convinced him that the Five Year Plan was simply a blueprint for a long-overdue national renaissance that aimed to promote, as Messersmith explained to Washington, "greater participation by the Argentine in her own development and a greater measure of social justice." Its inspiration, he decided, came not from Europe but, rather, from the New Deal. He professed to see "considerable similarity" between the proposed legislation and "some of the measures which were put into effect in the United States in the earliest days of the Roosevelt Administration."[72]

But other things were happening in Argentina, things that should have made the comparison to Roosevelt stick in Messersmith's throat. Perón himself gave the lie to the contention that he was a misunderstood democrat amenable to American leadership. A purge of the Argentine universities was already underway; by the end of 1946, 70 percent of the faculty had been replaced. Organized labor continued to make tremendous gains, but at the price of its independence. Restrictions were imposed on the press. Newspaper "holidays" were declared, ostensibly for the benefit of the vendors. The anti-Peronist justices on the Argentine Supreme Court were impeached. There *were* similarities between the Agricultural Adjustment Administration (AAA) and the Five Year Plan, but Perón's Tugwell, the plan's reputed mastermind, was José Figuerola, a close adviser to Spanish dictator Primo de Rivera during the 1920s. And there were many much worse than Figuerola in Perón's coterie.[73]

"I know something about dictatorships," Messersmith insisted on 25 September in a forty-three-page letter to the *New York Times*'s Arthur Sulzberger, "and this is not [one] in the sense that we understand the term." Joseph Page's definitive 1983 biography of Perón shows that he was essentially correct. Even at its worst, which was yet to come, Peronism was nothing like the unalloyed totalitarian evil that Braden and his newspaper friends continued to savage. But it was dictatorship enough to confirm their preconceptions. Nor did Messersmith help himself by trying to set the reporters aright; both sides were long past the point of sober discourse. He had it out with Virginia Prewett, which made wonderful copy for her. When Frank Kluckhohn similarly resisted reeducation, Messersmith went over his head in the aforementioned long and ill-advised letter to Sulzberger.[74] In it, after complaining about Kluckhohn, Messersmith went on to attack Braden in terms only slightly milder than he was using in his letters to Truman and Byrnes. Braden, of course, was almost certainly doing the same to him, but he had the good sense to do it secretly. For his part, Messersmith made the mistake of sending a copy of his Sulzberger letter to Byrnes, which earned him a humiliating rebuke. Byrnes ordered him to "immediately desist from writing to representatives of the press letters criticizing the Assistant Secretary of State, Mr. Braden. The United States cannot operate with one appointee of the President writing to a representative of the press in criticism of another of his appointees." As far as Byrnes was concerned, Braden was the aggrieved party. Byrnes had never heard Braden less than "enthusiastic in expressing his high opinion of your qualifications and his personal esteem for you," and this was how Messersmith was paying him back. Regarding the "alleged" Spaeth-Burrows conversation, Byrnes noted that "you not only convicted [Spaeth] of making the statement, but you also convicted Mr. Braden of inspiring or approving it without any evidence to justify it." "I want you to understand," Byrnes warned, "that if at any time you have any complaints about Mr. Braden . . . I expect you to advise me"—which, of course, Messersmith had been doing since August.[75]

It was a brutal slap in the face, clear evidence that he no longer had his superiors' confidence—if, indeed, he had ever had it. Messersmith was "deeply distressed" by Byrnes's chastisement, but he still did not appreciate the gravity of his situation. Any "misunderstanding" of his actions, he assured Byrnes, could be cleared up "in five minutes" face to face. The secretary agreed that he should return home for talks.[76]

The official announcement, which had him coming north for medical treatment, fooled no one. The Braden-Messersmith feud was a leading topic on the Washington cocktail circuit this holiday season. George Messersmith, who only wanted to do what he had been sent to do, found himself on the cover of *Time* magazine (2 December) for having done it too well. Pressed by reporters on 20 December, Byrnes allowed that some discussion of "South America in general" might take place during the ambassador's stay in the capital. Without anyone asking him, Byrnes added that he had "no intention of asking for Mr. Messersmith's resignation," which only served to fuel speculation that he would not be returning to his post.[77]

Byrnes surprised everyone and resigned first, on 7 January. General George C. Marshall was named to succeed him. In talks with another Byrnes ill-wisher, White House Chief of Staff Admiral William D. Leahy, Messersmith evinced unbounded relief over the sudden turn of events. What had become clear after his icy first "five minutes" with Byrnes on New Year's Day was that their differences were fundamental and unbridgeable. Marshall, on the other hand, was presumably imbued with the Pentagon's sense of urgency about Rio. In an 11 January speech, Vandenberg, now speaking for a Republican Senate majority, renewed his call for "our indispensable Pan American solidarity," a call it was predicted that Marshall would heed. And there was good news from Buenos Aires, in the arrest and deportation of notable Nazis and the final liquidation of all enemy property. Citing these acts of compliance, the British government renounced the Gentleman's Agreement, and openly entered the race for Argentina's arms business.[78]

The gathering momentum for reconciliation and his daily treatments at Bethesda did wonders for Messersmith's stomach. He met with Truman at the White House at 12:15 on 15 January, and the president used "some very strong language with regard to Braden." Messersmith agreed that Braden had "done enough harm." As he left the building Messersmith was intercepted by reporters who asked him to comment on the persistent rumors of his own imminent resignation. Tired of ducking the issue, and with Truman's encouraging words still ringing in his ears, he allowed himself an intemperate off-the-record reply. After the Cianfarra episode in Mexico City, he should have known better than to trust in the reporters' discretion. He blamed the resignation rumors on Miss Prewett, "a very active but very malicious little lady . . . who would be better off in a sanitarium than writing news stories about me." Her *Chicago Sun* printed the "ungallant remark," along with a scathing editorial.

> We have known for a long time that Ambassador Messersmith wanted to get Virginia Prewett, our correspondent in Buenos Aires, out of his hair. Miss Prewett has insisted, in her dispatches to this paper, on telling the truth about Peron's rotten fascist regime. Mr. Messersmith, anxious to appease Peron, wants to soft-pedal the truth.
>
> The Ambassador has now resorted to one of the most despicable tricks of the trade. . . . he launched a vicious tirade [and] undertook to make his remarks "off the record," which is a diplomat's way of refusing to assume public responsibility for his remarks. The Sun won't stand for that kind of malevolent irresponsibility. If Mr. Messersmith wants to blow his top about Miss Prewett's reporting in a way calculated to injure her reputation as a newspaperwoman, he can do it publicly and take the consequences.

His abdomen flared up again.[79]

Worse was to come. Truman was still playing both ends against the middle. On the morning of 21 January Marshall was sworn into office in a White House ceremony. When it was over the president drew Braden aside to let him know that "that s.o.b. Messersmith" would shortly be fired. Braden had survived the transition. A few days later he and Acheson briefed Marshall on Argentine policy. Just before returning to his post, Messersmith called on the new secretary to plead for rapprochement. Marshall was noncommital on that score, and went on to tell him in no uncertain terms that he would, no more than Byrnes, tolerate his taking his case to the press.[80]

Meanwhile a hero's welcome was being readied for him in Buenos Aires. But Messersmith, who stopped over in Rio on the night of 31 January, learned of the plan, and prevailed upon the Argentines by phone to cancel the brass bands. As it was, Juan and Eva Perón were on hand to greet him at the airport, and a damning photograph of him grinning in Perón's embrace appeared in a number of American newspapers.[81]

By that time Messersmith was immersed in discussions with Perón and the embassy staff to assay the progress toward compliance while he was away. From opposite perspectives, he and Braden both missed the irony: American conditions *were* rapidly being met, in large part because the emerging authoritarian character of Perón's regime gave him the freedom to do so. On 7 March Messersmith formally recommended that Marshall certify Argentine compliance, preferably before he left for the Moscow foreign ministers meeting later in the month. But Braden convinced Acheson that Argentine action was incomplete and insincere. Because a number of accused Nazis remained on the loose, Braden insisted, Argentina had "not yet met the test." And Marshall, testifying before the House Foreign Affairs Committee, promised a review of the administration's hemispheric policy, which would be "neither a Braden policy nor a Messersmith policy," but not until he returned from Moscow.[82]

A waiting game began. Messersmith expressed confidence in his eventual vindication. When Marshall finally sat down and reviewed all the facts, he assured Sumner Welles, whose syndicated column had begun speaking out in Messersmith's defense, the secretary would be "completely disgusted and exceedingly disturbed" by Braden's underhandedness. But Messersmith was "fearful we are reaching [the] time limit on Argentina." If Perón continued to be rebuffed, he wrote Arthur Sulzberger—itself a rash act of defiance—he might be toppled in favor of "a very radical government" that would take weapons from the many countries, including Russia, eager to sell.[83]

The issue, however, was out of Messersmith's hands; he knew it, and felt it too. As a youth he had looked older than his years; now, at the age of sixty-four, he looked older still. The eyes burned with the old intensity, but the flesh encircling them was puffy with weariness. He sagged badly at the jaw, and the whole face was deeply furrowed with the scars of a hundred battles, and especially this latest one. His stomach, always the barometer of his well-being, had never been worse since 1919. Then, in May, he fell down a long flight of stairs at a friend's country home, which fortunately for him resulted in nothing worse than badly bruised ribs. Still, bound in bandages, he grimaced with every breath.[84]

But a resolution of the Argentine issue was near. Pressure was building in Washington. The Cold War was on in earnest. Vandenberg and his committee refused to await Marshall's return from Moscow before settling up the hemisphere. On 12 March Truman asked Congress to authorize a massive aid program to fight Communism in Greece and Turkey and wherever else it threatened free people. Catching Nazis in Argentina plunged on the foreign-policy agenda. On the House floor Braden was denounced as a "muddling jug head," doing Moscow's work by holding up the Rio pact.[85]

Vandenberg, Connally, and Acheson—but, significantly, not Braden—were at Truman's side on 31 March when Ambassador Ivanissevich came to call at the White House by secret invitation. The ambassador, who was about to return to his country, was asked to convey the administration's desire for the "most friendly relations with the Argentine people and government." All that remained, Truman continued, was the deportation of "some 20 to 30 dangerous Nazis" still at large. Ivanissevich stiffened. He declared that there were no Nazis in Argentina and "that it was calumny to say there were." He would nonetheless deliver the president's message to Perón.[86]

Messersmith was "grateful" for this initiative. Unfortunately, he wrote Acheson, the Argentine ambassador was "completely uninformed on the alien question and what Perón is doing about it," and had therefore inadequately presented his government's case. Messersmith unwisely took the task upon himself. "Special squads," he reported, were out "scouring the country" for the fugitives, who had had a critical head start. Many had undoubtedly fled the country; the border with Chile alone was nearly 2,500 miles long, and impossible to police. He questioned whether those still at large could be considered "dangerous," inasmuch as they would be apprehended the moment they "show their heads." Surely when "the President spoke of these '20 or 30 aliens left' . . . he had in mind the adequate efforts of the Argentine Government and not that we would insist that every one must be found before we take appropriate action." Perón was doing all that could be done; nothing more could reasonably be expected.[87]

But Messersmith's opinion no longer counted. Undone by his own too avid advocacy, himself a victim of the "localitis" he deplored in others, he had already been written off as an apologist for Perón. Marshall's response (he had returned to Washington on 26 April) took Argentine bad faith for granted: despite the "highly conciliatory" approach to Ivanissevich, he complained to Messersmith, those "dangerous agents" were still not in custody. It was all faintly ludicrous in view of what a later generation would learn about real Nazi war criminals like Klaus Barbie being smuggled *into* South America around this time with the connivance of United States intelligence officials. Wearily, Messersmith tried again to explain Perón's problems. The point was that his government was doing its best, a point "I do not seem to have been able to make clear to the Department." It was as close to an admission of defeat as he ever uttered.[88]

Expediency won the day. The compliance question, the focal issue in Argentine–United States relations for almost two years, had been a fraud from the first. A few deportations more or less were immaterial. Meeting even Braden's exacting standards of compliance said next to nothing about Perón's motives or fitness to participate in a Rio pact. Even as Marshall was denouncing him for nonperformance, plans to proceed with the meeting and to ease Braden out of the picture were going forward. The secretary's Moscow experience had finally convinced him of Soviet intransigence and the need to arm the hemisphere. When he returned, he stripped Braden of responsibility for the stalled Latin American arms standardization program and gave it to General John H. Hildring, whom he named assistant secretary of state. On 1 May the Inter-American Military Cooperation bill, with the Pentagon and the State Department now united in support, was resubmitted to Congress.[89]

Braden finally saw the handwriting on the wall. What happened next depends upon which version of his one chooses to believe. According to his memoirs, when he learned that he had lost the arms program he stalked in to tell Marshall and Acheson that he was "resigning forthwith," but they "begged" him to wait until they could fire the "insubordinate" Messersmith. In a 1967 interview with historian David Green, Braden recalled being "quietly informed that his services would no longer be needed. He agreed to resign 'voluntarily'"—that is, without going public—"on condition that Messersmith also be recalled."[90]

It amounted to the same thing for Messersmith. He was to be sacrificed in order to spare the administration the political embarrassment that Braden, with his press connections, definitely had the power to cause. But the execution was badly botched. On 3 June Truman announced that the way was now clear for Rio. The next day came Braden's resignation, "reluctantly" accepted. Messersmith's mission was declared accomplished. What this meant he discovered early in the morning of the 5th: through the window of his Buenos Aires office, he heard a paperboy hawking the headline of his "resignation." An hour later this was confirmed by telegram from Marshall: "your resignation is accepted." He was instructed to notify the Argentine foreign office of this at once, preparatory to a Truman press conference the next day.[91]

This outcome surprised no one, probably not even Messersmith. Since the feud with Braden went public, even their partisans conceded that both protagonists would undoubtedly have to go. Marshall had hinted as much during his February testimony to Congress. As early as May, James Bruce, a fifty-four-year-old corporate executive, was correctly identified as the next ambassador to Buenos Aires. The suddenness of it all took Messersmith aback, but he was by now inured to the indignities of foreign service, and so accepted the news with good grace—that is, without fully understanding its implications for his career. He did not agree, he wrote Marshall calmly, that his mission had been completed; he had hoped it "would continue several months longer in order to consolidate . . . [the] very great progress [that] . . . has been made." Still, he had been on the verge of writing Truman that he was almost ready "to accept another suitable post in the field." His only concern was that "nothing may interfere with the course of [improved] relations so happily begun."[92]

His equability was short-lived. First, there were signs to which he called attention that his withdrawal might indeed harm relations with Argentina. He broke the news to Perón over lunch on the 5th, and, despite Messersmith's own reported efforts to soothe him, the Argentine president was all indignation and outrage. That afternoon, after getting off the phone with Buenos Aires, Ambassador Ivanissevich went to the State Department, where he registered Perón's wish that the decision be canceled and that Messersmith, "champion of the great cause of panamericanism and brilliant exponent of the democratic spirit," stay on. The Peronist press denounced the "dismissal" of the envoy who had "performed a miracle" in improving relations as an "unfriendly act."[93]

While Messersmith and Perón were commiserating with each other over lunch, Truman was facing reporters in Washington. The president raised more questions about Messersmith's status than he answered. No, Truman said, the ambassador had not resigned, nor had he been recalled. He had gone to Argentina with the understanding that he would return once his specific mission—repairing relations with Perón—had been accomplished. It now was. The president "professed no knowledge of Mr. Messersmith's future plans." That evening the State Department further muddied the waters with the announcement that his "resignation had been accepted."[94]

Messersmith's anxiety was now palpable. "I am completely in the dark as to what has been happening and the reasons therefor," he cabled Marshall the following afternoon: "As I have not submitted my resignation to the President, has my 'resignation' been accepted by him?" The national interest and inter-American relations still came first, but he was "sure that the President and you will wish to see that I receive that consideration which is decent and proper." After all, the understanding under which he had agreed to leave Mexico and that he had had the foresight to have Byrnes put in writing during their January talks called for reassignment when the Argentine job was finished. Refusing to believe, much as had Braden, that Truman would not honor his commitment, he comforted himself with the thought that the president had simply not yet decided what his new post would be.[95]

At the department's insistence, Messersmith and his wife, Marion, made haste to sail. They had had half a lifetime of practice at it together. As always for them, the disorderly drudgery of moving on was partially mitigated by fond farewells. The 18 June gala at the Casa Rosada brought together 200 eminent Argentines in a spirited tribute. The Argentine Congress voted him the jewel-encrusted Grand Cross of San Martín, the highest honor conferred on a foreigner. Lured by public notices describing him as a "great friend of all Argentines," more than 10,000 turned out at dockside on 21 June, joining their president and dozens of lesser officials, whose goodbyes delayed the sailing for over an hour. Perón was last to leave their ship. A roar went up from the crowd as he and Messersmith embraced at the railing. The chant "Perón! Messersmith! Perón! Messersmith!" echoed until the ship was out of sight.[96]

Epilogue

George and Marion Messersmith had "a delightful trip north." "For the first time in months," he recalled, "I was able to eat normally." They mulled over their future. He was sure that Truman would offer him another post, but "disgusted" by the way he and Argentina had been mishandled, "I felt that I could accept nothing from him." Messersmith was sixty-five; he was ready to retire. He had some writing projects in mind: memoirs, perhaps, and a treatise on foreign service administration. They landed in New Orleans on 9 July, and someone delivered a message from Truman, asking him to withhold comment on Argentina, promising that "an important European post" would soon be his. But Messersmith had made up his mind. He cabled the department requesting retirement. In Washington he decided not to call on the president, in order to "avoid recriminations." After all, Truman was "on the whole a man of many decencies. He had made a political bargain in which I became impersonally involved." There was no point in pressing the matter.[1]

That was not quite the way it happened. Messersmith left Argentina still hoping to be rewarded for bringing Perón into camp, and fully intending to take whatever was offered him. But he now recognized that Truman might have different plans, and when he got to Washington, his fears were confirmed. Meeting with Assistant Secretary of State Norman Armour on 17 July, Messersmith learned that he was finished. "I told him," Armour reported to Marshall, "that you, the Department, and many of us felt that he had gone too far in carrying his case to the press, the Hill, and elsewhere." That was only a pretext. But it was a good one. Clearly he had spoken his mind more than once too often, and to the wrong people. The next day he saw Marshall, who had absolutely nothing to say on the subjects Messersmith was there to discuss. Moreover, the record shows that it was Truman and not he who decided that it would be best that they not meet; the White House turned down his request for an interview. Messersmith persisted, and in late August, Treasury Secretary John Snyder, who had befriended him in Mexico, arranged for him to have what turned out to be a vacuous ten minutes with Truman. Braden was similarly favored. During his ten minutes with the president, Braden bitterly recalled, "the topic of conversation was a gabardine suit I was wearing."[2]

Messersmith and Braden, a scholar notes, "both lost the battle; Messersmith won the war." This was clear at the time. Even newspapers that had enthusiastically backed Braden, like the *New York Herald-Tribune*, gave a sigh of relief that "the long, maladroit, and unhappy history of the U.S. policy toward Argentina has at last reached a climax." The result was "a substantial defeat for Mr. Braden's views." The *Washington Post* donned sackcloth and ashes, acknowledging that the compliance controversy had really been an effort gone awry to influence "the character and composition of the Argentine government." Perón's triumph, the *Post* admitted, had demonstrated that "we do not know the sentiments of the Argentine people." The *New York Times* reserved its fears that the Perón regime was "still potentially a seedbed of Fascism in this continent," but agreed that "the course now chosen will restore that hemispheric unity which has been strained by the long impasse between our country and . . . Argentina." Comedian Bob Hope arrived in Buenos Aires to poke fun at the past and to christen the new cordiality. On 15 August the Rio conference got hastily underway, with Bramuglia heading the Argentine delegation and Marshall the American.[3]

Meanwhile, the American most responsible for this rapprochement was quietly vacating the scene. The announcement of Messersmith's retirement passed almost unnoticed. This did not seem to perturb him at all. His conscience was clear; that was the important thing to him. Recognition and approval meant less to him than to most successful men, which was one reason he was less successful than he might have been. His inability or unwillingness to accommodate the political cross-pressures on his Argentine mission had vitiated what need not have been his final diplomatic triumph. He did not appreciate, or did not care, how galling that triumph was to so many at home. Ironically, United States hostility had only served to make Perón a more sympathetic figure in his eyes than was warranted by the facts. Messersmith had responded too avidly to Argentina's courtship and had made serious errors in judgment, but in the end hemispheric solidarity and the Good Neighbor had prevailed, and that was reward enough for him. The Foreign Service house organ offered a fitting epitaph to a distinguished career: "[He] has stood by his principles courageously, independently, and inspiringly. His course has often been turbulent and generally hazardous, but he has thrived on the going, his flag (or carnation) nailed to the mast. Uncle George's retirement means much to many Foreign Service officers."[4]

Boredom would not be a problem for him. The ink was scarcely dry on his retirement papers when the job offers started rolling in. Stettinius offered him a position in a multinational corporation he was putting together. Other admirers broached business propositions that, though potentially lucrative, required extensive travel and long hours that he feared would leave him no time to write. Then he heard from Daniel Heineman, a friend since Antwerp and a major stockholder in the Toronto-based Mexican Light and Power Company, which provided 50 percent of the country's electrical energy. Mexico's power needs were growing, as Messersmith well knew, and the company, whose president had just stepped down, was set to launch a major expansion program. Was Messersmith interested in his job?[5]

He was indeed. Heineman promised improbably that it would involve only a "few" hours a week of his time. The salary was "attractive," too. Although the records do not disclose what he was to be paid, it was undoubtedly in excess of the $34,000 he was earning at the time of his retirement from the government. On top of his $8,100-a-year pension, the Messersmiths would want for little that money could buy. But neither luxury nor leisure were deciding factors, not for him. Mexlight was his opportunity to resume the work interrupted by Byrnes's phone call on 1 April 1946: promoting Latin development through private enterprise in order to raise the Latin standard of living and foster democratic stability. These were the objectives to which he had dedicated himself since Cuba, but with the Cold War they seemed more urgent than ever. Even as he was paving the way for Rio, he was also warning against overreliance on military or political countermeasures to Commmunist penetration in the hemisphere. In 1947 the worst trouble spot was Chile, where the Communists constituted a growing power in the labor movement and in the government of President Gabriel González Videla, whom they had helped elect. Across Chile's longest border, Perón had worried out loud to Messersmith that the American Republics might soon have to use force to stop the Communist cancer from spreading. But Messersmith, who was no less concerned about the Chilean situation and no more timid when it came to the use of armed force, had a different view. What he believed the south needed was more of the social responsibility that he admired in Peronism. Guns, he understood, were no answer to the human misery on which revolution fed. The only way to stability, he told Perón, "was no hunger and distress in these countries, for hunger and distress were the surest ways of bringing on Communism."[6]

So it was in the not entirely unfamiliar role of capitalist crusader that Messersmith accepted the Mexlight job, on condition that there be no objection from the Mexican government. There was none. He had a warm talk with President Alemán, who welcomed him "home." Their opulent new residence, around the corner from the American embassy compound, made him feel as though they had never left. They also leased a weekend retreat in Cuernavaca, with Camacho and other personages as neighbors.[7]

Time for recreation proved short, however. Messersmith poured himself into his new duties with characteristic vigor. He, and certainly Marion, should have known better than to think that anything he considered worth doing could be done part time. Between the long days and frequent travel, he was "working as hard as ever," "fighting the battle of private enterprise in Latin America." He developed another ulcer, in a good and successful cause. By 1954 over $80 million had been invested in new electrical generating capacity. That year Mexlight paid its first dividend since 1931.[8]

Messersmith was not too busy to stay abreast of world affairs. As a private citizen he was still less inhibited in criticizing American foreign policy for neglecting Latin America and appeasing the Soviet Union. In October 1948 he was invited to lecture at the Army Air War College at Maxwell Field, Alabama, and he stunned his audience with a clarion call for preventive war. Recalling his own battles with the appeasers of the 1930s, he condemned their Cold War counterparts as "sentimentalists" unable to face the hard facts about Soviet power. "The lesson of the last war," he declared, "showed that there is only one way in which such a force as that generated by Nazi Germany and now by Soviet Russia can be met and that is by the use of greater and overwhelming force to stop it in its tracks before it can involve [us] in an even more devastating conflict." He returned to the college in April 1950 to deliver the same message—only now the Russians had the atomic bomb themselves. "Time is no longer working in our favor," he warned; the United States must use its military advantage while it still existed. He was not invited back to speak a third time.[9]

By then he had begun curtailing his business activities as well. His trips north were increasingly for medical care. In April 1954, six months past his seventieth birthday, Messersmith retired from Mexlight. In line with his much reduced income, they gave up the Mexico City house for more modest quarters. The weekends at Cuernavaca grew longer. He puttered about his rose garden and contemplated the writing projects long in abeyance. A suggestion from his old school friend and collaborator, Owen Sypherd, that he consider leaving his papers to his Delaware "alma mater" prompted him to sit down to examine them for the first time. Ever absorbed in official business, never really convinced of his importance to posterity, he had been careless in keeping his personal files, which showed it. Their disarray led him to abandon the idea of a scholarly autobiography, but not of memoirs, in the literal manner more to his taste. He purchased dictaphones, hired secretaries, and, early in 1955, began to relive and recite his diplomatic life. In a matter of weeks he had dictated more than 800 pages, with 400 to follow. Messersmith was struck anew by how interesting and varied his experiences had been, and Harvard Professor William L. Langer, to whom he showed the transcripts during a stay in Boston for treatment, pronounced them of high historical importance. But the real work, turning these random reminiscences into a coherent narrative, lay ahead, and Messersmith, never the wordsmith, had no taste for the task. The project languished, becoming part of the collection he had agreed should go to the University of Delaware upon his death.[10]

The years began catching up to him. A string of small ailments made him miserable. He underwent surgery for his sinus and periodontal problems, which left him weaker still. Pleurisy sent him to Dallas's Methodist Hospital in January 1960. On the 29th, three months past his seventy-sixth birthday, George Strausser Messersmith died. He was buried in Marion's family plot in Lewes, Delaware. Opting for a life of luxury with friends abroad rather than a more modest existence with family back in the States, she returned to Mexico, where she spent her remaining years. She died in 1966, at the age of seventy-nine.[11]

Messersmith's death occasioned little more comment than his retirement. If Marion saved the messages of condolence she undoubtedly received, they were lost somewhere in the shipment of her effects back to Delaware, where her nieces liquidated her estate. It fell to history to judge him, a task already underway at his death. Writing with the benefit of longer hindsight and archives unavailable to Langer and Gleason and the others who had said such gratifyingly kind things about him toward the end of his life, the next generation of writers on 1930s diplomacy delivered essentially the same verdict. In his *American Appeasement* (1969), Arnold Offner deplored, among other things, the failure of Messersmith's State Department colleagues to heed "perhaps [their] country's most astute diplomatic analyst." Holding up Messersmith's reports on nazism as the standard against which all others must be judged, Robert Dallek, in a 1967 article, concluded that those of William E. Dodd "do not compare unfavorably" to his in accuracy or prescience—Dallek's point being that Dodd should have enjoyed equal reportorial renown at the State Department. Few monographs on any of the questions with which

Messersmith was concerned during his European and Washington years fail to note his contribution in a similarly approving way.[12] So does a recent textbook in diplomatic history, where space permits mention of only the most outstanding secondary figures. If not today a household word, even where diplomatic historians congregate, Messersmith has deservedly escaped the anonymity inherent in his profession. In October 1982 he gained a measure of posthumous public recognition, when the United Nations Association of Delaware saluted him at its annual dinner. His aged nieces were on hand to receive a pewter tray, on which was engraved the following words: "To George S. Messersmith, for his splendid contribution to the Conduct of Diplomacy in the Pursuit of Peace."[13]

The Messersmith that emerges from the far-smaller literature of United States–Latin American relations during the 1940s, however, cannot be the same person who fought so valiantly for human rights against the Nazis. In these works he is the prototypical Ugly American: a narrowminded defender of a benighted status quo; an insensate crusader for Open Doors in whom native Fascists invariably found a friend. Last impressions tend to linger longest, and his relationship with Perón, whom Americans are just beginning to understand as the complex figure he was, was hard to forget. Braden may have lost the war for Argentine policy, but the battle turned him into a kind of martyr among the foreign-policy liberals he generally despised. In 1947 and for a time thereafter, he was roundly praised for putting up a good fight in a good, if losing, cause, while Messersmith was cast in the infamous image of the diplomats who had toadied to Hitler and Mussolini the decade before.[14]

But Messersmith had compiled an impressive roster of liberal detractors before 1946. The list included some of his warmest admirers from the 1930s: Harold Ickes, Henry Wallace, and, counseled by Dean Acheson, Felix Frankfurter. All Washington heard the horror stories of the BEW and OCIAA functionaries who had the misfortune to cross his path in Cuba and Mexico. Before long, the top New Dealers had their own stories to tell. They learned from experience why the Nazis respected him so. Ickes and Wallace, who were nothing if not determined men, found him more than a match in bureaucratic combat, and they were outspokenly ungracious in defeat. Braden's calumnies fell on many receptive ears.[15]

The point is that to the very limited extent that they have heretofore been examined, both phases of Messersmith's mature career have been largely misunderstood. As the present study has tried to show, his 1930s service was a decidedly mixed success. His valor in Nazi Berlin was a wonder and an inspiration. He grasped the evil in

Hitlerism almost from the first. But the magnitude of this reality blinded him to others. He clung to his chimeras about Germany almost as long as the appeasers held onto theirs, and for many of the same reasons. Though both camps saw themselves as the authentic realists on the subject—and both were, though on different aspects of it—a common idealism helped lead them both astray. The appeasers assumed that because the German regime had popular support, it could not possibly be as bad as Messersmith made it out to be; and he concluded that because the regime was every bit as bad as he was saying, it would not be indefinitely tolerated by the fundamentally decent German people. What another student has suggested is true: Messersmith's reports on Europe "were a mixture of reality and illusion . . . [that] sometimes deserved [the] neglect" they received. He was not "his country's most astute analyst" of the Nazi phenomenon, not by a long shot. Though nazism appalled him no less, Raymond Geist's reports over the decade were models of cool and unflinching perspicacity. But Geist, unlike Messersmith, was too modest to call attention to himself and, perhaps as a result, never got the recognition he deserved. History needs to make amends.[16]

While Geist toiled in heroic obscurity, Messersmith was being rewarded with promotions. But Vienna and Washington brought him more frustration than satisfaction. His conscience urged him to speak out in warning about the unfolding tragedy, and he did, on and on. The State Department had good reason to dread him and his letters; he was a graceless and unrelenting prophet of doom. As assistant secretary of state, he was shunted aside to administration— consuls' work—and he left the Foreign Service a far stronger outfit than the one he took over in 1937. But isolation, his country's and his own, continued inexorably on, until German aggression stripped away the last illusions. Messersmith was vindicated but not rehabilitated; for by then, the stains on his credibility had set fast in his colleagues' minds.

Aside from Breckinridge Long, who inherited his administrative travails, everyone was well pleased when he shipped out to Havana. The State Department got him out of its hair, and he put the strains of Washington behind him. But once he had adjusted to the Cuban heat and the fact that Cuban politicians lived by their own code of ethics, he found unanticipated personal fulfillment. There and in Mexico he finally had the opportunity that isolationism had denied him in Europe, the opportunity to put his boundless energy to work for the values he cherished. For Messersmith, democracy was no mere abstraction, but rather, the path to human betterment he had walked himself. And he wanted nothing more for others than the same freedom he had enjoyed to achieve and to advance accordingly in the world. That these were universal aspirations he never doubted. But he was no doctrinaire as to what it would take to achieve them, and was chronically at odds with those who were, in the State Department and the New Deal. When he fought for free enterprise in Latin America he did so least of all for its own sake, and only secondarily for the sake of the United States economic interests there, but rather, because he passionately believed that it was the best way available to bring about the development and distribution of Latin resources for the common good. But, understanding as few did that capitalism as North Americans practiced it might not be suited to nations with different traditions and in earlier stages of development, he encouraged the Latins to come up with their own formulae, for he knew that they were going to do so with or without American approval. The alternatives to protectionism and statism, he warned Washington, would be more sweeping and far less palatable. In Cuba particularly, time would again bear him out.

Messersmith's enlightened pragmatism found little favor with Roosevelt and Truman administration ideologues left and right, who were determined to impose their own standards on the south. But it was completely compatible with Roosevelt's personal approach to both domestic and foreign affairs. During the Mexican years particularly, they worked together to make the system work for all, in the spirit of the New Deal. That was their Good Neighbor: a New Deal for the south. The principles it embodied—the principles of justice and empathy that Messersmith championed throughout his life— form as sound a prescription for foreign policy in our times as they did in his.

Notes

Abbreviations Used in the Notes

CF   Clippings File, George S. Messersmith Papers, the University of Delaware Library, Newark, Delaware

Conf.   Conference

CUOH   Columbia University Oral History Project

Desp.   Despatch

FDR   Edgar B. Nixon, ed., *Franklin D. Roosevelt and Foreign Affairs*
and FA

FDRL   Franklin D. Roosevelt Library, Hyde Park, New York

FRUS   United States Department of State, *Foreign Relations of the United States: Diplomatic Papers*

GSM   George S. Messersmith

GSMM   George S. Messersmith typescript memoirs, Messersmith Papers

HSTL   Harry S. Truman Library, Independence, Missouri

I   Items from the Messersmith Papers

Instr.   Instruction

OF   Official File

PF   George S. Messersmith personal file, 123 M 561, documents numbered sequentially until 1945, SD MS.

PSF   President's Secretary's File

SD MS   United States Department of State, Record Group 59, National Archives, Washington, D.C.

SF   Speech File, Messersmith Papers

Tel.   Telegram

USIAAO   United States Inter-American Affairs Office

Introduction

1. *New York Daily Mirror*, 14 December 1943, p. 12.

Chapter I

1. "First Days in the Service," I 1924, GSMM. Ward, "Introductory History," pp. 5–13. Wagner, *The Story of Berks County*, pp. 36–37.

2. The history of the Messersmiths in Fleetwood has been pieced together from Montgomery, *History of Berks County*, pp. 31, 481, 919–21, 924; headstones in the town cemetery, Fleetwood; *Reading Eagle*, 20 May 1889; "Last

Will and Testament of Charles A. Messersmith," 3 June 1889, Berks County Historical Society, Reading; interview with Mrs. Quentin Messersmith (George's cousin), 22 June 1980.

3. GSM to Herbert Feis, 30 December 1935, Feis Papers, "First Days," I 1924, GSMM.

4. Ibid.

5. "Tradition and Legend," I 2033, GSMM.

6. Telephone conversation with Ann L. Scott (Messersmith's niece), 11 April 1980. "First Days," I 1924, GSMM. John Bassett Moore to GSM, 4 July 1937, Moore Papers. GSM to Moore, 29 July 1937, ibid.

7. Dean to Dawson, 23 September 1974, I 2059.

8. "Anthony Drexel Biddle," I 1976, GSMM. GSM to Perkins, 8 December 1955, I 1917. See the publisher's blurb in the copy of his *Government* in the Berks County Historical Society Library. N.a., *Delaware: A History*, 4:418–19.

9. GSM to Sypherd, 31 July 1953, I 1904. Scott to author, n.d. (April 1980).

10. *New York Times*, 21 March 1934, p. 13. Hull to Roosevelt, 23 March 1934, PF 419. *Reading Times*, 3 July 1937, CF. Delaware College Faculty, Minutes of Meetings 1908–16, University of Delaware Archives.

11. John M. Clayton (university archivist) to author, 7 September 1979.

12. Wiebe, *The Search for Order*, pp. 118–20. Cremin, *The Transformation of the School*, pp. 85–89 and passim. Wilson, *Dreams and Realities*, p. 138.

13. Kennan, *Memoirs 1925–1950*, p. 66.

14. Weeks, *History of Public School Education in Delaware*, p. 138. Taggart, "The Modernization of Delaware's School Tax System," pp. 153–79.

15. "First Days," I 1924, GSMM. *Reading Eagle*, 21 March 1934, p. 3.

16. "Tradition and Legend," I 2033, GSMM.

17. "First Days," I 1924, GSMM.

18. GSM to Wilbur J. Carr, 8 July 1924, Carr Papers.

19. Israel, "A Diplomatic Machine," p. 148. Crane, *Mr. Carr*, pp. 121–34, 152. Heinrichs, Jr., "Bureaucracy and Professionalism," p. 136. Ilchman, *Professional Diplomacy*, pp. 69ff. Werking, "Selling the Foreign Service," pp. 185–207. Werking, *Master Architects*, pp. 88–120. Schulzinger, *Diplomatic Mind*, pp. 5–32.

20. "Fort Erie Days," I 1925, GSMM. Carr to Harvey, 12 June 1914, 123 H 26/8a. GSM desp., 8 August 1915, 125.3873/8.

21. Carr to Harvey, 12 June 1914, 123 H 26/8a. GSM desp., 8 August 1915, 125.3873/8.

22. "Fort Erie," I 1925, GSMM.

23. Alford, "Introduction," 1:ii–iii. GSM #35, 1 June 1916, 125.387/1.

24. "Curaçao," I 1926, GSMM.

25. "The Policy of the Dutch Government toward Curaçao," I 1928, GSMM.

26. GSM #8, 1 August 1916, 125.3473/18. GSM #11, 29 August 1916, 125.3472/19. GSM #249, 17 October 1918, PF 38.

27. GSM #249, 17 October 1918, PF 38. GSM desp. 14 September 1916,

PF 26. "Kind Offer by the Maduro Family," I 1941, GSMM.

28. GSM #39, 19 March 1917, 831.00/787. "Gómez, Dictator of Venezuela," I 1940, GSMM.

29. GSM #178, 14 May 1918, 862.20256b/6. GSM #66, 3 September 1917, 763.72112/4764.

30. "The Ordinary and Unusual Risks of the Foreign Service Officer," I 2032, GSMM.

31. "A Fortunate Discovery," I 1930, GSMM. GSM desp., 11 September 1917, 702.62/13. GSM #144, 3 April 1918, 862.20237/11. Carr to GSM, 27 April 1918, ibid. Hengstler to GSM, 3 September 1918, ibid.

32. GSM #248, 16 October 1918, PF 37.

33. Carr to GSM, 29 January 1919, PF 41a. "Transfer to Antwerp," I 1933, GSMM.

34. Ibid.

35. GSM #473, 29 March 1921, PF 75.

36. GSM to Lansing, 21 August 1919, PF 57.

37. "The Practice of Giving for Charity," I 1944, GSMM. GSM tel., 26 February 1920, PF 61. Carr to GSM, 12 March 1920, ibid.

38. GSM to Breckenridge Long, 25 June 1936, Long Papers. Messersmith apparently underwent a gastrectomy with a duodenal resection. GSM #473, 29 March 1921, PF 75. GSM to Dunn, 3 July 1936, I 689.

39. See an undated (prob. January 1940) "Washington Merry Go-Round" column, CF. Braden, *Diplomats*, p. 421.

40. GSM #282, 30 September 1920, PF 71. GSM #1994, 8 May 1925, PF 121. GSM desp., 9 November 1921, 855.00/234. GSM #140, 4 February 1920, 855.156/5.

41. "Transfer to Antwerp," I 1933, GSMM. Dept. tel. 422, 3 May 1919, 121.56/383. "Brief History of the American Consular Establishment at Antwerp," 21 June 1923, 125.143/13.

42. "Some Observations on the Protection and Promotion of American Trade Abroad," I 1921, GSMM. GSM #2838, 31 May 1927, PF 145. Of the large literature on U.S. business expansionism in Europe during the 1920s, Melvyn P. Leffler's *The Elusive Quest* and Frank Costigliola's "The United States and the Reconstruction of Germany" are particularly relevant here.

43. Post report, 16 December 1920, 125.143/10. GSM #240, 28 July 1920, 855.43Am3. GSM #774, 23 December 1921, 125.1436/46. GSM #640, 29 September 1921, 655.11171/7. Wright to Hughes, 13 April 1921, PF 76.

44. GSM #1994, 8 May 1925, PF 121. GSM #839, 23 February 1922, 855.1561/1. Love to Carr, 15 November 1922, PF 103.

45. GSM #823, 13 February 1922, 600.00/88. Carr to GSM, 14 March 1922, 125.1435/46a. The consulate, beginning in May 1922, volunteered massive monthly reports on "Market, Financial, and Shipping Conditions in Antwerp," as well as annual summaries (655.0001).

46. GSM #1994, 8 May 1925, PF 121. GSM #1790, 18 December 1924, 655.1125/2. GSM #2069, 7 July 1925, PF 125. GSM #3082, 2 April 1928, 655.1125/5.

47. Unnumbered desp., 5 September 1928, PF 190. Wright to Hughes, 13 April 1921, PF 76. Eldridge to Carr, 30 March 1923, PF 95. Chrysler to Kellogg, 25 August 1926, PF 140. Rumely to Castle, 27 September 1928, PF 192.

48. Entry for 10 September 1923, William Phillips Diary. GSM #2279, 20 January 1926, 125.1436/62. Carr to GSM, 10 June 1926, 125.1436/64. Carr to GSM, 11 October 1923, 125.143/13a. Paul C. Daniels oral history interview, pp. 1–2. Carr to GSM, 7 June 1924, PF 108a. GSM to Carr, 3 July 1924, Carr Papers.

49. GSM #1994, 8 May 1925, PF 121.

50. GSM to John C. Wiley, 28 August 1935, Wiley Papers. "Golf Game with President Ávila Camacho," I 1996, GSMM.

51. Telephone conversation with Ann L. Scott, 11 April 1980. GSM to Carr, 2 September 1920, 125.1436/36. GSM #1994, 8 May 1925, PF 121.

52. Bendiner, *Riddle*, p. 132. Telephone conversation with Rodney M. Layton (Messersmith's nephew), 15 April 1980. Scott to author, n.d. (April 1980). "Recommendations of the Foreign Service Personnel Board for Promotion to the Rank of Minister," 17 March 1933, Carr Papers. Carr to Hull, 30 July 1934, ibid.

53. GSM to Carr, 8 July 1924, ibid. GSM to Duggan, 3 December 1945, PF 748.

54. Scott to author, n.d. (April 1980). Virginia Layton Orr (Messersmith's niece) to author, 17 April 1980.

55. Carr to GSM, 29 May 1926, PF 126a. Carr to GSM, 8 July 1926, PF 136c.

56. GSM to Kellogg, 14 July 1926, PF 137.

57. GSM to Carr, 12 March 1928, 125.1433/177. GSM #3082, 2 April 1928, 655.1125/5. GSM #3046, 2 February 1928, PF 165. GSM #2713, 18 February 1927, 655.11/3. Mitchell, ed. *European Historical Statistics*, pp. 507–8.

58. GSM #3147, 14 June 1928, PF 175. GSM desp. 5 September 1928, PF 190. GSM #3176, 12 July 1928, PF 182. Johnson to GSM, 28 July 1928, PF 183. Sands, *Jungle Diplomacy*, p. 193.

59. GSM desp., 5 September 1928, PF 190. GSM #3185, 8 August 1928, PF 185. Wiley to GSM, 21 October 1935, Wiley Papers.

60. GSM to Spruille Braden, 23 April 1946, Braden Papers. GSM #15, 17, 31 October 1928, PF 200, 201.

61. GSM #55, 5 January 1929, PF 203.

62. Ilchman, *Professional Diplomacy*, pp. 150ff. Crane, *Mr. Carr*, pp. 245–68. Heinrichs, Jr., "Bureaucracy and Professionalism," pp. 161–63, 172. Barnes and Morgan, *Foreign Service*, pp. 203–9.

63. "Inspection Trips as Consul General in Buenos Aires," I 1946, GSMM.

64. McGann, *Argentina, the United States, and the Inter-American System*, passim. Whittaker, *The United States and Argentina*, pp. 3–95.

65. Whittaker, *The United States and Argentina*, pp. 99–100.

66. Peterson, *Argentina and the United States*, pp. 351–55.

67. Ibid., pp. 355–57. "Ordinary Risks," I 2032, GSMM. GSM desp., 19 September 1929, 611.4117/58.

68. Hurd to Carr, 7 March 1929, PF 207. Janovici to Department of Commerce, 12 June 1929, PF 217.

69. GSM desp., 8 July 1929, PF 220. Mrs. Quentin Messersmith interview, 22 June 1980. *Reading Eagle*, 9 November 1929.

70. Carr to GSM, 28 November 1929, PF 231. "Observations on Trade Conferences," 11 February 1930, 120.375/429.

71. Carr to GSM, 13 March 1930, PF 239a. Barnes and Morgan, *Foreign Service*, p. 238.

72. "Inspection Trips," I 1946, GSMM. State Department to Rio embassy, 15 March 1930, 125.7676/59.

73. GSM #1, 28 April 1930, PF 253. GSM desp., 28 April 1930, 125.7671/115. GSM desp., 28 April 1930, 125.7672/198.

74. "Inspection Trips," I 1946, GSMM. *FRUS 1930*, 1:464–74. State #1532, 123 M 82/218. State #46, 19 April 1933, 123 M 82/262. Gibson #61, 16 April 1934, 123 M 82/277.

75. "Inspection Trips," I 1946, GSMM.

76. Stimson to GSM, 6 May 1930, PF 245. GSM #17, 13 November 1930, PF 276.

Chapter II

1. McKenzie, *Weimar Germany*, pp. 207–18. Eyck, *A History of Weimar*, 2:278–98. Halperin, *Germany Tried Democracy*, pp. 403–16.

2. GSM #17, 13 November 1930, PF 276. GSM #31, 29 November 1930, PF 280. GSM #113, 23 January 1933, PF 352.

3. Ilchman, *Professional Diplomacy*, p. 230. Stuart, "The Diplomacy of Intelligence," p. 26. Stuart, *Department of State*, pp. 326–27. Barnes and Morgan, *Foreign Service*, pp. 217–19.

4. GSM to Mitchell, 28 December 1932, I 99. "Distressed Condition of Many German Officers," I 1967, GSMM.

5. GSM #139, 18 March 1929, 123G 796/18. State desp. 13 June 1934, 123 G 796/89. State desp. 29 March 1935, 123 G 796/113.

6. *Register of the Department of State 1948*, p. 225. GSM #340, 13 July 1932, 123 G 271. GSM #1405, 30 June 1933, 123 G 271/167. GSM #34, 26 June 1934, 123 G 271/182.

7. GSM to Phillips, 18 June 1936, I 688. Entry for 24 April 1936, Carr Diary. Adolf A. Berle to GSM, 17 December 1943, Berle Papers.

8. Geist to GSM, 13 April 1940, I 1343. Sketch 3898, Associated Press Biographies. Geist to GSM, 14 June 1934, I 380.

9. GSM to Carr, 22 May 1933, I 182. GSM to Carr, 17 March 1933, I 121.

10. GSM #597, 9 December 1932, 125.855/24. Cologne desp. 9 October 1931, 125.3271/55. Stuttgart #528, 15 December 1931, 125.8851/50. GSM #1076, 20 December 1932, 120.1/222.

11. Ilchman, *Professional Diplomacy*, p. 242.

12. GSM to Carr, 12 May 1933, I 182. GSM #1076, 20 December 1932, 120.1/222.

13. GSM to Stone, 28 December 1932, OF 896, Franklin D. Roosevelt Papers. Entry for 30 July 1937, Jay Pierrepont Moffat Diary. Entry for 5 July 1934, Phillips Diary. M. Dodd, *Through Embassy Eyes*, p. 20.

14. Barnes and Morgan, *Foreign Service*, pp. 214ff. Heinrichs, Jr., "Bureaucracy and Professionalism," p. 182.

15. "Appointment—Dr. William Dodd," I 1956, GSMM. GSM #216, 30 March 1931, PF 286. Stuttgart #319, 11 April 1931, PF 288.

16. Sackett #338, 28 June 1930, 124.621/150. Sackett #199, 4 September 1930, 124.621/154. State Department press release, 8 September 1931, 124.621/221. Sackett #45, 15 April 1931, 124.621/180. Gordon #2278, 31 March 1932, 124.621/278.

17. GSM to Bundy, 23 November 1932, 120.00/144. For evidence of Carr's bureaucratic conservatism, Carr to Bullitt, 27 March 1937, 120.1/301. Phillips memo, 11 December 1933, 124.621/303.

18. GSM to Stone, 28 December 1932, OF 896, Roosevelt Papers.

19. *New York Times*, 4 December 1932, p. 1; 6 December 1932, p. 1; 7 December 1932, p. 4; 8 December 1932, p. 20; 10 December 1932, p. 6; 11 December 1932, p. 3; 13 December 1932, p. 15.

20. *Detroit News*, 7 December 1932; *Los Angeles Times*, 8 December 1932; *Santa Barbara Press*, 9 December 1932, all CF. *New York Tribune*, 6 December 1932, p. 14. GSM memo, 10 December 1932, I 53.

21. GSM to Villard, 20 December 1932, I 87; 27 December 1932, I 98.

22. GSM to Villard, 27 December 1932, I 98. Entry for 10 December 1932, Stimson Diary. Transcript of Stimson press conference, 10 December 1932, I 49. *New York Tribune*, 12 December 1932, p. 16. *Antwerp Neptune*, 17 December 1932, I 81.

23. GSM to Gary, 27 December 1932, I 97.

24. GSM to Villard, 20 December 1932, I 87. Friedel, *FDR: Launching*, p. 360.

25. GSM to Stone, 28 December 1932, OF 896, Roosevelt Papers.

26. "Cordell Hull," I 2035, GSMM. Hull, *Memoirs*, p. 81. Drummond, "Hull," p. 185.

27. McKenzie, *Weimar*, p. 229. Fest, *Hitler*, pp. 345–69.

28. GSM quoted in Fromm, *Blood and Banquets*, pp. 65–66. Mommsen, "Reichstag Fire," pp. 129–222.

29. For his perceptive reporting, Sackett to Stimson, 3 March 1933, *FRUS 1933*, 2:201–4; 9 March 1933, ibid., pp. 204–9.

30. Offner, *American Appeasement*, pp. 54–55. Dallek, *Dodd*, pp. 187–90.

31. Bullock, *Hitler*, pp. 277–80.

32. GSM #1214, 31 March 1933, I 131. GSM #1210, 28 March 1933, I 128.

33. "Dodd," I 1956, GSMM.

34. GSM #1234, 11 April 1933, I 146.

35. GSM #1184, 14 March 1933, I 118. GSM #1210, 28 March 1933, I

128. Wheaton, *Prelude*, pp. 276–77, 280.

36. GSM #1205, 25 March 1933, I 125. GSM #1214, 31 March 1933, I 131. GSM #1216, 3 April 1933, I 133.

37. GSM # 1195, 14 March 1933, I 118. *New York Times*, 20 April 1933, p. 11. Göring quoted in Wheaton, *Prelude*, p. 225.

38. GSM #1212, 31 March 1933, I 130.

39. GSM #1421, 10 July 1933, I 211. GSM #1326, 22 May 1933, I 184. Peterson, *Hitler's Limits*, pp. 90–91. Wheaton, *Prelude*, p. 298. GSM #1405, 30 June 1933, 123 G 271/167. GSM #1421, 10 July 1933, I 211.

40. GSM #1216, 3 April 1933, I 133. GSM #1232, 11 April 1933, I 144. GSM #1252, 25 April 1933, I 153. GSM #1295, 9 May 1933, I 165.

41. GSM #1252, 25 April 1933, I 153. Wheaton, *Prelude*, pp. 301–2.

42. GSM #1208, 28 March 1933, I 127. GSM #1216, 3 April 1933, I 133. Peterson, *Hitler's Limits*, pp. 47–48.

43. GSM #1233, 11 April 1933, I 144. GSM #1243, 18 April 1933, I 148. GSM #1370, 19 June 1933, I 197. GSM memo, 8 May 1933, I 163.

44. GSM #1531, 23 August 1933, I 268. GSM #1243, 18 April 1933, I 148. GSM #1296, 9 May 1933, I 166. GSM #1273, 2 May 1933, I 156. Offner, *American Appeasement*, pp. 64–65.

45. GSM #1273, 2 May 1933, I 156. GSM #1322, 22 May 1933, I 181. GSM #1489, 9 August 1933, I 246. Peterson, *Hitler's Limits*, pp. 47–48.

46. GSM to Phillips, 14 August 1933, I 255. GSM #1413, 6 July 1933, I 208. GSM #1590, 10 August 1933, I 250. GSM #1741, 14 November 1933, I 338.

47. GSM #1301, 12 May 1933, I 171. GSM #1329, 23 May 1933, I 185. GSM #1330, 23 May 1933, I 186. GSM #1335, 24 May 1933, I 191.

48. GSM to Moffat, 20 May 1933, I 180.

49. Carr to GSM, 7 June 1933, I 192. Phillips to GSM, 10 May 1933, I 167. Phillips to GSM, 13 July 1933, PF 365: "You and Gordon have shown yourselves an admirable team [!] and your reporting, as well as your success in protection cases, has received the highest praise." Hull, *Memoirs*, pp. 236–37. Offner, *American Appeasement*, pp. 71–72. Pratt, *Hull*, 1:180–81.

50. Fromm, *Blood and Banquets*, pp. 126, 162. Armstrong, *Peace and Counterpeace*, p. 530. Mowrer, *Journalist's Wife*, p. 302.

51. "General Ernst," I 1952, GSMM. "Dr. Hanfstengel" [sic], I 1960, GSMM. "Character of Nazi Leaders," I 1963, GSMM. "Goering Doesn't Become Foreign Minister," I 1953, GSMM.

52. "Dr. Hanfstengel," I 1962, GSMM. GSM to Moffat, 13 June 1933, I 378.

53. Fromm, *Blood and Banquets*, p. 162. At least two American diplomats in Berlin—Second Secretary A. W. Kliefoth and Ambassador William E. Dodd—assumed that Messersmith was Jewish, or half-Jewish, in Dodd's case. GSM to Moffat, 14 June 1935, Moffat Papers. Dodd to R. Walton Moore, 21 June 1934, Moore Papers. GSM to Moffat, 13 June 1934, I 378.

54. "Addition to Memo on Attempts on My Life," I 1997, GSMM. "Dr. Goebbels," I 1953, GSMM. "Goering," I 1952, GSMM. The last prewar U.S. ambassador to Germany, Hugh Wilson, was also convinced that the propa-

ganda ministry had bugged the American consular and diplomatic offices in Berlin. A planned inspection by U.S. Navy eavesdropping experts apparently never took place. Wilson to GSM, 17 March 1938, Wilson Papers. GSM to Wilson, 6 April 1938, ibid. GSM #1464, 28 July 1933, PF 366.

55. "Dodd," I 1956, GSMM. Dallek, "Beyond Tradition," pp. 240–41. Entry for 28 March 1934, Carr Diary.

56. "Dodd," I 1956, GSMM. GSM to Phillips, 14 August 1933, I 255. GSM to Phillips, 28 October 1933, I 324. Dallek, *Dodd*, pp. 198–202. Ford, "Three Observers," pp. 450–51.

57. "Dodd," I 1956, GSMM. M. Dodd, *Through Embassy Eyes*, pp. 22–23. Entry for 13 July 1933, *Dodd Diary*, p. 12.

58. "Dodd," I 1956, GSMM. Dallek, "Beyond Tradition," pp. 240–41. Dallek, *Dodd*, pp. 205, 231. Dodd to Roosevelt, 23 December 1933, Nixon, ed. *FDR*, 1:548. Dodd to Moore, 17 August 1936, Moore Papers. Pratt, *Hull*, 1:185–86.

59. "Dodd," I 1956, GSMM. Entries for 28 March 1934, 24 April 1936, Carr Diary. Dodd to Moore, 21 June 1934, Moore Papers. Dodd to Moore, 17 August 1936, ibid. GSM to Hull, 24 October 1939, Hull Papers.

60. Mowrer, *Journalist's Wife*, p. 297. GSM #1303, 12 May 1933, I 172.

61. Hull memo, 11 August 1933, *FRUS 1933*, 2:403. Moffat memo, 19 August 1933, ibid., pp. 403–4.

62. GSM #1499, 10 August 1933, I 249. Mowrer, *Journalist's Wife*, pp. 297, 307–8. M. Dodd, *Through Embassy Eyes*, p. 39. Entries for 16 August, 22 August 1933, *Dodd Diary*, pp. 24, 26. Offner, *American Appeasement*, pp. 69–70. Dallek, *Dodd*, pp. 201–2.

63. GSM #1448, 22 July 1933, I 221. GSM #1454, 26 July 1933, I 223. GSM #1496, 9 August 1933, I 247. GSM #1520, 19 August 1933, I 263. Pratt, *Hull*, 1:182. "Conversation with Goering," I 1958, GSMM.

64. GSM #1564, 1 September 1933, I 287. "Hans von Kaltenborn," I 1960, GSMM.

65. GSM #1521, 21 August 1933, I 265. Entries for 14 September, 29 September 1933, *Dodd Diary*, pp. 36, 42. Dodd to Hull, 7 September 1933, *FRUS 1933*, 2:464–67. Dallek, *Dodd*, p. 208. Offner, *American Appeasement*, pp. 72–74.

66. GSM #1741, 14 November 1933, I 338. GSM #1413, 6 July 1933, I 208. GSM #1453, 26 July 1933, I 224. GSM #1696, 1 November 1933, I 326.

67. GSM to Phillips, 28 October 1933, I 324. GSM to Phillips, 14 August 1933, I 255. GSM to Phillips, 29 September 1933, I 312. GSM #1596, 21 September 1933, I 305.

68. "Character of Nazi Leaders," I 1963, GSMM. GSM #1590, 16 September 1933, I 303. Entry for 14 September 1933, *Dodd Diary*, p. 36. GSM #1610, 25 September 1933, I 306.

69. Hull to Dodd, 4 September 1933, *FRUS 1933*, 2:388–89. Dodd to Hull, 8 September 1933, ibid., p. 389. Hull to Dodd, 12 October 1933, ibid., pp. 393–94. Hull memo, 12 October 1933, ibid., pp. 393–94. Dodd to Hull, 14 October 1933, ibid., pp. 394–95. Entry for 11 October 1933, *Dodd Diary*, p. 44.

70. "Conversation with Goering," I 1958, GSMM. Entry for 17 October 1933, *Dodd Diary*, p. 49.

71. GSM to Phillips, 19 October 1933, I 320. Dodd to Hull, 17 October 1933, *FRUS 1933*, 2:396–97.

72. Offner, *American Appeasement*, pp. 67, 71–74. Hull, *Memoirs*, pp. 238–40. Hull to Dodd, 21 September 1933, *FRUS 1933*, 2:467–68. Pratt, *Hull*, 1:185–87. Entries for 29 September, 17 October 1933, *Dodd Diary*, pp. 42, 49.

73. Pratt, *Hull*, 1:186. GSM to Phillips, 29 September 1933, I 312. GSM to Phillips, 26 June 1933, *Peace and War*, pp. 191–92. GSM to Phillips, 28 October 1933, I 324. GSM #1741, 14 November 1933, I 338. Craig, "German Foreign Office," pp. 406–36.

74. GSM to Phillips, 19 October 1933, I 320. GSM to Phillips, 26 June 1933, *Peace and War*, p. 192. GSM to Phillips, 23 November 1933, ibid. GSM to Phillips, 29 September 1933, I 312.

75. Wheaton, *Prelude*, p. 383. Weinberg, *Hitler's Foreign Policy*, pp. 164–67. GSM #1733, 14 November 1933, I 337.

76. Dallek, *Dodd*, p. 209. Weinberg, *Hitler's Foreign Policy*, p. 167. GSM to Phillips, 19 October 1933, I 320. GSM to Phillips, 23 November 1933, *Peace and War*, pp. 194–95.

77. GSM to Phillips, 24 March 1934, I 357. GSM to Phillips, 29 March 1934, I 361.

78. GSM #1965, 22 March 1934, I 356. GSM to Phillips, 13 April 1934, I 364.

79. GSM to Phillips, 29 September 1933, I 312. "Goering," I 1952, GSMM.

80. GSM to Phillips, 29 September 1933, I 312.

81. Ibid. GSM to Phillips, 23 November 1933, I 342. GSM to Phillips, 28 October 1933, I 304. GSM #1741, 14 November 1933, I 338. GSM #1964, 22 March 1934, I 356. GSM to Phillips, 13 April 1934, I 364. GSM to Phillips, 21 April 1934, I 367.

82. GSM to Phillips, 19 October 1933, I 320. GSM to Dodd, 4 April 1934, I 363. Geist to GSM, 22 January 1939, I 1136. GSM to Phillips, 8 January 1935, I 460. Moss, "Diplomacy of Limits," p. 114.

83. GSM #1670, 18 October 1933, 611.623/66. Moffat to Phillips, 23 November 1933, 611.623/68. GSM #1964, 22 March 1934, I 356. GSM to Phillips, 13 April 1934, I 364. GSM to Moffat, 14 April 1934, I 365. GSM to Phillips, 27 April 1934, I 369.

84. Billikopf to Mack, 14 September 1933, I 298. GSM to Phillips, 28 October 1933, I 324.

85. Wise quoted in Shafir, "Messersmith," p. 35. GSM-Frankfurter correspondence in Box 83, Frankfurter Papers. Brandeis to Szold, 22 October 1940, Urofsky and Levy, eds., *Brandeis Letters*, 5:646.

86. Morse, *Six Million*, pp. 150–71. Carr to GSM, 1 June 1933, Carr Papers. Carr to GSM, 1 August 1933, I 238. GSM to Hull, 21 July 1933, I 220. Shafir, "Messersmith," p. 36 and passim.

87. Billikopf to Mack, 14 September 1933, I 298.

88. GSM to Moffat, 13 November 1933, Moffat Papers. GSM to Dodd, 11 December 1933, Dodd Papers.

89. GSM to Filene, 19 October 1933, PF 373. GSM to Dodd, 15 January 1934, Dodd Papers.

90. Ibid. Entry for 12 December 1933, Moffat Diary.

91. GSM to Filene, 19 October 1933, PF 373. Filene to Hull, 4 November 1933, ibid. Bodziak to Hull, 27 November 1933, PF 381 and PF 374ff.

92. GSM to Dodd, 15 January 1934, Dodd Papers. Entry for 25 January 1934, Stimson Diary. Entries for 15 December and 20 December 1933, Phillips Diary.

93. *Reading Eagle*, 28 December 1933, p. 3. Moffat to GSM, 17 January 1934, Moffat Papers. GSM to Moffat, 17 January 1934, ibid. GSM to Moffat, 18 January 1934, ibid.

94. GSM to Dodd, 15 January 1934, Dodd Papers. GSM to Filene, 19 October 1933, PF 373. Phillips to Roosevelt, 16 October 1933, 862.00/3097 1/2. Phillips memo, 23 November 1933, OF 896, Roosevelt Papers. Villard to Howe, 22 December 1933, ibid.

95. Weil, *A Pretty Good Club*, pp. 67–74. Entry for 28 June 1934, Phillips Diary. Roosevelt to Hull, n.d., PSF 87, Roosevelt Papers. Crane, *Mr. Carr*, p. 314.

96. Villard to Phillips, 19 December 1933, OF 896, Roosevelt Papers. Phillips to Villard, 20 December 1933, ibid. Mowrer to Knox, n.d., Box 4, Knox Papers.

97. Entry for 29 January 1934, Phillips Diary. *Reading Eagle*, 11 February 1934, p. 1.

98. Adams, "Messersmith's Appointment," p. 23. Phillips to Roosevelt, 23 November 1933, OF 501, Roosevelt Papers. Entry for 29 January 1934, Phillips Diary.

99. Weil, *A Pretty Good Club*, p. 73.

100. Entry for 10 March 1934, *Dodd Diary*, p. 92. GSM to Dodd, 3 April 1934, I 363.

101. Earle to Roosevelt, 10 March 1934, OF 969, Roosevelt Papers. Entry for 16 March 1934, Phillips Diary. Phillips memo, 18 March 1934, PF 411.

102. Roosevelt to Guffey, 21 March 1934, OF 166-B, Roosevelt Papers. Gunther, *Roosevelt in Retrospect*, p. 23.

103. GSM to Phillips, 24 March 1934, I 357. GSM to Moffat, 14 April 1934, I 365. *New York Times*, 23 March 1934, p. 22.

104. *New York Times*, 25 March 1934, p. 4.

105. Fromm, *Blood and Banquets*, p. 158. GSM to Dodd, 13 April 1934, Moore Papers.

Chapter III

1. Hitler, *Mein Kampf*, p. 16. Stadler, *Birth of Austria*. Gulick, *Habsburg to Hitler*, pp. 43–65, 778–82. Schuschnigg, *Austrian Requiem*, pp. 53–57, 69–82. Edmondson, *Heimwehr*, pp. 3–72.

2. Stadler, "Austria," p. 90. Gehl, *Austria*, pp. 1–24, 59. Rich, *Hitler's War Aims*, pp. 90–93. Weinberg, *Hitler's Foreign Policy*, pp. 88–99. Pauley, *Forgotten Nazis*, pp. 104–21.

3. GSM to Moffat, 20 September 1934, Moffat Papers. Brook-Shepherd, *Dollfuss*, pp. 1–48. Gehl, *Austria*, pp. 46–100. Mack Smith, *Mussolini*, p. 182.

4. Brook-Shepherd, *Dollfuss*, p. 122–55. Edmondson, *Heimwehr*, pp. 151–205. Gulick, *Habsburg to Hitler*, pp. 1266–1359. Lowe and Marzari, *Italian Foreign Policy*, pp. 231–39. Kliefoth #79, 20 February 1934, 863.00/891. Atherton #518, 19 February 1934, 863.00/900.

5. Barnes and Morgan, *Foreign Service*, p. 236. Carr memo, 27 June 1934, Carr Papers. Hull to GSM, 14 April 1934, PF 427.

6. Marriner to Carr, 30 April 1934, PF 439.

7. GSM #2026, "Reorganization of the Agencies of the Government of the United States in Paris," 14 May 1934, 124.516/150 1/2.

8. Carr memo, 27 June 1934, Carr Papers. Entries for 28 June, 24 September 1934, Phillips Diary. Roosevelt to Carr, 25 August 1934, 124.516/154 1/2.

9. Straus to Hull, 2 May 1934, PF 433. GSM to Moffat, 6 June 1934, I 375. "Presentation of Letters on Arrival in Vienna," I 1973 GSMM.

10. Selby, *Diplomatic Twilight*, p. 37. GSM to Dodd, 2 June 1934, I 374. GSM to Moffat, 6 June 1934, I 375. GSM to Hull, 12 June 1934, I 377.

11. GSM to Phillips, 18 June 1934, I 381. Brook-Shepherd, *Dollfuss*, p. 91.

12. GSM to Phillips, 18 June 1934, I 381; 14 August 1934, I 399.

13. GSM to Moffat, 6 June 1934, I 375. GSM to Phillips, 18 June 1934, I 381. Gehl, *Austria*, p. 93. Writing from Paris, William L. Shirer characterized Starhemberg as "a playboy ignoramus" and Fey as a "hatchet-faced and brutal reactionary." Entry for 12 February 1934, *Berlin Diary*, p. 9.

14. GSM to Phillips, 18 June 1934, I 381; 5 July 1934, I 385.

15. GSM #73, 21 June 1934, *FRUS 1934*, 2:28. GSM to Geist, 28 June 1934, I 384. Gehl, *Austria*, pp. 91–92. Weinberg, *Hitler's Foreign Policy*, pp. 100–101. Mack Smith, *Mussolini*, pp. 184–85.

16. Hull memo, 2 March 1934, *FRUS 1934*, 2:416–17. Sayre memo, 12 April 1934, ibid. pp. 420–21.

17. GSM to Phillips, 24 March 1934, I 375; 29 March 1934, I 361; 13 April 1934, I 364; 27 April 1934, I 369; 3 May 1934, I 370. In the same vein, commercial attaché in Berlin Douglas Miller's report of 17 April 1934, in Miller, *Via Diplomatic Pouch*, pp. 133–62.

18. Offner, *American Appeasement*, pp. 94–97. Phillips to GSM, 10 May 1934, I 372. Gardner, *Economic Aspects*, p. 101. Schlesinger, Jr., *New Deal*, pp. 57–59. Fite, *Peek*, pp. 271–77.

19. Dallek, *Roosevelt's Foreign Policy*, pp. 84–85. Livesay memo, 26 April 1934, *FRUS 1934*, 2:421–23.

20. Entry for 5 November 1934, Phillips Diary. Weil, *A Pretty Good Club*, p. 87. Phillips to Roosevelt, 5 June 1934, enclosing Feis to Phillips, 4 June 1935, *FDR and FA*, 2:139–42. State Department memo, 12 October 1934, *FRUS 1934*, 2:448–53. Hull to Roosevelt, 14 December 1934, PSF 44, Roosevelt Papers.

21. Hull *Memoirs*, pp. 370–74. Schlesinger, Jr., *New Deal*, pp. 255–57. Offner, *American Appeasement*, pp. 99–102.

22. Gallo, *Long Knives*. Wheaton, *Prelude*, pp. 435–45. GSM to Phillips, 5 July 1934, I 385. GSM to Moffat, 17 July 1934, I 389.

23. Selby, *Diplomtic Twilight*, pp. 29–31.

24. GSM tels. #80, 25 July 1934, (5 P.M.), 863.00/955; #81 (8 P.M.), 863.00/956; #82 (10 P.M.), 863.00/957; #83 (midnight), 863.00/958. Maass, *Assassination in Vienna*. Brook-Shepherd, *Dollfuss*, pp. 231–84. Pauley, *Forgotten Nazis*, pp. 122–37.

25. "Dollfuss-Assassination," I 2015, GSMM.

26. GSM to Phillips, 1 August 1934, *FRUS 1934*, 2:35–37. GSM to Phillips, 9 August 1934, I 397.

27. GSM to Feis, 31 July 1934, Feis Papers. GSM to Harry Hopkins, 28 July 1934, Hopkins Papers. GSM #89, 28 July 1934, *FRUS 1934*, 2:35–47. GSM to Phillips, 7 September 1934, I 411. Lowe and Marzari, *Italian Foreign Policy*, pp. 238–39.

28. GSM #87, 28 July 1934, *FRUS 1934*, 2:33–34.

29. Gehl, *Austria*, p. 104. Weinberg, *Hitler's Foreign Policy*, pp. 102–5.

30. Weinberg, *Hitler's Foreign Policy*, pp. 104–5. GSM to Phillips, 1 August 1934, *FRUS 1934*, 2:35–47. Marriner #574, 2 August 1934, 863.00/990. Benton #39, 27 July 1934, 863.00/969.

31. GSM to Phillips, 17 August 1934, I 403. Wheaton, *Prelude*, pp. 455–58.

32. GSM to Phillips, 1 August 1934, *FRUS 1934*, 2:35–47; 17 August 1934, I 403. GSM #94, 9 August 1934, 863.00/1032.

33. GSM to Phillips, 9 August 1934, I 397; 23 August 1934, I 407.

34. GSM #168, 5 October 1934, *FRUS 1934*, 2:49–51. GSM #176, 16 October 1934, ibid., pp. 52–54. GSM to Phillips, 5 October 1934, I 426. GSM desp., 9 October 1934, 863.00/1078. GSM to Phillips, 17 October 1934, I 428. Undated (prob. October 1934) "Résumé of European Factors," I 434.

35. Selby, *Diplomatic Twilight*, pp. 40–41. GSM to Phillips, 17 October 1934, I 428. "Conversations with Von Papen in Vienna," I 1978, GSMM.

36. "Conversations with Von Papen," I 1978, GSMM. GSM memo, 14 November 1934, I 441.

37. GSM to John F. Montgomery, 20 November 1934, Montgomery Papers. GSM to Phillips, 12 September 1935, I 570. GSM memo, 23 September 1935, I 580.

38. GSM to Phillips, 18 January 1935, I 464. GSM to Moffat, 15 February 1935, I 482; 1 March 1935, I 488.

39. GSM to Phillips, 14 August 1934, I 399; 31 August 1934, I 409; 18 January 1935, I 462. GSM to Moffat, 20 September 1934, I 420. GSM #158, 2 October 1934, I 424.

40. GSM to Phillips, 14 August 1934, I 399; 31 August 1934, I 409; 26 October 1934, I 433; 8 November 1934, I 439. GSM to Moffat, 18 October 1934, I 429. GSM memo, 19 March 1935, I 492.

41. GSM to Phillips, 8 January 1935, I 460; 11 January 1935, I 462; 14 February 1935, I 481; 27 February 1935, I 486. Gehl, *Austria*, pp. 113–14.

42. GSM to Phillips, 23 February 1935, I 484; 27 February 1935, I 486. Schuschnigg, *Austrian Requiem*, pp. 137–64.

43. GSM to Phillips, 6 February 1935, I 478; 23 February 1935, I 484; 9 March 1935, I 490. Selby, *Diplomatic Twilight*, pp. 42–43.

44. GSM to Moffat, 19 January 1935, I 465. Berger Waldenegg quoted in GSM to Phillips, 9 March 1935, I 490.

45. GSM to Phillips, 14 February 1935, I 481. GSM to Montgomery, 24 November 1934, Montgomery Papers. Gehl, *Austria*, pp. 105–6, 114. Schuschnigg, *Austrian Requiem*, p. 5.

46. Phillips to GSM, 15 August 1934, I 400. GSM to Dunn, 3 July 1936, I 689.

47. "Conversations with Von Papen," I 1978, GSMM.

48. Mitchell, ed., *European Historical Statistics*, p. 261. Moffat memo, 21 February 1934, *FRUS 1934*, 2:59.

49. Schoenfeld memo, 11 May 1935, *FRUS 1935*, 2:98; 24 June 1935, ibid., p. 99.

50. Dunn memo, 13 October 1936, *FRUS 1936*, 2:4–5.

51. GSM to Feis, 21 July 1936, Feis Papers. For GSM's handling of discrimination charges, his #163, 3 October 1934, 636.116/66. GSM #994, 16 December 1936, I 800. GSM to Moffat, 4 October 1934, I 425.

52. GSM to Moffat, 14 January 1936, Moffat Papers.

53. GSM memo, 16 November 1935, I 615.

54. GSM to Moffat, 6 June 1934, I 375; 18 October 1934, I 429; 19 January 1935, I 465. GSM to Wiley, 23 October 1935, Wiley Papers. GSM #601, 13 November 1935, 124.636/80. GSM memo, 8 April 1935, 124.631/70. GSM #616, 29 November 1935, 124.631/89.

55. GSM to Dunn, 10 January 1935, I 461. GSM to Phillips, 17 December 1935, I 632. GSM #439, 29 May 1935, 124.631/72.

56. State Department to GSM, 24 June 1935, 124.63/72; 10 October 1935, ibid./79. GSM to Montgomery, 17 September 1935, Montgomery Papers; 2 January 1936, ibid. GSM #551, 19 September 1935, 124.631/78. Entry for 5 October 1935, Phillips Diary. State Department to GSM, 11 October 1935, 124.631/81.

57. State Department #14, 11 May 1935, 123 K 684/94. GSM to Moffat, 14 June 1935, Moffat Papers. Entry for 13 June 1935, Phillips Diary.

58. Carr memo, 15 April 1935, Carr Papers. GSM to Moffat, 14 June 1935, Moffat Papers. State Department #25, 123 K 684/134.

59. GSM to Moffat, 8 November 1934, Moffat Papers.

60. GSM to Moffat, 14 June 1935, Moffat Papers. Moffat to GSM, 28 June 1935, ibid. Carr memo, 2 May 1934, 123 H 24/644 1/2. Carr to Hackworth, 18 June 1935, Carr Papers. Carr to Hull, 29 August 1935, ibid. GSM #54, 12 July 1935, 123 H 24/663.

61. State Department to GSM, 22 June 1935, 123 K 36/196. GSM to Wiley, 9 September 1935, Wiley Papers; 23 October 1935, ibid. State Department tel., 3 September 1935, 123 Y 82/239. Kennan, *Memoirs*, pp. 65–66.

62. GSM to Phillips, 17 August 1934, I 403. GSM to Moffat, 21 August 1934, I 405. Sherwood, *Roosevelt and Hopkins*, pp. 62–63. Feis to GSM, 10

December 1934, Feis Papers. Scott to author, April 1980. GSM to Montgomery, 4 February 1935, Montgomery Papers.

63. GSM to Montgomery, 20 December 1934, Montgomery Papers. GSM to Moffat, 14 December 1934, I 453.

64. GSM to Montgomery, 20 December 1934; 12 February 1935; 24 June 1935; 16 December 1935; 20 December 1935; 22 January 1936, Montgomery Papers. GSM to Moore, 16 January 1937, I 819. GSM to Leland Harrison, Jr., 19 October 1936, Harrison Papers. Scott telephone conversation, 11 April 1980.

65. Entry for 13 June 1935, Phillips Diary. Dunn to GSM, 9 July 1935, I 519. Hull to GSM, 10 March 1937, I 877. GSM to Geist, 22 January 1937, I 828.

66. GSM to Feis, 20 December 1935, Feis Papers. GSM to Hull, 6 November 1936, I 752. GSM to Phillips, 18 June 1936, I 682. GSM to Dunn, 9 October 1936, I 734.

67. "Scope of Memoirs," I 1934, GSMM. See, e.g., summaries of his letters of 14 August, 28 August, 10 September 1936, prepared by Joseph Flack of Division of Western European Affairs, Hull Papers.

68. Heinrichs, "Bureaucracy and Professionalism," p. 190. Entry for 28 August 1934, Phillips Diary. GSM to Carr, 28 December 1936, I 811. GSM to Moore, 22 December 1936, I 807. GSM to Moore, 16 January 1937, I 819. GSM to Hull, 30 January 1937, I 838; 9 February 1937, I 849.

69. GSM to Carr, 23 February 1937, I 861. GSM to Long, 26 June 1940, I 1385.

70. Weil, *A Pretty Good Club*, p. 61. Entry for 1 June 1934, Phillips Diary. Long to Hull, 1 April 1935, *FRUS 1935*, 1:212–16.

71. Maddux, "Watching Stalin," pp. 140–54. Maddux, "American Diplomats," pp. 468–87. Maddux, "Henderson," p. 154. De Santis, *Diplomacy of Silence*, pp. 27–44. Weil, *A Pretty Good Club*, pp. 50–63, 101. Farnsworth, *Bullitt*, p. 150.

72. GSM to Lewis, 23 September 1936, I 723a. GSM to Montgomery, 24 November 1936, Montgomery Papers. GSM to Moore, 5 December 1936, I 790. GSM to Feis, 30 December 1935, Feis Papers. GSM to Hull, 9 February 1937, I 849.

73. GSM to Phillips, 8 July 1935, I 518. GSM to Moore, 5 December 1936, I 790. GSM to Dunn, 20 December 1935, I 634.

74. GSM to Phillips, 27 February 1935, I 486. Bullock, *Hitler*, pp. 322–31.

75. GSM to Moffat, 14 December 1934, I 453; 19 January 1935, I 465.

76. GSM memo, 21 March 1935, I 495. GSM desp. 25 March 1935, I 497. GSM to Selby, 25 March 1935, I 496.

77. GSM to Montgomery, 25 March 1935, Montgomery Papers.

78. GSM desp. 25 March 1935, I 497. GSM to Selby, 25 March 1935, I 496.

79. Entries for 10 April and 2 May 1935, Phillips Diary. Feis to Hull, 25 March 1937, Hull Papers. Dodd #1465, 14 November 1934, *FRUS 1934*, 2:251–53. Jenkins #642, 4 November 1935, *FRUS 1935*, 2:266–72. Geist to

Moffat, 26 January 1935, I 470. De Santis, *Diplomacy of Silence*, p. 70.
    80. GSM to Dodd, 1 July 1935, Dodd Papers. Feis to GSM, 18 March 1937, Feis Papers.
    81. GSM to Dodd, 1 July 1935, Dodd Papers.
    82. On the Washington negotiations, *FRUS 1935*, 2:441–51. Offner, *American Appeasement*, p. 99.
    83. Entries for 13 February 1934 and 12 April 1935, White House Usher's Diary, PSF, Roosevelt Papers. Crane, *Mr. Carr*, p. 314. Cf. Lash, *Eleanor and Franklin*, p. 571. Sherwood, *Roosevelt and Hopkins*, p. 63. Roosevelt to Caffery, 20 March 1935, *FDR and FA*, 2:450.
    84. Friedel, *Launching*, p. 362. Hull, *Memoirs*, p. 200. "Scope of Memoirs," I 1934, GSMM. Moore to Roosevelt, 27 November 1936, PSF 32, Roosevelt Papers, enclosing GSM to Hull, 6 November 1936, I 752. GSM to Moore, 9 November 1936, I 756; 16 November 1936, I 763. The only other Messersmith letters to Roosevelt from Vienna are routine thanks for the White House's annual Christmas greetings, PSF 44.
    85. Dallek, *Roosevelt's Foreign Policy*, p. 102. Kinsella, Jr., *Leadership in Isolation*, pp. 2–3, 33–44. "Scope of Memoirs," I 1934, GSMM. Schlesinger, Jr., *New Deal*, pp. 522–23. Roosevelt to Mack, 4 December 1935, *FDR and FA*, 3:111.
    86. GSM to Hull, 6 November 1936, Hull Papers. "A Résumé of the General European Situation Today," 10 October 1935, I 591.
    87. Weinberg, *Hitler's Foreign Policy*, pp. 210–16. Selby, *Diplomatic Twilight*, pp. 48–49.
    88. GSM to Phillips, 6 August 1935, I 539.
    89. GSM to Phillips, 6 June 1935, I 504. Mack Smith, *Mussolini*, p. 191.
    90. Gehl, *Austria*, pp. 117–18. Taylor *Origins*, pp. 88–90, 109. Lowe and Marzari, *Italian Foreign Policy*, pp. 240–90.
    91. GSM to Phillips, 20 September 1935, I 576.
    92. GSM to Phillips, 27 September 1935, I 582; 4 October 1935, I 588. GSM #573, 11 October 1935, I 592.
    93. "Résumé," 16 October 1935, I 591. GSM to Phillips, 15 October 1935, I 595.
    94. Braddick, "Hoare-Laval," pp. 152–71. GSM to Phillips, 17 December 1935, I 632.
    95. GSM to Dunn, 20 December 1935, I 634. "A Brief Résumé of the European Situation Today as Seen from Vienna," 12 February 1936, I 650.
    96. "Movement of the German Army across the Rhine," I 1975, GSMM. GSM #721 and enclosures, 9 March 1936, I 667, 668. GSM to Phillips, 13 March 1936, I 670. GSM memo, 27 March 1936, I 677. Weinberg, *Hitler's Foreign Policy*, pp. 239–63.
    97. GSM to Dunn, 21 June 1935, I 511. GSM #475, 3 July 1935, I 516. GSM #484, 10 July 1935, I 520. GSM #493, 13 July 1935, I 524. GSM to Phillips, 23 August 1935, I 556; 12 September 1935, I 570. Gehl, *Austria*, pp. 109–11, 122.
    98. Enclosure #1 to GSM desp., 27 March 1936, I 677. Weinberg, *Hitler's*

Foreign Policy, pp. 264–66. Schuschnigg, *Brutal Takeover*, p. 138.

99. GSM to Phillips, 18 June 1936, I 682. Edmondson, *Heimwehr*, pp. 256–59. Gehl, *Austria*, pp. 128–30.

100. Gehl, *Austria*, pp. 130–32. GSM to Hull, 8 July 1936, I 691.

101. GSM to Hull, 12 July 1936, I 693. GSM to Dunn, 20 July 1936, I 698. GSM to Hull, 31 July 1936, I 703.

102. GSM to Hull, 12 July 1936, I 693. GSM #857, 10 August 1936, I 709. GSM #908, 18 September 1936, I 719. GSM to Hull, 2 November 1936, Hull Papers. Gehl, *Austria*, pp. 147–48. Pauley, *Forgotten Nazis*, pp. 163–71.

103. GSM to Armstrong, 4 August 1936, I 706. GSM to Hull, 14 August 1936, I 710.

104. Gehl, *Austria*, p. 133. Weinberg, *Hitler's Foreign Policy*, pp. 264–71. GSM to Frankfurter, 9 July 1936, I 692. GSM to Hull, 31 July 1936, I 703; 21 August 1936, I 711; 16 October 1936, I 735; 6 November 1936, I 752. GSM to Moore, 5 December 1936, I 790.

105. Weinberg, *Hitler's Foreign Policy*, pp. 331–37. Mack Smith, *Mussolini*, pp. 206–8. Lowe and Marzari, *Italian Foreign Policy*, pp. 297–309. GSM to Hull, 6 November 1936, I 752.

106. GSM to Moore, 23 November 1936, I 771. Ciano quoted in Gehl, *Austria*, pp. 136–37.

107. GSM #960, 16 November 1936, I 766. GSM to Moore, 23 November 1936, I 771; 30 November 1936, I 784. GSM #979, 30 November 1936, 762.63/331. GSM #1023, 21 January 1937, I 827. GSM to Mowrer, 24 February 1937, I 829.

108. GSM to Moore, 16 January 1937, I 819. GSM #1022, 18 January 1937, I 823. GSM to Dunn, 23 January 1937, I 829. GSM #1035, 29 January 1937, I 837. GSM to Hull, 23 February 1937, I 860. GSM #1067, 26 February 1937, 762.63/344. GSM #1078, 8 March 1937, 863.00/1337. "Vienna-Von Neurath," I 1979, GSMM.

109. GSM to Hull, 8 October 1936, I 733. GSM to Dunn, 16 October 1936, I 736. "Memorandum Covering Aspects of the Present Situation in Germany," 15 December 1936, I 798. GSM to Hull, 30 January 1937, I 838. GSM to Moore, 16 January 1937, I 819. Weinberg, *Hitler's Foreign Policy* II, p. 268.

110. GSM to Moore, 30 November 1936, I 784. GSM to Hull, 8 March 1937, I 837; 3 April 1937, I 888. Mack Smith, *Mussolini*, p. 213.

111. GSM to Hull, 13 March 1937, I 878; 30 January 1937, I 838.

112. GSM to Phillips, 2 April 1937, I 887.

113. See, e.g., GSM to Stresemann, 9 November 1936, I 759. Moffat to Norman H. Davis, 7 October 1936, Davis Papers. "Visits to Berlin and London," I 1977, GSMM. Dodd knew that Messersmith was one of the people seeking his job. Dodd to Moore, 17 August 1936, Moore Papers. See also entry for 24 April 1936, Carr Diary: "Messersmith . . . wants to succeed Dodd though he denies he has any desire to do so. His technique is to [sic] apparent. But he would be several hundred per cent better than Dodd." Dallek, *Dodd*, implicitly disputes the senility diagnosis.

114. "New York—Meeting with Colonel House," I 1980, GSMM.

115. See, e.g., Bullitt's #1537, 20 April 1936, in Bullitt, ed., *For the President*, pp. 154–57. Davies, *Mission to Moscow*, pp. xii–xiv, 140, 143. Davis to Wilson, 8 February 1937, Davis Papers. GSM to Dunn, 22 March 1937, I 883.

116. GSM to Moffat, 24 May 1935, Moffat Papers.

117. Phillips to GSM, 12 May 1937, PF 482. GSM to McIntyre, 20 May 1937, OF 896, Roosevelt Papers. "Conversations on Return to the Department," I 1981, GSMM.

118. Hull to GSM, 24 June 1937, PF 514. GSM to Hull, 28 June 1937, I 894. GSM to Harrison, 7 July 1937, Harrison Papers.

119. Young #1169, 17 July 1937, PF 526. *New York Times*, 12 July 1937, p. 6. Selby to GSM, 18 October 1939, I 1292.

Chapter IV

1. *New York Times*, 3 July 1937, p. 13. Moley, *After Seven Years*, p. 13. Entry for 6 March 1933, *Moffat Papers*, pp. 89–90. Acheson, *Present at the Creation*, pp. 33–34. Hull, *Memoirs*, pp. 509–10. Stuart, *Department of State*, p. 328. Jablon, *Crossroads*, pp. vii–viii, 131–32.

2. Weil, *A Pretty Good Club*, pp. 71–74, 77–78, 82–83, 129–31. Roosevelt to Caffery, 20 March 1935, *FDR and FA*, 2:450. Cronon, *Daniels*, pp. 146–47.

3. Crane, *Mr. Carr*, pp. 310–19, 323–25. *Newsweek*, 10 July 1937, p. 33. But see Moore to Roosevelt, 6 September 1935, PSF 94, Roosevelt Papers, defending Carr's performance on personnel.

4. *New York Times*, 28 May 1937, p. 8; 8 June 1937, p. 11; 3 July 1937, p. 13. *New York Times Magazine*, 22 August 1937, p. 8.

5. *Newsweek*, 17 July 1937, p. 44. *New York Times*, 10 July 1937, p. 14.

6. *Newsweek*, 10 July 1937, pp. 10–11, 33.

7. *Washington Post*, 13 July 1937, CF. *New York Times*, 10 July 1937, p. 14. *Newsweek*, 10 July 1937, p. 33.

8. *New York Daily Mirror*, 28 July 1937, p. 14; 20 July 1937, p. 24.

9. *New York Times*, 10 July 1937, p. 14.

10. *New York Daily Mirror*, 13 September 1937, p. 16. Bendiner, *Riddle*, pp. 184, 187–88.

11. *New York Daily Mirror*, 13 September 1937, p. 16; 24 July 1937, p. 14.

12. *New York Times*, 23 July 1937, p. 3. GSM to Montgomery, 3 August 1937, Montgomery Papers. Hull to Wilson, 11 May 1937, Hull Papers. Wilson to Davis, 5 June 1937, Davis Papers. Davis to Wilson, 10 June 1937, ibid. State Department #43, 17 July 1937, 123 W 693/489. Entry for 25 July 1937, Moffat Diary.

13. Entry for 25 July 1937, Moffat Diary. "Conversations on Return to the Department," I 1981, GSMM.

14. Crane, *Mr. Carr*, p. 328. Entries for 27–28 July 1937, Carr Diary. Entry for 27 July 1937, Moffat Diary.

15. State Department order #702, 26 July 1937, 111.017/210. Order

#703, 29 July 1937, 111.017/211. "Some Aspects of the Assistance Rendered by the Department of State," 3 November 1937, 111.12/16. GSM memo, 20 October 1937, 120.3/487 1/2. Before leaving Vienna, Messersmith prepared five long memoranda for *his* successor. See box two, Wiley Papers.

16. Stuart, *Department of State*, pp. 330–31. "The Reorganization of the Department of State," I 1985, GSMM. GSM to Stuart, 9 April 1940, I 1337. GSM to Selby, 26 February 1938, I 957.

17. Hosmer memo, 2 September 1937, 113/767.

18. *New York Times*, 22 May 1937, p. 8. Barnes and Morgan, *Foreign Service*, p. 247.

19. GSM memo, 11 November 1937, 113/773A. GSM to McIntyre, 11 November 1937, ibid. Bell to Hull, 16 November 1937, 113/774 1/2.

20. Bacharach to Kellogg, 15 December 1927, PF 154. House Ways and Means Subcommittee Hearings, 70th Cong., 1st sess., pt. 2, pp. 254–62, 271–73. Crane, *Mr. Carr*, p. 328.

21. *New York Daily Mirror*, 13 September 1937, p. 16. Entry for 13 September 1937, Moffat Diary. GSM memo, 8 December 1937, 113/777. Department of State Appropriations Bill for 1939, Hearings, 75th Cong., 3rd sess., pp. 24, 28–29, 180–85.

22. *Congressional Record*, 75th Cong., 3rd sess., 83:2159–61. GSM memo, 18 February 1938, 113/789.

23. *Congressional Record*, 75th Cong., 3rd sess., 83:2902, 4217–19, 4263–68, 5623, 5630–31, 5758, 6047.

24. GSM to MacDonald, 1 February 1938, 111.12/42. GSM to Villard, 2 June 1938, 113/799 1/2. GSM memo, 28 May 1938, ibid. State Appropriation for 1939 Hearings, pp. 84–85. Bendiner, *Riddle*, p. 213. Weil, *A Pretty Good Club*, p. 21.

25. GSM to Francis P. Corrigan, 7 February 1938, Corrigan Papers. Hosmer to GSM, 11 January 1938, 111.12/39. "Address to National Foreign Trade Convention, Cleveland," 3 November 1937, State Department Commercial Policy Series #40. "Speech to the Conference on the Cause and Cure of War, Washington," 19 January 1938, SF. "Speech to the National Council of Jewish Women, Pittsburgh," 26 January 1938, 112.12/40. "Speech to the New York City Federation of Women's Clubs," 4 February 1938, SF.

26. *New York Times*, 5 February 1938, p. 14. *Congressional Record*, 75th Cong., 3rd sess., 82:409–11, 414–15, 707–9. Schain to GSM, 24 January 1938, 113/831 1/2. GSM memo, 28 May 1938, 113/799 1/2. GSM memo, 16 June 1938, 113/801 1/2. Murphy memo, 20 June 1938, 113/802 1/2. GSM to Villard, 10 June 1938, 113/800 1/2.

27. GSM to Villard, 15 July 1938, 113/803 1/2.

28. GSM to Welles, 30 December 1938, 120.1/392. Hull, *Memoirs*, p. 375. Dallek, *Roosevelt's Foreign Policy*, p. 92.

29. "Address to National Foreign Trade Convention," 3 November 1937, 111.12/16. GSM memo, 7 February 1939, 120.1/399. Carr memo, 17 December 1936, 120.1/309.

30. "The Reorganization," I 1985, GSMM. Copy of S. 988, 120.1/302.

31. Carr to Welles, 27 July 1937, 120.1/305.

32. Leuchtenburg, *Roosevelt and the New Deal*, pp. 231–44.

33. Hosmer to GSM, 12 March 1938, 120.1/316. Polenberg, *Reorganizing.* Murphy memo, November 1937, 120.1/309.

34. GSM memo, 12 August 1937, 120.1/307. Duggan to GSM, 14 December 1937, 120.1/313. GSM memo, n.d., 120.1/315. GSM memo, 30 December 1937, I 922. Lockett to GSM, 24 May 1938, I 988.

35. Welles to GSM, 20 October 1937, 111.12/16. Murphy memo, November 1937, 120.1/309. *New York Daily Mirror*, 21 October 1937, p. 22. GSM to Hull, 6 November 1937, Hull Papers.

36. "Some Aspects of Assistance," 111.12/16.

37. Estrin to GSM, 8 November 1937, 111.12/17. GSM memo, 29 December 1937, 120.1/314.

38. Patterson, *Congressional Conservatism*, pp. 216–21. Duggan to GSM, 14 December 1937, 120.1/314.

39. GSM to Welles, 8 January 1938, 120.1/289 1/2. "Some Observations on the Position and Functions of Attachés and Offices of Other Departments of Our Government Stationed Abroad," 20 December 1937, ibid.

40. Welles to GSM, 10 January 1938, 120.1/289 1/2. GSM memo, 11 January 1938, ibid. GSM memo, 1 February 1938, I 935.

41. GSM to Roosevelt, 10 February 1938, 120.1/289 1/2.

42. GSM to Bullitt, 16 March 1938, 120.1/289 1/2. Polenberg, *Reorganizing*, p. 175. Patterson, *Congressional Conservatism*, p. 226.

43. GSM to Lockett, 17 May 1938, 120.1/323 1/2. Hosmer to GSM, 12 March 1938, 120.1/316. Memo to GSM, n.a., 14 April 1938, 120.1/318.

44. GSM memo, 16 April 1938, I 976.

45. GSM memo, 18 April 1938, 120.1/320.

46. GSM memo, 22 April 1938, 120.1/321.

47. Welles to Roosevelt, 27 April 1938, 120.1/321a. Welles to GSM, 25 April 1938, 120.1/322. Welles to Roosevelt, 11 May 1938, OF 3C, Roosevelt Papers. Roper to Roosevelt, 16 May 1938, ibid. GSM to Lockett, 17 May 1938, 120.1/323 1/2.

48. GSM to Welles, 28 April 1938, I 982.

49. GSM to Hull and Welles, 16 May 1938, 120.1/325. GSM to Lockett, 17 May 1938, 120.1/323 1/2. *New York Times*, 15 May 1938, p. 8, and clippings filed under 120.1/399 1/2.

50. GSM to Welles, 20 May 1938, 120.1/327. GSM to Lockett, 27 May 1938, 120.1/327 1/2. GSM to Hull and Welles, 28 May 1938, I 1000. GSM memo, 2 June 1938, 120.1/329. Roosevelt to Hull, 11 June 1938, OF 3C, Roosevelt Papers.

51. *Congressional Record*, 75th Cong., 3rd sess., 68:8233–34.

52. GSM memo, 9 June 1938, I 1005.

53. Ibid. The copy in the State Department archives (120.1/333) bears Messersmith's handwritten postscript on Welles's talk with Roosevelt. GSM memo, 14 June 1938, 120.1/388. *Congressional Record*, 75th Cong., 3rd sess., 68:1938.

54. GSM to Lockett, 17 August 1938, 120.1/341a.

55. Dallek, *Roosevelt's Foreign Policy*, pp. 148–49. Jacobs, "Roosevelt's Quarantine Speech," pp. 488–99. Divine, *Roosevelt and World War II*, pp. 18–19.

56. Dallek, *Roosevelt's Foreign Policy*, pp. 151–55. Divine, *Illusion of Neutrality*, pp. 219–20.

57. "Comparisons: President Roosevelt-Winston Churchill," I 2013, GSMM. Roosevelt's penchant for personal diplomacy has been noted by others. See, e.g., Hull, *Memoirs*, pp. 297–98. Divine, *Roosevelt and World War II*, p. 21. Welles memo, 6 October 1937, *FRUS 1937*, 1:665–66.

58. GSM memo, 11 October 1937, *FRUS 1937*, 1:140–45.

59. Entry for 24 March 1938, Stimson Diary. Hull, *Memoirs*, pp. 546–48. Langer and Gleason, *Challenge*, pp. 22–23. GSM to Dean, 22 July 1950, I 1898. GSM memo (covering), 11 October 1937, I 901. Welles, *Seven Decisions*, p. 24.

60. Dallek, *Roosevelt's Foreign Policy*, pp. 149–53. GSM to Heineman, 21 December 1937, I 914.

61. GSM to Geist, 7 December 1937, I 910. Davies, *Mission to Moscow*, pp. 254–56. Roosevelt's desire for a "distinctly formal" appointment to Berlin explains why his first choice was perhaps his least favorite among the career men, Hugh Gibson. Gibson declined the honor, citing the financial burden, and retired instead. Welles to Roosevelt, 26 November 1937, PSF 88, Roosevelt Papers.

62. GSM to Selby, 26 February 1938, I 956. "Cordell Hull and My Personal Relationships with Him," I 2035, GSMM. Weil, *A Pretty Good Club*, pp. 75–78. Bendiner, *Riddle*, p. 184.

63. Entry for 10 January 1938, Moffat Diary. Welles memo, 10 January 1938, *FRUS 1983*, 1:115–17. Offner, "Appeasement Revisited," pp. 379–80.

64. Halifax and Chamberlain quoted in Bullock, *Hitler*, p. 367. Chamberlain to Roosevelt, 14 January 1938, *FRUS 1938*, 1:118–20. Roosevelt to Chamberlain, ibid., pp. 120–22.

65. Bullock, *Hitler*, p. 367. Brook-Shepherd, *The Anschluss*, pp. 42–63. Schuschnigg, *Austrian Requiem*, pp. 19–32.

66. GSM to Hull and Welles, 18 February 1938, I 950.

67. Brook-Shepherd, *The Anschluss*, pp. 137–79. Bullock, *Hitler*, pp. 425–35. Fest, *Hitler*, pp. 545–49.

68. Richardson to Hull, 25 March 1938, I 970. Rogers to GSM, 1 April 1938, I 972. GSM to Montgomery, 5 April 1938, Montgomery Papers. Montgomery to GSM, 25 March 1938, ibid.

69. Wiley #134, 22 March 1938, 124.636/94. Wiley #159, 30 March 1938, 124.63/103.

70. Entry for 29 March 1938, Moffat Diary. Geist to GSM, 21 October 1938, I 1051. GSM memo, 6 April 1938, 124.63/108. Offner, *American Appeasement*, pp. 238–39.

71. Wiley to GSM, 8 June 1938, I 1004. Feingold, *Politics of Rescue*, pp. 22–26.

72. Feingold, *Politics of Rescue*, pp. 9–13. Entry for 18 April 1938, Moffat Diary.

73. GSM to Brandeis, 24 October 1938, I 1054. GSM to Geist, 30 November 1938, I 1084; 20 December 1938, I 1099.

74. GSM to Hull, 31 March 1938, 840.48/84 1/2. GSM to Welles, 7 April 1938, 150.01/34. Hull to GSM, 17 April 1938, ibid. Wyman, *Paper Walls*, pp. 67–71.

75. GSM to Wiley, 28 June 1938, I 1012. GSM to Montgomery, 3 April 1938, Montgomery Papers. GSM to Dodd, 21 June 1938, Dodd Papers, wherein Messersmith railed at would-be refugees "not willing to come here in the spirit of the pioneers who helped to build up this country." Shafir, "Messersmith," p. 41.

76. *Danziger Vorposten*, quoted in Morse, *Six Million*, p. 214. Wyman, *Paper Walls*, pp. 44–51. Feingold, *Politics of Rescue*, pp. 29–40. GSM to Geist, 7 November 1938, I 1066.

77. GSM to Geist, 7 November 1938, I 1066. Bullock, *Hitler*, pp. 442–44. Wheeler-Bennett, *Munich*, pp. 45–48, 71–93. Weinberg, *Hitler's Foreign Policy II*, pp. 313–77. Taylor, *Munich*, pp. 390–95.

78. Taylor, *Munich*, pp. 407–10. Weinberg, *Hitler's Foreign Policy II*, pp. 424–27. Entry for 13 September 1938, Moffat Diary.

79. On the Chamberlain-Hitler negotiations, see Taylor, *Munich*, pp. 732–53, 795–830.

80. Entries for 24–25 September 1938, *Moffat Papers*, pp. 211–13. Entry for 27 September 1938, Berle Diary, p. 187.

81. Bullock, *Hitler*, pp. 464–65. Offner, *American Appeasement*, pp. 270–71. Taylor, *Munich*, pp. 896–97 and passim. Weinberg, *Hitler's Foreign Policy II*, pp. 452–55.

82. Entries for 28 and 30 September 1938, Berle Diary, p. 188. GSM to Hull, 29 September 1938, *FRUS 1938*, 1:704–7.

83. Churchill quoted in Fest, *Hitler*, p. 567. GSM to Heineman, 7 December 1938, I 1092; 7 November 1938, I 1067. Langer and Gleason, *Challenge*, pp. 35–37.

84. *New York Times*, quoted in Morse, *Six Million*, pp. 221–26. Levin, *The Holocaust*, pp. 78–88. Wyman, *Paper Walls*, pp. 71–75.

85. GSM to Hull, 14 November 1938, *FRUS 1938*, 2:396–98.

86. GSM to Geist, 30 November 1938, I 1084.

87. GSM memo, 1 February 1938, I 935. GSM to Geist, 7 February 1938, I 941.

88. Wilson to State Department, 5 April 1938, 123 W 693/536; 21 March 1938, 123 W 693/558. GSM to Geist, 5 April 1938, I 974. Geist to GSM, 5 June 1938, I 1002.

89. Geist to GSM, 21 October 1938, I 1001. Wilson #399, 31 October 1938, 123 W 693/565.

90. Wilson to Roosevelt, 3 March 1938, in Wilson, Jr., *Career Diplomat*, p. 18. Wilson to Hull, 24 May 1938, ibid., pp. 33–35. Wilson to Roosevelt, 11 August 1938, ibid., pp. 44–45.

91. Wilson to Hull, unsent, in Wilson, Jr., *Career Diplomat*, pp. 51–53. Wilson to Hull, 21 May 1938, *FRUS 1938*, 1:506–7. Offner, *American Appeasement*, p. 251. Weil, *A Pretty Good Club*, pp. 60–61. For a milder view of Wilson, see Weinberg, *Hitler's Foreign Policy II*, p. 254.

92. Wilson to Hull, 30 July 1938, in Wilson, Jr., *Career Diplomat*, p. 43. Wil-

son to Hull, 18 October 1938, *FRUS 1938*, 1:799.

93. Geist to GSM, 1 March 1938, I 958; 20 April 1938, I 977; 5 June 1938, I 1002; 21 October 1938, I 1051; 5 December 1938, I 1087.

94. GSM to Geist, 7 November 1938, I 1066.

95. Hull, *Memoirs*, p. 599. Hull to Wilson, 14 November 1938, 123 W 693/571. Entry for 14 November 1938, *Moffat Papers*, pp. 221–22. *New York Times*, 15 November 1938, p. 1.

96. GSM to Montgomery, 17 November 1938, Montgomery Papers. GSM to Heineman, 28 November 1938, I 1083. GSM to Geist, 30 November 1938, I 1084; 8 December 1938, I 1093.

97. Press conference 500, 15 November 1938, *Complete Press Conferences*, 12:225–27.

98. Feingold, *Politics of Rescue*, pp. 43–51. Wyman, *Paper Walls*, pp. 56–58. Rublee to Hull, 15 December 1938, *FRUS 1938*, 1:873–74.

99. GSM to Geist, 20 December 1938, I 1099.

100. Welles to Rublee, 19 December 1938, *FRUS 1938*, 1:876–78; 21 December 1938, ibid., pp. 879–80. Feingold, *Politics of Rescue*, pp. 51–64.

101. Feingold, *Politics of Rescue*, pp. 64–68. Morse, *Six Million*, pp. 241–51.

102. Wilson to Mrs. Wilson, 31 December 1938, 123 W 693/587.

103. Geist to GSM, 22 January 1939, I 1136. Welles memo, 18 November 1938, *FRUS 1938*, 2:402–3. Bullitt to Hull, 28 February 1939, 1:212.

104. GSM memo, 21 December 1938, I 1100; 22 December 1938, I 1105; 5 January 1939, I 1128, 23 January 1939, I 1137.

105. GSM memo, 15 February 1939, I 1157.

106. GSM to Geist, 16 February 1939, I 1158. Entries for 13 February and 15 March 1939, *Moffat Papers*, pp. 229, 231–32. Entries for 3 March, 11–12 March 1939, Moffat Diary.

107. Entry for 15 March 1939, Moffat Diary. Entry for 16 March 1939, Berle Diary, p. 200. Langer and Gleason, *Challenge*, pp. 67–68.

108. Wilson to Mrs. Wilson, 20 March 1939, 123 W 693/603. Wilson, Jr., *Career Diplomat*, pp. 107–8.

109. GSM to Hull, 8 October 1939, Hull Papers.

110. GSM to Hull, 26 March 1940, I 1328. GSM to Long, 27 March 1940, I 1330; 11 April 1940, I 1341. Berle to GSM, 25 March 1940, Berle Papers. Wilson to Roosevelt, 7 March 1940, PSF 90, Roosevelt Papers. Welles, *Time for Decision*, pp. 73–74.

111. GSM to Sypherd, 29 November 1954, I 1906. He expressed particular pleasure at the judgments rendered by Langer and Gleason (*Challenge*, pp. 21–22, 125–27) and by Franklin L. Ford, in his "Three Observers," esp. p. 460.

112. "Influence of Fear in the Attitude toward War," I 2012, GSMM.

113. GSM to Geist, 27 November 1937, I 908. GSM to Heineman, 21 December 1937, I 914. GSM to Wilson, 25 August 1938, I 1026.

114. *Register of the Department of State 1939*, p. 4. Entries for 10 January 1938, 11 February 1938, 26 March 1938, Berle Diary, pp. 159, 164, 169–70. Entry for 5–6 November 1938, Moffat Diary.

115. Entry for 1 June 1938, Moffat Diary. Geist to GSM, 5 June 1938, I 1002; 21 October 1938, I 1051. GSM to Fodor, 18 August 1938, I 1022. GSM to Heineman, 7 November 1938, I 1067.

116. GSM statement, 15 September 1938, 113/824B. Hull to Bell, 26 August 1938, 113/816B. GSM to Bell, 28 September 1938, 113/817A. GSM memo, 26 September 1938, 113/824B.

117. Department of State Appropriation Bill for 1940, Hearings, 76th Cong., 1st sess., pp. 24–26, 205, 209–12, 290–94. Geist to GSM, 7 November 1938, I 1068. Geist #174, 16 March 1939, 124.621/480.

118. *Congressional Record*, 76th Cong., 1st sess., 84:5733–35, 6742. State Department Appropriation for FY 1940, 10 July 1939, 113/852.

119. Achilles to GSM, 15 July 1938, 120.3801/159 1/2. GSM memo, 18 March 1939, 120.3801/161. Hosmer to Skinner, 5 April 1939, ibid. Entry for 14 April 1939, Moffat Diary. *Congressional Record*, 76th Cong., 1st sess., 84:2298–2300, 4192, 4391.

120. GSM memo, 22 August 1938, I 1025. GSM to Hull, 25 June 1938, 120.1/340. GSM memo, 19 August 1938, 120.1/342. GSM to Bankhead, 14 September 1938, I 1038.

121. GSM to Hull, 7 September 1938, I 1030.

122. GSM memo, 8 October 1938, 120.1/349. Abbink to GSM, 27 October 1938, 120.1/365. Bookman to GSM, n.d., 120.1/380. Patterson's "Brief," 28 November 1938, I 1083a.

123. GSM memo, 19 October 1938, I 1050. GSM to Dickerman, 24 October 1938, I 1052. Thomas to GSM, 5 October 1938, 120.1/347. GSM to Thomas, 7 October 1938, ibid. Thomas to GSM, 7 October 1938, 120.1/348. GSM to Thomas, 8 October 1938, ibid. Thomas to GSM, 27 October 1938. *New York Times*, 3 November 1938, p. 1. GSM memo, 8 November 1938, I 1069.

124. Polenberg, *Reorganizing*, pp. 180–85. GSM to Lockett, 17 August 1938, 120.1/341a. GSM memo, 8 November 1938, I 1069.

125. GSM memo, 26 September 1938, 120.1/345. GSM to Hull, 18 November 1938, 120.1/347. GSM to Hull and Welles, 9 November 1938, I 1071 (copy to Roosevelt, 12 November 1938).

126. GSM to McMillan, 5 December 1938, I 1088. GSM to Gray, 9 December 1938, 120.1/386a.

127. GSM to Welles, 19 December 1938, I 1097. GSM to Boal, 15 December 1938, 120.1/385.

128. Roper, *Fifty Years*, pp. 347–50. Tugwell, *Democratic Roosevelt*, pp. 268, 361.

129. Sherwood, *Roosevelt and Hopkins*, pp. 93–98.

130. GSM to Welles, 30 December 1938, I 1112. GSM to Hull, 11 January 1939, I 1131. Patterson to Hopkins, 5 January 1939, Hopkins Papers. Roosevelt to Hopkins 19 December 1938, ibid. GSM to Hopkins, 11 February 1939, ibid. GSM to Welles, 5 January 1939, 120.1/395. GSM to Daniels, 26 January 1939, 120.1/398a. GSM to Hull and Welles, 2 March 1939, 120.1/400. "The Reorganization," I 1985, GSMM.

131. Polenberg, *Reorganizing*, pp. 186–88. GSM to Lockett, 27 March 1939, 120.1/401. Patterson, *Congressional Conservatism*, pp. 300–302.

132. GSM to Hopkins, 25 March 1939, Hopkins Papers; 13 April 1939, 120.1/399 1/2. "The Reorganization," I 1985, GSMM. Wallace to GSM, 21 April 1939, I 1197. Hull to Wallace, 21 April 1939, I 1198. GSM to Erhardt, 25 April 1939, I 1201.

133. GSM to Meyer, 26 April 1939, I 1206, and items 1207–1225. See editorial clippings in folder five, 120.1. Newbranch to GSM, 12 May 1939, I 1243, Polenberg, *Reorganizing*, p. 188.

134. GSM to Erhardt, 25 April 1939, I 1201. Ilchman, *Professional Diplomacy*, p. 241. Barnes and Morgan, *Foreign Service*, p. 365.

135. GSM to Shaw and Huddle, 21 October 1939, 120.1/459 1/2. GSM to Noble, 14 July 1939, 120.1/439.

136. Circular instr., 21 March 1939, citing that of 19 September 1938, *FRUS 1939*, 1:143–48. Department serial 3122, 28 August 1938, ibid., p. 150. Stuart, *Department of State*, pp. 340–41. Hull, *Memoirs*, pp. 663–64. Entry for 17 August 1939, *Moffat Papers*, pp. 247–48. Entry for 29 August 1939, Moffat Diary. Entries for 17 August and 21 August 1939, Berle Diary, pp. 237–39.

137. Robert H. Jackson oral history interview, p. 758. Entry for 1 September 1939, Berle Diary, p. 248. Hull, *Memoirs*, pp. 671–74. Entry for 1 September 1939, *Moffat Papers*, pp. 259–61. Entry for 2 September 1939, *Long Diary*, pp. 1–4.

138. Entries for 3–6 September 1939, *Long Diary*, pp. 4–10. Entry for 8 September 1939, *Moffat Papers*. Entries for 25 September and 29 September 1939, Moffat Diary. GSM to Herschel V. Johnson, 27 December 1939, Johnson Papers. GSM to Fullerton, 6 October 1939, I 1287; 7 November 1939, I 1297. GSM memo, 3 November 1939, 120.1/462.

139. Entry for 14 September 1939, *Long Diary*, p. 13. GSM to Montgomery, 30 November 1939, Montgomery Papers.

140. Entry for 5–6 November 1939, Moffat Diary. GSM to Harrison, 28 December 1939, Harrison Papers. GSM to Selby, 12 November 1938, I 1074. GSM to Burlingham, 13 July 1939, I 1259. State Department order #767, 13 July 1938, 111.12/52. State Department order #816, 15 September 1939, 111.12/72. The executive assistants were Fletcher Warren and Laurence C. Frank.

141. GSM memo, 1 February 1938, I 935. GSM to Montgomery, 14 November 1939, Montgomery Papers. GSM to Fullerton, 6 October 1939, I 1287; 7 November 1939, I 1297.

142. GSM to Baerwald, 13 January 1940, I 1316. GSM to Van Cauwelaert, 7 February 1940, I 1320. GSM to Backer, 24 April 1940, I 1354.

143. Entries for 10 January, 12 January, 20 January, 30 January 1940, Moffat Diary. Duggan to GSM, 31 January 1940, I 1319. GSM to Baerwald, 13 January 1940, I 1316. Entry for 23 January 1940, *Long Diary*, p. 55. GSM to Fullerton, 22 April 1940, I 1357. *New York Times*, 1 March 1940, p. 7. Long to GSM, 7 March 1940, Long Papers. Acheson, *Present at the Creation*, p. 35.

Chapter V

1. Beaulac to Hull, 2 March 1940, PF 544. Beaulac, *Career Ambassador,* p. 149. GSM to Long, 21 August 1940, Long Papers. Long to GSM, 27 August 1940, ibid.

2. Wood, *Good Neighbor,* pp. 48–117.

3. Gellman, *Roosevelt,* pp. 138–65.

4. Ibid., pp. 166–67.

5. Smith, *U.S. and Cuba,* pp. 171–75. "Summary of U.S.-Cuban Relations since November 1938," 26 January 1940, I 1319, prepared for Messersmith by Phillip Bonsal of the Division of the American Republics.

6. Gellman, *Roosevelt,* pp. 163–64, 175. Beaulac, *Career Ambassador,* pp. 147–48.

7. Smith, *U.S. and Cuba,* pp. 172–74. Gellman, *Roosevelt,* pp. 170–71.

8. Gellman, *Roosevelt,* pp. 168–69, 172–74, 178.

9. Ibid., pp. 174, 177–78. GSM to Hull, 9 March 1940, *FRUS 1940,* 5:742. GSM to Hull, 19 March 1940, ibid., pp. 745–49.

10. GSM to Long, 21 March 1940, Long Papers. GSM to Hull, 26 March 1940, I 1328.

11. GSM to Long, 21 March 1940, Long Papers. "Summary," 26 January 1940, I 1319. GSM to Hull, 26 March 1940, I 1328. GSM to Hull, 19 March 1940, *FRUS 1940,* 5:745–49.

12. GSM to Welles, 12 April 1940, I 1342. GSM to Hull, 19 March 1940, *FRUS 1940,* 5:745–49. "Cuba—Road Debt Settlement," I 1989, GSMM. GSM to Duggan, 10 April 1940, I 1338. GSM to Hull, 28 March 1940, *FRUS 1940,* 5:749–50.

13. GSM to Hull, 16 March 1940, 837.00/8707. GSM to Hull, 26 March 1940, I 1328. GSM to Hull, 10 April 1940, I 1339. GSM to Welles, 19 April 1940, I 1348; 12 July 1940, I 1390.

14. GSM to Hull, 26 March 1940, I 1328. GSM to Hull, 3 April 1940, 837.011/340. GSM to Frankfurter, 11 April 1940, I 1340. GSM to Welles, 24 April 1940, I 1352; 29 May 1940, I 1368; 1 June 1940, I 1371. Farber, *Revolution and Reaction,* pp. 93–98.

15. GSM to Welles, 29 May 1940, I 1368; 1 June 1940, I 1371.

16. GSM to Welles, 29 May 1940, I 1368. Beaulac memo, 31 May 1940, I 1369.

17. GSM to Welles, 1 June 1940, I 1371; 12 July 1940, I 1390.

18. Duggan memo, 21 May 1940, *FRUS 1940,* 5:15–16. Welles to GSM, 29 May 1940, ibid., pp. 94–95. GSM to Welles, 10 June 1940, ibid., pp. 96–97. GSM to Hull, 16 July 1940, ibid., p. 98.

19. Beaulac memo, 31 May 1940, I 1369.

20. GSM to Hull, 26 March 1940, I 1328. GSM to Long, 11 April 1940, I 1341.

21. GSM to Geist, 26 March 1940, I 1329. GSM to Long, 27 March 1940, Long Papers. GSM to Stuart, 9 April 1940, I 1337. GSM to Feis, 1 April 1940, Feis Papers. GSM to Moffat, 29 May 1940, I 1367. GSM to Frankfurter, 31 May 1940, I 1370.

22. Gellman, *Good Neighbor*, pp. 95–96. GSM to Barton, 22 June 1940, I 1384. GSM to Duggan, 14 June 1940, I 1380. GSM to Long, 26 June 1940, I 1385.

23. GSM to Welles, 5 June 1940, I 1374. "Observations," 3 June 1940, I 1373. Frye, *Nazi Germany and the American Hemisphere*, pp. 126–28.

24. GSM to Welles, 12 July 1940, I 1390. GSM to Long, 26 June 1940, I 1385.

25. GSM to Welles, 12 June 1940, I 1390.

26. GSM to Frankfurter, 31 May 1940, I 1370. "Observations," 3 June 1940, I 1373. "July 4 Speech," I 1389. "Speech at Lions International Convention," 24 July 1940, PF 563. *New York Times*, 9 July 1940, p. 3; 25 July 1940, p. 3. GSM to Ausenberry, 27 June 1940, I 1386.

27. "Observations," 3 June 1940, I 1373. GSM to Ausenberry, 27 June 1940, I 1386. GSM to Welles, 2 July 1940, I 1388. On the cartel, see Langer and Gleason, *Challenge*, pp. 630–35.

28. GSM to Hull, 15 June 1940, I 1381. Hull to Chiefs of Mission, 17 June 1940, *FRUS 1940*, 5:181. Langer and Gleason, *Challenge*, p. 689.

29. For Messersmith's role in the agenda negotiations, *FRUS 1940*, 5:182–256. Frye, *Nazi Germany and the American Hemisphere*, pp. 126–28. Langer and Gleason, *Challenge*, pp. 635, 691–95. Gellman, *Good Neighbor*, pp. 93–94.

30. GSM to Duggan, 14 June 1940, I 1380. GSM to Hull, 15 June 1940, Hull Papers. GSM to Welles, 2 July 1940, I 1388.

31. GSM to Welles, 12 July 1940, I 1390; 15 August 1940, I 1397. GSM to Harrison, 31 May 1940, Harrison Papers.

32. GSM to Hull, 15 July 1940, 837.00/8806. GSM #93, 9 July 1940, 5:196. Entry for 2 August 1940, Berle Diary, pp. 328–31. Bemis, *Latin American Policy*, pp. 367–71. Logan, Jr., *No Transfer*, pp. 326–40.

33. GSM to Hull, 28 June 1940, 711.37/336. GSM to Hull, 31 July 1940, *FRUS 1940*, 5:756–57.

34. GSM to Welles, 8 August 1940, I 1396.

35. GSM to Welles, 15 August 1940, I 1397. "Cuba—Road Debt Settlement," I 1989, GSMM. GSM to Hull, 4 September 1940, *FRUS 1940*, 5:761–62.

36. *New York Times*, 6 September 1940, p. 8. GSM to Beaulac, 14 September 1940, I 1400. Welles to Morgenthau, 14 September 1940, *FRUS 1940*, 5:778–79. Hull to Beaulac, 16 September 1940, ibid., pp. 779–80.

37. Hull to Morgenthau, 4 October 1940, *FRUS 1940*, 5:780–81. Martínez Fraga to Welles, 14 October 1940, ibid., p. 783. GSM to Hull, 3 October 1940, I 1401.

38. GSM to Welles, 19 October 1940, I 1404. GSM to Hull, 29 October 1940, *FRUS 1940*, 5:783–84. GSM to Welles, 8 November 1940, I 1412.

39. GSM to Welles, 18 October 1940, I 1403; 25 October 1940, I 1407; 8 November 1940, I 1412; 8 November 1940, I 1413; 10 December 1940, I 1420; 11 December 1940, I 1421; 11 December 1940, I 1422. Welles to Martínez Fraga, 4 December 1940, *FRUS 1940*, 5:785–88. Hull memo, 17 December 1940, Hull Papers.

40. GSM to Welles, 8 December 1940, I 1425. GSM memo, 25 December 1940, I 1427.

41. GSM to Welles, 8 November 1940, I 1412. GSM memo, 8 January 1941, *FRUS 1941*, 7:127–33. GSM to Welles, 19 October 1940, I 1404; 22 October 1940, I 1405; 7 November 1940, I 1411; 18 December 1940, I 1425.

42. GSM to Hull, 8 September 1940, *FRUS 1940*, 5:99–100. Gellman, *Roosevelt*, p. 209. GSM to Welles, 18 December 1940, I 1425. GSM memo, 25 December 1940, I 1427.

43. GSM memo, 8 January 1941, *FRUS 1941*, 7:127–33.

44. GSM to Hull, 31 January 1941, 837.61351/2419. Beaulac to Hull, 8 January 1941, *FRUS 1941*, 7:228. Hull to Beaulac, 9 January 1941, ibid., p. 229. Walmsley memo, 16 January 1941, ibid., pp. 230–31. GSM to Hull, 22 January 1941, ibid., pp. 231–32. GSM to Welles, 15 January 1941, I 1428; 18 January 1941, I 1429. GSM to Hull, 24 January 1941, I 1431. GSM to Welles, 31 January 1941, I 1433; 22 March 1941, I 1450.

45. GSM to Welles, 23 January 1941, I 1430; 27 January 1941, I 1432; 31 January 1941, I 1433. "Havana-Graft," I 1991, GSMM.

46. Gellman, *Roosevelt*, pp. 186–87. GSM to Welles, 3 February 1941, I 1434. GSM to Hull, 3 February 1941, I 1435. "Havana—Abortive Revolution," I 1993, GSMM.

47. GSM to Welles, 5 February 1941, I 1436. GSM to Bonsal, 10 February 1941, I 1437.

48. GSM to Hull, 16 January 1941, 837.00/8920. GSM to Hull, 25 January 1941, 837.00/8925. GSM to Welles, 14 February 1941, I 1438; 17 February 1941, I 1493; 25 February 1941, I 1441; 1 March 1941, I 1442.

49. GSM to Long, 26 February 1941, Long Papers. GSM to Long, 7 April 1941, I 1452.

50. GSM to Roosevelt, 19 April 1941, OF 896, Roosevelt Papers. GSM to Hull, 20 April 1941, I 1455. Walmsley memo, 28 April 1941, *FRUS 1941*, 7:156–57. Welles memo, 5 May 1941, ibid., p. 157. GSM to Hull, 8 May 1941, ibid., pp. 157–65.

51. GSM to Welles, 1 March 1941, I 1442. Hull to GSM, 10 May 1941, *FRUS 1941*, 7:166–67. Collado memo, 23 May 1941, ibid., p. 170. GSM to Hull, 5 June 1941, Hull Papers. Gellman, *Roosevelt*, p. 190. GSM to Hull, 7 June 1941, 837.00/8992; 21 June 1941, 837.00/8994.

52. GSM to Pierson, 21 May 1941, I 1460; 27 May 1941, I 1463. GSM to Bonsal, 5 June 1941, I 1464. GSM to Hull, 15 May 1941, *FRUS 1941*, 7:167–70. GSM to Hull, 5 June 1941, Hull Papers. GSM to Welles, 5 June 1941, I 1465; 5 June 1941, I 1466.

53. Hull to GSM, 13 June 1941, *FRUS 1941*, 7:171. Hull to George, 7 June 1941, Hull Papers. On lend-lease negotiations, *FRUS 1941*, 7:116–26. On airfield negotiations, ibid., pp. 104–9. GSM to Bonsal, 17 November 1941, I 1482.

54. GSM to Welles, 14 June 1941, I 1467. GSM to Hull, 17 June 1941, *FRUS 1941*, 7:176–83.

55. Thus concluded the March 1941 U.S. Department of Agriculture

study of diversification prospects, I 1447.

56. Cortina memo, 14 April 1941, *FRUS 1941*, 7:196–97; 18 April 1941, ibid., pp. 197–98.

57. GSM to Hull, 17 July 1941, ibid., pp. 200–201. Hull to Briggs, 27 September 1941, ibid., pp. 202–8. GSM to Hull, 12 December 1941, ibid., pp. 214–20.

58. Gellman, *Roosevelt*, pp. 202–3. GSM to Long, 13 May 1941, Long Papers. Hull to GSM, 21 October 1941, *FRUS 1941*, 7:238–39.

59. GSM to Welles, 24 October 1941, I 1479.

60. GSM to Hull, 24 October 1941, *FRUS 1941*, 7:239–41. GSM to Hull, 27 October 1941, I 1474. GSM to Hull, 6 November 1941, 837.00/9052. GSM to Clayton, 8 November 1941, I 1481.

61. GSM memo, 25 November 1941, *FRUS 1941*, 7:240–42.

62. Hull to GSM, 1 December 1941, *FRUS 1941*, 7:242–43; 4 December 1941, ibid., pp. 209–13.

63. GSM to Hull, 8 December 1941, *FRUS 1941*, 7:35–36. Batista to Roosevelt, 8 December 1941, ibid., p. 37. GSM to Hull, 12 December 1941, ibid., p. 214. GSM to Welles, 22 January 1942, I 1485.

64. GSM to Welles, 8 December 1941, I 1483. GSM to Hull, 12 December 1941, *FRUS 1941*, 7:214–20. "Cuban Agreement on Sugar Quota," I 1990, GSMM.

65. Walmsley memo, 17 December 1941, *FRUS 1941*, 7:223–24. Hull to GSM, 17 December 1941, ibid., pp. 224–26. Cortina to GSM, 14 December 1941, ibid., pp. 246–49. GSM to Hull, 28 January 1942, ibid., pp. 249–50. *New York Times*, 24 December 1941, p. 27. Hull memo, 18 February 1942, 611.6135/914.

66. "Transfer and Travel to Mexico," I 1995, GSMM. Hull to Roosevelt, 12 November 1941, OF 896, Roosevelt Papers. Hull to Johnson, 28 November 1941, PF 620. GSM to Van Cauwelaert, 15 December 1941, I 1484.

67. GSM to Hull, 28 November 1941, Hull Papers. GSM to Welles, 28 November 1941, PF 627. Welles to GSM, 6 December 1941, PF 628. GSM to Welles, 8 December 1941, I 1483. GSM to Hull, 15 December 1941, PF 626.

68. GSM to Welles, 21 February 1942, I 1486. GSM to Frankfurter, 2 December 1941, Frankfurter Papers. GSM to Spruille Braden, 15 January 1942, Braden Papers.

69. Briggs to Bonsal, 28 January 1942, PF 673. Briggs to Hull, 9 February 1942, PF 655. GSM to Welles, 21 February 1942, I 1486.

70. Briggs to Hull, 27 January 1942, PF 642. GSM to Bonsal, 17 November 1941, I 1482. "Cuban Agreement on Sugar Quota," I 1990, GSMM.

71. Gellman, *Roosevelt*, pp. 201–6. GSM to Hull, 17 June 1941, *FRUS 1941*, 7:172–75.

72. GSM to Hull, 5 June 1941, Hull Papers.

73. Welles to GSM, 6 December 1941, PF 628. GSM to Braden, 15 January 1942, Braden Papers. GSM to Welles, 25 October 1942, I 1551.

Chapter VI

1. Bonsal to Welles, 7 February 1942, PF 652. GSM to Welles, 21 February 1942, I 1486. "Transfer and Travel to Mexico," I 1995, GSMM.

2. GSM to Welles, 24 February 1942, I 1489. GSM to Long, 4 March 1940, Long Papers. Larkin memo, 28 January 1938, 124.121/291.

3. Cronon, *Daniels*, pp. 278–79. GSM to Welles, 24 February 1942, I 1486. GSM to Geist, 7 May 1942, I 1502.

4. Cronon, *Daniels*, pp. 154–84. Stegmaier, Jr., "Confrontation to Cooperation," pp. 1–39. GSM to Heineman, 7 November 1938, I 1607. Wood, *Good Neighbor*, pp. 202–33. Gardner, *Economic Aspects*, pp. 112–19.

5. Cronon, *Daniels*, pp. 200–201. Clash, "United States-Mexican Relations," pp. 7–37. Gellman, *Good Neighbor*, pp. 52–55. Schapsmeiers, *Prophet in Politics*, pp. 40–43. Schmitt, *Mexico and the United States*, p. 185. Camacho quoted in Archer, *Mexico and the United States*, p. 142.

6. Stegmaier, Jr., "Confrontation to Cooperation," pp. 197–229. Cronon, *Daniels*, pp. 230–71. Koppes, "Mexican Oil," pp. 62–81. *New York Times*, 22 April 1942, p. 22.

7. Stegmaier, Jr., "Confrontation to Cooperation," pp. 162–96, 229–40. Harrison, "Military Collaboration," pp. 123–58. Conn and Fairchild, *Hemispheric Defense*, pp. 334–38.

8. GSM to Hull, 6 May 1942, I 1501. GSM to Welles, 21 February 1942, I 1486. "Golf Game with President Ávila Camacho," I 1996, GSMM. GSM to Welles, 20 March 1942, I 1487. Cronon, *Daniels*, pp. 52–55. *El Continental* (El Paso, Texas), 26 February 1942, CF. New York *Sun*, September 1943, CF.

9. *New York Times*, 25 February 1942, p. 6. Finley to Hull, 28 February 1942, PF 669.

10. GSM to Van Cauwelaert, 15 December 1941, I 1484.

11. *New York Times*, 15 February 1942, p. 30. "Commencement Address at the American School," 25 July 1942, I 1516.

12. "Remarks to Pan-American Round Table," 14 April 1942, I 1494. "Remarks at American Colony Dinner," 4 July 1942, I 1520.

13. "Remarks to Foreign Service Conference," 28 April 1942, I 1499. "Remarks at American Colony Dinner," 22 April 1942, I 1497.

14. GSM to Henry Wallace, 17 July 1942, Wallace Papers. GSM to Welles, 20 March 1942, I 1487. GSM to Hull, 6 May 1942, I 1501. GSM to Shaw, 7 August 1942, Hull Papers.

15. GSM to Hull, 6 May 1942, I 1501. GSM to Acheson, 7 August 1942, Hull Papers. GSM to Roosevelt, 10 July 1942, ibid. "Stenographic Report of Ambassador's Remarks," n.d. (late April 1942), I 1500.

16. GSM to Welles, 24 March 1942, I 1488. GSM to Hull, 6 May 1942, Hull Papers. Creel to Hull, 2 January 1942, ibid. GSM to Hull, 20 May 1942, I 1503. GSM to Welles, 1 April 1942, I 1490. GSM to Wallace, 21 July 1942, I 1528.

17. Navy intelligence report, 26 March 1942, 812.00 Cárdenas, Lázaro/257. Entry for 22 May 1942, Stimson Diary. GSM to Hull, 29 May 1942, I 1506.

18. GSM to Hull, 1 September 1942, I 1538. GSM to Hull, 4 January 1944, Hull Papers.

19. Cline, *U.S. and Mexico*, pp. 268–69.

20. GSM to Hull, 6 May 1942, I 1501.

21. GSM to Hull, 20 May 1942, I 1503. "Mexico Declares War—Joins the Allies," I 2000, GSMM. Stegmaier, Jr., "Confrontation to Cooperation," pp. 273–75. *New York Times*, 24 May 1942, p. 3; 29 May 1942, p. 4. GSM to Padilla, 5 June 1942, I 1510. Padilla to GSM, 9 June 1942, I 1511.

22. GSM to Hull, 20 May 1942, I 1503. GSM to Welles, 3 June 1942, I 1509.

23. Harrison, "Military Collaboration," pp. 134–40. GSM to Welles, 17 June 1942, I 1514.

24. Enclosure to GSM #1716, 29 May 1942, I 1505. GSM to Welles, 3 June 1942, I 1508; 17 June 1942, I 1514. Stegmaier, Jr., "Confrontation to Cooperation," pp. 251–54.

25. Stegmaier, Jr., "Confrontation to Cooperation," pp. 245–46, 254–56. Conn and Fairchild, *Hemispheric Defense*, pp. 356–60. GSM to Hull, 1 September 1942, I 1538. GSM to Welles, 17 September 1942, I 1545.

26. GSM to Welles, 21 September 1942, I 1546.

27. Johnson to GSM, 12 December 1942, I 1557.

28. GSM to Johnson, 27 December 1942, I 1561.

29. Stegmaier, Jr., "Confrontation to Cooperation," pp. 248–62.

30. USIAAO, *History of the Coordinator*, pp. 3–10, 181. Thomson and Laves, *Cultural Relations*, pp. 48–50. Haines, "Under Eagle's Wing," pp. 379–88. Erb, "Prelude," pp. 250–51.

31. GSM to Caffery, 5 August 1941, Claude Bowers Papers.

32. GSM to Braden, 26 March 1942; 24 April 1942, Braden Papers. USIAAO, *History of the Coordinator*, p. 251 and insert between pp. 258–59.

33. Duggan to Dreier, 8 May 1942, PF 682 1/2.

34. GSM to Duggan, 27 July 1942, I 1530. GSM to McDermott, 21 August 1942, I 1537. GSM to Duggan, 18 November 1942, I 1554. Berle to GSM, 21 July 1943, Berle Papers. Morris Rosenthal oral history interview, p. 258.

35. GSM to Geist, 7 May 1942, I 1502.

36. GSM to Wallace, 17 July 1942, Wallace Papers. GSM to Shaw, 7 August 1942, Hull Papers. Shaw to Josephus Daniels, 14 November 1945, Daniels Papers. GSM to Duggan, 24 June 1942, I 1515. "The Busiest Spot in Mexico," *Christian Science Monitor*, 20 February 1943, p. 2.

37. GSM to Welles, 3 April 1942, I 1491. GSM to Bowers, 23 March 1944, Bowers Papers. GSM to Bonsal, 8 April 1942, Alan Bateman Papers. Bernstein, *Mexican Mining*, p. 226. Eckes, Jr., *The Search for Minerals*, pp. 94–100.

38. GSM to Welles, 10 June 1942, Bateman Papers. "Procurement Activities—Mexico during the War," I 1999, GSMM. Welles to GSM, 19 March 1942, *FRUS 1942*, 7:483–84. Hull to GSM, 14 May 1942, ibid., pp. 484–85.

39. *New York Times*, 8 April 1942, p. 10; 22 April 1942, p. 22. GSM to Welles, 3 April 1942, I 1491.

40. GSM to Welles, 3 April 1942, I 1491. GSM to Duggan, 24 June 1942,

I 1515. Duggan to GSM, 28 April 1942, 812.6363/7680. Welles to GSM, 22 May 1942, *FRUS 1942*, 6:525–26. Collado to Hull, 1 January 1944, *FRUS 1942*, 7:1234–37. "Railway Mission to Mexico," I 2003, GSMM. "Report on Minerals and Metals Mission to Mexico," Bateman Papers.

41. Hull, *Memoirs*, pp. 1154–57.

42. Acheson, *Present at the Creation*, pp. 68–72. GSM to Hull, 6 May 1942, Hull Papers. GSM to Geist, 7 May 1942, I 1502. Press conf. 823, 1 May 1942, *Complete Press Conferences*, 19:314–15.

43. GSM to Geist, 7 May 1942, I 1502. Markowitz, *The People's Century*, pp. 68–69.

44. GSM to Geist, 7 May 1942, I 1502. GSM to Bateman, 2 June 1942; 10 June 1942; 30 June 1942, Bateman Papers. Hull to GSM, 14 May 1942, *FRUS 1942*, 6:484–85. GSM to Shaw, 7 August 1942, Hull Papers.

45. GSM to Shaw, 7 August 1942, Hull Papers. "Report on Minerals," Bateman Papers. GSM to Bonsal, 26 July 1942, I 1529. Bernstein, *Mexican Mining*, p. 227.

46. Grayson, *Mexican Oil*, pp. 21–23, 239–41. Cline, *U.S. and Mexico*, p. 440. Hull to GSM, 6 August 1942, *FRUS 1942*, 6:528–33.

47. Hull to GSM, 6 August 1942, *FRUS 1942*, 6:528–33. Hull to GSM, 25 July 1942, ibid., pp. 526–27. GSM to Hull, 28 July 1942, ibid., pp. 527–28. Hull to GSM, 20 August 1942, ibid., pp. 533–34.

48. Thornburg to Hull, 3 December 1942, ibid., p. 535. "Report of Mexican Technical Mission," 27 October 1942, 1942, 812.6363/7766. Ickes to Hull, 4 August 1942, OF 146, Roosevelt Papers. Stoff, *Oil, War, and American Security*, pp. 62–68. Feis, *Three International Episodes*, pp. 93–101.

49. Entries for 2 April 1938 and 10 December 1938, *Ickes Diary*, 2:352–53, 521–22. Ickes to Roosevelt, 20 February 1942, OF 56, Roosevelt Papers. Roosevelt to Ickes, 28 February 1942, ibid. Koppes, "Mexican Oil," p. 78.

50. Thornburg to Bonsal, 28 April 1942, 812.6363/7675. Welles to GSM, 22 May 1942, *FRUS 1942*, 6:525–26. Pauley to Roosevelt, 20 April 1942, OF 146a, Roosevelt Papers. Jones to Roosevelt, 27 April 1942, ibid. Ickes to Hull, 4 August 1942, OF 146, ibid. "Conversations with the Mexican Government on the Oil Question," I 2004, GSMM. Details of the Pauley plan came out in February 1946 during Senate confirmation hearings on his abortive nomination as undersecretary of the navy by President Harry S. Truman. *New York Times*, 1 February 1946, p. 3.

51. Ickes to Hull, 4 August 1942, 812.6363/7703. Entries for 21 December 1940 and 12 October 1941, *Ickes Diary*, 3:392, 624–25. Gardner, *Economic Aspects*, pp. 206–7. Koppes, "Mexican Oil," p. 74.

52. Hull to GSM, 6 August 1942, *FRUS 1942*, 6:528–33.

53. GSM to Hull, 1 September 1942, I 1538. Ickes to Roosevelt, 18 October 1941, OF 12, Roosevelt Papers. GSM to Hull, 20 December 1943, *FRUS 1943*, 6:473. GSM to Welles, 3 June 1943, I 1569.

54. Camacho to Roosevelt, 18 April 1942, OF 146, Roosevelt Papers. GSM to Hull, 1 September 1942, I 1538. GSM to Welles, 3 November 1942, 812.6363/7811. GSM to Bonsal, 8 July 1942, I 1524.

55. Welles memo, 2 October 1942, 812.6363/7767. Bonsal to GSM, 24 No-

vember 1942, 812.6363/7814. GSM to Welles, 7 January 1943, *FRUS 1943*, 6:449–52. GSM to Welles, 8 January 1943, 812.6363/7823.

56. GSM #2563, 6 July 1942, 812.6363/7693. "Conversations on Oil," I 2004, GSMM.

57. "Conversations on Oil," I 2004, GSMM. GSM to Welles, 7 January 1943, *FRUS 1943*, 6:452. Pauley's behavior was apparently in character. Testifying at the 1946 confirmation hearings, Max Thornburg, State Department petroleum adviser, revealed that Pauley had also threatened to "liquidate" him unless he, Thornburg, removed his opposition to the Mexican project. *New York Times*, 1 February 1946, p. 3. Pauley defended himself, accusing "Mr. Thornburg and his stooges" of "selfish and dilatory practices" that deprived the United Nations of Mexican oil products during the war. See box 402, Ickes Papers.

58. Roosevelt to Ickes, 23 November 1942, OF 146, Roosevelt Papers. Hull to Roosevelt, 27 November 1942, ibid. Hull to Roosevelt, 14 December 1942, ibid. Ickes to Roosevelt, 16 February 1943, PSF 75, ibid. Duggan to Thornburg, 2 December 1942, 812.6363/7802. Roosevelt to Welles, 19 February 1943, *FRUS 1943*, 6:455. Welles to Roosevelt, 1 March 1943, ibid., pp. 456–57. Ickes to Roosevelt, 20 April 1943, PSF 75, Roosevelt Papers. Hull to Roosevelt, 1 May 1943, OF 146, ibid. Koppes, "Mexican Oil," p. 78.

59. Scruggs, "Mexican Farm Labor Agreement," pp. 140–45. Jones, *Mexican Farm Workers*, p. 1. Hull to GSM, 8 June 1942, *FRUS 1942*, 6:537.

60. GSM to Hull, 23 June 1942, *FRUS 1942*, 6:540–45. GSM to Hull, 8 June 1943, *FRUS 1943*, 6:554–56. Scruggs, "Mexican Farm Labor Agreement," pp. 142–43.

61. GSM to Hull, 23 June 1942, *FRUS 1942*, 6:546. GSM to Wallace, 17 July 1942, Wallace Papers.

62. GSM to Hull, 24 July 1942, *FRUS 1942*, 6:546. Scruggs, "Mexican Farm Labor Agreement," pp. 148–49. Jones, *Mexican War Workers*, pp. 1–14. Craig, *Bracero Program*, pp. 42–50.

63. Jackson to Roosevelt, 1 October 1942, OF 146, Roosevelt Papers. Roosevelt message, n.d., ibid.

64. Scruggs, "Mexican Farm Labor Agreement," pp. 148–49. GSM to Hull, 8 January 1943, *FRUS 1943*, 6:531–32. Bursley to Hull, 18 January 1943, ibid., pp. 534–35. GSM to Hull, 15 April 1943, ibid., pp. 544–45.

65. Hull to Rockefeller, 15 April 1942, 812.77/1484. Lord to Welles, 14 May 1942, 812.77/1494. GSM to Winters, 15 May 1942, 812.77/1495. GSM to Duggan, 14 August 1942, I 1535. GSM to Welles, 27 September 1942, I 1547.

66. Institute of Inter-American Transportation, *Railway Mission in Mexico*, pp. 84–88. USIAAO, *History of the Coordinator*, pp. 32–36. "Railway Mission," I 2003, GSMM.

67. "Railway Mission," I 2003, GSMM. *New York Times*, 3 March 1943, p. 7. *Railway Mission in Mexico*, pp. 3–7, 15–18, and passim. Collado to Hull, 1 January 1944, *FRUS 1944*, 7:1234–37. Clash, "United States-Mexican Relations," pp. 140–57.

68. GSM to Duggan, 24 November 1942, I 1555.

69. Schapsmeiers, *Prophet in Politics*, pp. 44–45. Walker, *Wallace*, pp. 95–96.

70. "Procurement Activities," I 1999, GSMM. GSM to Welles, 3 June 1943, I 1569. GSM to Duggan, 26 February 1944, I 1583.

71. GSM to Wallace, 27 November 1942, I 1556. GSM to Wallace, 16 December 1942, Wallace Papers.

72. GSM to Duggan, 24 November 1942, I 1555. Daniels to Roosevelt, 14 January 1943, PSF 61, Roosevelt Papers. GSM to Cellar, 20 August 1942, I 1536.

73. "Procurement Activities," I 1990, GSMM. Wallace to GSM, 23 November 1942, Wallace Papers. GSM to Wallace, 16 December 1942; 24 December 1942, ibid. GSM to Braden, 6 January 1943, Braden Papers.

74. *New York Times*, 16 January 1943, p. 4. Entry for 27 November 1942, Wallace Diary. "Memorandum of Conversation on the Activities of the Board of Economic Warfare in Mexico," 31 January 1943, I 1562. Entry for 23 January 1945, *Wallace Diary*, pp. 168–70. "Procurement Activities," I 1999, GSMM. Morris Rosenthal, BEW import chief in charge of the rubber program, later admitted that it was "a mess," that "it was a damn good thing all around" when the program was transferred back to RFC in February 1943. Rosenthal oral history interview, pp. 236–42.

75. Entry for 27 January 1943, *Wallace Diary*, p. 170. GSM to Duggan, 26 February 1944, I 1583.

76. Schapsmeiers, *Prophet in Politics*, pp. 50–71. "Procurement Activities," I 1999, GSMM. GSM to Bowers, 30 September 1946, Bowers Papers. GSM to Byrnes, 21 September 1946, 811.002/9–2146. Entry for 9 August 1945, *Wallace Diary*, pp. 472–73. Entry for 7 August 1942, Wallace Diary.

77. *New York Times*, 3 February 1943, p. 3. "Exchange of Visits—FDR and Ávila Camacho," I 2005, GSMM.

78. "Exchange of Visits," I 2005, GSMM. Reilly, *Reilly of the White House*, pp. 131–34. GSM to Welles, 8 March 1943; 22 March 1943, PSF 61, Roosevelt Papers. *New York Times*, 21 April 1943, pp. 1, 11. *Time*, 19 April 1943, cover and pp. 33–37.

79. "Exchange of Visits," I 2005, GSMM. Bonsal to Early, 24 April 1943, OF 200–63, Roosevelt Papers. *New York Times*, 21 April 1943, p. 11. *Time*, 3 May 1943, p. 20.

80. Daniels to Constantine, 28 April 1943, Daniels Papers. GSM to Will Clayton, 29 April 1943, Clayton Papers. GSM to Welles, 30 April 1943, PSF 61, Roosevelt Papers.

81. *Time*, 19 April 1943, pp. 33–34. "Mexico: One Year at War," *Fortune*, August 1943, p. 151. GSM to Hull, 8 April 1943, 812.50/311. GSM #9262, 14 April 1943, I 1565.

82. GSM to Hull, 28 April 1943, PSF 61, Roosevelt Papers. State Department Press Release, 29 April 1943, *FRUS 1943*, 6:417. GSM memo, 27 January 1944, *FRUS 1944*, 7:1198–1201. Mosk, *Industrial Revolution in Mexico*, pp. 91–93.

83. GSM speech before Congress of Public Welfare, 17 August 1943, PF 740. GSM to Welles, 3 June 1943, I 1569. Report of the Mexican-American

Economic Commission, 2 July 1943, OF 5378, Roosevelt Papers.

84. *New York Times*, 1 June 1943, p. 4. GSM to Welles, 3 June 1943, I 1569. Constantine to Daniels, 4 June 1943, Daniels Papers. USIAAO, *History of the Coordinator*, p. 124.

85. GSM to Welles, 3 June 1943, I 1569; 2 June 1943, I 1568.

86. GSM to Bonsal, 29 November 1943, I 1576. Hull to GSM, 26 July 1943, *FRUS 1943*, 6:43. Bonsal to GSM, ibid., p. 433.

87. "Exchange of Visits," I 2005, GSMM. Roosevelt to GSM, 15 October 1943; 25 October 1943, PSF 61, Roosevelt Papers.

88. Stuart, *Department of State*, pp. 382–83. Gellman, *Good Neighbor*, pp. 176–82. Weil, *A Pretty Good Club*, pp. 142–50.

89. GSM to Roosevelt, 23 September 1943, OF 896, Roosevelt Papers.

90. Roosevelt to GSM, 29 September 1943, *FRUS 1943*, 6:436. Berle to GSM, 13 October 1943, ibid., pp. 436–37. Roosevelt to Jones, 14 October 1943, OF 146, Roosevelt Papers. Berle to Roosevelt, 16 October 1943, ibid. Stettinius to Roosevelt, 25 October 1943, ibid. Entry for 15 October 1943, Wallace Diary.

91. Stettinius to GSM, 25 October 1943, *FRUS 1943*, 6:424–26. Duggan to Welles, 9 June 1943, 812.50/346.

92. GSM to Hull, 19 November 1943, *FRUS 1943*, 6:426–29. GSM to Stettinius, 12 December 1943, Berle Papers.

93. Whitaker, ed., *Inter-American Affairs 1943*, p. 44. Gellman, *Good Neighbor*, pp. 175–76. Hull, *Memoirs*, p. 743. Acheson, *Present at the Creation*, p. 62. Entry for 26 January 1945, Berle Diary. "Oumansky in Washington and Mexico City," I 2024, GSMM.

94. "Oumansky in Washington and Mexico City," I 2024, GSMM. Entry for 28 July 1943, Berle Diary, p. 441. GSM to Bonsal, 29 November 1943, I 1576; 13 December 1943, I 1577.

95. GSM to Bonsal, 29 November 1943, I 1576. GSM to Hull, 4 January 1944, Hull Papers.

96. GSM to Hull, 4 January 1944, Hull Papers. GSM to Bonsal, 13 December 1943, I 1577.

97. GSM to Bonsal, 29 November 1943, I 1576; 13 December 1943, I 1577.

98. GSM to Duggan, 10 December 1943, PF 748. GSM to Roosevelt, 31 December 1943, OF 146, Roosevelt Papers. *New York Times*, 1 February 1944, p. 2. GSM memo, 27 January 1944, *FRUS 1944*, 7:1198–1201. Stettinius to GSM, 26 February 1944, ibid., p. 1201. GSM to Hull, 9 March 1944, ibid., pp. 1202–3. Hull to Nelson, 31 March 1944, ibid., pp. 1203–5.

99. State Department to Mexican Embassy, 14 January 1944, *FRUS 1944*, 7:1213. Bursley to Hull, 15 January 1944, ibid., pp. 1213–15. Izquierdo, "Protectionism in Mexico," p. 264.

100. Hull to Bursley, 1 February 1944, *FRUS 1944*, 7:1215–18. GSM to Hull, 12 February 1944, ibid., pp. 1218–19. GSM to Hull, 17 February 1944, ibid., p. 1220.

101. Duggan memo, 5 February 1944, 812.50/2–2544. Phelps to Bonsal,

14 February 1944, 812.50/473a. Bonsal to Duggan, 10 May 1944, *FRUS 1944,* 7:1206–7.

102. GSM #16,364, 9 March 1944, I 1587. GSM to Duggan, 13 April 1944, 812.50/542. GSM to Hawkins, 26 May 1944, I 1593.

103. GSM to Hull, 13 May 1944, *FRUS 1944,* 7:1221–22. Hull to GSM, 29 May 1944, ibid., pp. 1222–24. Acheson to GSM, 12 June 1944, ibid., pp. 1227–28. GSM to Hull, 24 June 1944, ibid., pp. 1228–29. Hansen, *Mexican Development,* p. 48.

104. Bonsal memo, 11 April 1944, 812.50/538. GSM to Duggan, 13 April 1944, 812.50/542. GSM to Duggan, 28 April 1944, I 1591. GSM to Hull, 1 May 1944, 812.50/547. GSM to Hawkins, 9 July 1944, Hull Papers. Hawkins to GSM, 17 July 1944, 812.50/7–944.

105. Hull to GSM, 25 May 1944, 812.50/547. GSM to Hawkins, 9 July 1944, Hull Papers. Stettinius to Roosevelt, 18 January 1945, OF 146a, Roosevelt Papers. State Department *Bulletin,* 4 February 1945, pp. 155–60.

106. State Department *Bulletin,* 4 February 1945, pp. 155–60. Berle to GSM, 20 September 1944, *FRUS 1944,* 7:1230–31. Clayton to GSM, 12 January 1945, *FRUS 1945,* 9:1173–74. GSM to Stettinius, 2 February 1945, ibid., pp. 1174–78. GSM to Byrnes, 13 December 1945, ibid., pp. 1178–87. GSM to Byrnes, 18 January 1946, *FRUS 1946,* 11:1039–41. Bohan to Byrnes, 13 March 1946, ibid., pp. 1043–46. *New York Times,* 16 December 1945, p. 13. GSM to Clayton, 25 January 1946, Clayton Papers. Clash, "U.S.-Mexican Relations," pp. 128–30.

107. Hull to GSM, 12 November 1943, *FRUS 1943,* 6:469–70. GSM to Hull, 30 November 1943, ibid., pp. 470–71.

108. GSM to Hull, 20 December 1943, ibid., pp. 471–72. Duggan memo, 7 December 1943, 812.6363/8059. Powell, *Mexican Petroleum,* p. 194.

109. GSM to Hull, 4 January 1944, Hull Papers. GSM memo, 7 January 1944, PSF 61, Roosevelt Papers. GSM to Hull, 18 April 1944, 812.6363/8165. "Conversations on Oil," I 2004, GSMM.

110. "Conversations on Oil," I 2004, GSMM. GSM to Hull, 24 July 1944, Hull Papers. GSM to Hull, 1 July 1944, *FRUS 1944,* 7:1336–37.

111. GSM to Hull, 22 December 1943, Hull Papers. GSM to Stettinius, 18 February 1944, I 1581. GSM to Roosevelt, 29 June 1944, PSF 61, Roosevelt Papers. GSM to Hull, 1 July 1944, *FRUS 1944,* 7:1336–37. Hull to Roosevelt, 4 July 1944, OF 146, Roosevelt Papers.

112. *New York Times,* 8 July 1944, p. 4. Watson to Crim, 7 July 1944, OF 146, Roosevelt Papers. GSM to Hull, 21 July 1944, Hull Papers.

113. Duggan to GSM, 15 July 1944, *FRUS 1944,* 7:1342. Hull memo, 12 July 1944, ibid., pp. 1338–39. Entry for 6 July 1944, Ickes Diary.

114. GSM to Duggan, 19 July 1944, *FRUS 1944,* 7:1343–46. GSM to Hull, 24 July 1944, Hull Papers. "Conversations on Oil," I 2004, GSMM.

115. Roosevelt to Hull, 19 July 1944, *FRUS 1944,* 7:1346–47. GSM to Hull, 11 September 1944, ibid., pp. 1348–51. GSM to Watson, 12 September 1944, OF 146, Roosevelt Papers. GSM to Roosevelt, 27 November 1944, PSF 61, ibid. "Conversations on Oil," I 2004, GSMM. GSM memo, 19 De-

cember 1944, *FRUS 1944*, 7:1356–58. GSM to Roosevelt, 8 January 1945, PSF 61, Roosevelt Papers. GSM #22,273, 3 January 1945, I 1669.

116. Hull to GSM, 21 July 1944, I 1607. GSM to Hull, 25 July 1944, I 1608; 27 July 1944, I 1616. Padilla to GSM, 26 July 1944, I 1609. Gray to GSM, 28 July 1944, I 1619.

117. GSM to Hull, 5 July 1944, Hull Papers.

118. GSM to Hull, 27 November 1944, I 1659.

119. GSM to Hull, 31 July 1945, Hull Papers. Hull, *Memoirs*, pp. 1715–19. Krock, *Memoirs*, p. 210.

120. "Department—The President," I 2014, GSMM.

121. Stuart, *Department of State*, pp. 412–15. Weil, *A Pretty Good Club*, pp. 178–86. Dallek, *Roosevelt's Foreign Policy*, pp. 502–3. Sherwood, *Roosevelt and Hopkins*, pp. 834–35. Entry for 18 October 1944, *Long Diary*, pp. 387–88. Entry for 28 December 1944, *Wallace Diary*, pp. 418–19. Entry for 27 November 1944, *Stettinius Diary*, pp. 184–87. May, *"Lessons" of the Past*, pp. 3–18. Blum, *Morgenthau Diaries: War Years*, p. 392.

122. Gaddis, *Origins of the Cold War*, pp. 96–97.

123. "Is There Such a Thing as a Good German?" I 1966, GSMM. GSM to Carrigan, 22 March 1945, I 1700. GSM #24,115, 23 April 1945, I 1714.

124. Dallek, *Roosevelt's Foreign Policy*, pp. 472–77.

125. Stuart, *Department of State*, pp. 397–99. Acheson, *Present at the Creation*, pp. 35–37, 131–32. *Berle Diary*, pp. 506–12. Entry for 28 November 1944, *Long Diary*, pp. 390–91. Hopkins to Roosevelt, 28 November 1944, Hopkins Papers.

126. *New York Times*, 15 December 1944, p. 4.

127. Roosevelt to GSM, 14 December 1944, PSF 61, Roosevelt Papers. Roosevelt handed this letter to him during their 19 December conversation. GSM to Stettinius, 17 April 1945, PF.

128. Connell-Smith, *Inter-American System*, pp. 129–30. Gellman, *Good Neighbor*, pp. 202–3. Whitaker, ed., *Inter-American Affairs 1944*, pp. 67–70. Dozer, *Good Neighbors?* pp. 234–36.

129. Gellman, *Good Neighbor*, pp. 187–96. Peterson, *Argentina and the U.S.*, pp. 423–37. Woods, *Roosevelt Foreign Policy Establishment*, pp. 61–160. Smith, Jr., *Yankee Diplomacy*, pp. 66–125. Paz and Ferrari, *Argentina's Foreign Policy*, pp. 117–20. Wood, *Dismantling*, pp. 43–75.

130. GSM to McGurk, 7 August 1944, I 1625. GSM to Hull, 14 August 1944, I 1629. Dozer, *Good Neighbors?* pp. 139–44.

131. Gellman, *Good Neighbor*, p. 196.

132. Embassy memo 3223, 3 November 1944, I 1639. GSM #21,242, 7 November 1944, I 1643. GSM to Hull, 8 November 1944, *FRUS 1944*, 7:39–41. Stettinius to Roosevelt, 11 November 1944, ibid., pp. 42–43. GSM #21,309, 9 November 1944, I 1648. GSM to Armour, 9 November 1944, I 1649. GSM #21,401, 13 November 1944, I 1653. GSM #21,476, 17 November 1944, I 1655. Stettinius to GSM, 17 January 1945, *FRUS 1945*, 9:8. GSM to Stettinius, 18 January 1945, ibid., pp. 9–10. Rockefeller to GSM, 19 January 1945, ibid., pp. 11–12. Peterson, *Argentina and the U.S.*, pp. 440–44.

Woods, *Roosevelt Foreign Policy Establishment*, pp. 160–65. Paz and Ferrari, *Argentina's Foreign Policy*, pp. 127–31.

133. Gellman, *Good Neighbor*, pp. 201–2. Kolko, *Politics of War*, pp. 458–59. Green, *Containment*, pp. 163–68. Campbell, *Masquerade Peace*, pp. 115–17.

134. GSM to Hawkins, 26 May 1944, I 1593. Paterson, *On Every Front*, pp. 33–46.

135. GSM to Roosevelt, 29 June 1944, PSF 61, Roosevelt Papers. GSM to Hull, 4 August 1944, Hull Papers. GSM to McGurk, 24 August 1944, I 1633. GSM #23,057, 11 February 1945, I 1676. GSM to Rockefeller, 12 February 1945, I 1677. "Oumansky," I 2024, GSMM. "Notes for Air War College Lecture, 8 October 1948," I 1894. Cline, *U.S. and Mexico*, pp. 297–98.

136. Woods, *Roosevelt Foreign Policy Establishment*, pp. 56–60, 147–51. Peterson, *Argentina and the U.S.*, pp. 437–40.

137. GSM to Armour, 18 November 1944, I 1657.

138. GSM to Stettinius, 16 January 1945, Edward R. Stettinius Papers. GSM to Stettinius, 25 January 1945, I 1672.

139. GSM to Stettinius, 25 January 1945, I 1672; 13 February 1945, *FRUS 1945*, 7:110–11.

140. Entry for 26 January 1945, Berle Diary. Entry for 20 February 1945, *Berle Diary*, pp. 470–71. Gellman, *Good Neighbor*, pp. 204–5. Warren Austin to GSM, 15 February 1945, Austin Papers.

141. GSM to Stettinius, 9 March 1945, I 1680; 16 January 1945, Stettinius Papers. GSM to Austin, 12 February 1945, Austin Papers. GSM to Newhall, 20 March 1945, I 1698. GSM to Roosevelt, 12 March 1945, I 1684. "Inadequacies of Stettinius as Secretary of State," I 2027, GSMM.

142. Entry for 6 March 1945, Berle Diary, pp. 472–74. American delegation to Grew, 8 March 1945, *FRUS 1945*, 7:149–50. Stettinius statement, 8 March 1945, State Department *Bulletin*, 11 March 1945, pp. 398–400. GSM to Roosevelt, 12 March 1945, I 1684. GSM memo, "The Political Situation in Mexico: Reaction to the Recent Inter-American Conference," 16 March 1945, 812.00/3–1645.

143. Duggan, *The Americas*, p. 116. Connell-Smith, *Inter-American System*, pp. 131–38. Gellman, *Good Neighbor*, pp. 204–9. Campbell, *Masquerade Peace*, pp. 111–29. Woods, *Roosevelt Foreign Policy Establishment*, pp. 182–92. Wood, *Dismantling*, pp. 85–92.

144. Baily, *Development of South America*, pp. 45–48. Department of State, *Report of the Delegation to the Inter-American Conference on Problems of War and Peace, Mexico City*, pp. 277–80. Green, *Containment*, pp. 201–7.

145. State Department *Bulletin*, 4 March 1945, pp. 334–38.

146. Entry for 27 February 1945, *Stettinius Diary*, pp. 277–78. Cline, *U.S. and Mexico*, pp. 280–81. Whitaker, ed., *Inter-American Affairs 1945*, pp. 12–13. For the U.S. draft proposals, State Department *Bulletin*, 4 March 1945, pp. 243–50. Mosk, *Industrial Revolution in Mexico*, pp. 17–19, 33–34.

147. GSM to Carrigan, 22 March 1945, I 1700. Crowley to Roosevelt, 20 March 1945, OF 146, Roosevelt Papers. GSM to Clayton, 11 April 1945, I

1705; 16 January 1946, I 1767. GSM #23,909, 10 April 1945, *FRUS 1945*, 9:1163–68.

148. Hundley, Jr., *Dividing the Waters*, pp. 19–96. GSM to Stettinius, 27 November 1944, I 1661. State Department to Mexican Embassy, 11 February 1942, *FRUS 1942*, 6:547–48. Bursley to Duggan, 10 February 1943, *FRUS 1943*, 6:592–95. Hackworth to Hull, 23 April 1943, ibid., pp. 608–10. GSM to Welles, 13 May 1943, ibid., pp. 611–13. McGurk to Bonsal, 16 August 1943, ibid., pp. 620–21.

149. Duggan to Stettinius, 11 December 1943, *FRUS 1943*, 6:628–29. "Water Treaty between the United States and Mexico," State Department *Bulletin*, 23 March 1944, pp. 282–92.

150. Knox to Roosevelt, 3 February 1944, OF 146a, Roosevelt Papers. Hewes to Roosevelt, 4 February 1944, ibid. Barnes to Roosevelt, 25 April 1944, OF 146, ibid. Roosevelt to Barnes, 28 April 1944, ibid.

151. Hundley, *Dividing the Waters*, p. 145. Roosevelt to GSM, 27 November 1944, PSF 61, Roosevelt Papers. GSM to Rockefeller, 4 January 1945, I 1670.

152. GSM to Meyer, 3 February 1945, I 1673. GSM to Hull, 20 April 1943, *FRUS 1943*, 6:548–50ff. On the air squadron, Harrison, "Military Collaboration," pp. 228–51. "Military Collaboration by Mexico during the War—Squadron 201," I 2031, GSMM.

153. GSM to Meyer, 3 February 1945, I 1673. GSM #25,473, 14 August 1945, Clayton Papers. Food statistics in Duggan, *The Americas*, p. 27. Cline, *U.S. and Mexico*, pp. 284–89.

154. *Washington Post*, 13 February 1945, p. 12. Hundley, *Dividing the Waters*, pp. 160–63. State Department *Bulletin*, 28 January 1945, pp. 122–23. Donovan, *Conflict and Crisis*, pp. 3–4. Truman, *Year of Decisions*, pp. 14–16.

155. "Comparisons: President Roosevelt—Winston Churchill," I 2013, GSMM. GSM to Stettinius, 13 April 1945, Stettinius Papers.

156. GSM #24,106, 21 April 1945, I 1713. GSM to Stettinius, 19 April 1945, I 1710.

157. "What the Passing of President Roosevelt Means to the American Republics," 14 April 1945, I 1707. GSM memorial addresses, 15 and 17 April 1945, attached to GSM to John W. Snyder, 26 April 1945, Snyder Papers. Truman message to Pan American Union Governing Board, 14 April 1945, State Department *Bulletin*, 15 April 1945, p. 669.

158. GSM to Truman, 17 April 1945, PF.

159. GSM to Truman, 25 April 1945, OF 370, Harry S. Truman Papers. Entry for 7 July 1945, *Truman Diary*, pp. 48–49. Truman to Morgan, 28 January 1952, ibid., pp. 234–35. President's Appointments, 29 September 1945, Truman Papers.

160. "First Meeting with President Truman," I 2006, GSMM. GSM to Stettinius, 18 May 1945, Stettinius Papers.

161. GSM to Stettinius, 14 June 1945, Stettinius Papers. GSM to Hull, 31 July 1945, Hull Papers.

162. GSM to Stettinius, 14 June 1945, Stettinius Papers; 12 July 1945,

ibid. Cline, *U.S. and Mexico*, pp. 307–8. Whitaker, ed., *Inter-American Affairs 1945*, pp. 73–74.

163. GSM to Hull, 31 July 1945, Hull Papers; 2 August 1945, ibid. Smedley, "Mexican-U.S. Relations," pp. 95–96.

164. GSM #27,755, 19 December 1945, I 1758. GSM #27,796, 27 December 1945, 812.00/12–2745. *New York Times*, 18 December 1945, p. 17. GSM to Carrigan, 12 January 1946, I 1763.

165. GSM to Carrigan, 12 January 1946, I 1763. GSM #27,773, 21 December 1945, 812.00/12–2145. *New York Times*, 22 December 1945, p. 20.

166. GSM to Rockefeller, 23 March 1945, I 1703. GSM #27,755, 19 December 1945, I 1758. GSM to Carrigan, 27 December 1945, 812.00/12–2745; 12 January 1946, I 1763. GSM to Acheson, 12 January 1946, *FRUS 1946*, 11:971–73. GSM to Braden, 31 January 1946, 812.00/1–3146. GSM to Byrnes, 29 March 1946, 812.00/3–2946. GSM to Carrigan, 26 March 1945, 812.00/3–2646. La Feber, *America, Russia, and the Cold War*, pp. 21–36.

167. GSM to Bowers, 14 February 1946, Bowers Papers.

168. Woods, *Roosevelt Foreign Policy Establishment*, pp. 192–203. Peterson, *Argentina and the U.S.*, pp. 446–49. Smith, *Yankee Diplomacy*, pp. 151–54. Vanucci, "U.S.-Argentine Relations," pp. 194–99. Frank, *Perón vs. Braden*, pp. 57–79.

169. GSM to Braden, 25 July 1945, Braden Papers. Braden to GSM, 18 August 1945, ibid. GSM to Hull, 5 September 1945, Hull Papers.

170. Smith, *Yankee Diplomacy*, pp. 154–60. Peterson, *Argentina and the U.S.*, pp. 450–54. Welles, *Where Are We Headed?* pp. 216–33. Whitaker, *The U.S. and Argentina*, pp. 148–50. *Consultation among the American Republics with Respect to the Argentine Situation: Memorandum of the United States Government* [the *Blue Book*], p. 131. Cabot #490, 14 February 1946, *FRUS 1946*, 11:212. Cabot #465, 13 February 1946, ibid., pp. 210–11. Cabot #671, 7 March 1946, ibid., pp. 229–32.

171. Braden to GSM, 8 March 1946, *FRUS 1946*, 11:232–33. GSM to Braden, 14 March 1946, I 1774; 16 March 1946, I 1775. *New York Times*, 22 March 1946, p. 1.

172. "Harry S. Truman," I 2007. GSMM. GSM to King Carol of Romania, 10 October 1945, I 1738. GSM to Hull, 15 September 1945, I 1728. GSM statement, 7 August 1945, Robert Jackson Papers. *New York Times*, 29 November 1945, p. 1.

173. GSM to Carrigan, 26 January 1946, 812.6363/1–2645. Byrnes to Truman, 11 October 1945, OF 146, Truman Papers. GSM #27,613, 5 December 1945, I 1753. D. Bonsal to GSM, 27 March 1945, PF. Cline, *U.S. and Mexico*, pp. 312–17. Dozer, *Good Neighbors?* p. 233. Smedley, "Mexican-U.S. Relations," p. 116.

174. "Truman," I 2007, GSMM. GSM to Russell, 11 May 1946, PF. Byrnes to Truman, 9 January 1947, PF.

175. *New York Times*, 9 April 1946, p. 1. Havana #1408, 8 April 1946, PF. GSM #29,139, 9 April 1946, PF. Buenos Aires #1057, 12 April 1946, *FRUS 1946*, 11:245.

176. GSM to Carrigan, 23 April 1946, PF. GSM #29,285, 24 April 1946, PF. GSM #29,276, 24 April 1946, PF, quoting Felix F. Palavicini.

Chapter VII

1. *Baltimore Sun*, 11 April 1946, p. 14. *Philadelphia Inquirer*, 10 April 1946, p. 22. *Christian Science Monitor*, 10 April 1946, p. 16. *U.S. News*, 19 April 1946, pp. 78–80. *Time*, 15 April 1946, p. 21.
2. Pach, Jr., "The Containment of U.S. Military Aid," pp. 225–35. Green, "The Cold War Comes to Latin America," pp. 166–67.
3. Vandenberg, Jr., *Vandenberg Papers*, pp. 186–89. *New York Times*, 18 October 1945, p. 4; 23 October 1945, p. 10; 9 April 1946, p. 1. "Washington Merry Go-Round," 23 April 1946 (in *San Francisco Chronicle*, p. 12). Wood, *Dismantling*, p. 102.
4. *New York Times*, 12 April 1946, p. 16. President's Appointments, 11 April 1946, Truman Papers. Schlesinger, Jr., "Good Fences Make Good Neighbors," *Fortune*, August 1946, p. 165. Braden, *Diplomats*, pp. 1–91, 99–100, 116–17.
5. Braden, *Diplomats*, pp. 11, 24–25, 77–80, 99–100, 116–17.
6. For a Latin indictment, Pepper, *I Accuse Braden*. Bushnell, *Santos*, pp. 24–29, 39, 46–48. Gellman, *Roosevelt*, pp. 198–220. An interesting analysis of the "Braden corollary" to the Good Neighbor policy is in Dozer, *Good Neighbors?* pp. 211–20.
7. Braden, *Diplomats*, pp. 316–17. Kelly, *Ruling Few*, p. 307.
8. Kelly, *Ruling Few*, p. 310. Ferns, *Argentina*, p. 185. Alexander, *Perón*, pp. 15, 36–39. Page, *Perón*, p. 70. Braden to GSM, 18 August 1945, Braden Papers. Hodges, *Argentina 1943–1976*, pp. 14–16. Alexander, *Perón Era*, pp. 20–32. Vanucci, "United States–Argentine Relations," pp. 97–109. Wood, *Dismantling*, pp. 97–98.
9. Vanucci, "United States–Argentine Relations," pp. 103–7. Frank, *Perón vs. Braden*, p. 77. Braden, *Diplomats*, p. 376. See, e.g., his tel. 1498, 11 July 1945, *FRUS 1945*, 9:391–93; tel. 2066, 4 September 1945, ibid., pp. 406–8.
10. Page, *Perón*, pp. 24–25. "Notes of Braden Press Conference by Collins of United Press, 18 September 1945," I 1730.
11. Green, *Containment*, p. 252. Kelly, *Ruling Few*, pp. 288, 295. Vanucci, "United States–Argentine Relations," pp. 299–318. Blanksten, *Perón's Argentina*, pp. 199–211. Entry for 15 October 1946, Leahy Diary.
12. Tel. 1387, 30 June 1945, *FRUS 1945*, 9:508–10. Tel. 1388, 30 June 1945, ibid., p. 511. Page, *Perón*, p. 98. "Our Argentine Blunder," *Commonweal*, 8 February 1946, pp. 422–26. Braden, "Germans in Argentina," *Atlantic Monthly*, April 1946, pp. 43–45. Frank, *Perón vs. Braden*, p. 69.
13. GSM to Clayton, 27 April 1946, 812.5018/4–2746. GSM to Russell, 11 May 1946, PF. Spruille Braden oral history interview, p. 744. GSM to Braden, 23 April 1946, Braden Papers. "Harry S. Truman," I 2007, GSMM. A former consul who had made his reputation protecting Americans in Spain during the civil war, Thurston had followed Messersmith's career

path closely. "The U.S. Foreign Service," *Fortune*, August 1946, p. 84.

14. Braden, *Diplomats*, pp. 358–59. May, "The 'Bureaucratic Politics' Approach," pp. 151–53. Messer, *End of an Alliance*, pp. 181–94. Byrnes, *Speaking Frankly*, p. 61.

15. Acheson, *Present at the Creation*, pp. 254–56. "Procurement Activities," I 1999, GSMM. "Developing Events Which Led to the Termination of My Work in Buenos Aires," I 1946, GSMM. Merwin L. Bohan oral history interview, pp. 33–34.

16. GSM tel. 381 (Mexico City), 15 May 1946, *FRUS 1946*, 11:1051–52. GSM to Clayton, 27 April 1946, 812.5018/4–2746. Clayton to Stillwell, 3 May 1946, ibid. Instr. 69, 11 July 1946, PF. Braden oral history interview, pp. 890–91. GSM to Braden, 23 April 1946, Braden Papers.

17. *Time*, 3 June 1946, p. 40.

18. *New York Times*, 23 May 1946, p. 10. *Christian Science Monitor*, 10 April 1946, p. 14.

19. *San Francisco Chronicle*, 21 April 1946, p. 5. *Time*, 3 June 1946, p. 40. Paz and Ferrari, *Argentina's Foreign Policy*, pp. 137–43. "Profiles: Ambassador John Moors Cabot," pp. 39–90, CF. Cabot #2483, 10 April 1946, *FRUS 1946*, 11:241–44.

20. *New York Times*, 24 May 1946, p. 20; 25 May 1946, p. 8. GSM to Byrnes, 6 June 1946, PSF 170, Truman Papers. Braden to Connelly, 20 June 1946, 711.35/6–646.

21. "Conversations with Perón—Buenos Aires," I 2008, GSMM. GSM to Byrnes, 29 May 1946, I 1780.

22. GSM to Byrnes, "Personal for the Secretary," 15 June 1946, PSF 170, Truman Papers. GSM to Byrnes, 15 June 1946, I 1781.

23. GSM to Byrnes, 15 June 1946, I 1781.

24. *New York Times*, 26 June 1946, p. 1; 5 July 1946, p. 1. Irigoyen to GSM, 15 June 1946, I 1782. GSM #219, 24 June 1946, I 1784. GSM memo, 24 June 1946, I 1783. GSM #230, 25 June 1946, I 1786. GSM memo, 24 June 1946, I 1785. *Washington Post*, 27 June 1946, p. 9.

25. *Washington Post*, 27 June 1946, p. 9. GSM #256, 28 June 1946, PF. GSM to Pawley, 6 August 1946, I 1793.

26. GSM to Flack, 5 August 1946, I 1792.

27. Acheson to GSM, 2 July 1946, *FRUS 1946*, 11: 268–69. GSM to Byrnes, 26 July 1946, ibid., pp. 285–89. "Harry S. Truman," I 2007, GSMM. Braden, *Diplomats*, pp. 255, 261, 305, 309. Braden to GSM, 7 October 1942, Braden Papers.

28. GSM to Braden, 6 January 1943, Braden Papers. Rosenthal oral history interview, pp. 258–59.

29. GSM to Hull, 5 September 1945, Hull Papers. GSM to Braden, 6 January 1946, Braden Papers.

30. GSM to Braden, 16 March 1946, I 1775. Braden, *Diplomats*, p. 359.

31. Braden, *Diplomats*, p. 359. "Harry S. Truman," I 2007, GSMM.

32. GSM #26,949, 21 October 1945, 612.325/10–2145. GSM #29,023, 30 March 1946, 612.325/3–3046. Anderson to Byrnes, 23 April 1946, 612.325/4–2346. GSM to Braden, 25 April 1946, 612.325/4–2546.

33. Instr. 8608, 29 April 1946, 612.325/4–846. GSM #29,357, 612.325/5–846.

34. Division of Mexican Affairs memo, 7 May 1946, 612.325/5–746. Acheson to GSM, 7 May 1946, 612.325/5–746.

35. GSM #29,357, 8 May 1946, 612.325/5–846. GSM to Braden, 8 May 1946, Braden Papers. GSM to Acheson, 8 May 1946, ibid.

36. "History of Importation of Zebu Cattle into Mexico," 17 January 1947, *FRUS 1946*, 11:1048–51. Relating the episode in his 1969 memoirs, Acheson wrote that "the bulls were landed with—it was charged—Messersmith's collusion, if not consent" (p. 257). This was one of many factual errors in the passage that moved Merwin Bohan to a heated complaint to the author. Acheson wrote back explaining that the cattle question "was one of the very few incidents that were written of solely from memory," and pleaded *nolo contendere*, promising to try to have the errors corrected. In the second printing, the chronology, which had had Messersmith moving *from* Argentina *to* Mexico, was straightened out, but the charge of collusion remained. See the Bohan correspondence, I 2058 a–h, Messersmith Papers. Entry for 14 October 1946, Leahy Diary.

37. "History of Zebu Imports," 17 January 1947, *FRUS 1946*, 11:1048–51. On the control effort, Machado, Jr., *Aftosa*. Braden, *Diplomats*, p. 359.

38. GSM to Bowers, 11 June 1946, PF.

39. Acheson to GSM, 2 July 1946, *FRUS 1946*, 11:268–69.

40. Braden to GSM, 22 July 1946, I 1788.

41. Allen and Shannon, *Truman Merry-Go-Round*, p. 25. Braden, *Diplomats*, pp. 360–61.

42. Acheson to Truman, 12 July 1946, *FRUS 1946*, 11:270–78. Truman to Acheson, ibid., p. 282. Braden memo, 12 July 1946, PSF 170, Truman Papers. Braden to GSM, 30 July 1946, ibid.

43. *Washington Post*, 21 July 1946, p. 4b; 9 August 1946, p. 17; 11 August 1946, p. 2b. *New York Times*, 8 July 1946, p. 4; 11 July 1946, p. 4; 19 July 1946, p. 10; 2 August 1946, p. 5; 10 August 1946, p. 12.

44. Burrows memo, 12 August 1946, I 1794.

45. GSM to Byrnes, 16 August 1946, PSF 170, Truman Papers, is printed in *FRUS 1946*, 11:302–3, which, however, omits mention of the Burrows-Spaeth conversation.

46. GSM #561, 12 August 1946, PSF 170, Truman Papers.

47. GSM tel. 1082, 15 August 1946, I 1795. GSM #583, 15 August 1946, PSF 170, Truman Papers. GSM to Truman, 16 August 1946, ibid., GSM to Byrnes, 16 August 1946, ibid., GSM to Acheson, 16 August 1946, ibid.

48. *Washington Post*, 27 July 1946, p. 1; 17 August 1946, p. 1. Acheson to GSM, 29 August 1946, *FRUS 1946*, 11:309–10. On the same date, Acheson wrote Truman that Messersmith's suspicion of Braden was neither "fair (n)or justified." PSF 170, Truman Papers.

49. For Wallace's view of Perón, Thurston to Braden, 3 September 1946, 711.61/9–346. Entry for 28 August 1946, Wallace Diary. This passage is deleted in the published *Wallace Diary*, p. 610.

50. *Wallace Diary*, p. 610 n. 1. Braden, *Diplomats*, p. 359. *Frankfurter Diary*, p. 277, n. 6. Allen to Truman, 23 January 1946, 812.00/1–2346. Braden to Allen, 23 January 1946, 812.00/1–2346. GSM #28,201, 29 January 1946, 812.00/1–2946. Desp. 99 (Nuevo Laredo), 4 February 1946, 812.00/2–446. "Procurement Activities," I 1999, GSMM.

51. *New York Times*, 12 May 1946, p. 28.

52. *Daily Worker*, 27 August 1946, pp. 1–2; 28 August 1946, p. 7, demanding editorially that Messersmith be fired. Entry for 28 August 1946, *Wallace Diary*, pp. 610–12.

53. *New York Times*, 5 September 1946, p. 3. GSM to Braden, 3 September 1946, 711.61/9–346; 18 September 1946, 711.61/9–1846, enclosing American Legion *Bulletin*, September 1946.

54. De Santis, *Diplomacy of Silence*, pp. 170–98. Herken, *Winning Weapon*, pp. 97–100. La Feber, *America, Russia, and the Cold War*, p. 54.

55. De Santis, *Diplomacy of Silence*, p. 3. GSM to Braden, 3 September 1946, 711.61/9–346.

56. Entries for 21 November 1945 and 28 August 1946, *Wallace Diary*, pp. 518, 611.

57. *New York Times*, 29 August 1946, p. 8; 31 August 1946, p. 7; 3 September 1946, p. 8. "Ratification of the Acts of Chapultepec," I 2009, GSMM. GSM #651, 28 August 1946, PSF 170, Truman Papers. Paz and Ferrari, *Argentina's Foreign Policy*, pp. 141–42. GSM #730, 10 September 1946, I 1803. GSM to Byrnes, 30 October 1946, I 1813.

58. Mann to GSM, 30 September 1946, *FRUS 1946*, 11:317–19. Acheson to GSM, 25 September 1946, ibid., pp. 311–16. GSM #1004, 15 October 1946, ibid., pp. 325–32.

59. On Russian activities, GSM to Acheson, 2 October 1946, 711.61/10–246AW. GSM to Clayton, 31 October 1946, I 1815. GSM to Sulzberger, 25 September 1946, I 1807. On arms overtures, GSM #969, 9 October 1946, PSF 170, Truman Papers. GSM #983, 11 October 1946, ibid. GSM #1309, 25 November 1946, I 1819.

60. Paz and Ferrari, *Argentina's Foreign Policy*, pp. 155–56. Alexander, *Perón Era*, pp. 156–58. Blanksten, *Perón's Argentina*, pp. 240–41.

61. *New York Times*, 1 August 1946, p. 9. GSM to Clayton, 3 September 1946, PSF 170, Truman Papers.

62. GSM to Clayton, 3 September 1946, PSF 170, Truman Papers.

63. GSM to Clayton, 5 September 1946, ibid.; 19 September 1946, ibid. *Washington Post*, 17 September 1946, p. 1. *New York Times*, 18 September 1946, p. 13.

64. *La Prensa* (Buenos Aires), 19 August 1946, quoted in Paz and Ferrari, *Argentina's Foreign Policy*, p. 158. *Washington Post*, 20 September 1946, p. 20. *New York Times*, 18 September 1946, p. 13.

65. Leeper to GSM, 21 September 1946, PSF 170, Truman Papers. GSM to Clayton, 25 September 1946, ibid.

66. GSM to Clayton, 19 September 1946, ibid. Bowen, "The End of Hegemony," ignores the larger context of Argentine-American relations in an un-

successful attempt to explain Messersmith's intervention, pp. 21–22. Kolkos, *Limits of Power*, p. 77. GSM to Acheson, 2 October 1946, 711.61/10–246AW. "British-Argentine Agreement for the Purchase of Meat," I 1947, GSMM.

67. Correspondence between Treasury Secretary John Snyder and Hugh Dalton, chancellor of the exchequer, cited in Gardner, *Sterling Dollar Diplomacy*, pp. 319–20. On the British loan, see Gardner, *Sterling*, pp. 208ff., and Gardner, *Architects of Illusion*, pp. 113–38. *Washington Post*, 10 October 1946, p. 2. *New York Times*, 1 November 1946, p. 10.

68. GSM to Truman, 12 October 1946, PSF 170, Truman Papers. GSM to Byrnes, 12 October 1946, ibid. GSM to Byrnes, 15 October 1946, ibid. GSM to Acheson, 16 October 1946, ibid.

69. Donovan, *Conflict and Crisis*, pp. 229–31. *New York Times*, 22 October 1946, p. 1; 23 October 1946, p. 30; 27 October 1946, 4:12. GSM to Truman, 23 October 1946, PSF 170, Truman Papers. Entry for 21 October 1946, *Frankfurter Diary*, p. 278.

70. *New York Times*, 1 November 1946, p. 10; 22 October 1946, p. 13. Alexander, *Perón Era*, pp. 159–60. Blanksten, *Perón's Argentina*, pp. 254–55. Page, *Perón*, pp. 168–70.

71. *New York Post*, 24 October 1946, p. 12.

72. Ibid. GSM to Byrnes, 30 October 1946, I 1814.

73. Blanksten, *Perón's Argentina*, p. 254. Whitaker, *U.S. and Argentina*, pp. 153, 230–31. Alexander, *Perón Era*, pp. 184–86. Page, *Perón*, pp. 68–69, 164–67. Alexander, *Perón*, pp. 54–66. *New York Times*, 31 August 1946, p. 7; 9 November 1946, p. 16; 11 November 1946, p. 4.

74. GSM to Sulzberger, 25 September 1946, I 1807. GSM #1199, 13 November 1946, I 1818. GSM #1365, 2 December 1946, I 1822. For typically sensational Prewett stories, see *Washington Post*, 2 October 1946, p. 14, and her "Colonel Perón's New Order," *The Nation*, 8 June 1946, pp. 685–86. Prewett, *Beyond the Great Forest*, pp. 26–28. Kluckhohn was separated from the *Times* early in 1947. See GSM #2400, 29 April 1947, I 1876.

75. GSM to Byrnes, 3 October 1946, 111.12 Braden/10–2946. Byrnes to GSM, 29 October 1946, ibid.

76. GSM to Byrnes, 30 October 1946, PSF 170, Truman Papers. GSM to Byrnes, 19 November 1946, *FRUS 1946*, 11:333–35.

77. *New York Times*, 17 December 1946, p. 4; 18 December 1946, p. 25; 21 December 1946, p. 5; 24 December 1946, p. 8. *Time*, 2 December 1946, cover and pp. 22–24. Entry for 7 January 1947, Berle Diary.

78. *New York Times*, 2 January 1947, p. 15; 8 January 1947, pp. 1, 11; 12 January 1947, p. 1. For the talks with Byrnes, "Harry S. Truman," I 2007, GSMM. Clippings filed under 711.35. Entries for 10 and 23 January 1947, Leahy Diary. O'Donoghue to Marshall, 24 January 1947, *FRUS 1947*, 8:169–70. Acheson memo, 27 January 1947, ibid., pp. 171–72. Tewksbury to Marshall, 31 January 1947, I 1842. Paz and Ferrari, *Argentina's Foreign Policy*, p. 143. Wood, *Dismantling*, pp. 117–18.

79. Woodward to Connelly, 10 January 1947, OF 370, Truman Papers. President's Appointments, 15 January 1947, ibid. "Harry S. Truman," I

2007, GSMM. *Newsweek*, 27 January 1947, p. 51. *Chicago Sun* editorial quoted in Prewett, *Beyond the Great Forest*, pp. 27–28.

80. Braden, *Diplomats*, p. 363. Acheson, *Present at the Creation*, p. 285. *Newsweek*, 3 February 1947, p. 48. Mann memo, 21 January 1947, *FRUS 1947*, 8:166–68. GSM to Marshall, 21 January 1947, 711.35/1–2147. GSM memo, 24 January 1947, I 1841. GSM to Marshall, 4 February 1947, PF.

81. *New York Times*, 1 February 1947, p. 2; 2 February 1947, p. 17. GSM to Littell, 12 March 1947, I 1859. GSM to Arthur Bliss Lane, 7 February 1947, Lane Papers. Wood, *Dismantling*, p. 117.

82. GSM tel. 134, 7 February 1947, *FRUS 1947*, 8:173–76. Braden to Acheson, 7 February 1947, ibid., pp. 176–78. State tel. 112, 12 February 1947, ibid., pp. 179–81. GSM to Pawley, 7 February 1947, I 1844. GSM #1850, 13 February 1947, I 1846. GSM to Marshall, 21 February 1947, I 1851. GSM #1883, 21 February 1947, I 1852. *New York Times*, 19 February 1947, p. 14.

83. GSM to Welles, 12 March 1947, I 1858. See Welles's 12 February 1947 column, *Washington Post*, p. 14. GSM to Sulzberger, 3 April 1947, I 1871.

84. GSM to Deerwester, 2 April 1947, I 1867.

85. Ibid. De Conde, "Marshall," pp. 250–51. Mann memo, 3 March 1947, 711.35/3–347.

86. State tel. 252, 2 April 1947, *FRUS 1947*, 8:186–87. *New York Times*, 15 April 1947, pp. 1, 16.

87. GSM to Acheson, 3 April 1947, I 1870; 11 April 1947, I 1872; 25 April 1947, I 1875. GSM #2462, I 1879.

88. Marshall to GSM, 7 May 1947, *FRUS 1947*, 8:193. GSM to Marshall, 8 May 1947, I 1880. *New York Times*, 23 September 1983, p. 1.

89. Pach, Jr., "The Containment of U.S. Military Aid," p. 215.

90. Braden, *Diplomats*, p. 367. Green, "Cold War Comes to Latin America," p. 171.

91. *New York Times*, 3 June 1947, p. 1; 5 June 1947, pp. 1, 28. Layton telephone interview. Marshall to GSM, 4 June 1947, I 1887.

92. *Buenos Aires Standard*, 28 January 1947, CF. "Braden or Messersmith," *The Nation*, 1 February 1947, pp. 116–17. *Newsweek*, 26 May 1947, p. 15. GSM to Marshall, 5 June 1947, I 1889.

93. "Developing Events," I 1949, GSMM. Ivanissevich to Truman, 5 June 1947, OF 270, Truman Papers. Truman to Ivanissevich, 14 June 1947, ibid. *New York Times*, 7 June 1947, p. 8. GSM to Truman and Marshall, 6 June 1947, I 1893.

94. GSM to Truman and Marshall, 6 June 1947, I 1893. GSM to Marshall, 5 June 1947, I 1890. Memo on Truman announcement, n.d. (5 June 1947), I 1891–92. *New York Times*, 6 June 1947, p. 8.

95. GSM to Truman and Marshall, 6 June 1947, I 1893. Byrnes to Truman, 9 January 1947, PF.

96. Desp. 2706, 19 June 1947, I 1893a. *New York Times*, 19 June 1947, p. 18; 22 June 1947, p. 34. *Washington Post*, 22 June 1947, p. 1. *Newsweek*, 30 June 1947, p. 40. Desp. 2726, 25 June 1947, PF.

Epilogue

1. "Developing Events," I 1949, GSMM.

2. Ibid. GSM to Clayton, 16 June 1947, Clayton Papers. Armour to Marshall, 17 July 1947, PF. Woodward to Connelly, 17 July 1947, OF 370, Truman Papers. President's Appointments, 27 August 1947, ibid. Braden, *Diplomats*, p. 370.

3. Trask, "The Messersmith and Braden Conflict." Summary of United States newpaper comment, CF. *Washington Post*, 30 June 1947, p. 11. Paz and Ferrari, *Argentina's Foreign Policy*, pp. 144–47. Peterson, *Argentina and the U.S.*, pp. 466–67.

4. *New York Times*, 28 August 1947, p. 5. GSM memo, 23 July 1947, PF. *American Foreign Service Journal*, August 1947, p. 20.

5. "Developing Events," I 1949, GSMM.

6. Ibid. GSM to Braden, 18 September 1946, I 1804. GSM to Bowers, 23 May 1947, Bowers Papers. *New York Times*, 14 October 1947, p. 16. Entry for 12 November 1947, Leahy Diary.

7. "Developing Events," I 1949, GSMM. GSM to Corrigan, 11 April 1948, Corrigan Papers. GSM to Sypherd, 1 May 1951, I 1901.

8. GSM to Sypherd, 31 July 1953, I 1904; 29 November 1953, I 1906. On Mexlight, Wionczek, "Electric Power," pp. 75–77. Combined Mexican Working Party, *Economic Development*, pp. 270–71.

9. "Notes for Air War College Lecture, October 8, 1948," I 1984. "Notes for Air War College Address, April 25, 1950," I 1896. "Influence of Fear in Attitude toward War," I 2012, GSMM.

10. GSM to Bohan, 22 December 1950, Bohan Papers. Sypherd to GSM, 24 February 1951, I 1899. GSM to Sypherd, 29 November 1954, I 1906; 12 April 1955, I 1910; 10 August 1955, I 1915; 6 September 1955, I 1916. "Scope of Memoirs," I 1934, GSMM. "Memo to Myself," I 1936, GSMM.

11. GSM to Sypherd, 21 April 1955, I 1912. *New York Times*, 20 January 1960, p. 21; 2 February 1960, p. 35; 18 November 1966, p. 43.

12. Bohan to Mrs. GSM, 30 January 1960, Bohan Papers. Layton telephone interview. Offner, *American Appeasement*, p. 237. Dallek, "Beyond Tradition," p. 237. Weinberg, *Hitler's Foreign Policy II*, pp. 254–55.

13. "Recognition at Last for a Diplomat," *Wilmington* [Delaware] *News-Journal*, 20 October 1982. Mary Ann Pike to author, 5 January 1983. See, e.g., Paterson et al., *American Foreign Policy*, pp. 329, 402.

14. See, e.g., Koppes, "Mexican Oil," p. 75. Green, *Containment*, pp. 302–3, 327–29. Kolko, *Politics*, pp. 459–61. Smedley, "Mexican-U.S. Relations," p. 114, n. 18. Taylor, "Axis Replacement Program," p. 153.

15. Offner, *American Appeasement*, pp. 239–44. Cf. entry for 23 January 1944, Ickes Diary. Entry for 21 August 1946, *Frankfurter Diary*, p. 278. Rosenthal oral history interview, p. 258.

16. Moss, "Messersmith and the Diplomacy of Limits," p. 114.

Bibliography

Archives and Manuscript Collections

Bloomington, Indiana
Lilly Library, Indiana University
   Claude Bowers Papers.

Burlington, Vermont
Bailey/Howe Library, University of Vermont
   Warren Austin Papers.

Cambridge, Massachusetts
Houghton Library, Harvard University
   William Phillips Diary and Papers.
   Jay Pierrepont Moffat Diary and Papers.

Charlottesville, Virginia
Alderman Library, University of Virginia
   Edward R. Stettinius Papers.

Hyde Park, New York
Franklin D. Roosevelt Library
   Adolf A. Berle Diary and Papers.
   Francis P. Corrigan Papers.
   Harry Hopkins Papers.
   R. Walton Moore Papers.
   Franklin D. Roosevelt Papers.
   Henry Wallace Papers (microfilm).
   John C. Wiley Papers.

Independence, Missouri
Harry S. Truman Library
   Merwin S. Bohan Papers.
   Will Clayton Papers.
   Robert Jackson Papers.
   Herschel V. Johnson Papers.
   John Snyder Papers.
   Harry S. Truman Papers.

Newark, Delaware
University of Delaware Archives

Department of Special Collections, University of Delaware
George S. Messersmith Papers.
Ruth Alford, "Introduction to the Messersmith Papers" (typescript index).
Hugh R. Wilson Papers (photocopies).

New Haven, Connecticut
Yale University Library
Alan Bateman Papers.
Arthur Bliss Lane Papers.
John F. Montgomery Papers.
Henry L. Stimson Diary and Papers.

New York, New York
Rare Book and Manuscript Library, Columbia University
Spruille Braden Papers.
Henry Wallace Diary.

Reading, Pennsylvania
Berks County Historical Society Library.
Local records.

Washington, D.C.
Manuscripts Division, Library of Congress
Wilbur Carr Diary and Papers.
Josephus Daniels Papers.
Norman Davis Papers.
William E. Dodd Papers.
Herbert Feis Papers.
Felix Frankfurter Papers.
Leland Harrison, Jr., Papers.
Cordell Hull Papers (microfilm).
Harold Ickes Diary and Papers.
Frank Knox Papers.
William D. Leahy Diary.
Breckinridge Long Papers.
John Bassett Moore Papers.

Washington, D.C.
National Archives
United States Department of State, Central Decimal Files, Record Group 59.

Interviews

Fleetwood, Pennsylvania
Mrs. Quentin Messersmith (by author).

Independence, Missouri
Harry S. Truman Library
  Merwin S. Bohan.
  Paul C. Daniels.

New York, New York
Columbia University Oral History Project
  Spruille Braden.
  Robert Jackson.
  Morris Rosenthal.

Yonkers, New York
  Rodney Layton (by author).
  Virginia Orr (by author).
  Ann Scott (by author).

Other Unpublished Material

Clash, Thomas Wood. "United States-Mexican Relations, 1940–1946: A Study of U.S. Interests and Policies." Ph.D. dissertation, State University of New York, Buffalo, 1972.

Harrison, Donald Fisher. "United States-Mexican Military Collaboration During World War II." Ph.D. dissertation, Georgetown University, 1976.

Moss, Kenneth. "Bureaucrat as Diplomat: George S. Messersmith and the State Department's Approach to War, 1933–1941." Ph.D. dissertation, University of Minnesota, 1978.

Smedley, Max Jewel. "Mexican-American Relations and the Cold War, 1945–1954." Ph.D. dissertation, University of Southern California, 1981.

Stegmaier, Jr., Harry I. "From Confrontation to Cooperation: The United States and Mexico, 1938–1945." Ph.D. dissertation, University of Michigan, 1970.

Trask, Roger R. "The Conflict between George S. Messersmith and Spruille Braden, 1945–1947." Paper delivered to a Symposium on "Conflict in the Department of State over Latin American Policy, 1937–1947," 29 December 1979, at the annual meeting of the American Historical Association, New York, New York.

Vannucci, Albert Philip. "United States–Argentine Relations, 1943–1948: A Case Study in Confused Policy Making." Ph.D. dissertation, New School for Social Research, 1978.

Documents

The Complete Press Conferences of Franklin D. Roosevelt. Vols. 12–20 (1938–43). New York, 1972.

Messersmith, George S. "Address to the National Foreign Trade Convention, Cleveland, Ohio, Nov. 3, 1937," State Department Commercial Policy Series No. 40. Washington, D.C., 1937.

Mitchell, B. R., ed. *European Historical Statistics*. New York, 1975.

Nixon, Edgar B., ed. *Franklin D. Roosevelt and Foreign Affairs*. 3 vols. Cambridge, Massachusetts, 1969.

United States Congress. *Congressional Record*. 75th–77th Congress. Washington, D.C., 1937–40.

————. House Appropriations Subcommittee Hearings. 75th–76th Congress. Washington, D.C., 1938–39.

————. House Ways and Means Committee Hearings. 70th Congress. Washington, D.C., 1928.

United States Department of State. *Bulletin, Department of State*, 1942–47.

————. *Consultation among the American Republics with Respect to the Argentine Situation: Memorandum of the United States Government*. Washington, D.C., 1946.

————. *Foreign Relations of the United States: Diplomatic Papers*. Annual vols., 1929–47. Washington, D.C., 1946–74.

————. *Peace and War: United States Foreign Policy, 1931–1941*. Washington, D.C., 1942.

————. *Register of the Department of State*. Annual vols., 1914–47. Washington, D.C., 1915–48.

————. *Report of the Delegation to the Inter-American Conference on Problems of Peace and War, Mexico City, Feb. 21–Mar. 8, 1945*. Washington, D.C., 1946.

Books and Articles

Acheson, Dean. *Present at the Creation*. New York, 1969.

Adams, D. K. "Messersmith's Appointment to Vienna in 1934: Presidential Patronage or Career Promotion?" *Delaware History* 18 (Summer 1978): 17–27.

Alexander, Robert J. *Juan Domingo Perón: A History*. Boulder, Colorado, 1979.

————. *The Perón Era*. New York, 1951.

Allen, Robert S., and William V. Shannon. *The Truman Merry-Go-Round*. New York, 1950.

Archer, Jules. *Mexico and the United States*. New York, 1973.

Armstrong, Hamilton Fish. *Peace and Counterpeace from Wilson to Hitler*. New York, 1971.

Baily, Samuel L. *The United States and the Development of South America, 1945–1975*. New York, 1976.

Barnes, William, and John Heath Morgan. *The Foreign Service of the United States*. Washington, D.C., 1961.

Beaulac, Willard L. *Career Ambassador*. New York, 1951.

Bemis, Samuel Flagg. *The Latin American Policy of the United States*. New York, 1967 edition.

Bendiner, Robert. *The Riddle of the State Department.* New York, 1942.

Berle, Beatrice Bishop, and Travis Beal Jacobs. *Navigating the Rapids 1918–1971: From the Papers of Adolf A. Berle.* New York, 1973.

Bernstein, Marvin D. *The Mexican Mining Industry 1890–1950.* Albany, New York, 1965.

Blanksten, George I. *Peron's Argentina.* Chicago, 1953.

Blum, John Morton. *From the Morgenthau Diaries: Years of War, 1941–1945.* Boston, 1967.

———, ed. *The Price of Vision: The Diary of Henry A. Wallace, 1942–1946.* Boston, 1973.

Bowen, Nicholas. "The End of British Hegemony in Argentina: Messersmith and the Eady-Miranda Agreement." *Inter-American Economic Affairs* 28, no. 4 (Spring 1975): 3–24.

Bracher, Karl Dietrich. *The German Dictatorship.* New York, 1970.

Braddick, Henderson B. "The Hoare-Laval Plan: A Study in International Politics." In Hans W. Gatzke, ed., *European Diplomacy between Two Wars 1919–1939*, pp. 152–71. Chicago, 1972.

Braden, Spruille. *Diplomats and Demagogues.* New Rochelle, New York, 1975.

Brook-Shepherd, Gordon. *The Anschluss.* Phildelphia, 1963.

———. *Dollfuss.* London, 1961.

Bullitt, Orville H., ed. *For the President Personal and Secret: Correspondence between Franklin D. Roosevelt and William C. Bullitt.* Boston, 1972.

Bullock, Alan. *Hitler: A Study in Tyranny.* New York, 1964.

Bushnell, David. *Eduardo Santos and the Good Neighbor 1938–1942.* Gainesville, Florida, 1967.

Byrnes, James F. *Speaking Frankly.* New York, 1947.

Campbell, Thomas M. *Masquerade Peace.* Tallahassee, Florida, 1973.

———, and George C. Herring, eds. *The Diaries of Edward R. Stettinius, Jr., 1943–1946.* New York, 1975.

Cline, Howard F. *The United States and Mexico.* New York, 1963 edition.

Combined Mexican Working Party. *The Economic Development of Mexico.* Baltimore, 1953.

Conn, Stetson, and Byron Fairchild. *The Framework of Hemispheric Defense.* Washington, D.C., 1960.

Connell-Smith, Gordon. *The Inter-American System.* London, 1966.

Costigliola, Frank. "The United States and the Reconstruction of Germany in the 1920's." *Business History Review* 50, no. 4 (1976): 477–502.

Craig, Gordon A. "The German Foreign Office from Neurath to Ribbentrop." In Gordon C. Craig and Felix Gilbert, eds., *The Diplomats 1919–1939*, vol. 2, pp. 406–36. New York, 1963.

Craig, Richard B. *The Bracero Program.* Austin, Texas, 1971.

Crane, Katherine. *Mr. Carr of State.* New York, 1960.

Cremin, Lawrence A. *The Transformation of the Schools: Progressivism in American Education, 1876–1957.* New York, 1962.

Cronon, E. David. *Josephus Daniels in Mexico.* Madison, Wisconsin, 1960.

Dallek, Robert. "Beyond Tradition: The Diplomatic Careers of William E.

Dodd and George S. Messersmith, 1933–1938." *South Atlantic Quarterly* 66, no. 2 (Spring 1967): 233–44.

———. *Democrat and Diplomat: The Life of William E. Dodd*. New York, 1968.

———. *Franklin D. Roosevelt and American Foreign Policy 1932–1945*. New York, 1979.

Davies, Joseph E. *Mission to Moscow*. New York, 1941.

De Conde, Alexander. "George Catlett Marshall." In Norman A. Graebner, ed., *An Uncertain Tradition: American Secretaries of State in the Twentieth Century*, pp. 245–66. New York, 1961.

De Santis, Hugh. *The Diplomacy of Silence*. Chicago, 1980.

Divine, Robert. *Roosevelt and World War II*. Baltimore, 1969.

Dodd, Martha. *Through Embassy Eyes*. New York, 1939.

———, and William E. Dodd, Jr., eds. *Ambassador Dodd's Diary, 1933–1938*. New York, 1941.

Donovan, Robert J. *Conflict and Crisis: The Presidency of Harry S. Truman 1945–1948*. New York, 1977.

Dozer, Donald M. *Are We Good Neighbors?* Gainesville, Florida, 1959.

Drummond, Donald F. "Cordell Hull." In Norman A. Graebner, ed., *An Uncertain Tradition: American Secretaries of State in the Twentieth Century*, pp. 184–209. New York, 1961.

Duggan, Laurence. *The Americas*. New York, 1949.

Eckes, Alfred E., Jr. *The United States and the Global Search for Minerals*. Austin, Texas, 1979.

Edmondson, C. Earl. *The Heimwehr and Austrian Politics 1918–1936*. Athens, Georgia, 1978.

Erb, Claude C. "Prelude to Point Four: The Institute of Inter-American Affairs." *Diplomatic History* 9, no. 3 (Summer 1985): 249–69.

Eyck, Erich. *A History of the Weimar Republic*. 2 vols. Cambridge, Massachusetts, 1963.

Farber, Samuel. *Revolution and Reaction in Cuba, 1933–1960*. Middletown, Connecticut, 1976.

Farnsworth, Beatrice. *William C. Bullitt and the Soviet Union*. Bloomington, Indiana, 1967.

Feingold, Henry L. *The Politics of Rescue*. New Brunswick, New Jersey, 1970.

Feis, Herbert. *1933: Characters in Crisis*. Boston, 1966.

———. *Three International Episodes Seen from E.A.* New York, 1966 edition.

Ferns, H. S. *Argentina*. New York, 1969.

Ferrell, Robert H., ed. *Off the Record: The Private Papers of Harry S. Truman*. New York, 1980.

Fest, Joachim. *Hitler*. New York, 1973.

Fite, Gilbert C. *George N. Peek and the Fight for Farm Parity*. Norman, Oklahoma, 1954.

Ford, Franklin L. "Three Observers in Berlin: Rumbold, Dodd, and François-Poncet." In Gordon C. Craig and Felix Gilbert, eds., *The Diplomats*, vol. 2, pp. 437–76. New York, 1963.

Frank, Gary. *Juan Perón vs. Spruille Braden: The Story behind the Blue Book*. Lanham, Maryland, 1980.

Freidel, Frank. *FDR: Launching the New Deal.* Boston, 1973.

Fromm, Bella. *Blood and Banquets: A Berlin Social Diary.* New York, 1942.

Frye, Alton. *Nazi Germany and the American Hemisphere.* New Haven, Connecticut, 1967.

Gaddis, John Lewis. *The United States and the Origins of the Cold War, 1941–1947.* New York, 1972.

Gallo, Max. *The Night of the Long Knives.* New York, 1972.

Gardner, Lloyd C. *Architects of Illusion.* Chicago, 1970.

_____. *Economic Aspects of New Deal Diplomacy.* Boston, 1971.

Gardner, Richard N. *Sterling-Dollar Diplomacy.* London, 1956.

Gehl, Jürgen. *Austria, Germany, and the Anschluss 1931–1938.* London, 1968.

Gellman, Irwin F. *Good Neighbor Diplomacy: United States Policy in Latin America 1933–1945.* Baltimore, 1979.

_____. *Roosevelt and Batista.* Albuquerque, New Mexico, 1973.

Grayson, George W. *The Politics of Mexican Oil.* Pittsburgh, 1980.

Green, David. "The Cold War Comes to Latin America." In Barton Bernstein, ed., *Politics and Policies of the Truman Administration,* pp. 149–95. Chicago, 1970.

_____. *The Containment of Latin America.* Chicago, 1971.

Gulick, Charles. *Austria from Habsburg to Hitler.* 2 vols. Berkeley, California, 1948.

Gunther, John. *Roosevelt in Retrospect.* New York, 1950.

Haines, Gerald K. "Under Eagle's Wing: The Franklin Roosevelt Administration Forges an American Hemisphere." *Diplomatic History* 1, no. 4 (Fall 1977): 379–88.

Halperin, S. William. *Germany Tried Democracy.* New York, 1946.

Hansen, Roger D. *The Politics of Mexican Development.* Baltimore, 1971.

Heinrichs, Waldo H., Jr. "Bureaucracy and Professionalism in the Development of American Career Diplomacy." In John Braeman et al., *Twentieth Century American Foreign Policy.* Columbus, Ohio, 1971.

Herken, Gregg. *The Winning Weapon.* New York, 1981.

Hitler, Adolf. *Mein Kampf.* Translated by Ralph Manheim. Boston, 1971.

Hodges, Donald C. *Argentina 1943–1976.* Albuquerque, New Mexico, 1976.

Hooker, Nancy Harvison, ed. *The Moffat Papers.* Cambridge, Massachusetts, 1956.

Hull, Cordell. *The Memoirs of Cordell Hull.* New York, 1948.

Hundley, Norris, Jr. *Dividing the Waters.* Berkeley, California, 1966.

Ilchman, Warren F. *Professional Diplomacy in the United States 1779–1939.* Chicago, 1961.

Institute of Inter-American Transportation. *The United States Railway Mission to Mexico 1942–1946.* Washington, D.C., 1947.

Isquierdo, Rafael. "Protectionism in Mexico." In Raymond Vernon, ed., *Public Policy and Private Enterprise in Mexico.* Cambridge, Massachusetts, 1964.

Israel, Fred L., ed. *The War Diary of Breckinridge Long.* Lincoln, Nebraska, 1966.

Israel, Jerry. "A Diplomatic Machine: Scientific Management in the Department of State, 1906–1924." In Jerry Israel, ed., *Building the Organizational State*. New York, 1972.

Jablon, Howard. *Crossroads of Decision: The State Department and Foreign Policy 1933–1937*. Lexington, Kentucky, 1983.

Jacobs, Travis B. "Roosevelt's Quarantine Speech," *The Historian* 24 (August 1962): 488–99.

Jones, Robert C. *Mexican War Workers in the United States*. Washington, D.C., 1945.

Kelly, Sir David. *The Ruling Few*. London, 1962.

Kennan, George F. *Memoirs 1925–1960*. Boston, 1967.

Kinsella, William E., Jr. *Leadership in Isolation: FDR and the Origins of the Second World War*. Cambridge, Massachusetts, 1978.

Kolko, Gabriel. *The Politics of War*. New York, 1968.

Kolko, Joyce, and Gabriel Kolko. *The Limits of Power*. New York, 1972.

Koppes, Clayton R. "Good Neighbor Policy and the Nationalization of Mexican Oil: A Reinterpretation." *Journal of American History* 69 (June 1982): 62–81.

Krock, Arthur. *Memoirs*. New York, 1968.

La Feber, Walter. *America, Russia, and the Cold War, 1945–1966*. New York, 1967.

Langer, William L., and S. Everett Gleason. *The Challenge of Isolation*. New York, 1952.

Lash, Joseph P. *Eleanor and Franklin*. New York, 1971.

———, ed. *From the Diaries of Felix Frankfurter*. New York, 1975.

Leffler, Melvyn P. *The Elusive Quest: America's Pursuit of European Stability and French Security, 1919–1933*. Chapel Hill, North Carolina, 1978.

Leuchtenburg, William E. *Franklin D. Roosevelt and the New Deal 1932–1940*. New York, 1963.

Levin, Nora. *The Holocaust*. New York, 1973.

Logan, John A., Jr. *No Transfer: An American Security Principle*. New Haven, Connecticut, 1961.

Lowe, C. J., and F. Marzari. *Italian Foreign Policy 1870–1940*. London, 1975.

Maass, Walter B. *Assassination in Vienna*. New York, 1972.

McGann, Thomas F. *Argentina, the United States, and the Inter-American System 1880–1914*. Cambridge, Massachusetts, 1957.

Machado, Manuel A. *Aftosa: A Historical Survey of Foot and Mouth Disease and Inter-American Relations*. Albany, New York, 1969.

McKenzie, John R. P. *Weimar Germany 1918–1933*. Totowa, New Jersey, 1977.

Maddux, Thomas R. "American Diplomats and the Soviet Experiment: The View from the Moscow Embassy." *South Atlantic Quarterly* 74 (Autumn 1975): 468–87.

———. "Loy W. Henderson and Soviet American Relations: The Diplomacy of a Professional." In Kenneth Paul Jones, ed., *U.S. Diplomats in Europe 1919–1941*, pp. 149–61. Santa Barbara, California, 1981.

———. "Watching Stalin Maneuver between Hitler and the West: American

Diplomats and Soviet Diplomacy, 1934–1939." *Diplomatic History* 1 (Spring 1977): 140–54.

Markowitz, Norman D. *The Rise and Fall of the People's Century: Henry A. Wallace and American Liberalism 1941–1948*. New York, 1973.

May, Ernest R. "The Bureaucratic Politics Approach: U.S.-Argentine Relations, 1942–47." In Julio Cotler and Richard R. Fagan, eds., *Latin America and the United States: The Changing Political Realities*. Stanford, California, 1974.

_____. *"Lessons" of the Past*. New York, 1973.

Messer, Robert. *The End of an Alliance*. Chapel Hill, North Carolina, 1982.

Messersmith, George S. *The Government of Delaware*. New York, 1908.

Miller, August C., Jr. "The New State Department." *American Journal of International Law* 33 (July 1939): 500–18.

Miller, Douglas. *Via Diplomatic Pouch*. New York, 1944.

Moley, Raymond. *After Seven Years*. New York, 1939.

Mommsen, Hans. "The Reichstag Fire and Its Political Consequences." In Hajo Holborn, ed., *Republic to Reich*, pp. 129–222. New York, 1972.

Montgomery, M. L. *History of Berks County in Pennsylvania*. Phildelphia, 1886.

Morse, Arthur D. *While Six Million Died*. New York, 1968.

Mosk, Sanford A. *Industrial Revolution in Mexico*. Berkeley, California, 1954.

Moss, Kenneth. "George S. Messersmith: An American Diplomat and Nazi Germany." *Delaware History* 14 (Fall 1978): 236–49.

_____. "George S. Messersmith and Nazi Germany: The Diplomacy of Limits in Central Europe." In Kenneth Paul Jones, ed., *U.S. Diplomats in Europe*, pp. 113–26. Santa Barbara, California, 1981.

Mowrer, Lillian. *Journalist's Wife*. New York, 1937.

Ninkovich, Frank A. *The Diplomacy of Ideas: U.S. Foreign Policy and Cultural Relations 1938–1950*. Cambridge, 1981.

Offner, Arnold A. *American Appeasement: United States Foreign Policy and Germany, 1933–1938*. Cambridge, Massachusetts, 1969.

_____. "Appeasement Revisited: The United States, Great Britain, and Germany, 1933–1940." *Journal of American History* 64 (September 1977): 373–93.

Pach, Chester J., Jr. "The Containment of U.S. Military Aid to Latin America." *Diplomatic History* 6, no. 3 (Summer 1982): 225–35.

Page, Joseph. *Perón: A Biography*. New York, 1983.

Paterson, Thomas G. *On Every Front*. New York, 1979.

_____ , et al. *American Foreign Policy*. Lexington, Massachusetts, 1983.

Patterson, James T. *Congressional Conservatism and the New Deal*. Lexington, Kentucky, 1967.

Pauley, Bruce F. *Hitler and the Forgotten Nazis: A History of Austrian National Socialism*. Chapel Hill, North Carolina, 1981.

Paz, Alberto Conil, and Gustavo Ferrari. *Argentina's Foreign Policy 1930–1962*. Translated by John J. Kennedy. Notre Dame, Indiana, 1966.

Pepper, José Vincent. *I Accuse Braden*. Trujillo City, Dominican Republic, 1947.

Peterson, Edward N. *The Limits of Hitler's Power.* Princeton, 1969.

Peterson, Harold F. *Argentina and the United States 1810–1960.* New York, 1964.

Polenberg, Richard. *Reorganizing Roosevelt's Government 1936–1939.* Cambridge, Massachusetts, 1966.

Powell, J. Richard. *The Mexican Petroleum Industry, 1938–1950.* New York, 1972.

Pratt, Julius W. *Cordell Hull.* 2 vols. New York, 1964.

Prewett, Virginia. *Beyond the Great Forest.* New York, 1953.

Reilly, Michael F. *Reilly of the White House.* New York, 1947.

Rich, Norman. *Hitler's War Aims: Ideology, the Nazi State, and the Course of Expansion.* New York, 1973.

Roper, Daniel C. *Fifty Years of Public Life.* New York, 1968 edition.

Sands, William F. *Our Jungle Diplomacy.* Chapel Hill, North Carolina, 1944.

Schapsmeier, Edward L., and Frederick H. Schapsmeier. *Prophet in Politics: Henry A. Wallace and the War Years.* Ames, Iowa, 1970.

Schlesinger, Arthur M., Jr. *The Coming of the New Deal.* Boston, 1958.

Schmitt, Karl M. *Mexico and the United States 1821–1973.* New York, 1974.

Schulzinger, Robert D. *The Making of the Diplomatic Mind.* Middletown, Connecticut, 1975.

Schuschnigg, Kurt von. *Austrian Requiem.* New York, 1946.

_____. *The Brutal Takeover.* Translated by Richard Barry. New York, 1971.

Scruggs, Otey M. "The Evolution of the Mexican Farm Labor Agreement of 1942." *Agricultural History* 34 (July 1960): 140–45.

Selby, Sir Walford. *Diplomatic Twilight 1930–1940s.* London, 1953.

Shafir, Shlomo. "George S. Messersmith: An Anti-Nazi Diplomat's View of the German-Jewish Crisis." *Jewish Social Studies* 35, no. 1 (January 1973):32–41.

Sherwood, Robert E. *Roosevelt and Hopkins.* New York, 1950.

Shirer, William L. *Berlin Diary.* New York, 1941.

Smith, Denis Mack. *Mussolini.* New York, 1941.

Smith, O. Edmund, Jr. *Yankee Diplomacy.* Dallas, Texas, 1953.

Smith, Robert F. *The United States and Cuba.* New York, 1960.

Stadler, Karl R. "Austria." In S. J. Woolf, ed., *European Fascism.* New York, 1968.

_____. *The Birth of the Austrian Republic 1921.* Leyden, Netherlands, 1966.

Stoff, Michael B. *Oil, War and American Security: The Search for a National Policy on Foreign Oil.* New Haven, Connecticut, 1980.

Stuart, Graham H. *The Department of State.* New York, 1949.

_____. "George S. Messersmith: The Diplomacy of Intelligence." In J. T. Salter, ed., *Public Men In and Out of Office.* Chapel Hill, North Carolina, 1946.

Taggart, Robert J. "The Modernization of Delaware's School Tax System during the 1920s." *Delaware History* 18, no. 3 (Spring–Summer 1979): 153–79.

Taylor, A. J. P. *The Origins of the Second World War.* New York, 1961.

Taylor, Graham D. "The Axis Replacement Program: Economic Warfare and the Chemical Industry in Latin America." *Diplomatic History* 8, no. 2 (Spring 1984): 145–64.

Taylor, Telford. *Munich: The Price of Peace.* Garden City, New York, 1979.

Truman, Harry S. *1945 Year of Decision.* New York, 1955.

Tugwell, Rexford G. *The Democratic Roosevelt.* Baltimore, 1967 edition.

United States Inter-American Affairs Office. *History of the Coordinator of Inter-American Affairs.* Washington, D.C., 1947.

Urofsky, Melvin I., and David W. Levy, eds. *The Letters of Louis D. Brandeis.* Albany, New York, 1971.

Vandenberg, Arthur H., Jr., ed. *The Private Papers of Senator Vandenberg.* Boston, 1952.

Wagner, A. E., et al. *The Story of Berks County.* Reading, Pennsylvania, 1913.

Walker, J. Samuel. *Henry A. Wallace and American Foreign Policy.* Westport, Connecticut, 1976.

Ward, Mrs. Laurence. "Introductory History." In *Living History: Exploring the Heritage of Berks County, Pennsylvania.* Reading, Pennsylvania, n.d.

Weeks, Steven B. *History of Public School Education in Delaware.* Washington, D.C., 1917.

Weil, Martin. *A Pretty Good Club: The Founding Fathers of the U.S. Foreign Service.* New York, 1978.

Weinberg, Gerhard L. *The Foreign Policy of Hitler's Germany: Diplomatic Revolution in Europe 1933–1936.* Chicago, 1970.

———. *The Foreign Policy of Hitler's Germany: Starting World War II.* Chicago, 1980.

Welles, Sumner. *Seven Decisions That Shaped History.* New York, 1950.

———. *The Time for Decision.* New York, 1944.

———. *Where Are We Headed?* New York, 1946.

Werking, Richard Hume. *The Master Architects: Building the United States Foreign Service 1890–1913.* Lexington, Kentucky, 1977.

———. "Selling the Foreign Service: Bureaucratic Rivalry and Foreign Trade Promotion, 1903–1912." *Pacific Historical Review* 45 (May 1976): 185–207.

Wheaton, Eliot Barculo. *Prelude to Calamity: The Nazi Revolution 1933–1935.* New York, 1968.

Whitaker, Arthur P. *Inter-American Affairs 1943.* New York, 1944.

———. *Inter-American Affairs 1944.* New York, 1945.

———. *Inter-American Affairs 1945.* New York, 1946.

———. *The United States and Argentina.* Cambridge, Massachusetts, 1954.

Wiebe, Robert. *The Search for Order 1877–1920.* New York, 1967.

Wilson, Etta J. *Dreams and Realities.* Newark, Delaware, 1968.

Wilson, Hugh R., Jr. *A Career Diplomat.* Westport, Connecticut, 1973 edition.

Wionczek, Miguel S. "Electric Power: The Uneasy Partnership." In Raymond Vernon, ed., *Public Policy and Private Enterprise in Mexico,* pp. 19–110. Cambridge, Massachusetts, 1964.

Wood, Bryce. *The Dismantling of the Good Neighbor Policy.* Austin, Texas, 1985.

————. *The Making of the Good Neighbor Policy.* New York, 1967 edition.
Woods, Randall Bennett. *The Roosevelt Foreign Policy Establishment and the "Good Neighbor."* Lawrence, Kansas, 1979.
Wyman, David S. *Paper Walls: America and the Refugee Crisis 1938–1941.* Amherst, Massachusetts, 1968.

Newspapers and Periodicals

American Foreign Service Journal, 1947.
Atlantic Monthly, April 1946.
Baltimore Sun, 1946.
Christian Science Monitor, 1943–46.
Commonweal, 8 February 1946.
Daily Worker, 1946.
Fortune, August 1943 and August 1946.
The Nation, 8 June 1946 and 1 February 1947.
Newsweek, 1937–47.
New York Daily Mirror, 1937–43.
New York Post, 1946.
New York Times, 1920–66.
Philadelphia Inquirer, 1946.
Reading [Pennsylvania] *Eagle,* 1929–40.
San Francisco Chronicle, 1946.
Time, 1937–47.
U.S. News, 1946–47.
Washington Post, 1945–47.

Index

Phillips, William, 46, 53, 65, 70, 76,
79, 86, 92, 93, 97, 98, 109; on
GSM, 16, 54–55, 77; and diplo-
matic appointments, 52, 54–55;
and trade with Germany, 61–62,
81; on Hitler vs. communism, 78
Phipps, Eric, 80
Pierson, Warren L., 148, 163–64,
217
Pittman, Key, 106, 114
Poland, 56, 121, 123, 132, 143
Prewett, Virginia, 233, 256, 258
Price, Ward, 60
Prochnik, Edgar, 71

Quebec, conference at, 210

Ramírez, Pedro, 211, 232
Ransom, Floyd, 183–84, 185, 186,
192
Reconstruction Finance Corpora-
tion, 165, 183, 184, 195, 305
(n. 74)
Reece, B. Carroll, 115
Reed, Edward L., 97, 98
Rhineland, 87
Ribbentrop, Joachim von, 129, 134
Rieth, Kurt, 63, 65
Rintelen, Anton, 63
Rio de Janiero: U.S. mission at, 24–
25; conference at (1942), 172,
211, 243; proposed conference at,
223, 224, 228, 229, 230, 235, 239,
246, 250, 257, 259, 260; confer-
ence at (1947), 265, 266
Rio Grande River, 217, 218
Rivera, Miguel Primo de, 256
Rockefeller, Nelson A., 180–82,
193, 198, 200, 215, 218, 241, 245
Rogers, Alan, 74–75
Rogers, Edith Nourse, 53
Rogers Act, 21, 24, 29, 53, 97, 110,
142
Romania, xii, 56, 57
Rome Protocols, 57, 69–70, 79, 80
Roosevelt, Franklin D., 41, 50, 73,

77, 78, 93, 94, 103, 105, 106, 119,
120, 123, 128, 129, 137, 172, 182,
184, 212, 214, 215, 218, 231, 232,
234, 237, 255; attitude toward
State Department and Foreign
Service, 32, 52, 53–55, 82, 96–97,
102, 103, 209, 220; and ambassadorship in Germany, 34, 94, 131,
134, 135, 292 (n. 61); and GSM,
53–55, 82–83, 95, 103, 167, 198–
99, 207, 208, 210, 219–20, 271,
308 (n. 127); and foreign trade
policy, 62, 81; and fascism, 83,
116–17, 121, 135; and executive
reorganization, 110, 112–15, 139–
41; and refugees, 123, 125, 131–
32; and Czech crisis, 125–26; and
preparations for war, 127, 143;
and Cuba, 146, 148, 162, 166;
and Mexican oil, 171, 189–90,
206–7; and Board of Economic
Warfare, 185, 195; and *braceros*,
191; visit to Mexico of, 195–96,
197, 198, 200; and Camacho,
195–96, 199; and Mexican economic development, 197, 202,
204, 217; and Stettinius, 209; and
postwar Germany, 209, 210; and
international rivers, 218; death of,
219–20
Roosevelt, Mrs. Franklin D., 50, 196
Roosevelt, Theodore, 217, 231
Roper, Daniel C., 109–15, 138–41
Rosenthal, Morris, 241, 305 (n. 74)
Rubber Reserve Company, 183
Rublee, George, 125, 130, 131, 133

Saar, 68
Sackett, Frederic M., Jr., 29, 33–34,
35, 73
Saint-Germain, treaty of, 56, 70
Saladrigas, Carlos, 159, 160
San Francisco, conference at, 216,
223, 239, 240, 246, 251
Santos, Eduardo, 231
Sayre, Francis, 52, 71, 111